What if There's Nothing **Wrong?**

Alison J. Kay, PhD

BALBOA.
PRESS
A DIVISION OF HAY HOUSE

ISBN: 978-1-4525-6146-2 (sc)
ISBN: 978-1-4525-6147-9 (e)
ISBN: 978-1-4525-6148-6 (hc)

Library of Congress Control Number: 2012920019

Balboa Press books may be ordered through booksellers or by contacting:

Balboa Press
A Division of Hay House
1663 Liberty Drive
Bloomington, IN 47403
www.balboapress.com
1-(877) 407-4847

Because of the dynamic nature of the Internet, any web addresses or links contained in this book may have changed since publication and may no longer be valid. The views expressed in this work are solely those of the author and do not necessarily reflect the views of the publisher, and the publisher hereby disclaims any responsibility for them.

The author of this book does not dispense medical advice or prescribe the use of any technique as a form of treatment for physical, emotional, or medical problems without the advice of a physician, either directly or indirectly. The intent of the author is only to offer information of a general nature to help you in your quest for emotional and spiritual well-being. In the event you use any of the information in this book for yourself, which is your constitutional right, the author and the publisher assume no responsibility for your actions.

Any people depicted in stock imagery provided by Thinkstock are models, and such images are being used for illustrative purposes only.
Certain stock imagery © Thinkstock.

Printed in the United States of America

Balboa Press rev. date: 12/18/2012

Contents

Chapter 3—Becoming Reasonable, Yes? Scientific Materialism's Metaparadigm and the Emerging Industrial Era 115

Chapter 4-The Modern Industrial Age: How Did We End Up Where We Are? 145

Chapter 5—The Breakdown of Newtonian Physics and Scientific Materialism: Quantum Physics Emerges and Scientific Certainty Begins to Falter: Where Are We Headed? 201

Chapter 6—So if Our Basic Beliefs Have Become Outdated, What are Other Options? 239

Dedication

~~~~~~~~

This book is dedicated to all the courageous ones who choose
to make the tougher choices in those moments when no one is
watching—except themselves. Facing themselves, their stuff, their
truth, our stuff, our truth—and stepping forward into more of
themselves, their Higher Selves in the face of the fear, anyways.

For those who trust that largest perspective in the face of the ease of
shrinking back into that smaller me perspective—and allow themselves
to be uncomfortable at times, during this process of expansion.

Love, light & blessings to each and every one of us!

It does, and will continue to pay off in ways we're
not even able to be aware of, yet!

Acknowledgements

First and foremost, this book could not have been written without the experiences I have had due to my strength of spirit, fire, courage, vitality and tenacity. I am deeply grateful to whatever this source is for my magical being.

I am also grateful for any and all of the coaches, healers and teachers who have worked with me, to help me learn how to work with my power, my fire—rather than have it overwhelm me. And for my earliest teachers—the ones who helped me cultivate my meditation practice.

B. Alan Wallace for his teachings on making the mind serviceable, Eknath Easwaren for his *Conquest of Mind* and other teachings, The Dalai Lama for his supremely logically mind and humor and "his" Mind Life Institute summits with Western Scientists, Chogyam Trungpa for his massive accumulation of teachings, especially his *Shambhala: The Sacred Path of the Warrior*, my little dog-eared pocket version that fell apart due to my daily grabbing for it to get me through my most triggered period of my life, from the projections thrown onto me from a deeply foreign culture, in deeply foreign ways. Thank you Taiwan for becoming my second home. Thank you to the Taiwanese people, for your humanness, penetrating stares of curiosity, help and patience with my Chinese— and your smiles.

All my students, now friends, at the International Bilingual School of Hsinchu, aka NEHS—I want to express gratitude to you for sharing with me some of my most extremely precious years and experiences. Your unique Chinese American International beings, your brilliance, your curiosity to explore some of these questions with me, and especially the love, understanding and beauty with the class of 2010, writing that ridiculous amount of essays for your 10th grade American Literature Honors class, as we were so grateful to be together again. Thank you too, for that year with you as my 6th grade homeroom and Humanities students; that year was a phenomenal one. This doesn't negate all my other students too, of AP Psychology, Global Psychology, Fitness & Nutrition, you know who you are. Have fun we did, hey? I am a different person because of my decade there with you all in Taiwan, and am grateful too, to the parents of my students who reached out in all the ways you did to make my ex-pat life there better.

To my Reiki Master, Nancy Finck, for being by my side all the way, including my mom's healing from a brain tumor and the writing of this book, providing love, light and support as only a best friend who is also my Reiki Master could provide. Our connection, for me Nancy, is unparalleled. To my sweet, fiery, seeztah in South Africa, Rianna Peck, as I am her Reiki Master, who journeyed with me during our ex-pat days in Taiwan of finding ourselves amidst that surreal world. Thank you Rianna for the beauty you are and the love and friendship you've blessed me with and all the fun of our butterfly-like ways and mutual interests—and for your perfect welcoming of me to your home in South Africa this past year. My dear, sweet friend and "brother" Keith Eckerling who left his body last year. You were my first and best expat friend in Taiwan, my Chicago born and bred friend who was instantly familiar to me, owner of Rose Records turned social studies teacher and college counselor—you became my partner at work and play, especially in those early days in Taiwan and many trips to Thailand, Laos, Cambodia, the Philippines—but not Bali! Thank you for your Keithness. Your charm deserves a patent and this planet does not feel the same without you on it in your body. To my cousin Deb Katz, who straddled me and stared down my fear in the face of my leaving my life in the States as I trembled with a fear that was some sort of precognition or awareness of the supreme challenges to come for me in my life in Taiwan. Deb thank you for being a fellow, fierce warrior by my side through so much medicine work, especially those early days within the Native American community up in the mountains of California. Marjorie King I am also wanting to thank you my dear sweet friend, for your love, companionship, and fellow adventurous pioneering spirit. Your assistance in getting to that deeper level of understanding the Chinese culture, and for being the client providing the impetus that shifted me out of "just" a Reiki Master and into a holistic life coach are gems that permanently reside in my heart. Elizabeth Wyant, you were in the perfect place at the perfect time to help steer me in the direction of the Enlightenment —thank you.

I am also grateful for Amy Van Reeuwyk of Edmonton Canada, another who I am honored to be the Reiki Master of, who helped me understand more with her information, love and support, and who I am so proud of getting her masters of anthropology in Chinese—and so jealous of because you entered Taiwan once they had made learning Chinese more accessible to foreigners! Jia yo! And to complete the hat trick of my third expat woman I am the Reiki Master of, Christina Deviyani Ortaliz, whose purity of heart came in at just the right time in my life. Thank you Chris—especially for that trip to the "library" when you bought those few "books" with Amy and I. Priceless, sister!

And back in the States, thank you to my editor Betty Norlin, who took care of some of the more tedious details in order to push this book out, amidst my full time practice with clients and the online radio show. And for her willingness to seek out What Else is Possible. For Debbie Anderson, who has naturally supported my efforts, seeing the importance of my platform and championing my efforts with her gentle, humorous style. Darrin and Brook your support too has meant the world to me returning to live stateside once again. Thank you both! Dad, Alan Nathan, Heidi, David Matthew and Seth Isaac—thank you for being my family and loving me.

And finally, to the woman who seeded in so many ways, literally and metaphorically, this path of mine, that comes to you partially through this book—my mother, Libby Kay. I feel you around me Mummy, I know you're still with me. And no, it doesn't have to be this way, and no it doesn't have to be so hard, and YES there is a better way. And yes it can be easy. I love you.

Dear Reader

H I THERE. THIS BOOK IS a transmission to you, energetically encoded and written in a style to give you an experience, rather than a mind-to-mind, cognitive engagement of the mechanics of thinking, concluding, judging, categorizing and labeling as you go through the book. In fact, it's been written to help take you out of your mind. Your current mind, that is, and helps you step into something bigger within yourself so we can also step into something bigger as a society, collectively.

The reading of this book is a direct experience of what the ideas are suggesting.

This book is meant to connect to and ask questions of the higher part of you, beyond your everyday cognitive, "ego-mind." This discovery process has to happen experientially. Therefore, you have to go through it; it can't be delivered in quick bullet points. Otherwise, it becomes what it is intending to help dissipate.

The first pages of the first chapter will most likely not feel "right" to your mind. The wording will feel strange. Some of my preliminary readers who experienced this said they caught the rhythm around page forty. The ideas won't be directly delivered, but circular, almost in the obscure way a Master addresses her disciple, but always eventually delivering the teaching. Like a Chinese Chi Gong Master or a Zen Master with his koans. Frustrating at first. And this will cause reactions, judgment and conclusions as the mind acts in its predictable ways, wanting the meat to chew on-the conclusion. It will also possibly react to certain sections with impatience and frustration as your mind resists the information and the energy behind the ideas because *it is in fact challenging this very part of your mind by working around it.*

This is key to understand. Cultivate mental agility and flexibility; challenge that conformity to the mind's rigid demands for sound bites and quick delivery of tidbits of information. Get out of formulaic reading and thinking. Awaken even more, beyond your everyday thoughts and mind. Experience this book as if it is a workshop or retreat-or gym-in how to work with your mind. Indeed, that is exactly what this is.

As I tell my yoga and meditation students, and my clients who come to me for individualized meditation programs, you're meeting with resistance because you're just starting.

In meditation when we first sit down to observe our mind, it does not really react well at all. In fact, it tends to rebel. We notice more restlessness, more "monkey-mind" bounding from tree limb to tree limb, or thought-to-thought. Or conclusions about how there's no clear goal, or how we can't do this, or how we can't be this way, and off we go following the mind, quitting before anything in us beyond the mind has had time to be engaged.

There is a reason why you picked this book up. Trust that.

The more steadfastness you exert, the more you can stay right with what's being said in the line you're reading right at that moment. So you'll be more in the present moment, where energy expands and presence occurs, making less room for the cognitive mind. There will then be less clinging to the mind's judgments. Following your thoughts and going off on one of your mind's habitual trains of thought will happen less this way, too. This is one of the intended outcomes of taking in this book. I have written this as a meditator of twenty years, and a meditation and yoga teacher of fourteen years. You will feel this, eventually, under the words, if you don't right away. It will be re-working your cognitive mind's natural tendencies to be jumpy, easily distracted and busy with its concluding, labeling and judging, as if you were in fact meditating.

However, this is not a self-help book. Rather, it is a commentary on the state of our country, and the West in general, due to the obesity we have allowed the mind to become. However, in order to deliver this message, key aspects to how the mind became this way, and then other ways of being in our human minds with a lot more comfort, are presented.

So, the first part of the book is a clearing process. After a few years into my teaching career, I realized that I did this with my students during the first month of school-when I taught at the high school level. This was apparently not needed at the middle school level. The first part of the book, as you readjust, will most likely challenge your mind's demands to hurry up. Another key suggestion is that you engage the Observer in you. We each have this ability in us whether we're meditators or not. The Observer is on top of a boulder raised high above the little personality, "ego-mind" version of ourselves, looking down and simply observing itself make choices as it goes through life. Observe your impatience with wanting the point to be delivered immediately. Observe your desire for conclusions to be made so you can feel more comfortable being in the known rather than the question. Observe your mind's demand for a clear understanding right from the start. Practice the art of allowing. Allow the points being made to develop and unfold.

This is a transmission that is meant to be experienced. Reading this book will take you through a process of de-conditioning your mind from its feeling of being in control. The writing will softly, gradually, but very clearly put your mind in the back seat, while something Higher in your consciousness gradually begins to step forward and receive this book's content.

This book activates other parts of your human system, your intuitive inner knowing. This happens even though it goes in through your mind. The questions asked of you are connecting to something beyond the every day mind, asking this part of you to step more forward and interact with the ideas. It does not present issues or problems for the mind to chew on. It instead presents the way it has been in order to understand why it's the way it is now and gently asks you to consider seeing yourself, our society and our role on the planet in a different way now, here, in 2012 and beyond.

This different way is not from the mind. So, this book is not speaking to your mind. It's going at your heart, your wisdom and your Higher Self. The writing style is therefore not quick, sharp, demanding nor direct, as the mind is. It is instead, the same energy as where these ideas are meant to go to inside of you. And where it's meant to take each of you, and all of us. The hope here is to give you access to another energy, another way of being, another way of existing on this planet different than it has been.

So, that means a different way to deliver this message. I am loaning you a set of eyes from someone—me!—who was removed from our country two months prior to 9/11 and returning two years into Obama's administration. This country has changed. The content of the typical concerns, and the level of fear the average citizen seems to display, have changed. I can feel it so much so that within the first month back here I visualized an astronaut's helmet around my head. I did not want to absorb the general climate of thought as it has become here in the United States. It has apparently been a decade moving full throttle into fear. This has pulled at my heart, so much so that the labor behind this book increased in order to get this message out to more people. My workshops have increased and changed in their original intent and thus content, upon learning more and more what the everyday person here is worrying about.

Nevertheless, how about turning this inside out? Because that's what this book is going to do. I was turned upside down, and inside and out living in Asia for the past decade and have a mental flexibility and agility to my mind that my twenty years of meditation practice alone would not have given me. This removal of mine from our country appears to have been divinely timed. You can read my bio at www.healing-balance.com to understand that more. The consciousness behind my eyes-me!-has been a political consultant, has a masters in Public Administration focusing on Public Policy, has been a writer and teacher of English Literature and Administrator, a Yoga and Meditation Teacher, an Energy Healer and a daughter of a mom who needed my energy healing when diagnosed with a deadly brain tumor.

One more thing-this book is written from a deep belief in our ability to change in positive ways in America. I have been involved in nothing but helping people awaken and grow since my first profession as a political consultant. During that work, I used some of the most fundamental democratic practices of grassroots organizing to successfully get the candidates whose campaign I was working on elected. I watched at precincts as votes came in, and watched as my candidates pulled forward in the number of votes, to victory. I enlisted people to go out, volunteering their time, to register voters. I could go on; I won't.

I taught American Literature in my second career, finding myself teaching the Declaration of Independence, the writings of Thomas Jefferson, Thomas Paine, Benjamin Franklin's - one of our country's first millionaires - essay on moral perfection, Emerson, Thoreau, Walt Whitman, Fitzgerald's *The Great Gatsby*, the Beatniks and on up through to Post-Modern Literature. I read and reread year after year the founding principles of this country. I traced our development of a national character alongside the industrial revolution, some of it with the critiques of the Transcendentalists as industrialization kicked into full gear in the late 1800's.

I believe in our country's ideals. The American ingenuity, idealism, passion and belief in something better being possible is what our country is founded on. So are my business, my book, my radio show ("http://www.voiceamerica.com" www.voiceamerica.com), and my belief that something far greater than what we're currently allowing ourselves to be is possible. Maybe part of my Bostonian upbringing has something to do with this. Therefore, it is with this spirit that I have painstakingly labored at times over the communication of these ideas in this book because it feels somewhat like my contribution to my fellow Americans. Please remember that as you read what are critiques, not criticisms, of our country.

I invite you to get out of your own way even more, allowing yourself to be even bigger than you currently are. Living in a more alive way, living in a more authentic way that you are on fire about, having more vitality, passion and enthusiasm for yourself growing into being more than you ever thought possible. That is my hope for each of us. More health, more wealth (if that's what you desire, especially if you were tripped up into the mentality that there isn't enough to go around) and more joy. If we each were to live at this level-with an aware, alive joy-then could you even begin to imagine what it would be like to be in community? And what this would do for the collective good of us in America? And in the West? And on our little planet? Now is the time! And a part of you already knows this; otherwise, you never would have picked up this book. Trust that part of you. And me. Namaste.

Welcome

YOU'VE MADE A MAJOR DECISION just by picking up this book. I say the same thing to my clients. It appears, after doing energy healing and being in the holistic health and natural healing field for 20 years, that I seem to attract people who are ready for something much greater than where they're currently operating. In fact, I have been nicknamed a "lightning bolt" due to the way my work quickly pierces to the very core of what my clients are truly needing. You can view video testimonials saying as much at www.healing-balance.com. I don't mess around. One client puts it, "What I like about you Alison is that this is not a romance, it's not a dance. You, like an arrow, get straight to where it is that I was blocked and we went right at releasing it."

So I congratulate you on being attracted to what is in this book. It says something about you! It will no doubt challenge you in ways that you've most likely not been before, challenging your most deeply held, cherished beliefs -many of which you are unconscious of even holding. Many of these same beliefs are at the core of how our society has functioned for the past 300 years or so, and thus what your mind has taken in as "the way things are."

What you will get from this book are many things.

1. This book is about power. Power for individuals; societal and universal power. You will be able to see how you can have more ease and vitality. You'll be guided how to restore or increase the "magic" in your life. You'll be shown how to directly access this power source for yourself, flushing your life with this power in a very practical way. This book also delivers very clear

instruction on how to work with our thoughts to move beyond the mind in order to access this power. Where this power resides according to the wisdom from ancient cultures and the new cutting edge sciences, a.k.a. "The New Sciences" will also be presented. Much of this is from the author's own experience from living and working in Asia for a decade while researching ancient practices for vitality, longevity and power, working as a successful energy healer, yoga teacher, meditation teacher, chi gong teacher, vegetarian personal trainer and body builder for the past 20 years.

2. You will gain a crystal clear picture of why life in the United States in particular feels so unstable, comparatively, say to about ten years ago. This is beyond the commonly blamed sources. American society in particular, but Western society in general, has been and continues to be vulnerable to losing its power right now. You'll be given a window to see how our society has been trained to turn away from the power in subtle energy and consciousness while also be given quite a solid understanding about how subtle energy and consciousness is seen as THE source of power in the East. This comparison will help you appreciate just how much we leave out in our society's views on life, and what we're missing out on.

3. You'll then gain a clear view of how Western culture is in the midst of a mostly unspoken shift that is changing the way we "do life." This is a massive shift, or "macroshift" from a society structured by Newtonian Physics, based on denser energy and a more physical understanding of our world. The times we're heading into are more of Quantum Physics, based on a lighter, more fluid, quicker, more random energy. You'll learn how Newtonian Physics deals with the physical, while Quantum Physics deals with consciousness. The understanding that old structures society-wide are crumbling because they are based on doing things in this old way, and this is no longer possible will calm you. Hence, they're crumbling. This is not bad. This is change. In addition, it's where we are. Anything too dense is being forced to change. This appears to us as breaking down,

or crumbling. It is at both the individual and societal level this density is being broken down. You'll also have a sense of how this all coincides with the nature of the years immediately preceding and following 2012, a time predicted to be The Great Awakening for humanity.

4. You'll see how this translates in a very real way to how we in the West, particularly America, are being commanded to adopt a new *fundamental* way of doing things. The discussion will show you how at the start of modernization and industrialization Western science had its focus more towards the physical, in reaction to the main sentiments of their times. You'll gradually have the picture painted for you of how this old model, or metaparadigm, is no longer relevant to our times now. So you'll then understand a great part of why it feels so unstable today in the USA and the West overall. We are at a turning point; there is a global macro-shift underway. These changes are causing us to feel unstable, individually and collectively, throughout the top organizations and sectors of our society.

5. Very clearly, you will be shown that in order for us to remain competitive and viable as individuals and as a leading nation on this planet we must deal with the most basic aspect of being human, our minds. You'll see how this connects to consciousness, the period we're entering into. This means dealing with our thoughts, beliefs, emotions, behaviors and choices, rather than focusing mostly on the physical. Globalization has given us a new world. Equally, the very nature of 2012 is as a turning point.

6. Finally, it will be absolutely redundant that you see it is time to take your power back from wherever you've given it away. And you'll be shown how. This may be from clergy to tell us about our own relationship to divinity and to our own souls. You'll come to distinguish where you've given away your power to doctors to tell us about our own bodies as if they know them better than each of us do (or can), the food industry to trust with such an intimate aspect of life, the medical system that we hope

has our best interests at heart, or the government to take care of you. So, in order to do this, this book is also focused at a very personal level, examining how our choices have been shaped by our society's metaparadigm. Meaning our core beliefs, since the start of the modern industrial era, have been very much influenced by what our society's authority figures have told us is real and true. You will see first hand with practical examples of how these ideas have become outdated in this emerging age of consciousness or holism. These very foundational ideas have shaped how each of us frames what is and what isn't possible. So as we work backwards from the societal beliefs of our metaparadigm, you will be able to see how and where to work with your own thoughts to take your own power back.

Wow! Right? This is huge! This book presents both the macro and the micro, weaving them together as if a dance between the two. In order to do so, the ideas take a while to come to shape for you, my dear reader. So please engage patience. The complexity of these many ideas does come together, however you just have to wait for it to unfold for you.

To help you better grasp some of these ideas that may erupt your world, you have access to my online radio show. Go to voiceamerica.com and put, "Create Your Best Life Ever!" in the search and you will get to my show. On it are the leading thinkers, movers, shakers, and doers of this time interviewed by me, as well as myself on the show helping to drive these points home. There are also loads of free clearings, healings, holistic lifestyle tools and tips with which to test, apply and work with the ideas presented here.

This book came from a decade that rocked my world. That is, more so than the other decades of my life. Ask any of my long-term friends, or even my newer friends, and this is something that one gets quite quickly about me. "I could sense there was something alive over there in the corner, and I realized it was you once you got up and walked to the podium to speak," said one of my more recent acquaintances-and client. My life has not been one of status quo, choosing along with what everyone else has done. And feeling comfortable.

I have traveled around the world, lived in Asia for a decade, living in all regions of our globe and all regions of the United States for shorter time periods than that. I did not have a bucket list; I was living a bucket list before the term got trendy. I visited the very same aboriginal healer in Bali that Elizabeth Gilbert writes about in *Eat, Pray, Love* before she did. I had already written much of this book when I completed my PhD, moved back to the United States and started my business. Elizabeth just got it penned and submitted quicker! You can see pictures of me getting the actual treatment on my content rich website, alisonjkay.com (go to the "A Note From Alison" page under the About tab http://www.alisonjkay.com/Note.php)

In fact, suffice it to say my truth is that I have lived the life of a pioneer, having ideas in me usually about ten years ahead of the curve. This has caused my family to refer to my food at the dinner table as "jungle food" back in the start of my now 20 years of being a vegetarian. It has caused me to from college on seek out the most progressive pockets of our country and planet to live in so I could thrive. Otherwise, my constant existence of expansion as if a growing tree would have been stifled. I have never been married, I have never had kids. I have been a leader my entire life, and not realizing it until about my late teens. I have always been a floater never a member locked into just one group of friends because I have always wanted to be able to change at my rate, and not be locked in to the group rate of change, nor group think.

I have lived what I write about here. This includes my own personal story of seeing how the natural healing world conflicted with the biomedical system's delivery of healthcare when it came to my mom's diagnosis of a brain tumor and a prognosis of three months. This prognosis I did not know when I packed up my belongings and left my logjam in Istanbul, where I was under contract as the Middle School English Department Chair and 6th-8th grade Humanities teacher at an international IB school. I came back to Florida and immediately got underway to treat my mom with energy healing and the reconditioning of her beliefs that this brain tumor was not going to take her in 3 months. I backed off all of my family members including my Dad somewhat, telling them to stay away until they could get their fear under control. I acted as the proverbial brown bear wrapping her protective arms around her cub with my mom's head, containing both the tumor and the thoughts and beliefs that could either help her or hurt her. In the end, we were successful. The brain tumor was wiped away and off the MRI, leaving the doctors at the local cancer center, Moffit, to declare my mom a miracle case.

This book is born from living a very different life than most of the people I meet. And it is my gift to you, dear reader. It is a way for you to stop allowing yourself to just be ordinary. Because that somehow is not the nature of being alive here on this planet in 2012 and beyond. It seems we are being asked to be the fullest version of ourselves, individually and collectively. And it is with this in mind that I do the most basic American thing I can: express my ideas within a democracy that has citizens who have freedom of choice.

Know that you can make very different and slightly different choices in each moment. Know that your choices in the way you spend your time, your money and your thoughts are actually choices too. Know that this is where your power is. And truly-let freedom ring! You can do this, it is more than just possible, it is the single most liberating thing any human can be shown. And it is within these pages that this expansive energy will be explored, unraveling for you the way it has been tied up, and freeing up space for a new way, a new moment, a new day. Welcome to your best life, *our* best life, ever! Choice is frequently underrated.

Preamble: Who Is Doing This Thinking? The Issue in a Nutshell

I N WESTERN THOUGHT THE TASK of defining the mind body connection is not at all simple. In fact, it's one of the central issues within western existence. Known as the "mind body problem," it's defined by Dictionary. com as "the problem of explaining the relation of the mind to the body."

Realistically, this issue extends from, "Who or what is doing this thinking and commanding of my body being able to breath itself" to questioning if the body is mechanical only, or if there is something more driving its functioning.

This question is central to our increasing our health and well-being. Because if our mind and body are connected, and it's not just a mechanical relationship, then that means we have the ability to affect our health and well-being ourselves, without waiting for an outside authority source to tell us what our state of health is. It also helps us to see the need for tools to aid us in working with our minds, so we can have that increase of health and well-being. But if we view it as merely mechanical, then we won't think we have any influence over our own state of physical and mental well-being. Do you see?

And then, continuing on, the bottom line question to this line of thinking typically then becomes, "So then, if it's all mechanical, or if it's all not—from what source do human beings come?" Since science came on the scene this issue is the dividing line in the West now. For example, if one's belief is in the physical as the underlying source, then it's the brain that drives the mind.

Therefore everything is driven by the physical; and then, for instance, one would therefore believe in Darwin's survival of the fittest, evolution and our genes being a main determinant. And us at the mercy of our environment and the situations in our lives that come at us, that affect us.

If we believe that there is a mind body connection, we see our thoughts affect our bodies, and contribute to creating our state of health or disease, happiness or suffering. When viewing the world this way, it's also seen how we have a great deal more influence over our own well-being and what goes on in our lives. So this view doesn't leave us at the mercy of our environments and the situations in our lives. Typically, it becomes understood at some point within this worldview, that our choices made from our beliefs are the turning point for any and all situations.

For example, for those who meditate, it's known we're able to pull our attention from our thoughts and back to our breath. If we're able to observe ourselves thinking and then choose to discipline our mind's incessant stream of thoughts by refocusing our attention, or awareness, onto our breath – who's exerting this discipline?

Is it a higher mind or another level of our mind?

Lower brain, higher brain?

Lower mind, Higher Self? We don't even have a working vocabulary within English to discuss this.

How do we explain the mysterious things in life that appear unexplainable? Like thinking about someone we haven't spoken to in a long time and then they call that same day? Or having a dream and having it come true? Or déjà vu? Do we thus discount these occurrences? Typically it seems we do.

How do we explain that which is beyond the physical, or *that which is metaphysical*? Dictionary.com offers, "a prefix with the meanings 'after,' 'along with,' 'beyond' and 'behind' for the definition of 'meta.'" Ultimately this leads to questions such as, does some sort of higher intelligence, or a divine source exist? Then the ensuing explanations to these questions typically lead to the divide between what is tangible, concrete and physical, from which is intangible, mysterious and metaphysical. Historically in the West, this been the division between matter and the non–material, or secular vs. spiritual once church vs. state-with-science separations came on the scene.

Some stop at the level of the physical, believing in nothing more than what can be seen–many do, in fact–and this is the materialist belief that's been the dominant paradigm for the past three hundred years or so in the West. This belief comes to us from science first, then got reinforced by the industrialization and medicine based on this science.

To the metaphysician, these questions are a matter of that which is physical, and then that which goes beyond, or transcends the physical, is then therefore, metaphysical. Both the physical and metaphysical exist together, with the physical more easily identified by the physical five senses, and the metaphysical connected to the physical and then above and beyond it—and behind it. The metaphysical then requires beyond the physical five senses to be perceived.

The mind body connection "problem" also leads us to then ask if everything is, in fact, able to be broken down to the physical, or matter, and that if this is the underlying basic force in the universe, then how do we have the capacity to even ask these questions? Meaning, where does this capacity come from; again, what is the driving force behind the brain? Is it the mind? And if it's the mind, what's its source? Consciousness? And so what is this source?

So then is the mechanical, or the physical, supported by the metaphysical? It would seem that ancient cultures, including the Chinese, Hindu Indian and ancient Romans say yes. But why would we look to ancient cultures? It's the post-modern era now. We've had so much development in our science, technology and therefore understandings of how the world works, why would we bother to consider these outdated beliefs? Because they're dealing with the most fundamental questions of life, and these questions are being asked again in today's globalized world.

This year, this time in human evolution is demanding a merger between these two worlds within the Western hemisphere, the physical and metaphysical. We've spent the last 250 years or so steeped in developing the physical, with all of our societal systems supporting this premise in the way our society and its social and economic systems have been organized. Yet outside of the West, there have been other societies organizing around the opposite belief—the metaphysical being the primary organizing principle for their societies—from the start of their cultures. They still function from this belief today, without interruption, while having entered the global, modernized arena that is very much steeped in commercialism and the physical.

Alison J. Kay, PhD

Now is the time in our post-modern globalized world in the West, and particularly in the United States, as we see so many familiar systems within our society crumbling, to emerge with an entirely new model. A major part of this shift is helping folks understand why our society functions as it has, how this leads us to view life and think differently than those in other societies with different cultural values. Then helping these folks gain access to these other ideas, and see how to gracefully and easily change into the model we're now moving into.

British philosopher Gilbert Ryle gave a derogatory description of Rene Descartes' mind body dualism in his book *The Concept of Mind* in 1949. He introduced the "ghost in the machine" label to highlight the perceived absurdity of dualist systems like Descartes' –where mental activity carries on parallel to physical action, but where their means of interaction are unknown or, at best, speculative, and considered unimportant. The physical, being more accessible to the physical five senses we sense and perceive with, is the precedent within this duality, while the mind is rendered secondary. Yet upon closer inspection of Descartes' original idea, it wasn't to relegate the mind to a secondary position. Descartes actually believed in the soul, and the soul having a connection to the mind in some way. This was—the soul and its connection to the mind—considered by Descartes to be one of the two trump cards for the power of the physical. A divine source was considered the other. It was later scientists who eventually unraveled this last part from Descartes' theory. So Ryle is pointing out the absurdity of what the later scientists did with Descartes' original theory on the mind body connection.

This remake of Descartes' theory basically dismissed the power from the mind, or consciousness, without any answers about what is behind our thinking mind. So it seems we should then ask a question from epistemology—the field that studies the theory of knowledge, concerned with the nature, scope and limitations of knowledge—begun by the Greek philosophers Socrates, Plato and Aristotle. Typically such questions like, "How is knowledge acquired?" and "How do we know what we know?" are epistemological. So how do we know what we know? You just saw a trip through answering that question applied to how do we know what we know about how the mind effects the body?

Does the common belief of "something everyone just knows" really justify believing in something? Especially if there is continuing growth of evidence that the common belief is not accurate? That sounds a whole lot like, "Well it's how we've always done things!"

Asking this question again in today's world, is happening. With some of the effects from globalization being information from the ancient Eastern cultures, and then add to that quantum physics' discoveries over the past century, it might well be necessary, because it seems maybe we've been missing something.

If we are led to consider the dominant view we've held in the West since the advent of science in that our existence is based on the physical, so our mind is subsumed within our brain and it is the brain's neurons and synapses firing only that creates all emotions and thoughts – then, *what is responsible for getting the neurons and synapses to fire?*

Is it this "ghost in the machine?" If so, what *is* this ghost in the machine of the human brain? Where does it come from? What's its source? And this is not even addressing how can emotions be mechanical. Indeed, emotions are basically ignored as something valid and important within a human's health and well-being because they're so elusive to study and prove.

We'll get back to this later. For now, you can see how this belief that still functions at the core of our paradigm in the West is still in effect. And perhaps you already see how nonsensical it feels to us today. Yet it still totally effects life in the West, particularly the Unites States, in almost all ways. These ways will be explored, because many of them are not serving our society's needs. Again—how do we know what we know? Or: why do we believe what we believe? And why do we choose what we choose? Very much because of our beliefs. And what do we think is possible, that then informs our choices? Again, this is based on our beliefs. And where do we get our beliefs from? Our parents, friends, teachers, society, and government. Where do they all get their beliefs from? In the West, it's science more so than anywhere else. You'll see this eventually through the course of this book; it is quite insidious, but buried.

This brings us to the application of the mind body connection to medicine. It's one of the primary disciplines–the field of medicine, which includes mental health/psychology–that is at a nexus today in the West and even more so within our country. This turning point full of tension is centralized around this very contentious issue of the mind body connection, very much due to the growing evidence of the new discoveries within the "new sciences" in the study of subtle energies and consciousness.

New understandings have arisen about how our thoughts, emotions, and consciousness impact our body, health and well-being. These have been some of the strongest discoveries within the new sciences, revealing new ways to operate with health and well-being. Yet our mechanical, scientific materialist, physically focused medicine based on our science cannot incorporate these discoveries into its system, because it unravels how they approach medicine.

The physical level can only be treated with surgery or medicating symptoms that pop to the surface, but not regarded in any more depth than that because the tools developed for our medical system come from its narrow perspective on the physical as primary. It's easier to produce technology to diagnose, cut and band-aid with patents, than entering into the more individualized human systems of an intertwinement of mind-body-spirit, with emotions a part of this trinity. Intimately intertwined with medicine is one of the other major disciplines also in the midst of a paradigm shift– science.

So that finally, and of central importance to this observation that we are at a crossroads right now in history, is the mind body connections' relevance to the field of science. All of the questions asked above are contained within science as it is done in the West today. It has basically become the application of—or the avoidance of—the mind body connection within our sciences. There has been a new, emerging body of sciences, grouped as "The New Sciences" who are applying and unraveling the significance of the mind body connection, while orthodox science is holding tightly to the old thinking and paradigm.

Over the past twenty years or so, rather than being avoided, the mind body connection has been periodically explored, with the New Sciences being the main lens of inquiry *and much of the focus being the field of consciousness studies.* Additionally, the discoveries in quantum physics have caused ripples of a long, slow unfolding of the realization that we cannot go back to the way we once thought the world worked. That world, those beliefs are that the world is stable, relying on laws of gravity and the solidity of the Newtonian physics yielding the predictability our Western scientific tradition is based on.

This science is referred to in many sources as "orthodox science," and by implication is being termed here as "old science." One primary reason I'm choosing to term orthodox science, or Scientific Materialism based on

Newtonian Physics, "old science" is because of one of the key new discoveries from quantum physics. Energy as the primary building block of our universe replacing physical matter is a huge discovery—hence it being one of the key discoveries from quantum physics. It shifts everything if you take time to consider it.

One essential shift is that it directly effects moving from viewing the body and brain as purely mechanical—with the physical as the fundamental building block—to the mind and body as connected—with energy as the fundamental building block.

The second key discovery is that when our consciousness observes the phenomena being studied it effects the outcome of the experiment! This carries many implications. One of the most important questions we end up with as a result from this discovery is whether authentic scientific inquiry as it has been historically defined is even genuinely possible.

If when we observe something we effect it, then that implies an interconnection between all animate life, and thus objective scientific study using the scientific methods as it has traditionally been done within the "old" scientific model is rendered somewhat mute. It has to reconsider its methods, and whether what science seeks to "prove" can really be validly "proven."

This is radical, considering we've always been able to rely on science to distinguish for us fact from fallacy, or fact from subjective thinking. We've never considered the scientists themselves, who have their own mental perspectives that make them choose to study what they do. Nor is this considering the very practical issue of scientists studying what is getting funded, leaving behind studying anything that is not popular with where the money is for scientific studies.

Most recently, say the last twenty years or so, in the United States, the European Union, Israel, Taiwan and Russia among other more newly developed countries like India and China, much of the efforts within the new sciences have been attempting to use the old methodology applied now to studying a human being's system and the subtle energies that are involved in healing. These studies are focusing on how the more elusive aspects of life, or consciousness, or energy, that is in all animate life effects human health, vitality and healing.

This leg of the new sciences has compiled many studies of various complimentary and alternative medicine therapies. Notice that it brings us right back to medicine, and its application to the individual human being.

This is of central importance to how the times are changing due to the growing understanding of the mind body connection, the discoveries of quantum physics and globalization.

What's been realized clearly is that the mind body connection puts the power back in the hands of the individual, with the awareness of the power of our minds and the ability to work with consciousness. Along with hope, empowerment and health, there is also inherent resistance to this from different angles, which will be explored later. These are the times we are in now, and this is central to the great shift going on.

It is not just about natural healing methods. It's about a way of life, an entire paradigm, giving way to an emerging one as it becomes increasingly clear the old ways of doing life, business, education, politics, science, medicine, relationships and health are based on an incomplete view of the world. And this incomplete view of the world has become outdated.

Answering these fundamental questions about life and our existence in the universe formally began in the West back in Greece, with the establishment of the Western field of philosophy. Our science comes from philosophy. This is actually the foundation that the scientific community picked up in-part, and then somewhat developed during the Renaissance— and then completely locked into place during the Enlightenment.

Picking up the pace, our Western scientific model of scientific materialism went "full steam ahead" during the Industrial Age. The Industrial Age is the next age, after the Enlightenment; in fact, the Western scientific model was an outcome of the Enlightenment, although most would say it's indirect. And this science has been followed in increasing degrees up through the present day. This foundation is the concept–*and many say belief here in place of "concept"*–that there is an objective reality we can study, and know through the application of *logos*, or reason. It can be proven by applying reason within a sound methodology–the scientific method–to prove what the external is, outside of and separate from us. It is because of this separation that we can study it objectively and with reason.

However, gradually as the physical took primary positioning, that which science deemed "unprovable" was brushed under the carpet, not studied, or even acknowledged. If anyone was to deal with the unseen or subtle energies that supposedly are not as predictable as solid physical matter, it was the domain of religion–The Church–because they dealt with the irrational–or what was disregarded by science as unable to be proven.

Finally, another reason for this brushing aside of the subtle in favor of the physical within this scientific materialist *metaparadigm* has increasingly been fueled from the modern industrialized era. Our scientific materialism's primary focus on the more tangible aspects of life has a relative usefulness in its application to technology, whether steam engines, assembly lines, weapons, space exploration or biotech's pharmaceutical drugs production.

This division has been convenient to the sciences, and clearly implies that they have come down on one of the two sides of the central question behind the mind body connection. One of the key tenets of orthodox science has been from the start that all physical things in the universe are able to be reduced and then studied in parts. Once reduced the physical object or phenomena is studied and observed until the object's function in question is discovered and proven with scientific methodology. This is reductionism.

Once modern science took hold in around the 1950's, the practice became even more infused with the need for logical proofs, with the concept of logical empiricism. This was in resistance to what quantum physics had discovered back in the first decade of the 1900's. Discoveries had to be able to be proven again using the same methodology by others replicating the study. So it had to be reliable, and had to be consistent. To do this, reductionism was key. This is, in fact, the quintessential western modus operandi–reductionism. Just think of one of the most familiar examples–the specialists of each area of medicine who you get referred to from your primary care physician. Meanwhile modern science continued the Enlightenment scientists' choice to attribute "the other side" of this dualistic model in the West to that which is subtle, subjective—and likely not able to be explained by reason.

Not external, not physical, or not as easily measured, is how the subtle was viewed–and still mostly is. Thus the subtle was relegated mostly to the domain of religion–or whoever else handles the intangible which sometimes contains the seemingly irrational–but it is not the role for science, nor socio–economic politics. This belief in practice, as we shall see, stems from the Enlightenment and this choice made by the scientists during the Enlightenment, as science became an established field.

Therefore, in order to define the mind body connection we have to first understand the definition itself depends on what one's beliefs, foci and desires are. In order to better understand why at a mass level we have the cultural values and beliefs that we do about human and physical existence we need to explore how this issue has been dealt with historically in our culture, paying particular attention to *the implications behind*—for example, who benefits? who loses? what gets left behind?—the chosen definitions, and the methods used to support these definitions.

The beliefs driving the efforts with which this question has been attempted to be answered, or avoided, are key. What science's scientific materialism has produced for the West's version of how the world works is what has us in the West believing what we do!

This core belief is steeped in the metaparadigm of disbelief amongst the masses that there is a mind body connection, and being treated by our biomedical doctors as if it doesn't exist, for they don't get taught that it does exist. Meanwhile, we're living within a government supporting the sciences who give us this metaparadigm lens through which the unquestioning masses and government receive the scientists' interpretation of life and the world. Hence, it's a metaparadigm; we have all been given this version of the world–including the scientists themselves, that it is the physical that is primary and to reduce whole systems into parts in order to understand matter and life.

Science and mainstream society collectively have formed a paradigm under which the West has lived, at increasing levels of strict–and as we shall see, nearing fanatical–adherence to, in order to keep separate–and away–that which is secular from that which is spiritual. Thereby we close ourselves off to authentically exploring with as much authority and validity the subtle energy, or consciousness, by dealing mostly with that which is secular, tangible, and able to be proven.

What has occurred therefore is the hidden unconscious conclusion that it is the physical that is safe and reliable, while the subtle, or intangible, is neither safe nor reliable–or as important.

The fact is this question has risen again. Yet this time more insistently, central to a web of implications suggesting how we're still running our society has become dysfunctional and outdated. Furthermore with the "new sciences" finding a way to measure and validate the subtle as we have globalized, this issue is battling its way to center stage at this point in history, particularly within the United States.

We need to look at the different schools of thought about dealing with the physical and the intangible–or metaphysical –as they've existed in the West to see how we've adopted as a societal and scientific paradigm the paradigm of duality, of separating matter and the non–physical within the West; again more specifically in the United States. Then, once this understanding of why reality has been defined for us the way it has been, build from there to examine the current redefining of the mind and body's connections, as metaphysics once again comes into play at increasing rates throughout various sectors of our society.

This knock is increasingly and insistently at our doors with an incessant banging, forcing us to allow it inside our dominant cultural paradigm–and genuinely acknowledge, this time, incorporating it into our metaparadigm. Look at how the East has incorporated materialism and modernization. Are we as balanced in our restructuring post globalization?

Alfred North Whitehead (1861–1947) was a British mathematician, logician and philosopher best known for his work in mathematical logic and the philosophy of science, coauthoring the epochal *Principia Mathematica* with another leading scientist, Bertrand Russell. Whitehead contributed significantly to twentieth–century logic, philosophy of science and metaphysics. In 1925 he said,"When you are criticizing the philosophy of an epoch, do not chiefly direct your attention to those [explicit] intellectual positions which its exponents feel it necessary to defend. There will be *some fundamental assumptions* which adherents of all the variant systems within the epoch *unconsciously presuppose. Such assumptions appear so obvious that people do not know what they are assuming* because no other way of putting things has ever occurred to them. With these assumptions a certain limited number of types of philosophic systems are possible, and *this group of systems constitutes the philosophy of the epoch,*" (italics mine) (Whitehead, 1925).

The mind body connection is the idea that the mind affects physiological functions in the body (The Dalai Lama 1991). Another definition is that the mind body relationship is the relationship between a human body and its unique mind (Gummow 2007). Finally, a third definition: of, involving, or resulting from the interrelationship between one's physical health and the state of one's mind or spirit (Answers.com).

Examples of the Mind Body Connection

An example of a frequently overlooked mind body connection is when we are surprised or frightened our faces turn pale—because fear causes blood vessels to constrict, thereby decreasing the flow of blood to the skin because the body is responding to our fear, with the fight or flight mechanism carried over from our hunter and gatherer days, preparing us to use all our bodies' resources for the fight or the flight.

Another example is eating chocolate helps us emotionally feel more comfortable and happy while illustrating one of the most currently discussed discoveries within the new sciences; the emerging field of neuroimmunology. This discovery made in the early 1970's by Candace Pert, Ph.D., a neuroscientist and psychopharmacologist, identified the neuropeptide called the "opiate receptor" on various sites throughout the body, and the concept of neurostransmitters and their receptor sites in general.

This concept states that our brain communicates with our body using the communication between the brain's neurotransmitters and the receptors located on millions of receptor sites throughout our body. Another way to phrase this discovery of neurotransmitters and receptor sites throughout the body is that this is how the mind and body talk. This has become one of the key important advances in the recently increasing scientific understanding of the mind body connection within the "new sciences."

Following this study to its application to the immune system, hence neuroimmunology: "For many years we have known about interactions between the mind (nervous system) and the body (immune system) along with the effects of these interactions on diseases. It's a proven fact that the immune system is a target of signals from the brain and the endocrine system. Therefore, our experience, behavior, way of thinking and believing has a huge impact on the body and vice versa," (Yasha 2010).

But what does this have to do with our much beloved chocolate? Haven't you recently noticed, "Food is Medicine" more? This is connecting what we eat, to how the foods effect our body chemistry and physiological reactions—and obviously, to learn to eat for health. Chocolate effects the levels of endorphins in the brain. Eating chocolate increases the levels of endorphins released in the brain, giving credence to the claim that chocolate is a comfort food–endorphins work to lessen pain and decrease stress.

Another common neurotransmitter affected by chocolate is serotonin. Serotonin is known as an anti–depressant. One of the chemicals which causes the release of serotonin is tryptophan found in, among other things, chocolate. Then there's one of the more unique neurotransmitters released by chocolate–phenylethylamine. This so called "chocolate amphetamine" causes changes in blood pressure and blood–sugar levels leading to feelings of excitement and alertness. It works like amphetamines to increase mood and decrease depression, but does not result in the same tolerance or addiction, thankfully.

Phenylethylamine is also called the "love drug" because it causes the pulse rate to quicken, resulting in a similar feeling to when someone is in love. Amongst other remaining chemicals found in chocolate to give us these delicious feelings, is one more worth mentioning–theobromine, which can affect the nervous system. Besides having properties that can lead to mental and physical relaxation, it also acts as a stimulant similar to caffeine. Combined, they form a delicious blend of bodily and psychological responses; or the mind body connection in action in response to food, rather than thoughts. A cascade of biochemical reactions are set off with both food and thoughts, so it's all the mind body connection. Some food, just as some thoughts, make us feel more comfortable than others, yes?

An example of some of the proof coming out of mostly "the new sciences" of the mind body connection (being applied to what is now termed "mind body medicine") comes from a clinical trial's finding, as quoted in the *Journal of The American Board of Family Practitioners*: "Evidence emerging within the past several decades suggests that psychosocial factors from emotional states, such as depression, behavioral dispositions, such as hostility, and psychosocial stress can directly influence both physiologic function and health outcomes," (Astin 2003).

Another modern day example of the mind body connection applied to life is from one of the earliest in the field of mind body medicine, the pioneering work of Herbert Benson's, M.D., relaxation response therapy at The Benson–Henry Institute–BHI. Benson's work is possibly the most well known, researched, developed and respected program thus far of the mind body connection being addressed through mind body medicine; it is from a western trained M.D.. His development of the relaxation response therapy led him and his team to teach patients at Massachusetts' General Hospital a host of mind body medicine techniques.

Some of these techniques of the BHI's mind body medicine program are his renowned relaxation response, a meditative technique during which the patient observes the deep breathing of his or her body. Other techniques used are cognitive behavioral therapy, and physical activity including yoga, and nutrition. "The Benson–Henry Institute's work is based on the inseparable connection between the mind and the body–the complicated interactions that take place among thoughts, the body, and the outside world. Mind body medicine integrates modern science, medicine, psychology, nutrition, exercise physiology and belief to enhance the natural healing capacities of body and mind, where the end result is self–care, a complement to the conventional medical paths of surgery and pharmaceuticals," (Benson, M.D., 2010).

In 1977 psychiatrist George L. Engel at the University of Rochester published an article in *"Science,"* the academic journal of the American Association for the Advancement of Science and considered one of the world's most prestigious scientific journals, in which he proposed the biopsychosocial model, or "BPS," as an answer to the need for a new medical model.

BPS is a general model or approach that posits that biological, psychological (which entails thoughts, emotions, and behaviors), and social factors all play a significant role in human functioning in the context of disease or illness. Furthermore, health is best understood in terms of a combination of biological, psychological, and social factors *rather than purely in biological or physical terms.* Thus, this goes beyond the conventional biomedical model provided by the materialist scientific paradigm.

This BPS model is in direct contrast to the conventional, *reductionists' biomedical model of medicine supported by the AMA.* This conventional model suggests every disease process can be explained in terms of an underlying deviation from normal function such as a pathogen, genetic or developmental abnormality, or an injury.

These examples are all obviously contemporary and supportive of the belief in the mind body connection. However, this has not yet reached the majority of our population, although it is rapidly gaining ground. These changing minds—and perhaps you, the reader—are encroaching upon what will become critical mass that will tilt the scales permanently. This change will go beyond the current assigning to the sidelines the mind body connection and its ensuing medicine and accompanying therapies–what have been typically termed, "complimentary" or "alternative."

Our conventional, or biomedical, or allopathic medical system, supported by the AMA, henceforth in this work referred to as the biomedical model, will instead become even more threatened by the credence given to the mind body medicine therapies, and the dollars, restructuring itself after being forced by market-demands, as it has slightly been doing over the past five years or so. Our power is in our dollar; it is a strong voice.

Or perhaps the two models will work with equal stature, side by side, where each works best, respectively, in an integrated manner, such as the model of Integrative Medicine. This is somewhat the way it's done in India with Ayurvedic medicine and "Western Medicine"; and in China with its TCM (Traditional Chinese Medicine) and "Western Medicine."

The US' medical system's strength has been found by the WTO and Harvard Medical School's global study (discussed at length later) to be its trauma response–i.e. antibiotics or emergency room. While the strength of these other, *holistic* systems is to look at a person's vulnerabilities to the traumas caused (mostly) by a person's lifestyle choices (and the ancient wisdom of these holistic systems of how lifestyle choices interact with the natural biological and universal laws).

This examination of daily lifestyle choices only begins once the trauma has subsided. After the lifestyle is assessed, the patient makes the necessary adjustments in lifestyle choices, i.e., reduction of stressors in daily life, changes in diet and exercise, along with some form of a mind body series of treatments to change the person's bio–chemistry and/or vulnerability that lead to the physical diagnosis and trauma in the first place. This is healing at the level of cause when treated holistically, *not only* making symptoms go away by reducing the holistic human system to parts and treating symptoms only, as is done in the current biomedical model provided by the AMA.

Our still dominant biomedical model is the one that is being suggested here to be currently crumbling under its own outdated modus operandi and thus dysfunction. The people defending this model are the very same ones naming the mind body therapies as alternative or complimentary. Huh. Imagine that. Yet, the biomedical model comes from something larger–our culture's metaparadigm of scientific materialism.

In order to better understand the strong opposition and resistance to changing our current delivery of medicine means that we need to acknowledge the many arms that profit from maintaining this system, along with the enabling traditions – and finally, the many industries supporting it as practiced in the United States today.

Our Western scientific tradition of scientific materialism has had the central foothold as our metaparadigm, particularly since the Industrial Revolution. So this means we need to look at our science's history, then trace our biomedical model's development out of our sciences. Ironically, this will allow us to see back to when the various theories negating the mind body connection began and why, after our medical history in the West originally supported these. In fact, placebo—as in the placebo effect—was so generally acknowledged by doctors as pharmaceutical drugs first got introduced that the names of the beginning pharmaceutical drugs were named from word plays on placebo—but more on that later!

The Primary Mind Body Connection Theories in the West

The theories of the mind body connection can be most clearly initially divided into two: monistic and dualistic. *Monistic theories say that the mind and body are not separate substances; dualistic theories say that they are,* with the mind originally thought of as a substance other than a physical substance in dualism, but later this last aspect was lost within dualism, as we shall soon see. Meaning the common connotation for dualism eventually became the mind/body split, but there was more to it, as Descartes originally construed it.

Within each of these two main categories—monistic and dualistic, there are subcategories, further specifying the mind and body's interaction, or separation. Only the subcategories relevant to our discovery process here will be explored. Thinkers like Aristotle, Hobbs, Hegel, and the Behaviorists, collectively thought of as the *materialists,* postulated that *the mind was nothing more than a bodily function, or an extension of the brain.* We'll return to the materialist position shortly, as this is the dominant metaparadigm that has reigned throughout Western science, medicine and hence culture, bringing us to the crossroads we are at today.

Going back now to the non–dualistic school of thought, Berkeley, Leibniz, and Schopenhauer, collectively known as the *idealists,* were monists of a different sort; *they theorized that the body was simply a mental representation.* Meaning, what one knows to be real is in some way confined to the contents of one's own mind, and that *anything we experience through our senses is colored by how our mind perceives it.*

The theory further contends that ideas are dependent upon being perceived by minds for their very existence, a belief that became immortalized in the dictum, "esse est percipi," or "to be is to be perceived," stated in Berkeley's most widely–read work A *Treatise Concerning the Principles of Human Knowledge.* George Berkeley (1685 –1753), also known as Bishop Berkeley (Bishop of Cloyne), was an Anglo–Irish philosopher, and it was his primary achievement, this advancement of the theory he called "immaterialism,"–later referred to as "subjective idealism" by others, referred to as idealism within this discussion.

So that the idealists (or proponents of Berkeley's subjective idealism) collectively reflect much of what modern quantum physicists' core discoveries imply for human consciousness; it is only our thoughts and ideas that originate in our minds that we can immediately experience, and *know* and these thoughts influence what happens around us. *We are more participatory in the creating of the world of physical matter* than previously thought under the scientific materialism of Newtonian physics.

Idealism, a philosophy in the 18th century–even though amidst Newtonian physics–purports this same level of involvement by us and our minds that the 20th century quantum physicists found. Both of which, therefore, stand in stark contrast to the theory of materialism, *for materialism endorses that the physical, spatial, factual domain is the ultimate reality.*

Alfred Whitehead actually grouped the mind body connection theories into three, not only the two categories of monists and dualists. He stated that there are the *dualists, the materialists and the idealists;* remembering that materialists and idealists are both of the monist category initially mentioned, as the theory that the mind and body are not separate substances.

This is where science's history of stemming from both philosophy and science in the West shows up, and it can get confusing. How can the seemingly dichotomous theories of materialism–that the mind is a part of the body–and idealism–that the body is an outcome of the mind–both be in the same category? Because they're both saying there's only one–mono–existence, that there is no duality. Hence their separation from dualism.

But look at the two again side-by-side, materialism and idealism. They're both saying there is only one system; idealists say that the mind is primary, and the materialists say that the body is primary. Yet the dichotomy is so strong, so essential to how one views human existence, that, according to Whitehead and all who have followed since, materialism needs its own place, as does idealism. This puts the Berkeley, Leibniz and Schopenhauer group into their own primary category as Idealists, instead of being contained within the monist view.

Again, this points to the inherent difficulties within the essential issues contained within the mind body connection discussion, hence the label "the mind body problem." There's challenge even in how to discuss, or group, the various theories.

As the International Society for Complexity, Information and Design state on their website, "The mind body problem arises from an intuition that, somehow, the mind is fundamentally different than matter. If that is the case, at least two questions immediately arise. First, if mind is different than matter, then what is its nature? Second, if mind and matter are distinct, then in what way do they exert causal influence over each other? How does the mind affect the body?" (ISCID 2010).

Note the similarity of these questions to what was discussed earlier. Yet, in a current acknowledgment of what has been changing, ISCID goes on to further say, "Most modern philosophers have rejected the view that mind and matter are different substances, but many remain realists about the mind. In other words, *it has become increasingly difficult to draw a strict, reducible identity between brain states and the mind....Most philosophers have come to recognize the distinctive aspects of the mind, as, in some way, irreducible,*" (italics mine) (ISCID 2010).

Within the *initial dual* categorization of *monistic* and *dualistic* theories, double aspectism needs to be mentioned as one of the theories within the monistic category, for it involves an element of divinity. Benedict de Spinoza (1632 –1677) was a Jewish Dutch philosopher known as one of the great rationalists of 17th century philosophy. So much so, that Spinoza has been given the credit for laying the groundwork for the 18th century Enlightenment. By virtue of his masterpiece, the posthumous *Ethics,* in which he opposed Descartes' mind–body dualism, Spinoza is considered to be one of Western philosophy's most important philosophers.

He proposed that *mind and body were the manifestations of some third property–what he considered God.* Spinoza further asserted that the mind and body are *distinguishable* as separate, *but they are inseparable.* Cognitive and experiential aspects can be distinguished from physical aspects, so there is a separate mind and body, somewhat, but the separate mind and body are *two aspects of the same human,* hence its name double–aspectism. Ok.

Now the biggie: our current metaparadigm in the West -materialism. Materialism is one of the three main mind body models. Materialism has been the view that only physical matter is real. The body is governed by *strictly material, non–mental causes. Further, if mental properties do even exist, they have no causal effect on the physical body.* Strict materialists may "hard-headedly deny that anything mental exists at all," (Gummow 2007).

Others may admit that while yes the mind may exist, it is identical, or one and the same, as the brain. The earliest exponents of something resembling materialism dates back to the Greeks, with Democritus and Aristotle—important to note, is that Aristotle still gave massive credence to the mystical, or metaphysical.

An even more specific theory of materialism, and one held by much of Western scientists and medical doctors–neuroscientists and psychologists being two examples–is epiphenomenalism. This theory not only aligns with *the belief that only physical matter is real and that anything mental is questionable,* but even more biasedly towards the physical, this theory asserts that *the mind is limited to being just a byproduct of the physical brain.* Furthermore, that it is only the physical events in the brain (i.e. synapses and neurons firing) that have causal power.

An example of this can be seen applied to the field of psychology. It is replete with examples of how it has historically remained materialist when it comes to qualifying–meaning justifying–itself as a hard science, so that it would not be downgraded to "just being a soft science." This is reflective of our culture's bias towards materialism and our skepticism towards the validity of the intangible.

Epiphenomenalism is the basis of what we can term, for the sake of this discussion, the old neuroscience, comparative to the new sciences that are studying consciousness' role. Most neuroscientists still cling to epiphenomenalism's view, that the brain and physical matter, and hence the body, all have primary and even exclusionary positioning to that of the mind. Meaning, when epiphenomenalists speak of the brain, they are meaning a physical thing, because to them the brain is part of the body. In this view, the physical body affects–and even causes–the mind. However, because the mind is merely a byproduct, the mind does not affect the body.

According to William James, considered the father of modern Western psychology, mental events do not affect the brain activity that produces them "anymore than a shadow reacts upon the steps of the traveler whom it accompanies," (James 1879). For the sake of our discussion, when referring to the materialist view, it will include–and typically be speaking directly to–the epiphenomenalism view, for it is this more extreme version of materialism that is the foundation of our hard sciences. And it is the polar opposite to acknowledging that the mind influences the body's physiological states or chemistry, as the mind body connection is defined by the Dalai Lama

And now to the biggie: dualism, remembering this was originally one of the two initial categories of monism and dualism. Then there were three-dualism, monism—with materialism being monistic—and idealism. Popular dualists were, John Locke and William James. Dualism is typically credited to Descartes, as well as is the creation of the split between the mind and body in the West.

However, at first glance this seems ironic because Descartes acknowledges the mind, unlike the materialists who are monists saying it's all body and no mind, so why is he any different from the monists? He is different from the materialists of the monists because it is not one—or mono—system, but that the mind is split from the body because *it is of a substance other than a physical substance, hence two, or dual systems.*

This seems a bit similar to the idealists, who acknowledge the mind as well—unlike the materialists—but say that it is still a single—mono—system, but it is the mind exerting the primary force upon the body. Descartes' dualism also does acknowledge the mind and its power, as evidenced in his "I think therefore I am," realization in 1637.

However, Descartes also acknowledged the primary of the physical, in that we are physical beings because we are extended in space. Here's the split; yet we are also mental beings, because we think—I think therefore I am.

Now here's the reason for more confusion: the mind is not physical in any way, and it exists separately from the body. So how does it then, this non—physical mind, affect the physical body, and vice versa or does it ever do so?

Descartes accredited an interaction between the mind and body, saying it's in the pineal gland. He also said the pineal gland is where the soul is located; hence, Descartes retained a sense of the mystical in his dualistic approach, like his Greek forefathers, for he credited the mind as being its own substance separate from the physical, and containing the element of that which cannot be fully explained—or the mysterious or *mystical*—occurring within the soul which is physically seated within the brain's pineal gland.

Ironically, as we shall see, the "new sciences" scientific research within neuroscience is confirming that the pineal gland has soul level activity associated with it, while also simultaneously confirming as well an ancient

Eastern–Hindu–belief of the pineal gland's "mystical" or metaphysical powers, contained within the Yogic sciences.

Where the problem lies is the Western scientists and philosophers following Descartes and their erroneous interpretations and applications of his theory of dualism, focusing only on the body and leaving the mystical, or the other stuff of the "mind problem" to the Church.

So, due to the impact of the sciences in the West creating how we as a culture have perceived in general the mind body connection, before we can go any further, we need to look at Western science. As it will be made increasingly clear, the gradual dominance of the Western scientific model—based on materialism, reductionism and objective, logical empiricism—progressively squeezed out any substantial exploration into the subtle energies, or the mind and consciousness, as this was—and continues to be—seen by science as a "hard problem" due to the intangibility, and therefore immeasurability of its nature.

Within the western scientific and biomedical methodology of measurement provable in a laboratory, and standardized reliability applicable to every individual so that the results are consistently replicable by peer scientists in peer review journals, something as elusive or seemingly non-uniform as the human mind is neither of these—measurable and replicable—*easily.* Yet this is the nature of their profession; to measure stuff.

As one of the great physicists of the 20th century, Niels Bohr admitted: "The procedure of measurement has an essential influence on the conditions on which the very definition of the physical qualities rest," (Bohr 1935). Albert Einstein, continuing along this vein also stated that, "On principle, it is quite wrong to try founding a theory on observable magnitudes alone. In reality the very opposite happens. It is the theory that decides what we can observe," (Wallace 2008).

However, both of these great scientists did not come along until the twentieth century, and both were physicists, which has been the discipline within the sciences that has been turning the materialist paradigm upside down since around the 1920's, with both Bohr's and Einstein's—amongst others—discoveries about reality, matter, time and space.

Peter Russell is a British author of ten books, his most popular being *The Global Brain* (1983), and producer of three films on consciousness, spiritual awakening and their role in the future development of humanity. He went from being a self–proclaimed convinced atheist, studying mathematics and physics, to realizing a profound personal synthesis of the mystical and the scientific. He gained an honors degree in physics and experimental psychology at the University of Cambridge in England. He has been, also, a student of meditation and Eastern philosophy in India. After returning from India, he conducted extensive research into the neurophysiology of meditation at the University of Bristol. Russell is a perfect voice here. In his book *From Science To God: A Physicist's Journey Into the Mystery of Consciousness*, he says:

> "Today, after thirty years of investigation into the nature of consciousness, I have come to appreciate how big a problem consciousness is for contemporary science. Science has had remarkable success in explaining the structure and functioning of the material world, but when it comes to the inner world of the mind–to our thoughts, feelings, sensations, intuitions, and dreams–science has very little to say. And when it comes to consciousness itself, science falls curiously silent. *There is nothing in physics, chemistry, biology, or any other science that can account for our having an interior world.* In a strange way, scientists would be much happier if there were no such thing as consciousness," (italics mine) (Russell 2003).

Tales From a Holistic Practitioner

"**Y**ou've got to be kidding me. You can talk. You can so talk!"

The 82 year old jokester stood in front of me, smiling and shrugged his shoulders. He started to motion with his fingers, as if drawing in the air a letter, while some gurgling sound came out of his throat.

"Ed, you just said a bunch of stuff clearly, without hesitation, with me understanding you! What are you doing now? You can talk, but you can't spell!"

His eyes twinkled as he opened his mouth. I waited. He closed it. I smiled. "See, you just think you can't talk. And when you think it—you can't! As soon as you hesitate and start thinking about how you can't talk, then you can't."

"Really?" His eyes got really big.

"Yes, really." He thought for a minute. Then nodded. I thought for a minute. "Ok, so we can get to that belief with some subconscious reprogramming." There I went again, into my geek talk, as I looked at his blank stare. "I can use one of my energy medicine methods to help you with that belief and those thoughts that make you think you have a problem with talking."

"Ok," he said, looking surprised.

"Also, I can release whatever trauma surrounded the stroke, and all the stuff around all the speech therapy you've done these years, you know, that has reinforced the belief that you can't talk, or that you have a problem talking."

He stood there looking at me incredulously. "You understood what I just said, I know you did, Ed. You did, right?"

He nodded. I saw something come across his face, then he opened his mouth and said, "I think so. You mean when I think it's going to be a problem to talk, then it is." We stood there looking at each other, both of us grinning ear to ear, realizing he'd just said that sentence perfectly.

"Yup. You got it. You know for a retired Hallmark Card Sales Rep, you're not so soft." I clipped him on the shoulder and led him into the healing studio. "Come on, let's get at it."

Ed tromped into the room behind me, as if a child of six getting ready to go get some ice cream. I wondered what flavor he'd get. He was from New England originally, so probably something like Maple Walnut.

"Ed, what's your favorite ice cream?"

"Mint chocolate chip," again said perfectly. I chose to let that go and proceed.

"Hmmm. Really?"

He smiled as he sat down. "Yes. It's good!" A little slur to his words, but still understandable.

"You know that was my first boyfriend's favorite ice cream too. He had it on our first date. I'll never forget it. And my family and I used to ride our bikes up a couple of miles to the old fashioned ice cream stand on Sundays. Apparently, my mom told me this later, as a little girl of about six," I paused making sure he was with me, "I would go around and offer my ice cream cones to strangers at the stand to have a lick." I floated into the feeling of that memory for a moment.

"That's because ice cream is so good!" Ed kind of said that a bit more slowly, but most clients do the same at that point in the beginnings of the session as they start to feel the calming from the energy healing. I had been activating his pineal and pituitary glands for about three minutes. It always takes everyone—and me—out of their cognitive, linear mind as they start to float with the relaxing energy taking them down into alpha brain waves and then eventually theta brain waves, out of the everyday level of beta.

I thought about how Ed had been just two sessions before this one, his third. He had not spoken one sentence clearly. I was really excited to see how much progress we could make in another three sessions.

"Ed, if I had you listen to a few sound healing CD's on your computer to help reconnect your brain hemispheres, which would help your speech, do you think you would do that twice a day, with headphones?"

"Sure! I'll try anything! Why not?" He looked up at me, even though my hands were at his forehead and the top of his head, so my hands followed his head. His eyes were so happy, with a "I dare you!" look.

"Well now that's the spirit Ed! I tell you, Sir, if most people half your age had your attitude, there would be a lot happier bunch of people out and about, less achy and unhappy. You could teach them a thing or two, you know! So would you consider coming with me to one of my workshops? Maybe you'd rub off on them," I smiled down at him, even though he couldn't see me.

I could feel him hesitate.

"We'd make sure your speech would be just fine before that."

"Ok then. Sure!"

This was going to be fun, I thought to myself, as I switched to the second hand position, and began to treat Ed's brain stem and pineal gland to balance his central nervous system. He shifted his posture as I did, relaxing more in the chair he was in.

Wow! I thought to myself as Joy pulled back her bra and showed me the lump that had developed in the last three weeks since her last session. It was quite huge! I cleared my face of any reaction and resettled in my chair as I put my hand in the appropriate spots to begin the energy healing treatments on the lump. We proceeded to talk about how Joy had felt that this lump was somehow connected to her relationship with her 31 year old daughter. As we talked and new information came up, I steered Joy through the limiting beliefs she had taken on about her and her daughter.

After about 45 minutes I lifted my hand up off of the lump and looked down and exclaimed, "Oh my God Joy this thing has shrunk by about 2/3 the size!" She couldn't see because she was laying down.

"Really?" she was not incredulous because we'd been working together for two years by that point, and had dealt with quite a lot in that two years, and saw quite a lot of change in things considered "unchangeable." So she was ready to accept this.

"YES! This is fantastic!"

I was excited because my work deals so much in the invisible realms, without tangible proof validating the progress, save for the results my clients get back from tests from their doctors measuring the progression or regression of their illness or condition. Instead, the measures are typically quite subtle and I coax information out of my clients about their reactivity levels within sensitive areas of their lives (i.e., bosses, spouses, kids), their energy levels, their happiness levels, their sleep, and other measures of their well-being. But this was the first time I was dealing with a visible tumor that I could see shrink under my hands—and in a little under an hour! I was in awe for the rest of the night, and still kind of am, as I add this in after the original manuscript had already been completed. You can see Joy's testimonial on my blog. And get an update on her progress. Yesterday was the second treatment and it has shrunk even more, down to just a little peak.

"I don't feel like myself anymore. I used to be so happy. I want some help getting my joy back," said the woman's voice on the phone. I walked over to my window to get better cell reception. The sky was so blue at that moment, with fluffy white clouds and the sun blasting away on this sunny day in Florida. The sunshine state—no doubt! Flashing back on the grey skies in Taiwan that could last for months during the winter months, I brought myself back to the present, to the woman reaching out.

"Ok. Well this is definitely something that I help people with, and have had much success with alleviating it for people even in their first session. Depression tends to lift rather easily, compared to other issues I work with, and depending on if it's a weepy depression, or a deeper, more lethargic, long standing depression."

"Ok. Good. Well, I have good energy, it's not that. It's just feels like there's something suppressing my happiness. I cry a bit, yes, but not non-stop. And the crying is a part of this lack of joy, but it's not the major thing, I don't think. I'm just not happy, whereas I always have been. Up until recently. And I just can't seem to shake it."

"Mary, right?"

"Yes."

"Mary, this is more typical than I bet you're aware of. At least half of my client base is dealing with less joy than they once had, and that's why they're coming to me—along with whatever else the lack of joy comes with. There's this kind of thick, grey cloud over most of us nowadays, it's part of being on our planet right now. But typically, we just think it's us. In fact I have a weekly online radio show in order to help people know it's not just them, and to help people better understand the nature of what we're facing here in 2012. It's like it's our time to wake up. But before we do, we have this thickness over us, like what you're describing. Or for other people, they have a health, personal or financial crisis in their lives to get them to wake up to something beyond this everyday life we've created of being busy, making money, feeding and taking care of our families and homes, and doing it all over again each day, loaded with obligations that we may not want to be obligated to. It's also the reason why I've written a book that's due to be released soon. It's a common feeling right now. And it's not too terribly hard to address. Come in, and during this initial consult and energy healing session I'll get a better idea of your particular areas where the joy has been suppressed and we can go from there. You will get lighter, with more of a feeling of well-being just from the first session. You'll see—it's more something that needs to be experienced rather than described."

We talked just a bit more—she did not want to go into a big long story of the recent drama and struggles, as many do when they call—and then booked an appointment for the next week. I found myself already liking her, appreciating her style. I told her, "Ok, Mary. See you next week, then. Congratulations on taking this step towards your new life."

"Great. Thank you. See you next Thursday at 1:00."

"Yes, next Thursday at 1:00. And Mary?"

"Yes?"

"Keep your eyes open. And your ears. The universe seems to send some kind of message that affirms our taking steps towards our YES's to being happier, to being more. Once a person reaches out to work with me and commits to it, it's quite consistent throughout my client base's experience—in the first weeks especially until they get used to it happening so they see it everyday—when starting the holistic life coaching and energy healing with me. Kind of like we're given clues to follow, and then support after we follow the ones that will lead us to more expansion of ourselves. Do you know what I mean?"

"I think so, yes. Like something happens that could seem random, but has a sort of message to it. Like finding your ad in the Tampa Bay Wellness magazine when I was feeling this has got to change and finally admitted needing help? I had never picked up that magazine before. I was walking out of the health food store and it just kind of caught my eye, so without thinking

I took one. And when I opened it, it was to the page with your bright ad. It kind of leapt off the page at me."

"Yup. You got it. Fantastic!" I was excited to be able to work with someone who seemed already in tune to the way this higher field surrounding all life seems to interact with us. Some say God here. Some say "the universe." Whatever. It's all the same source. It is source! "Source energy," still others call it, come to think of it.

I was looking forward to helping someone already tuned in, and wanting to make new choices, who was reaching out for help. Yay! In fact, I recognized that I had been asking "the universe" for this type of client to fill up my client load and here she was! While about half of my clients already understood how the holistic model of the mind body connection paradigm worked and were looking for some more "fine tuning," the other half of my clients were dealing with the real heavy issues like cancer, digestive disorders, suicide attempts, prescription drug addictions, and some dark fears locked up into chronic pain. They were needing a heck of a lot of support, while only mildly understanding the mind body connection. And even less understanding of how energy healing works to help "unravel" what's been tied up within their chakras, or unconscious.

So, overall, this required a lot more explaining on all fronts. As we went through each week's session I told them what I found because it helped them better understand their physical, mental and emotional "symptoms," and why their body was doing what it was. Then also as I gave them the suggested holistic life coaching tools, I helped them to understand how these would help our overall program together. My clients used my program of both the energy healing sessions, coupled with the lifestyle changes from the holistic life coaching tools to support their changing at their daily life level. It's such a different way of doing things than the reductionist, specialist model of our current medical system's methods. It's holistic, and it addresses my clients' daily lifestyle choices.

Natural healing is not a quick fix. If it is meant to unravel an issue at its roots, it takes a bit of time for a person—and this varies according to the person's willingness to change—to release all the layers of what has built up in their system with the pattern that becomes the actual issue they're coming to me for. Because what we see as a physical issue has its roots in the daily, typical mental and emotional life of each of us, that then directs life force energy in the same way over and over again. And if this pattern isn't based on wholesome feelings and thoughts for a person—and this does have some variability between people like what different people view as stress—then it becomes an issue.

See! This is an example of the amount of education needed to translate the effects of and how natural healing works to people who are used to a system that treats surface symptoms, and can take pills or get surgeries to seemingly address their ills with almost immediate effects. But this is only addressing them at the surface level. Energy healing is fascinating in the way it can undo what's been done. I find it an incredibly elegant statement about the inherent beauty built into life in this universe. That if we mess something up, and even quite badly, it can still get cleaned up—or healed, as other people would put it.

Anyways, yes, back to explaining. So in order to understand the symptoms a person experiences as they let go of the layers of build up towards their issue, they need the bigger perspective on what's happening in their whole system of how their mind, body, spirit and emotions work together and direct flows of life force energy—or not—in their system. And when the life force energy isn't flowing energy to a certain area, issues start, that eventually, if not dealt with, become the physical symptoms that sends people to their doctors.

The next week a woman in her early 50's came to my healing studio's door, with huge sad blue eyes, vibrantly colored auburn and red hair and a soft voice. I greeted Mary, "Hi. Well you did good finding the place. Usually half the people call, lost, because it looks like a Monopoly board in here. Welcome. Would you mind taking off your shoes here, please? I'm glad you're here."

"You are?" She looks surprised, as she obligingly took off her strappy heels.

"Sure. You're ahead of the game, Mary. You recognized you needed support because you missed the alive juice in your life, without having a physical problem. And you reached out for help."

She smiled slightly, looking encouraged. "Really?"

I nodded, "Most people in our country only notice something is wrong when there are physical issues to deal with. Not as many catch slightly off feelings, or a bit of the blues and then reach out for help. Shows how in tune you are with yourself."

"Well that's funny, because I don't really feel that in tune with myself. That's part of why I'm here. I feel just off, like I said, not myself. That's interesting that you say that."

I handed her the clipboard with the two pieces of paper that were my intake forms, and motioned for her to come on in. A few minutes later, her paperwork filled out and signed and read by me, we began her first session. It silence, I stood by her side facing her side, while she sat in the chair looking straight ahead, and put my fingers on her forehead and the crown of her head. I began the alignment of her pineal and pituitary glands, as the master glands of the endocrine system, to activate and balance her hormonal system with the vital life force energy. But I like to start with this one because it's a really soothing hand position—all of them are, but particularly this one. I love doing it on myself, and do it at least a few times a week on myself. There's a quieting and calming that usually comes after the first three of the five minutes for this hand position.

"You feel really low energy, but not like your mind has been racing. Just slow, low, but still, good and grounded. Not like you're anxious and worried."

"Hmm. No I don't really get anxious, just more sad. I've been sad recently. And yes, not too worried or anxious. How did you know that?"

"I can tell from the activity under my fingers, across your forehead. Like if someone works on the computer a lot, there's this kind of buzzing, heightened energy at the top of the forehead. One of my clients, a programmer, his head is always buzzing like this. He comes to me straight from work, so it's right there. But yours is slow and without that buzzing."

"Wow. That's cool."

"Yeah."

We proceeded through the remainder of her session in silence. Afterwards, I met with her outside of the healing studio in another room, and we talked about what I had found, and she gave me her feedback on what life events were connected to what I was saying I found. "Yes, I have had a lot of people's anger coming at me over the past few years. Especially from two different people. That's what I think is really affecting my happiness. I mean, I know I am not doing all that I can for myself to be as happy as I can. But their anger is definitely a part of it."

"Yes. It does affect us, especially when we're more open to people and can kind of feel what they're feeling, which you seem to be. So their anger has affected you more. We can strengthen you ability to draw stronger boundaries, though, through working with your 2nd and 3rd chakras. It's not a problem. In fact, we've already started that process with today's treatment. Do you have a pattern in your life of people being angry at you?" I asked her, suspecting the answer she gave.

"Yes," and her story began to come out just a bit. I listened as she described the various circumstances that seemed the most pressing on her mind. When she finished, I suggested a few different holistic life coaching tools, loaned her a seminar on a 7 CD set, and made the appointment time for the next week. She appeared to be feeling encouraged.

"I feel lighter," Mary said, after putting her shoes back on, her hands on the door handle, as she met my eyes, looking a bit pleasantly surprised, as if she'd forgotten this feeling. She opened the door and I followed her out to the sunny day, standing on the grass.

"Oh this is just the beginning, Mary! Enjoy your day. You'll probably want more sleep tonight to help incorporate the session. I'll email you that document explaining the typical responses to energy healing tonight. For now, as you leave, please go slow."

"Ok," she smiled and walked towards her new Volvo.

I completed writing notes in her file, and said out loud, "Thank you universe!" Grateful for the opportunity to be in service to help another person lighten during this time, and grateful that this one was so easy, comparatively.

"I just kind of feel like I'm also being used to deliver some kind of message for others. What I just went through wasn't just for me. Does that make sense?"

I felt it out for a moment, as I sat there at May's head, holding the hand position for the energy healing process I was doing with her to help re-balance her brain chemistry. She had thus far shown herself to be one of those more rare people who is already listening to herself in a way I've found that most people don't seem to. There isn't the training nor milieu in our country to gear us to slow down, and introspect, comparatively. That's what they come to me for, somewhat. To help them interpret themselves. Sounds strange, but true. Like I was acting as translator of the deeper parts of themselves to their everyday cognitive mind of their more genuine motivations, fears and long standing energy patterns.

She interrupted my intuitive receptivity to her last statement by saying, "I mean I don't want to sound like I don't have responsibility here too and that this also hasn't been because of some of my stuff."

"No, May you are definitely in the middle of something much, much bigger than you. You're absolutely right. After your suicide attempt, your improvement that allowed you to be released, and then your panic attacks that led you back into the psyche ward—and I know you checked yourself back in those later times—that is all part of something much bigger."

"What do you mean?" She was really softened and receptive by this point due to the energy healing that had been flowing into her system for about 20 minutes.

"Well, it's what my book is all about, it's what my radio show is all about, it's what my business is all about! It's a dysfunctional system at this point, and at the level of the masses, it has never known how to effectively deal with mental pain and anguish. And in today's world, the suicide attempts are increasing, as are panic and anxiety attacks, depression and all the other psychological disorders—as are the medications for them. It does know how to deal with trauma, diagnose and give out medications, but how much has that helped you?"

I was wondering if her Prozac use was actually what had led her to the suicidal feelings and attempt, as it has with a high percentage of users. Or if it was that she was hitting the bottle pretty hard, and with alcohol being a depressant...Yeah. People are always more complex than a simple diagnosis, as convenient as they are.

"AA has helped me some, for sure. But it wasn't enough," she said that as if half asleep.

"I've had other clients who have said much the same. Like AA was a bridge for them, but it was missing the spiritual component. One said he was really only able to kick his habits—he came from both AA and NA—once he took up meditation."

"Hmmm. I'm just glad I was eventually led to someone like you who can look at the different layers of me, and get to the deeper me, help me you know? Guide me to hear my soul's needs better. Really help me on my path towards enlightenment."

I swallowed back responding to the bigness of the last word she'd used, and instead said, "Well that's what the suicide attempt was, that's what the alcoholism was about. You were searching for something with more meaning...searching for how to connect with something bigger and how to use your power. And look at two of the main traditions in your genes, Native American and African American. Both cultures are massively mystical, with rich traditions of honoring that part of life. But you, along with some of your ancestors—they just legalized Native Americans conducting their religious traditions and ceremonies again in the 1970's!—have had their source of power shut off from them. You were and are looking for yours. There was no turning it down. Even as you tried! No escaping it, so here you are learning to deal with it. And your being is powerful enough to have called me into your life. See how you are!"

I could feel her satisfaction in considering what I had just said. And her ease. And then her sleep. I switched my hands into a new hand position, one that treats the part of the brain to help release more of the happy feeling hormones.

"I just don't feel like myself anymore. I was never this lacking in confidence. I've always been strong, confident, happy. I don't know how to get myself back again." This was said to me during Mike's initial phone consult, on a sunny Saturday, early in the afternoon. I reprimanded myself for not letting the unknown number's call go to voicemail, and then addressing it on Monday.

When Mike came to my healing studio the following week, his long, drawn, fifty-something face reflected a mind locked in on itself. The first session Mike didn't say much, just that he had a recent bout with cancer, had done chemo and wasn't healed from it, so he had gone to Arizona to a doctor who gave him chelation therapy to detox the chemicals out of him, coupled with intravenous vitamin C, amongst other therapies. That was four months ago. He had been doing well up until last month, when he had developed a staph infection and found himself fed up with his lack of feeling good.

Mike's body, upon my initial assessment, felt weakened still in his immune system, but it didn't have the heavy energy that the presence of cancer has. He had already been told the cancer was gone by this doctor in Arizona. His system confirmed that to me.

We went for boosting his immune system through the energy healing and then using food as medicine, with food suggestions including Chinese medicinal mushrooms. The following week we began to address the "real reason"—meaning unknown by Mike, but one of the most frequent emotional connections to cancer— he had sought me out.

"I just don't know how to forgive these people who betrayed me. I still have a lot of anger towards them."

I looked up from his toes that lay on the rock salt foot lamps, where I was holding the end-points of the main meridians to complete his central nervous system balancing. I was startled that he let this out in the second session, and grateful because now we could actually make some progress towards bringing his system fully back.

"Mike, I hear you. Oh do I! Forgiveness is considered the pinnacle of the spiritual lessons a human being goes through. But with you releasing anger, blame, and resentment, you'll be able to open your heart chakra which will support your system being flushed with its more native energy, rebalancing the energy of cancer. What is known to be one of the main emotions behind cancer, if not THE main one, is anger, specifically one that is directed at others where feelings of betrayal or attack are perceived. So this is one of the strongest things we can do to assure your release of the pattern behind the cancer."

"Are you saying I caused my own cancer?"

This is such the first human response! "No Mike," I said this in such a serious tone, to match the heaviness of where he was at, hoping that the graveness would speak to him in a way he'd understand. "There is such a thing known as 'the toxic load' and it's a combination of chemical pollutants, toxicity that results from both physical means such as the chemicals in our food, chemo, pesticides, and then the subtle energies of the emotions you mentioned also being toxic. The contributions from the ongoing stress, anger, rage or bitterness can tip the scales of the toxic load, and frequently are the tipping point, into a disease state. It's the mind body connection, and no it's not your fault. But your emotions are a contributing factor. So the sooner we can release the residue of the anger, the pattern of the anger and feelings of betrayal, the sooner we'll shift your system closer to the body chemistry of health. We'll need to continue with the detoxing through your supplements you're currently doing, yes, and the fantastically healthy diet you're now eating, but the emotional and mental thought patterns we're going to need to unravel from your system. We can do that through the chakras' unconsciousness as well as some other means. I can use one of the energy healing modalities I work with to help with your thoughts and beliefs around the betrayal and hurt. I can use one of the other energy medicine modalities I work with to help boost your immune system, too."

Looking for this to give him relief, I instead was met with, "What about my mind? How can I get away from this negativity? I've never been like this before!"

"Mike, from what I can see at this point, your system has been in some shock from the cancer diagnosis. And you've been in the fight or flight response basically since then, tapping into your adrenals to the point of now you've gotten yourself into basically adrenal burnout, coupled with this cycle of anxiety driving your system to be in an ongoing fight or flight response. So I can work directly on the adrenals and hormonal system to help rebalance it through the chakras. But I can also use ThetaHealing to help with releasing the shock, and clearing your mind of its more deeply held negative beliefs and blocks at this point."

His body slumped back into the chair as I treated him at his toes, finishing the central nervous system balancing. He seemed relieved, as little as it was, it was still a lightening. I realized this man's mind had had a firm grip over him for quite a while. Meaning, he was getting swallowed up by his mind, with the incessant heavy thoughts suppressing the more heart based living that yields more joy and lightness. He carried this thick, grey cloud of seriousness all over him. I thought back to how his first session, after he'd left, I had to spend some extra time clearing the healing studio.

He then left "the golden throne" and got on the table and I did the ThetaHealing on his subconscious and conscious beliefs as I said I would. He really responded well, with a lot of emotional and mental charge locked up around not believing he was actually cancer free at that point. Even though we hadn't talked much about this, once I went up into the Theta brain wave state, my intuition guided me to see that he was still holding on to having the cancer.

I was pleased by the end of the whole session, having then treated his immune system and chakras, after the ThetaHealing, because I felt that I was able to get to much of what was weighing him down that first time going in with the ThetaHealing. At the end of that session that day, I gave him one of the primary books that I loan out to my clients; it's one I use to teach about the nature of the mind when teaching meditation classes. I walked him out to his vehicle, noticing as we walked that he had a lighter step.

"You seem lighter, Mike. That's great! I think we got something there! That clearing for you being able to believe it's finally over, the chase for a cure and that you're actually cured—it seems to have gotten at something, yah?"

"I hope so. Yes. I do feel better. Ok. See you next week, same time, right?"

I smiled at his vulnerability to this new land of believing he could actually be rid of this disease, this weight he'd been carrying for so long. That he could change, that it could change had also been part of the ThetaHealing, and it was what I felt had had the strongest impact on his consciousness. He had passed out at that point in the clearing. His needing to go to sleep actually told me that's how deeply traumatizing those beliefs had been. By knocking out the conscious, cognitive mind with sleep, the energy healing is able to get into the subconscious. Clients fall asleep when the high power of the energy healing needs to work on deep subconscious and unconscious beliefs. It's only my lighter—and better rested clients—that stay awake during sessions.

"Yes. Same time next week. Take good care of the book, and I'm ready for any questions you may have. It's new territory, this description of the way the mind works. So go slow. The information in the book is dense, the ideas are new and big."

He looked down at the book tentatively, opened his van's door and got in. I walked slowly back to the door of my healing studio, making sure to smile and wave as he pulled away. He was so tentative in that new feeling, as if he couldn't believe it. As if expecting it at any moment, his worries, his negativity, that darkness he'd been battling with to return.

"Hi Mike. Good to see you. Come on up." It was the next week, and I was standing at the top of the stairs looking down at him as he took his shoes off before entering beyond the foyer, where a Buddha statue and a Dalai Lama's textile, "The Paradox of our Age" hung that talked about how we had more ways to communicate now, but less communication.

"How did you do with the book?" I asked, as I saw he had it in his hands.

"Not good. I couldn't read it. For some reason, my mind really was negative with it," he said this quite forcefully, nearly spitting it out.

Extremely familiar with this somewhat homeopathic reaction the mind creates in response to something that could lead a person to making changes in the exact area that the mind feels like it doesn't want that exact change, because it's too close to a core pattern in a person, I pause, and wait in silence as Mike makes his way up the stairs.

It seems like the mind's view is that if this core pattern were changed, then the mind wouldn't be able to maintain its control through fear, because the person would've faced the very fear that the mind seems to hold on to, in order to keep the status quo of the mind's dominance, and the person not stepping into the next level of their power. Almost like it's afraid of the person evolving. Maybe it's because this power is infused with the person's Higher Self, so it's not from the mind. And for some reason, the mind, views that it'll be somewhat killed off if the person steps into this new level of operating from this different power source of the Higher Self, or new version of themselves. Plus, then the status quo is shaken up. The mind doesn't want this. It tries to protect us, and at times it takes its job very seriously. Too seriously, in fact!

Frequently it appears that a core pattern within a person (i.e., always messing up in that same way when presented with another new relationship, so the relationship falls apart in that same way again; or that same problem with bosses that comes up no matter what that new boss is like) is where the mind has created a consciousness loop, or a train of thought that keeps the mind in control, and the person fumbling, repeating cycles of behavior that consistently lead to an unfavorable outcome.

It's the mind feeling threatened by losing its sense of comfort with the status quo, pushing away any and all opportunities for change by strong reactions and resistance against change so the person who is believing their every thought buys into the lock-down the mind wants to have with staying the same. And so they don't make those new choices, almost as if the mind/ personality construes the new choices as rebelling against their mind's most dominant thought patterns and choices that lead to unfavorable outcomes. Deeply entrenched behaviors we're talking about here, like those ones that are as intimately familiar as that old t-shirt you always wear on Saturdays. Much of the time this is not a reaction that most people are aware of. They just don't take action towards changing that very base pattern that would then catalyze huge change in their lives. Instead, they run from the opportunities to change, with the mind leading right back into habitual behaviors.

So I said nothing but, "Ok. Come on in." Off we went into the healing studio.

A few minutes into the treatment, Mike said, "I don't know how to stop this negativity in my mind! It keeps me awake at night."

"Mike, have you noticed a difference in the level of it since last week?" I was fishing to see his response to the energy healing session from the week before. Most clients don't know how to gauge nor report their emotions, state of mind, physical shifts, dreams, incidents with wildlife out in nature, or interactions with others between sessions as information that shows how their system is integrating the influx of light, or life force energy, or energy healing. And gives them—and me—messages. So I fish.

"It almost feels more intense. Like I'm even more negative!" He sat there, seemingly excited to get to his healing, but frustrated.

"Mike, that's, um, actually a sign that what we did last week worked. It's called the healing crisis. If you felt comfortable getting emails at your place of work, then I would've sent you the document I always send out after someone's first treatment about what to expect. But do you remember me telling you that for three days after the treatment, what we were able to go in and get out with the energy healing has to leave your field, or the invisible bodies just beyond your physical body? That's your system releasing, letting go of what we got unstuck. And after the third day out, you will have integrated the energy healing, and your system would've shifted into a new state. The intensity is done. Do you remember me saying that?"

"I think so. Something like that."

"I know. Whenever clients are done with these treatments, they leave here floating, and the cognitive mind is quieted, so memory—not so good, " I smiled.

"But it's actually a great sign! As crazy as that sounds, the negativity increasing means we're getting to it. It's the healing crisis, which is homeopathic in nature, because it's the body's way of bringing itself back into balance, so it purges itself of what was stuffed down in there. Like how we get a fever to burn up an infection, but it has to peak before the fever breaks? That intensity level of the fever peaking is the same thing you experienced with your negativity. That intensity is a reflection of the level we got it to release last week, clearing it out of your system."

We remained in silence for quite a few minutes while he considered that and I tuned into his system more.

Mike broke the silence, saying, "I feel like I should tell you what happened that caused me so much hurt. But I just don't want to talk about, like I will be negative. And I am trying not to do that." He brought his hand up to his chin, placing it there as if in deep thought.

"Mike, complaining is one thing, where you're repeating the story over and over again about something bad that happened to you as the mind perceives itself like a victim. This does at some point make it worse, yes. It reinforces the story and solidifies more the old emotions from the event, yes, and so they're then lodged more in the physical body as blocks. That's when it's repeated over and over again and the person thinks of it as "their story." But then there's another way to deal with it, and that's not keeping emotions bottled up that have been, and need to be released. That's what we're doing here. But you don't have to talk to me about it, if you don't want. I'll see them anyways in your chakras, as I go to work on them. So no worries."

He considered that for a few moments. I cued him to now move to the "yellow golden sunshine throne" as I call it—a chair opposite the one clients sit in for the first ten minutes of the energy healing session. Once seated in the golden sunshine throne, he returned his feet back onto the Pakistanian pink rock salt foot blocks, heated by little light bulbs, that are used to clear my clients'—and mine!—field of EMF interferences from wifi, cellular towers and the like.

I took hold of his big toes. Looking up at him, as I knelt down on the floor in front of his feet, the rather big rock salt foot rests and him, he said, "I had these people, who I trusted, who took care of me because I had no one else—no wife, no kids, no parents, no one—when I first got diagnosed. They betrayed me. I couldn't and can't understand why or how people would do what they did." He was shaking his head back and forth.

Never specifying the exact betrayal, Mike continued, "They seemed like good people. From where I come from in Minnesota -"

"You're from Minnesota, hey?" I smiled, as some of my favorite expat colleagues at the international school I had taught at in Taiwan came to mind.

He seemed pleased by my response, continuing, "Yes. I would never hurt anyone. Like if a girl were alone at night in a parking lot, I'm not a threat.

It's not the way I am or the way people are where I come from. I just don't understand how people can hurt each other."

What could I say? Start lecturing on the nature of people and good and bad? God no. So I nodded, and said, "Mike, I know exactly what you mean." I looked him dead in the eye, and he could feel that I did. Because I did. Nothing more was said. Mike moved to the table at the end of the completion of his central nervous system balancing in the golden sunshine throne, and we began the next leg of the treatment.

"Mike, I think I'm going to try a different treatment this time with you. It's from a system created to deal with our negative and self-restrictive beliefs called Access Consciousness that I've been doing for about 6 weeks now. It's called a Bars treatment and it helps release the emotional and mental charge on our more limiting thoughts. It'll help free up your thoughts, the negative ones you're talking about, and allow for some new openings in your thoughts. Kind of like airing out your stale thinking."

"Yes! Anything that you can do to get at these negative thoughts! That'd be good!" He ran his hand through his hair and sighed, as I put the knee bolster under his knees.

After the session, as we did our wrap-up, I observed Mike. "You look good, Mike. The stress around your eyes and in your cheeks has gone. Your face has really opened up. You should go look in the mirror."

"Really?" He just kind of stood there, looking like a kid fresh from a nap, not really ready to talk.

So I gave him another one of my key teaching materials for the nature of the mind and meditation. "Here, try this one. It may go in easier, he's a soft spoken Indian, who left India to teach at Berkeley and was the first to teach meditation at the university level at University of California, Berkeley. He was also an English Literature teacher. So the writing is really clear. He puts stuff really simply, for such a complex subject."

Mike looked down at the little book in my hand, reached for it and walked down the stairs. I followed him, asking him if he'd been able to use his spirulina in his smoothies. "Yes, that's going well."

"Good. That'll help you have more light circulate in your system."

Two weeks and treatments later, after reading a bit in the second book that first week, he then returned it to me the second week at the start of this treatment, with the same reaction as he'd had to the first book. "I don't know. I just couldn't. It's not for me, maybe. I just can't seem to get out of this negativity." I continued to treat him silently.

A few moments later he said, "I am sleeping better."

"Excellent!"

Switching to the golden sunshine throne, where clients typically continue to give me updates as I ask questions prior to them getting on the table, where they usually drift off to some sort of sleep/la-la land, I asked him about his energy levels, and he reported, "Good."

I felt him out and said, "It's still not time yet, it seems, for you to get back into exercise. In my personal trainer training we're cautioned to take it slow, post chemo or surgeries. I know and can feel that we still need to replenish your deep supplies of energy and your immunity—your foundational system. But within the next few weeks, we could get you started with walking again. That'll help with your energy levels increasing, slowing down your mind's incessant chatter and being able to fall asleep easier. And if you could do that in nature you'd also be helping your heart chakra open up more, with forgiveness coming easier for you."

He didn't respond right away. When he eventually did, he said, "I've actually found myself being more kind to people. I'm making it a point to be more friendly when I'm out and about."

"Excellent Mike! That's a great sign that we're making progress with that fourth chakra."

Once he was on the table I got the leg booster, neck alignment pillow, and sacral alignment wedgy all in place so his spine would receive mild traction and an adjustment during the session. This alignment helped because it opened up the spine more and as a result his energy and emotions would all flow better too. We got into some more ThetaHealing to help with his negativity and his beliefs that this will change and that he had positive in him. This seemed to help him more than anything else we'd done thus far. His relief was tangible as he lay on the table receiving the clearing of the fear that he'd always feel this way. It went in to where it needed to, it felt. I also cleared more layers of shock and trauma from the diagnosis and the trail of doctors, treatments and healing he'd undergone. We then did some Bars and work with his chakras.

The next week Mike greeted me for the first time yet with a smile. I was really happy for this—both for Mike's sake and for mine. Yay! It'd be lighter to be around him, and treat him! He handed me the empty flower essence bottle, showing me he'd "been a good boy" and had finished them. I took the bottle from him, smiled back and made a motion for him to go on into the healing studio. We had a really great session, I could see the releasing his system was doing at the unconscious level through his chakras.

His system overall was lightening up, there was less suppressed density in it. We had clearly gotten through some layers and released them. His abdominal region was also feeling less constricted. This is such an important area because it's where our emotional bodies reside, and where our digestive tracks also sit, as well as the second and third chakras, which are what take the hit if people attack us, and if we feel unable to successfully navigate life out in the community. This area in particular drew my attention with Mike, because he had had liver cancer, he had been betrayed, was anxious and afraid. Sensing it lighter was hugely encouraging. I gave myself a mental pat on the back, and wrote down the progress in Mike's file after the session, while he left with his new flower essence blend in hand, still with that spring in his walk.

The following week Mike came in, and we started the session as normal, then moved to the table to continue, when he started having pain in the left side of his abdominal area. I told him to raise his left leg off of the table by about forty-five degrees and flick his foot, toes pointed. He did this a few times, and the pain apparently subsided.

"Mike some stuff is releasing from your abdominal area. We've hit a new level. We're getting in deeper now. It's excellent. Just breath through it. And continue to raise your leg in the air and flick it that way, it'll help the energy coming from the abdominal area that we're releasing flow out easier."

He did this a little bit more. There was still more pain; a whole lot was getting flushed and moved out that needed to leave his system. I could almost see the grey yuck around the left side of the table and at the base of his left foot. Thankfully, there was a window there, too. I made a mental command as

well, to help clear out the dank energy he was releasing. It had a completely nasty feeling to it.

A few minutes later, I mentioned another technique using his legs to help direct the loosening energy down and out through his legs. We proceeded further into the treatment. At one point, however, he abruptly jumped up off the table and stood, shaking his left leg. This was not normal behavior. I observed him, waiting while he did so. Once he stopped, I asked, "Better?"

He nodded his head and got back on to the table, and laid face down, as it was time to flip over. The rest of the treatment went well, no more pain. We ended the session, and as I went to make him his new flower essence blend he asked, "Do you think I really need this?"

"We usually continue a course of flower essence blends through until the issue dissolves, or feels like it's been fully addressed. If need be, that can be up to six months with the same essence, depending on how long it takes to clear a person's system of this pattern. They're helping you with the darkness that was in your system, so yes."

"Ok." I completed his blend, awed by the beauty once again that the flower essences have in their ability to get to a soul level issue that also addresses a mental, emotional, behavioral and/or interpersonal relationship issue, if not all at once, which is typically the case. Just astonishing, time and time again in their beautiful compliment to the energy healing sessions, specifically the unconscious patterns contained in the chakras and how they can address them. I can come out of a session with a client, straight from the energy healing, still retaining some of the connection with the client as I look into the Flower Essence's Practitioner Guide, and be guided directly to the right flower essences that precisely address what we were dealing with in the energy healing. Magic! And then I cut off the connection with them, and go back to being self-contained.

After I blended the essence, Mike met me outside, and as I handed him the essence blend, he said, "I think I'm going to take a break for a while."

I looked up at him, triggered by what he said. Oh no, here we go again, I thought. "Mike I would strongly suggest that you wait a few more sessions at least! We're right in the middle of a process! And we're just now starting to really get results!"

I looked at him, and he seemed to be hearing me, but he also looked like he had ants in his pants, really restless. I knew it was because that was the exact energy we were releasing. But he didn't. At least not cognitively.

This was the part of my work that was not fun because I've had other clients quit just when we begin to get to the root of the issues that they came to me for. It doesn't happen as quickly as our biomedical model and its chemicals or surgeries deliver changes. And yet this is a key stage because it is beginning to release. It's uncomfortable because what they feel releasing is the exact stuff that caused whatever they came to me for and they want it gone, understandably. Yet in the natural healing process, as the stuck stuff comes out of the system, which is beautiful in and of itself and says a lot about this universe we live in, it can cause discomfort.

Like a fever needing to peak, that's the way this once stuck stuff leaves our fields, once the energy healing's light goes in and jars it loose. If it wasn't jarred loose, then these stuck emotional patterns, thought patterns, behavioral patterns and thus biochemistry ends up in a diagnosed disease, typically. It's what we know in the holistic model. Ask a client when they have a diagnosis from a Western doctor about what strong emotions they went through within the three to five years prior to the diagnosis. It may take a while, but the person always, and I mean always, comes up with the, "Oh, well, yeah, there was this thing that happened when ..." and off they go naming different events, and getting to one that I just know—we both do—is the one containing the emotions that lead to this pattern that brought their whole system out of balance, and lead to the thing they went to the doctor of and got diagnosed as a disease.

I knew Mike and I were right at the cusp of the next wave of breakthrough with him; instinctively he knew that too. Hence his little ego-minded self feeling threatened with the pending change, even though he wanted it, and came to me for it and paid me for it, he feared the change, the new him more. I'd seen the resistance all the way through, but he had also liked feeling lighter and sleeping better and feeling stronger. It was that pain had started, as the more physical aspects of the emotional blocks and thought patterns stuck in his abdominal chakras' began to be jarred loose, and the chakras began to be functional again. I couldn't get him to see that it was only temporary, they were releasing. I'd had other post-cancer patients have a hell of a ride, releasing the emotions that had gotten patterned, and contributed to the toxic load tipping into cancer.

I gave it a last shot, "Mike, we're in the middle of a process here, and we're getting closer. Things are releasing! Cancer doesn't come from light emotions, it's pretty dense, so the stuff we're releasing is too. We need you to hang in there just a bit more, and trust this process. You've seen the results we've already been able to get just in this seven weeks. We need you to just be a bit more patient, and able to handle the discomfort just a bit more. At this point, with each of the upcoming sessions we'll be able to keep you more balanced through this ongoing process. And the flower essences will help, as will the spirulina."

I paused. I knew I'd already lost him. But I chose to give in to my having been triggered into frustration, and continued on, "Mike, we've been stirring the stuff up as we got the top layers in the beginning sessions, and then the denser more stuck stuff came closer to the surface, ready to be released. It's a gradual process; you didn't get all wound up like that and your cancer didn't happen overnight. But we will reach a certain threshold if you stay with it, when you will feel different and know that it has changed...But if you stop in the midst of this process, you're going to be walking around more opened and vulnerable without the support to continue to move through the release that's been activated and stirred up within you. This is a process, not a quick fix, and I need you, you need you, to be able to tolerate a little discomfort during the process, I'm sorry."

Normally, with clients, I have email correspondence with them, and can send them soothing sound healing frequencies that also help them retain a sense of calm through the healing crises that may come up during the natural healing process as a human being goes through changing themselves. And as they go along through their process of change, I also intuitively and holistically coach them personally, and I provide them from my vast library with books, articles, CD's and mp3's of workshops, selected by me to help inform their cognitive mind and soothe their fears, dietary adjustments, yoga postures, exercise suggestions, core strengthening exercises, essential oils, supplements and flower essences suggestions to round out their process, easing their release. Mike only did the flower essences. And the spirulina. He could only take so much help. In fact, it seemed like he could barely tolerate coming to get help with the energy healing sessions at all. So he barely wanted anything in addition to that.

He never returned. I hope he's well. And whatever we did achieve together, he's been able to make use of and expand on those releases.

Chapter 1—Science is Objective, Right? A Brief Look at the Choices of the West's Scientific Doctrine

"More than anything else, the future of civilization depends on the way the two most powerful forces of history, science and religion, settle into relationships with each other," Alfred North Whitehead, *Science and the Modern World*, 1925.

Facts are Facts, Right?

INTERESTINGLY AND IRONICALLY, THE WESTERN scientific tradition has its roots in philosophy; meaning the first scientists were philosophers. Originally the term "philosophy" was applied to all intellectual endeavors. Considered the first predecessor to our modern science, Aristotle studied what would now be called biology, meteorology, physics, and cosmology, alongside his metaphysics and ethics. It was even all the way until the eighteenth century that physics and chemistry were still classified as "natural philosophy," not yet subsumed under what was to become the establishment of the hard sciences within this period, the Enlightenment. Physics and chemistry were considered up through then as the philosophical study of nature. Today, physics and chemistry are popularly referred to as sciences, and are distinctively separate from philosophy. Philosophy has

Alison J. Kay, PhD

been informally ranked secondary to the primary function that the hard sciences provide in today's world.

Why this point is important, albeit perhaps boring, is because the distinction remains unclear; some philosophers still contend that science retains an unbroken—and unbreakable—link to philosophy. More importantly, others wish that science would have retained more of their link to philosophy so there would be more of a moralistic question within the halls of hard science as studies are devised and funded. H.H. The Dalai Lama says as much during his meetings with Western Scientists that have become a series of books available from the Mind Life Institute. The Mind Life Institute, headquartered in Boulder, Colorado, is an organization the Dalai Lama co-founded to see how a functional merger of Buddhism's science of the mind could inform the western sciences and vice versa.

Having philosophy as the roots from which our tradition of the hard sciences in the West grew from illustrates one of the essential points of our discussion. The discipline of Western sciences originally–and still does, while now it is a bit more masked–comes from *people with their own perspective on the world, and here "perspective" is meant to mean interpretation that comes from one's beliefs, ideas, biases and opinions.* As much as scientists claim that they have to be and are free of this, the more self–effacing and aware ones admit to this impossibility. To quote the great physicist Werner Heisenberg: "What we observe is not nature in itself but nature exposed to our method of questioning," (Heisenberg 1962).

B. Alan Wallace, both a scientist–BA in physics and philosophy of Science and Ph.D. in religious studies–and also a Tibetan Buddhist monk for fourteen years, has further insight. He points out how science is not even free of biases, even though both we as laypeople and scientists themselves have traditionally looked to science to be the one arena in life without biases, the one place we could go to for cold, indisputable facts.

"What we can see with our instruments–as well as the very instruments and experiments that scientists design–are determined by our expectations of what is out there to be found. Those expectations are based upon beliefs... They bring a lot of extra baggage with them when they step into the laboratory: their various spiritual, cultural, and philosophical backgrounds; their need for funding; their rivalries and disagreements with peers; their ambitions; their personal problems and so on. Many of them are believers in scientific materialism, even if they are unaware of the fact. Their expectations may be unconsciously guided by the tenets of scientific materialism..." Wallace then adds, "Ideally, the scientist maintains an open mind regarding the process of gathering data and devising and revising theories, but as we shall see, it is virtually impossible to meet such an ideal. The deck has already been stacked," (Wallace 2008).

The Age, Ironically, of Enlightenment

The Age of Enlightenment was an intellectual movement in 18th century Europe that led to the American Revolution and the Industrial Revolution. It is also during this period that what we know as our modern day sciences were created. The goal of the Enlightenment, as it has been explained, was to establish an authoritative ethics, aesthetics, and knowledge based on an 'enlightened" rationality—or reason. Interestingly, this is quite different from the Eastern use of the word "enlightenment," although we translate it as enlightenment nonetheless.

The Age of Reason was the age immediately preceding the time of the Enlightenment in Western history. Frequently, the Age of Reason is clumped in with the Age of Enlightenment, as one general period. Yet the concepts behind the Age of Reason—consider its title—were the foundation for the science that began in this Age of Reason (Copernicus, Galileo) then clearly emerged during The Enlightenment.

This period of the Enlightenment had leaders who viewed themselves as a courageous, elite body of intellectuals leading the world toward progress, out of a long period of irrationality, superstition, and tyranny that they saw from the historical period they called the Dark Ages. "The Dark Ages," also known as the Middle Ages, began with the fall of Rome, went through the religious wars known as the Crusades, the witch trials and lasted up through the Renaissance. Then began a new period, with the Age of Reason and the Enlightenment. This movement during the Enlightenment provided a framework not only for the American and French Revolutions, our modern day science and what we think of as the scientific method, but also the rise of capitalism and the birth of socialism. All of this period's significant changes are what our industrialized, modern West is based upon, giving us the beliefs that we operate from, and organize society around.

B. Alan Wallace gives us a window into this time, saying that eventually this thinking during the Enlightenment is what led to the science that helped force the split between Church and Science. He states that even though it was "inevitable that science would develop initially along Christian lines" that as science then evolved and its theories and experiments produced reliable, practical results, "a dialogue, often political in nature, took place between scientists and ecclesiastical authorities—a cautious dance of give and take. Much was at stake," (Wallace 2008). Much power and control, including the framing of how we view who or what began the world.

Wallace goes deeper into the process of the split: "Through the course of this exchange, the church was gradually forced to modify its opposition to science so much that by the twentieth century science had for many people replaced religion as the final authority on reality. Even so, scientific thinking never completely divested itself of ideas derived from Christian theology. They were too deeply embedded. As a consequence, the prevailing popular view of science in the West is based on the discoveries achieved by the scientific method, but infused with a hidden Christian view of nature. That view evolved from a set of metaphysical assumptions that underlie science and are believed by many scientists today—they're collectively called scientific materialism," (Wallace 2008).

So science has at its base beyond the reason and objectivity, its roots in the Christian belief that this is a world created by a singular God, and we are each in the image of God. Also there's the pivotal belief that "God is outside of us," and this is the key belief taken from Christian theology effecting our scientists from the start. At the roots of science is also the belief that God's creation, the external world, can be objectively studied, because of this external focus within the Christian-Judeo perspective.

It is not the same in the main philosophy that serves as their "religion" in the Eastern Hemisphere—Buddhism. Instead this sense of a divine presence is both outside and inside of us, and exists as a more "human neutral" consciousness, or "energy." It is not this paternal authority figure. Thus what has been studied varies between the two hemispheres, as do the values and world views. Meaning, one of the core central organizing principles—if not the core principle—behind the two hemispheres, differs.

That the scientists took this framework presented to them from the Church and Bible, and operated from that perspective is basically completely overlooked by us today. What if it had been another religion at its roots that believed in a polytheistic universe that had various gods ruling over various aspects of life, including the mental and emotional life? And another god for the central nervous system, and then another for the immune system? And then another for trees, and another for the land? Greece was like this polytheistic world just described, as are all ancient cultures. That is, Greece before Socrates, Plato and Aristotle with their introduction of logos, the foundation to logic.

Or what if the main religion had a belief in there being not one giant divine power outside of us and up in the sky/heavens, different and separate from us as Christianity and Judaism do, but instead, there was a divine intelligence that runs throughout the universe, and throughout all humans, and all animate life? Wouldn't the focus of our sciences then have been different, without this stark split between "out there" and "in here"? Are you starting to see now the picture of why we may have some of the beliefs in our culture that we do? But also, that there's other ways to think and other beliefs out there?

Interestingly, while our sciences have their roots also in Greek philosophy, in ancient Greece the strong split between what is mystical and what is secular was not at all distinguished. It is understood that this is because the church had not positioned itself as the authority yet on all things mystical. Instead, it was these very philosophers who were considered the scientists for their time, such as Socrates, Pythagoras, Plato and Aristotle, who dealt with the greater questions in life. This included both what was in nature and what was in humans, and the mysticism present in both.

They had mystery schools to honor the mystical, such as the Eleusinian mystery schools. Pythagoras, the West's father of geometry, had his own mystery school, highly mysterious and highly mystical. In fact, Pythagoras is credited with having had a great influence over Plato, with reports of Plato going to Pythagoras' highly secretive mystery school.

Socrates is credited as one of the founders of Western philosophy. He is an enigmatic figure known only through the classical accounts of his students, with Plato's dialogues being the most comprehensive to survive from antiquity. Socrates was born into a polytheistic, pagan, pre-Christian Greece, akin to how much of the world's cultures began—polytheistic and pagan, or earth based cultures worshipping gods who preside over the earth, and natural and human events, such as the harvests of crops.

Socrates' branding of atheism by his society was not that he did not believe in the power in what is mysterious, or metaphysical. Rather, he didn't believe in his society's version of worshipping without question the polytheistic gods and their purported powers. He absolutely believed in the mystical and metaphysics, it's a great portion of what he studied and discussed, leading both his students Plato and Aristotle to build on this focus.

In fact, Socrates ultimately was condemned to death because he did not agree to acknowledging the gods that Athens acknowledged. The typically barefoot, rather rotund and ebullient Socrates was considered an ascetic and accused of being an atheist. Why? Because he was also considered a threat, even with his loyalty to preserving democracy by serving on the council when it was his turn. His "Socratic method" of questioning his young students propelled them to think for themselves, and to critically consider what they were being handed down for systems of thought from their forefathers. This stirred up the status quo, so he was considered dangerous. Some things never change.

But much does. The brand of atheism Socrates was condemned for is altogether different than today's version, obviously, particularly the atheism scientists are expected to exhibit. There is a gradual turning away from the acknowledgment of the mystical within our scientific tradition as it develops further into what we have today. We will see this. However, for the present discussion, the modern, materialist atheistic scientist is quintessentially different from our founding fathers of philosophy in Greece and this is of central significance.

Compared to our scientists today, these early philosophers, as did the early "hard" scientists of the Enlightenment, both retained a sense of the mysterious, through the mystical metaphysics *from their cultural milieu behind their scientific investigations.* As materialism has increasingly taken over with the modern era and industrialization, this contemporary brand of atheism, devoid of a sense of the metaphysical, has become the status quo within the scientific community. Obviously, something got lost along the path of scientific inquiry in the West. The critical thinking, the philosophic, dialectical inquiry as cultivated by Socrates required release from the polytheistic, superstitious act of attributing all unexplainable power of the earth, of fertility, of fortune, of misfortune, illness and death to the gods. Yet it did not mean release from recognizing that which is metaphysical. In fact, he was criticized for his lack of focus on the material world.

"'Platonism' is a term coined by scholars to refer to the intellectual consequences of denying, as Socrates often did, the reality of the material world. In several dialogues, most notably *The Republic*, Socrates inverts the common man's intuition about what is knowable and what is real. While most people take the objects of their senses to be real if anything is, Socrates is contemptuous of people who think that something has to be graspable in the hands to be real. Furthermore, Socrates' idea that reality is unavailable to those who use their senses, is what puts him at odds with the common man, and with what common sense seems to demand of us, in a Newtonian, reductionist, materialist world. Yet, note that Socrates, as one of the fathers of philosophy—which leads into Western science—held this understanding of the intangible world, and in fact, placed priority on the intangible, or metaphysical, over the material world.

Turning Outward, Away From the Mind

In Dharamsala, India at the home of the Dalai Lama in 1987 the first of what was to become a series of conferences took place between His Holiness the Dalai Lama and a panel of Western Scientists on the theme of "Mind and Life." These meetings eventually lead to the establishment of The Mind and Life Institute in Boulder, Colorado; formally incorporated in 1990 with R. Adam Engle, a North American businessman and a Buddhist practitioner since 1974, as the Chairman. The Mind and Life Institute—MLI—has as their guiding vision, "to establish mutually respectful working collaboration and research partnerships between modern science and Buddhism—two of the world's most fruitful traditions for understanding the nature of reality and promoting human well-being."

In this first meeting of what was to become biennial meetings that took place in the Dalai Lama's residence in 1987, the first presenter was Jeremy W. Hayward. Hayward is one of the founders of the Naropa Institute, an accredited college in Boulder, Colorado based on Buddhist philosophy and the first of its kind in the USA. Hayward also is a Ph.D. of physics from Cambridge University and was a molecular biology research scientist at MIT; is author of *Perceiving Ordinary Magic*—which discusses the dialogue between science and spirituality, and *Shifting Worlds, Changing Minds*—which deals with the meeting of cognitive science and Buddhism. Hayward opened the meeting with establishing the need to first review briefly the history of science in the West for the Dalai Lama and for the purposes of their discussion.

He says, "The beginning of the opening up after these Dark Ages, the great flourishing during the early Middle Ages, was in large part due to the (re) discovery of Greek texts, particularly the writings of Aristotle. One result of reading Aristotle was that people began to conceive of nature as a realm that has its own reality, its own modes of functioning, and its own regularities, which people could come to know through careful use of their senses and reason. So a duality was postulated between the heavenly realm, knowable through faith, revelation, and deductive rational thought, and the earthly realm, knowable through the senses and inductive rational thought," (Hayward 1992). But notice that both of what was postulated as knowable are connected to studying the external world, whether the universe or the earth and the sensual experience of living here.

Neither pose the concept of turning inward and studying the human mind, emotions and consciousness. These earlier choices in our Western tradition imply two things. First, that these realms of the human experience are not knowable; and second, by implication they are not worthy of being known. This foundation to the metaparadigm of scientific materialism has its roots in the Christian world, and it has directed our focus in the West to the external. This direction has been *away from* studying the internal, particularly when contrasted to the Eastern tradition with Buddhism—also termed "science of —and the science of the Yogic path, another internally focused practice and tradition.

Chapter 2—Other Systems of Thought on Our Planet: Different Choices

"We get and we spend, we marry and we work, and yet inside ourselves, at that delicate frontier where the heart peers over an invisible horizon onto eternity, we have not confronted what is real. At best, society appoints a priesthood to be the caretakers of 'the big questions.' As individuals we live on the hopes that our souls will escape being troubled by those questions too much. (i.e. Do I have a soul? What happens after death? Why is anything real?) This form of escapism is deeply troubling," Deepak Chopra (Goswami 2000)

The Chaos

In visiting other countries outside of the United States, specifically Asian countries, to a Westerner, particularly an American, the typical view emerges that these countries are chaotic. This is particularly in the cities which are full of neon flashing lights and other high stimulus phenomena.

People are crowding, pushing and not orderly; each person seems to be doing their own thing and not working together; there is not a sense of infrastructure and planning that is easily apparent; the buildings seem thrown together, even leaning on each other; zoning restrictions are not a concept nor policy, so that businesses exist on the first floor or two, while residences are the top two or three floors, next to a bank, casino or modern supermarket; trash collection happens rather than once or twice a week, punctually at the same time every day, where people run out to the truck as it slowly creeps through neighborhoods as if an ice cream truck announcing itself with a tune, but the tune is Beethoven's fourth symphony, for example, while people either stand there waiting gathered in the streets as if a street festival talking and chatting, or some typically race after the truck either on foot or on scooter, depending on how poor their timing was that day with the typically pink garbage bags in hand; people yelling, megaphones without a live person but instead playing recordings and left laying on the ground out in front of the business, and people yelling with microphones screech out the latest fruit stand's bargains while trucks drive by advertising political candidates at seemingly all times of the year; temples wafting the smell of burning incense or fake money as offerings to the gods and ancestors are next to baseball stadiums; ATM's have voices that come at you from somewhere that guide you through a secure process and warn you about fraud, while others have armed guards outside of the glassed ATM "closet" to ensure your safe transaction; trash is in places where trash is thought not right to exist without garbage bins lining the streets; natural parks have speakers blasting what perhaps someone may consider peaceful music through them—with crowds, busses and women hiking in heels; motorcycles, or "scooters" zoom in and around pedestrians, bicyclists, motorized vehicles and utility poles while driving on sidewalks is also frequently seen; businesses exist out of the back of peoples' trucks pulled over to the side of the road without prominently displayed business permits or health inspector certificates, frequently selling traditional, local food, at times right next to McDonald's or Kentucky Fried Chicken's drive thrus; groups of meditators or chanting Buddhists meet in houses, or first floor community gathering rooms while next to them 7-11's have their doors opening and closing with a little tune from a bell ringing every time customers go in or out, with clerks calling out greetings each time the little tune goes off with a phrase to each person's exit or entry no matter how busy they are; Pizza Hut and McDonalds deliver with their uniformed deliverers driving around on their scooters with a refrigerated box on the back of the motorcycle prominently displaying their logo; little gadgets–key chains and walking, talking and tail wagging electronic dogs–are sold alongside underwear, winter comforters for beds, fine art, prom dresses, wooden or bronze buddha statues, and fine bamboo products all at quite discounted rates at the busier traffic intersections; one thing is said to each others' face while the exact opposite or something not in congruence with what was said to the face happens later; early morning markets bustle while early morning tai chi and chi gong and yoga practice occur in close proximity; traffic lights are considered more as warnings than law; speaking one's mind as an individual with freedom of expression in order to contribute to the collective voices of a democracy is not present in these collectivist, hierarchical societies, rather it's done in a more backdoor way through back–stabbing and actions; monks can be seen smoking cigarettes, talking on cell phones and riding on the metro in countries where mandatory monk service replaces mandatory military service (Thailand), while monks can also be seen walking down the street or driving scooters loaded with recyclable bags with fresh greens sticking out of them from the morning or evening market; digital televisions and digital billboards are everywhere there's room for one and even where there's not; "ok" or "yes" is said even when the real meaning is "no" and each person is left to read the contextual clues and body language to infer the genuine meaning; talking voices come out of the most peculiar places as recordings announcing various warnings and rules which not many seem to heed; dogs and cows–depending on which country–interweave with traffic, stopping cars; people pull their little blue trucks up to the harbor populated by fish and seaweed markets with amplifiers and microphones to sing seaside karaoke; stores frequently run out of products so that nothing is considered as regularly stocked items, leaving their shelves at times appearing as if everyone has stocked up due to a pending natural disaster which instinctively causes an American ex–pat concern; scientific/medical research is done on brain matter left on chop sticks that were somehow lodged into a man's brain, and then taken out in an emergency room, and handed to scientists to study stem cells without protests from any organizations; barber shops double as "special special" massage parlors –but only if you're in the "know"–as do skyscraper office looking buildings where men go in to sing karaoke as if their lives, or at least their reputations, depended on their performance, drink whisky and be attended to in secluded, living room style suites by the female "KTV" "friendly" workers; Michael Jackson is blaring out of one side of the street, while across the street amidst the smell of incense and people saying prayers is the gong of a temple; six story high statues of the Buddhist Goddess Kuan Yin loom on hills in Taiwan in front of the Buddhist monasteries, sometimes situated behind gas stations; pharmacies that sell over–the–counter antibiotics, tiger's penis used for male power, herbal teas for slimming, crushed oysters for a laxative, along with skin whitening products lining two–thirds of the shelves, sit next to traditional medicine clinics dispensing herbal remedies that have the odor of the earth, recently dug up; what looks like candy striper or cocktail waitress or butler uniform wearing elevator attendees help to announce arriving elevators and manage traffic flow at the larger department stores' elevator terminals; laws are on the books to be avoided or worked around without genuine threat of a punitive or judicial branch ensuring compliance; gigantic male gods seven stories high are constructed atop temples while seemingly slaying invisible dragons; all of this is happening in most Asian cities and villages, to varying degrees.

Singapore may be the only exception, and it just happens to be the banking and financial capital of Asia, the world's fourth top financial and trade center, with the sixth highest percentage of foreigners in the world–42% of the population in Singapore is foreigners. Overall, in Asia the sense of order is not present as a Westerner, particularly an American, is used to order–nor personal space. Yet the lack of order is not just high population rates per square mileage induced *at all*. That's only a small percentage of the reason. The chaos instead of order and seeming lack of emphasis placed on an individual's voice is in stark contrast to the Enlightenment ordered Western world. Again even more strongly is the contrast seen against America, rather than Europe, due to it's centuries of history in it's cities that newer American cities do not have.

Where Do We Have More Control? Our Internal or Our External Environments?

As Robert Thurman, Ph.D., and Jey Tsong Khapa, Professor of Indo–Tibetan Buddhist Studies at Columbia University, say in *Mind Science*, "In India, science and philosophy have never split, philosophy always having been thought essential to control the theoretical part of science and ultimately to be indivisible from the empirical part. And within philosophy's sciences, the inner science, philosophy/psychology has always been considered the king of all the sciences," (The Dalai Lama 1991). Furthermore, it is understood in India that the quest for the knowledge of reality has always been considered an eminently practical matter. There is the belief in India that if humanity wants to succeed in any sense, it must gain valid knowledge of reality–the reality of self and the reality of the environment. Implied in this is the reality of self *in* the environment. This brings thoughts up of India's chakra system, particularly the third chakra. It is the third chakra that deals with the self in the environment. (Chakras will be explored in just a bit.) In India, when the Buddha established the Buddhist educational institutions, reality was approached as both outer environment and inner self, the same as in the West. The inner self, however, was chosen as the more important to understand and the more practical to control and engineer to suit human needs, rather than the external, physical environment, as chosen in the West. This is a key difference, obviously.

Robert Thurman continues in his address, "In the West, scientists have predominantly thought of reality as external to the human thought world, as the physical world, the outer world, the world 'out there.' *It has seemed to scientists that the environment needed to be tamed, controlled and engineered to suit human needs.* Thus physics, chemistry, biology, and astronomy, armed with mathematics and geometry, have been considered the most important sciences in the West. The psyche was left to the priests, who eventually differentiated into philosophers, poets, artists, and psychiatrists. When psychology sought entry into the halls of science, rather recently, it tried to model itself on the 'hard' sciences. How could Western cognitive sciences best take advantage of what the Indo–Tibetan tradition has to contribute? *Exploring (this) first requires realizing that Western science is dominated by materialism* and *then taking a critical look at scientific materialism's prospects for success in understanding the mind reduced to brain processes,*" (italics mine) (The Dalai Lama 1991).

Thus, Thurman is acknowledging the study of the brain using the materialist approach as the primary approach that Western science has, when studying "the mind." The result of this is neuroscience overshadowing psychology. In fact, it's epiphenomenalism, and this relates to Western science's still dominant view of the mind body connection. This still dominant view is *it is the brain that contains whatever it is that may be the mind if there is any mind at all, and that it is the brain that is the primary mover electro–chemically in the physical existence of the body and brain. There is no room in this model for the consideration of the impact of any mental subjective experience, nor for any acknowledgement of something like consciousness nor emotions' role within consciousness.* This is throughout mainstream science. Whereas in the "new sciences," and amongst the neuroscientists who embrace the new sciences' discoveries, they have been quickly coming to see the many effects of the mind in the body beyond the more mechanical brain's cognitive functions.

Ancient Indian Culture: Yogic & Buddhist Science— Sciences of the Mind & the Mind Body Connection

Most people know that the practice of yoga makes the body strong and flexible. It is also well known that yoga improves the functioning of the respiratory, circulatory, digestive, hormonal, and nervous systems. Most people also know that yoga helps one to carve out a better shaped core and butt. And, most people are aware that yoga brings emotional stability and clarity of mind. But this is really only considered the beginning of the yogic journey within the yogic science in India. What is not typically known about yoga in the West is that there are even more subtle states of refined consciousness. These more refined states are reachable on the yogic path, the longer one practices. These more advanced subtle states are peaceful, detached, clear, and precise states of mind, and then states beyond this.

The advanced levels of mental power include eventually being coupled with another force that is mystical in nature. This then supports clear, alive, fired up, and empowered living. The definition of yoga is to yoke with or be in union with the Divine, meaning the Higher part of ourselves that is divine and thus connected to a larger divinity. This speaks to the higher, pristine states of clear consciousness that are not succumb to those lower states of distorted perception. An example of distorted perception is when one has a reaction from a distorted and misinterpreted interaction with someone because they misperceived, mislabeled, and misunderstood what the person meant. This then frequently results in taking personally something that has nothing to do with the perceiver. Most likely the distorted perception included some type of injury or offense to the inaccurate perceiver by the other. Typically too, this mistaken perception then leads to resulting conflict with ensuing worries, reliving the event, anger, and the other emotional states that typically accompany a conflict with someone. Mastery over the lower mind allows for a more peaceful, calm life. It also naturally then yields access to higher levels of consciousness, in which there is not the turmoil, but the clarity and an increased access to what seems like unlimited power one never knew they had. This is sometimes referred to as self–realization. Or enlightenment.

To be clear, yogic sages were doing their thing way before Buddha was born. Buddha used what these yogic sages had discovered to become enlightened. Buddhism grew out of yoga, then spread out of India, up through Tibet, on over to mainland China, up and over to Japan and down throughout the rest of Southeast Asia.

The ancient sages who meditated on the human condition starting about 5,000 years ago outlined four ways to self–realization: *jnana marg*, the path to knowledge, when the seeker learns to discriminate between the real and the unreal; *yoga marg*, the path by which the mind and its actions are brought under control; *karma marg*, the path of selfless service without thought of reward; and finally, *bhakti marg*, the path of love and devotion.

All these paths lead to the same goal – *samadhi*, which, at this level of our discussion, is considered to denote the maintenance of the intelligence, or the mind, in a balanced state. Samadhi is understood as a practical outcome of a sustained meditation practice. It is achieved when the knower, the knowable, and the known become one. Meaning, when the object of meditation engulfs the meditator and becomes the subject *so that there is no separation between what is "out there" and what is "in here."* Realistically, the meditator becomes the subject, so that a sense of self–awareness is lost, meaning self–consciousness that separates us as a separate self, or the ego identity. Notice how opposite this is from the Western scientific materialist paradigm, and the split we typically have here.

In other words, one has gotten themselves to an expanded consciousness through working with the mind that then opens up one's perception to see how everything is interconnected–or as a whole. American neuroscientist Andrew Newburg in *How God Changes The Brain* writes that he has discovered this is triggered by the anterior cingulate, a tiny section in the brain that gets activated through meditation or sustained prayer for at least twelve minutes. And once activated through meditation or extended prayer, it gives a sense of decreased boundaries between oneself and others during that time in meditation or prayer (Newburg 2009). I've noticed that it then cumulatively effects this perception overall in life, even when not meditating or praying.

This sense feels like the loss of the separate self and the realization that the self–consciousness that comes with this separate self is replaced by a feeling of oneness, or unity with everything.

This absorption is *samadhi,* and it is the fruit of yoga. The science of the mind that yoga started in 3,000 B.C. has been worked out through the over 5,000 years of self–observation and application by masters and sages. *It contains within it a thorough understanding of the more subtle states of mind and consciousness. They consider the mind the vital link between the body and the overall, circulating consciousness throughout us and all life, and the Divine.* The mind from the individual's consciousness – once the individual calms and quiets his mind enough to move or reach out somewhat beyond it– then is able to unite with this higher consciousness, which is considered a more divine force.

In yogic science they have discovered that we have five mental faculties which can be used in a positive or negative way. These mental faculties are: correct or clear observation and knowledge, perception, imagination, dreamless sleep, and memory. When the mind loses its stability and clarity, it is either incapable of using its various faculties properly, or uses them in a negative way.

The dedicated practice of yoga with meditation gradually leads one to use these mental faculties in a positive way, thereby bringing the mind to a more discriminative and attentive state. *Awareness together with discrimination target bad habits, which are essentially those that are basically repetitive actions based on mistaken perception.* Another way to say this: habitual behavioral patterns that keep us stuck in uncomfortable and even unhealthy habits we'd like to get rid of are able to be taken care of by cultivating awareness and discrimination.

Yogic science also distinguishes between five basic states of mind. These are not grouped in stages, nor are they, except the last, unchangeable. Patanjali, with his interpretation of the ancient Hindu Sutras, is considered the source to understanding yogic philosophy. According to Patanjali, these five states of mind are: *dull and lethargic, distracted, scattered, focused, and controlled.* The lowest level of the mind is dull, or *mudha.* A person in this state of mind is disinclined to observe, act, or react. This state is considered to be rarely inherent or permanent. It is usually, instead, caused by a traumatic experience. For example during bereavement. Or when a desired goal seems impossible to obtain after successive failures to take control of their lives, many people withdraw into dullness and lethargy. Often, this is exacerbated by either insomnia or over–sleeping, comfort–eating, or the ingestion of antidepressants and/or other substances which typically make the matters worse. Yoga gradually transforms this feeling of defeat and helplessness into optimism and energy.

The next state of mind, the distracted state, is one where thoughts, feelings, and perceptions churn around in the consciousness, but leave no lasting impressions and hence serve no purpose. Someone in this state, *ksipta*, is unstable, unable to prioritize or focus on goals, usually because of flawed signals from the sense of perception he or she accepts unquestioningly, and follows them into reaction–i.e., going and buying one of those great smelling sausages because we're distracted into following our sense perception. This easily distracted state clouds the intellect and disturbs mental equilibrium, so that it has to be calmed and brought to confront the actual factual knowledge or reality. Regular practice of yoga asanas and pranayama – various special breathing exercises that are one of the eight main "limbs" of a genuine yoga practice –help this.

The most common state of mind considered by the ancient sages is a scattered mind, *viksipta*. In this mind state, though the brain is active, it lacks purpose and direction, and it is constantly plagued by doubt and fear, alternating between decisiveness and lack of confidence. The regular practice of yoga gradually encourages the seeds of awareness and discrimination to take root, generating mental equilibrium, and a positive attitude.

The focused mind, *ekagra*, is one that indicates a higher state of being, and it is what is one of the goals within this science. *This is a liberated mind that has confronted afflictions, with afflictions defined as sticky places in our mind* like nagging fears, repeated aggressive thoughts, obsessive desire and obstacles. Such a liberated mind has direction, concentration and awareness. Living in the now, in the present moment without being caught up in what happened in the past or worrying or projecting or fantasizing into what may happen in the future, is a result of this level of mind. Hence, liberation.

Finally, the fifth and highest state of mind is the controlled, restrained mind, *niruddha*, and can be attained through the persistent practice of yoga, specifically meditation. A consistent practice has been shown to allow an individual to conquer the lower levels of the mind. At this level of the mind, the mind is linked exclusively with the object of attention. So the result of this is the mind is not darting to and fro while thinking of other things in a scattered or distracted way. Instead, it is able to focus and fully concentrate on what is in front of it here and now.

This choice in ancient India to focus on the inner self and to thus then develop both the Yogic Science and the science of the mind, as Buddhism is frequently referred to, *was because they believed this domain to be more likely what humans can exert more control over, remember?* Realistically, this choice had no connection to some deep, mystical truth realized in the caves of the Himalayas. Instead, it was based on a practical choice coming from a thorough and comprehensive knowledge of reality, on an already assessed, in depth understanding of self and environment–that is to say, from over 5,000 years of collected information from explorers of self–mastery. This eventually culminated with the development of the Yogic science, and eventually also Buddhism. Buddha used their material and applied it to himself, then eventually teaching others.

Observing one's mind during meditation is empirical observation. In Western scientific methodology meditation could be considered a case–study. Or when observing the mind in others, meditation can also be considered naturalistic observation. These case–studies were conducted by individuals who had evidently developed high levels of self–mastery over the typical, common person's mind full of mental chatter, contradictions, worries, regrets, fears, anger, sorrow, and other emotional labels–known in Buddhism as *afflictions*. These early sages are considered to have been at least close to enlightened, while it was (at least) the Buddha himself who was "The Enlightened One."

Without getting into a history of yoga or Hinduism which is clearly way beyond the scope of this discussion, nonetheless it is essential to gain a basic understanding in order to speak of the East and West comparatively. The discourses that occurred amongst the rather skilled practitioners of self–observation of their minds (meditation) and the practices of yoga including the better known postures, (asanas), then resulted in the sutras, recorded down finally by Patanjali. "Our opinion can be summarized by saying that all the techniques of raja yoga existed long before Patanjali, even if in a latent form within the collective unconscious mind. The *Yoga Sutras* are probably a compilation of previously known verses handed down from guru to disciple by word of mouth. It was the genius of someone called Patanjali who put the system into a comprehensive written whole," (Saraswati 1976).

The Yoga Sutras of Patanjali were not written for intellectual debate and speculation. They were written to explain the process and practical methods of raising levels of awareness, gaining deeper wisdom, exploring the potential of the mind and eventually going beyond the mind. The text is primarily practice–orientated; it is not intended to be an intellectual exercise on samadhi, that ultimate state of clear consciousness. Furthermore, many of the verses of Patanjali's Sutras indicate things that are beyond the range of normal mundane experience and comprehension. This is not done to bring intellectual understanding; again, it is for practical purposes, so that an aspirant who practices the yoga of Patanjali or any other yogic system will progressively gain insight and understanding of the deeper aspects of his being. It is all focused on self–observation and self–awareness, with the goal of self–mastery, or enlightenment.

When one is on this path of enlightenment, part of the outcome is also increased feelings of oneness, less separation. This is coupled with cultivation of compassion for all living things. Both the Buddhist and Yogic approach include service to others as a major part of the path towards self–mastery. Self–realized morality, in a sense.

Reincarnation and Holism: The Two Main Aspects to the East's Metaparadigm

The following is from Chakraburtty's *The Science of Meditation*: "...It is also a Vedic (ancient Hindu) philosophy, penned and saved for posterity in black and white, over five thousand years ago. He (a sage offering the underlying philosophy behind yogic science) perpetuated and proved that *Consciousness and Awareness are our real nature.* He said *evolution (of one human being, their soul) is fulfilled when we discover these states. Vedanta* pointed to the reflective writings of the Vedas. *They repeatedly affirm this world of sense objects is not genuine.* This also happens to be a Buddhist view." As we can see there is the connotation to some sense of divinity or a higher consciousness. Yet at the same time, it also fully allows for dealing with the phenomena of consciousness as just that—a phenomena, without a sense of spirituality. Nor is it connected to the dogma of a religious institution.

Chakraburtty's discussion then gets a bit more abstract, by saying that it is only with deep respect for both the process and oneself that one can grow from gaining self–awareness, *or* self knowledge, and then retreat back into the non–physical, having evolved. This reflects the Hindu belief in reincarnation, the life–death–rebirth cycle that runs throughout Asia, as Buddhism spread throughout Asia ultimately taking on three different main schools of Buddhism as it met the various local Asian cultures, thus *making the belief in reincarnation a metaparadigm for the East. This is in most ways, as subtle in its omnipresence as scientific materialism is for the West.*

Also influencing the East at a metaparadigm level is seeing things as a whole, rather than breaking the whole apart with reductionism, as is done in scientific materialism in the West. Chakraburtty describes an example in an entry entitled, "Awareness Flows Outward" within her *The Science of Meditation*, "The brain recycles itself every six years. The human body undergoes physical changes every twelve years. *A person's lifestyle influences these changes.* Wrong living habits hinder the mind and intellect's ingenious growth and change. Disease then sets in. The quality of life degenerates. The health and body and brain cells fall apart. When Awareness flows outwards, it is out of ownership and gets pulled by attachment. Wrenching towards Matter arrests liveliness of the higher chakras," (Chakraburtty 2009). (Higher chakras are the chakras more associated with enlightenment, and/ or spiritual activity, or "higher seeing," or "higher intellect.") Amongst the descriptions of how our bodies regenerate, of how getting pulled towards the material diminishes the brightness of the spirit is also this view of the integrated whole more than focusing on the parts. This is also clearly reflected in Chinese culture, which we shall look at next.

However, as Chakraburtty further reflects on the Sankhyan philosophy that, again, influenced both Yoga and Buddhism, (meaning the two main philosophies to emerge from Ancient India) "The 'reality' of a mirage also disappears as one approaches it...The world and individualistic egocentric ideas are a fantasy. The sense of a separate existence is a superimposition on Truth." This reflects the opposite view to the West's starkly drawn line that demarcates between the external and internal, or the objective and subjective and our science's assumed ability to separate the two. This has then been followed by their superimposition out onto the "Truth," or external reality with what their internal reality directed them to focus on, without much or any conscious awareness.

It also reflects an even more fundamental difference: in the West the predominant belief inherited from the dominant Judeo–Christian worldview is that humans are not able to access this non–egocentric personality, bigger Self on their own. Instead, an intermediary is required to help, such as a priest, minister, or rabbi. Chakraburtty continues with this point, deepening the appreciation for the distinctive differences between the Hindu Indian Buddhist and Yogic approach - or the East's metaparadigm - and the mainstream Western approach, "Because self–inquiry is the human mind's eternal search, Man always asks the same questions. What engulfs everything everywhere? Where does all this repose? The answers to this timeless inquisitiveness are universal. They are found in the words of sages of all times and climates. Kapila discovered the Absolute within himself. He knew the answers to Man's questions. *He knew the answers are not in the relentless search of the outward world.* Only by retracing steps from the outside to the inner world can Man find himself. *Man has to enter his own self first.* Yogis before him had done that, he said. *They identified the origin of the material world from within.* After all, the material world, like everything else, dissolves into the same Absolute Brahman or God," (italics mine) (Chakraburtty 2009). This view has been validated by the discoveries in quantum physics.

The Logic and Reason in Buddhism's Science of the Mind

Along with meditation, what is frequently not know by outsiders is that Buddhists also spend a great portion of their time reviewing the sacred Buddhist texts. They engage in long discussions and debates over what is meant in the sacred scriptures, which then has them discussing the fundamentals of life. This is on an equal level, if not at times more than the practiced, seated meditation on the cushion. Hence, the labeling of Buddhism as a "science of the mind," as it is one part empirical observation– the seated meditation. The other part is the critical thinking that involves questioning, examining, refining, and readjusting hypotheses and theories of the mind, of existence, of life, of consciousness—as the science.

Upon visiting a Buddhist monastery, one sees mostly classrooms. There are classrooms after classrooms for these lively discussions. We also see libraries, one or two big open rooms for general meetings, chanting and group meditations, and then some smaller rooms for the monks to go and practice their individual seated meditations. H. H. The Dalai Lama's style of logic coupled with humor is an excellent example of these critical thinking skills when cultivated alongside a consistent meditation practice,.

The Dalai Lama explains to a group of Western scientists at the first Mind and Life Institute summit: "...National origin is not an especially fundamental problem; differences arise unconsciously due to a variety of environmental factors. You are very sincerely trying to explain the truth, but due to other factors (i.e., perspective) you are unconsciously conditioned; as a result, you have a different explanation...[laughing] It is my view that generally Buddhism, and particularly Mahayana (Tibetan, Chinese) Buddhism, *is very close to a scientific approach.* Consider, for example, that the Lord Buddha himself gave different kinds of teachings, depending on whether they were given publicly or not. According to the general Mahayana point of view, there were three major turnings of the wheel, as the three main cycles of Buddha's teachings are traditionally called. The teachings that were given during these major turnings of the wheel are literally contradictory—some elements are really incompatible. Since all these teachings were genuine words of Buddha himself and they contradict each other, how do we determine which are true and which are not? If we were to make the distinction on the basis of some scriptural citation, then that again has to depend on something else to validate its authenticity. Therefore, eventually the final validation has to be done on the authority of reasoning, logic."

The Dalai Lama then goes on to apply this to an example within the sutras, where in one place Buddha says that things do not inherently exist and in another one he says that things do inherently exist. He goes on to explain, "Then where do you go? The only way is to establish a conclusion by reasoning and not simply further scriptural authority. Therefore Mahayana Buddhists divided the words of the Buddha into two categories: those that are definitive, and those that require further interpretation; those that are literal, and those that are not literal...*We find that analysis and examination through reasoning, the basic Buddhist attitude, is very important,*" (Hayward 1992). For the purposes of our discussion, what we can take from this is that this analysis and reasoning is done by a mind aware of its own biases, opinions, perspectives, and the conditioning from where and when one grew up—meaning the environmental (societal, familial, religious, etc.) context.

Whereas our ancestors making the choices of what to study in the beginning days of Western science, did not have an introspective practice that helped them be more aware of their own biases. The internal, subjective mind simply was not looked at in this systematic way. Upon studying any literature of the West from the Dark Ages on up through the Renaissance and then on up through the Enlightenment, or even the history, one can clearly see the references to and descriptions of the fear of the perceived irrationality contained within the mind.

Reaching Beyond into the Role of the Soul

The science that is the science of yoga, predates Buddha, remember? The self–observation that comes from a long tradition of seated meditation that the Buddha taught, also involves other practices. One of these other practices is the control over one's body through yogic asanas, or postures–what is typically thought of in the West as yoga. Another practice in yogic science are the kriyas. They're ways to cleanse one's mind and body, to keep healthy, alert, fresh and clean. These kriyas end up sharing an overlap into Ayurvedic treatments, the ancient medicine of India.

In fact, there are eight different stages to the Yogic Science, as recorded by Patanjali circa 400 BC, which is commonly known as Ashtanga Yoga–meaning the yoga of eight stages, or limbs. These eight different stages include *Yama*–guidance on one's civic behavior; *Niyama*– one's internal behavior and personal code within oneself; *Asana*–the body postures; *Pranayama*–breathing exercises to learn self control and mastery through controlling the life force, or prana; *Pratyahara*–considered sense withdrawal, which is gathering inwards by checking and curbing the outgoing tendencies of the mind so that awareness can be directed inwards. You'll notice almost the exact opposite to our daily life here in the West, where our attention and our focus is externally and stimulus driven, now much by consumerism. You'll also notice how this description of pratyahara is of a mind in the opposite direction of a typical ADD/ADHD mind, or even a mind with a short attention span.

These first five stages are considered the more external ones that progressively prepare the body–mind for the last three stages which deal with the more subtle energies. The next level of the last three stages begins with *Dharana*–considered seated meditation that includes an initial stage of focused attention; *Dhyana*–which is increased concentration and awareness that arises when one is able to maintain a smooth, unfluctuating flow of concentration towards an inner symbol for a period of time so that the flow of awareness *ultimately leads to an elimination of duality*, which then leads to the 8th stage–*Samadhi*, or superconsciousness, described by Patanjali as, "When the five senses of perception together with the mind are at rest, when even the intellect has ceased to function, that, say the sages, is the supreme state," (Saraswati 1976). You can see how far that is from a common, everyday Western mind. And again this is due in great part to our greater cultural milieu in the West, or our metaparadigm with its dominant cultures' values.

The Sanskrit root yuj means to bind, join, attach, and yoke, to direct one's attention on, to use and apply. It also means union, or communion. It is the true union of our will with the will of God. Thus, yoga translates into meaning, "the yoking of all the powers of body, mind and soul to God. It also means the disciplining of the intellect, the mind, the emotions, the will, which that Yoga presupposes; it means a poise of the soul which enables one to look at life in all its aspects evenly," (Desai in B.K.S. Iyengar 1966).

Really, yoga is an ancient art based on an extremely subtle science, that of the body, mind, and soul, so that clearly it presupposes an interconnection, or a model of integrated wholeness, where mind, body and spirit each have their equal role within the entire tri–system. In B.K.S. Iyengar's *Yoga: The Path to Holistic Health*, he states, "Yoga is an ancient art based on an extremely subtle science, that of the body, mind, and soul. The prolonged practice of yoga, will, in time, lead the student to a sense of peace and a feeling of being at one with her or his environment...The persistent practice of yoga allows you to conquer the lower levels of the mind and reach the peaks of self–realization... The primary aim of yoga is to restore the mind to simplicity, peace, and poise, to free it from confusion and distress," (B.K.S. Iyengar 2001).

The Chakras—Another Aspect of India's Mind Body Connection

In fact, in yogic science, or Hindu belief, the body and the mind are in a state of constant interaction. *Yogic science does not demarcate where the body ends and the mind begins, but approaches both as a single, integrated entity.* The turmoil of daily life brings stress to the body and the mind. This creates anxiety, depression, restlessness, and rage. Yoga asanas, or poses, while appearing to deal with the physical body alone, actually influence the chemical balance of the brain, which in turn improves one's mental state of being. One can look up in the better yoga books "afflictions," such as depression, and be given a list of asanas that help alleviate it, known somewhat loosely in the West as "yoga therapy."

Yoga asanas, or poses, also influence the opening of the chakras and the channels–the *nadis*–that run the subtle life force energy–the *prana*–so that it can flow freely and unhindered throughout a body's system, collecting at important physical nerve centers. These centers are also centers for certain types of subtle energy patterns called *"chakras,"* in Sanskrit, meaning "wheel." These patterns divide into aspects of life, such as basic survival, love, and self–empowerment. *Practicing yoga also has this science of subtle life force energy, or consciousness, contained within it with the goal being to have one's life force free flowing uninhibited throughout the body and mind, intersecting at the open and turning chakras, ideally.* This is frequently what leaves a person feeling so refreshed, balanced, and calm after yoga. This subtle energy is now opened in the body, so that it is gets unstuck in places where it may have been clogged due to certain issues centered around certain beliefs, which directs and focuses consciousness in a certain way, such as "people are so angry nowadays." Traditional Chinese Medicine's acupuncture, chi gong and reflexology (in a different way) also function to break up these blocks of subtle energy within the human body.

This flow of prana along the nadis energy "highways" running throughout our body– is almost the exact same theory as in the Chinese science of chi gong, or Traditional Chinese medicine that uses acupuncture, all of which work with getting chi to flow throughout the body's channels in a healthy flow, or working to treat pain or disease that has happened once the chi has stagnated. *Both Prana of the Hindu Indian system and Chi of the Chinese system are what can be considered "subtle energy."*

Ayurveda —India's Holistic Medical System

Another way to view yoga is it is Ancient India's system of the science of mind, lifestyle, and well–being, i.e., preventative medicine, still continuing to the modern day. Their specific medical system, Ayurveda, is seen as a system for health and longevity. Ayurveda comes from these same yogic sciences, and then expands into the more physiological and physical arm as their medical system.

Alison J. Kay, PhD

Ayurveda, India's traditional medical science, operates in the same way as traditional Chinese medicine in that the patient is treated as a whole. Their "signs" are solicited by a doctor's questions and observed through various diagnostic techniques. A complaint is the problem that brings a person to a physician, and the patient will usually mention his or her complaint. A sign, however, is something that the doctor looks for but that the patient would not necessarily know or talk about. *The patient is viewed not as a separate entity from their lifestyle, their daily work, their diet, their emotional life nor their basic constitution of one of the three doshas.*

Doshas are an Ayurvedic concept that recognizes three primary biological humors, and the life–forces in the body. Another way to understand the dosha system is it is a classification system that classifies all humans into three primary patterns of energy, "personality traits" (i.e. what we think of in the West as personality traits, such as anxious, worried, uptight, slow, lethargic) and physical, mental and emotional characteristics. The three doshas are called vata, pitta and kapha. Upon the Ayurvedic doctor targeting which of the three doshas is the patient's primary one, the patient is then typically guided towards specific dietary, lifestyle, and Ayurvedic mind body healing treatments as their "prescriptions." So that again, we are dealing in Ayurveda with a whole system concept, not a reductionist model.

Ayurveda goes beyond just being a non–reductionist model. Ayurvedic medicine, *the science of life, health and longevity,* is an ancient healing system, wherein *Ayu* means *Life* and *Veda* means *knowledge.* Ayurveda originated as part of 'Vedic Science'. The fundamentals of Ayurveda can be found in all the Vedic scriptures, the sacred texts of the Hindus. Ayurvedic doctors state that this is an integral spiritual science devised to give a comprehensive understanding of the entire universe, which it sees as working according to a single law. And that, contrary to the popular misbelief, Ayurveda is not a mere alternative therapy but a way of life, which, if strictly followed, can help one attain a better physical, emotional, social and spiritual life. For curing diseases, Ayurveda insists on treating and eradicating the root cause of the ailment instead of satisfying the patient with symptomatic relief.

The same great Vedic (ancient Hindu) seers and sages that produced India's original systems of yoga, meditation, and self–realization, established Ayurveda as well. According to the Vedic texts, Ayurveda was in practice before 4000 BC. Ayurveda obviously has modernized itself and it is still the main practiced form of medicine in India today. Yet due to globalization, the biomedical model is almost equal in use at this point there. In fact, many modern day Ayurvedic doctors are also American trained M.D.'s, having returned to India to practice both together, using the biomedical model when most appropriate–i.e., prescribing antibiotics in order to get rid of an infection.

According to my teacher of Ayurvedic medicine during my yoga teacher training in India, who is also a Western M.D., after treating the emergent symptoms with Western medicine at a "trauma" or emergent level, they then diagnose from an Ayurvedic perspective what lead to the body weakening that allowed for the trauma or the infection to invade. After identifying the body's imbalance that lead to the body being weakened so that it created, say, an infection to get rid of the invading microorganisms, they prescribe lifestyle changes to the patient on a more preventative basis. Prescriptions for these lifestyle changes can include: to reduce certain foods while increasing intake of others; the use of certain spices to balance out their body's dosha or biological humor; to make certain lifestyle changes; to do certain yoga asanas (postures); a certain herbal remedy (the Ayurvedic doctor frequently prepares him or herself), all as a course of treatment to take once the pharmaceutical antibiotics cycle is complete. Finally, the doctors implement a certain Ayurvedic treatment protocol, typically geared to cleansing, or purging the body, in some way.

They take the best of both systems–the trauma or response effectiveness of the biomedical model, alongside the more preventive and lifestyle geared holistic approach that takes the whole person's daily life and ensuing emotions and mental states (typical moods), corresponding physiological states, their diet and primary biological humor in mind. That's how it's done in India by a doctor of both Ayurveda and biomedicine. Note that this holistic consideration by the Ayurvedic doctor corresponds quite closely to a traditional Chinese doctor. They consider a patient's daily life; their typical state of mind, exercise, meals, etc.

As Scott Gerson, M.D., and Executive Director for Basic and Clinical Research, as well as Medical Director of Clinical Services at The National Institute of Ayurvedic Medicine in the United States says in his introduction to David Frawley's *Ayurvedic Healing: A Comprehensive Guide*, "We are in the midst of a global paradigm shift in health care. At the center of this change is Ayurvedic Medicine, a healing system which promotes health using natural, nontoxic substances and which recognizes the important role of the mind and emotions...In the same way, the medical paradigm shift which we are experiencing today represents a movement towards holism." Our current, yet outdated medical paradigm views the human being as a machine, with separate systems, organs, and tissues. It separates mind and body into distinct categories.

In this new paradigm Dr. Gerson speaks of acknowledging the mutual interdependence of the physical body and brain, mind, emotions, and the environment in creating health and disease. Dr. Gerson continues, "Neither is there separation in this emerging face of a new medical paradigm between physician and patient. The new paradigm has removed the absolute authority from the doctor and has re-fashioned a model of shared responsibility between patient and physician—much in the same way that an electron forming a bond is shared between two nuclei," (Frawley 2008). Hmmm. Imagine that.

Ancient Chinese Culture, Taoism and Chi Gong

Physicist Amit Goswami provides a good transition from Hindu and Buddhism to Taoism, or ancient Chinese culture, with his comment, "Spiritual traditions in the East dance to a different metaphysical tune. *Hinduism, Buddhism, and Taoism posit that a transcendent consciousness, rather than matter, is the ground of all being and that all else is epiphenomena [secondary phenomena], matter and self included.* These traditions see the spiritual quest for unblemished happiness as the quest for the true nature of our being, our wholeness. Eastern traditions solve the problem of dualism with the idea of transcendence and its proper understanding. Consciousness is both inside and outside the material, space-time reality. As transcendent-outside-it is pure consciousness, unmanifested. Immanent-inside-it appears split as self and the world, subject and object; but the split, the separateness, is epiphenomenal, brought forth by a mysterious force called *maya*, or illusion created by the human mind, in the Hindu tradition. I call this philosophy monistic idealism, but it is also called Vedanta in India and the Tao in China," (italics mine) (Goswami 2000).

"Qi, *or chi*, is the ancient Chinese word for 'life energy,' and according to Chinese medicine, qi is the animating power that flows through all living things. A living being is filled with it. A healthy individual has qi more than one who is ill. However, health is more than an abundance of qi. Health implies that the qi in our bodies is clear, rather than polluted and turbid, and flowing smoothly, like a stream, not blocked or stagnant," (Cohen 1997). It is also the life energy one senses in nature. The earth itself is moving, transforming, breathing and alive with qi. Taking the two Chinese words *qi* and *gong*, where *gong* means "work" or "benefits acquired through perseverance and practice," together, qigong means working with the life energy to learn how to improve the health, aliveness, and flexibility of oneself, in both mind and body. Qi, is therefore, also labeled as a *subtle energy*.

Chi gong techniques and schools also developed in response to influences from Indian Yoga and Tibetan Buddhism. Tibetan Buddhism, known as *Mi Zong*, or "Esoteric School" in Chinese, came to China in the eighth century A.D., where it was centered around the capital city of Chang An. Even amidst all the disruptions and fighting with Tibet and then Mao's rule, nevertheless, many present day chi gong masters claim Mi Zong Chi Gong lineage and include Tibetan or Sanskrit chants in their chi gong. Most commonly used are the chants *Om Mani Padme Hung*, or *Om Ah Hung*, which are invocations of the Buddhist personification of Compassion. The blending of Hindu practice into Chinese practice is not common, though, even with the basis of Chinese Buddhism coming from the Hindus of India.

The ancient Chinese were an agrarian people who learned the principles of chi gong naturally by observing the cycles of planting and harvesting, life and death. Both of which could be considered within the Western scientific model empirical observation via naturalist observation methodology. As Kenneth S. Cohen, considered one of the leading Western interpreters of Taoist Chinese practices, specifically Chi Gong, writes in *The Way of Qi Gong: The Art and Science of Chinese Energy Healing*, "A farmer cultivates his crops by carefully tending them, making sure they get the proper nourishment from soil and sun, and pruning his field to remove destructive or pathogenic influences," (Cohen 1997). Cohen then goes on to reflect more of this Chinese style of speaking and teaching through metaphor, as he further explains how one cultivates health and longevity within the body and mind by working with this subtle energy of chi.

He says, "Like farming, qigong requires daily attention, especially during the early hours of the day. The early stages of qigong practice are the most important, in order to ensure that the 'seed' of chi germinates and establishes strong, healthy roots. A healthy plant is filled with living, moving sap (chi). It is supple, yet strong. It sways with the breeze, but doesn't break. When the plant is sick, withered, or dead, it is stiff and rigid, easily broken. In a healthy field, several crops are grown, or crops are rotated. This creates a mineral–rich environment, in which no single crop will draw excessively on the balance of nutrients or deplete the soil. Similarly, the vast repertoire of qigong self–healing techniques allows us to deal effectively with different states of health or disease," (Cohen 1997).

Probably the earliest known qigong–like exercises in China are the animal dances of ancient Chinese shamans, during the Zhou Dynasty, 1028–221 B.C.. Many of today's chigong exercises are sets of linked postures, each flowing into the next, as in a beautiful, slow–motion dance, inspired by ancient ritual dances designed to alter consciousness. Some of these dances were believed to create health and increase longevity. The earliest documented reference to qigong as a healing exercise rather than dance is inscribed on twelve pieces of jade, dating back to the sixth century B.C., containing advice to collect the breath and allow it to descend in the body, presumably to the lower abdomen. By cultivating quiet, relaxed breathing, chi accumulates and "solidifies" making the body feel stable and balanced. Then the chi "sprouts" so that it is moving through the whole body, from the crown of the head to the soles of the feet, creating vitality and long life.

The Chinese culture's traditional roots actually spring from before the best known Chinese philosopher, Confucius, to Lao Tzu. Lao Tzu is considered the founding philosopher, or compiler, in much the same way Patanjali is for the Yogic Sciences. He put down the founding philosophies in writing for Taoism. Taoism contains the roots of what can be understood to most Westerners as Chinese culture and folklore. It is Taoism and not Confucianism that originated the yin–yang symbol and concept, feng shui, the I Ching, and the meridian systems for both acupuncture and chi gong.

David Rosen, in *The Tao of Jung: The Way of Integrity*, quotes the later part of the Enlightenment era's German philosopher Goethe on his first page, "East and West can no longer be kept apart," (Rosen 1996). "Jung," from Rosen's title, is the Austrian psychoanalyst Carl Jung. He was Freud's student who departed from Freud on his Oedipal and Electra complexes, and focused more on archetypes contained at a collective cultural level, creating the "collective unconscious" concept. Jung was also known for his exposure to Eastern thought. On the first page Rosen has the character–the Chinese pictograph that communicates a word and concept–for *The Tao*.

This is his explanation for it: "The Tao (the Way) is both fixed and moving at the same time. The Tao governs the individual just as it does visible and invisible nature (earth and heaven). On the left side of the ancient Chinese pictograph, which is linked to the earth, the upper part signifies going step-by-step, but the line underneath connotes standing still. On the right side is a head with hair above, which is associated with heaven, and interpreted as the beginning or source. The original meaning of the whole pictograph is one of the Way, which, though fixed itself, leads from beginning to end and back to the beginning," (Rosen 1996). And while chi is considered alive consciousness, the Tao is what its theories are based on. You can observe a sense of something much bigger in the Tao.

The Chinese Language, its Communication System and Holism

It is important to appreciate at a very rudimentary level how the Chinese mind may differ from the English-speaking mind, because it reflects their roots in the metaparadigm of holism. Note that all of this mentioned above with the characters for "The Tao" was communicated with what consists for the Chinese, as one word. Yet it is bringing a few different concepts together, albeit abstractly, into a more collective meaning, still containing a level of metaphor, but also to be interpreted as a concept that communicates meaning. In other words, a word.

In and of itself, this can help to explain a bit of the sense of the *Chinese focus on the whole*, as opposed to its parts. It's different than how the letter "a" comes together with the letter "r" and the letter "e" because neither the "a," "r," nor "e," contain any meaning in and of themselves whatsoever. Yet, when working at the level of roots, prefixes and suffixes within the English language, there is this same function of combining together different parts to form a whole. But it's done from a more logical and linear perspective, and not an abstract, metaphorical one that requires interpretation.

The last relevant difference between the two languages is the interpretation of something that originated from a picture. Interpreting art or metaphors from a picture is a task of the creative right brain, the more abstract brain of the two hemispheres. *It's also the side of the brain which is able to see things as their whole*, as opposed to the analytical left brain. The left brain is that analytical side, that breaks things apart and dissects them into reduced sections. It seems reasonable to say that the Chinese language is a more right-brained based language than perhaps an alphabet based language devoid of pictorial roots. The left brain analysis for reading (and even a bit of language based interpreting, but not art nor picture based interpretation), can be understood as a further reductionist, or non-holistic behavior, *comparatively*.

Thus, the Chinese language which is layered with metaphors, abstraction and interpretation, to some immeasurable degree also operates in the same way that a metaparadigm does. It underlies every day thinking and behavior and assumptions, both individually and collectively. Sanskrit does not have this; it has what is considered an alphabet. The Chinese language does not have an alphabet, per se, it has a list of basic characters–3,500 pictographs and radicals. Approximately 500 of the most frequently used ones are then what are initially memorized when someone learns the Chinese language. This list of the most used 500 characters allows one to be able to decipher and understand the multifarious combinations and recombinations used in communication through Chinese at a less advanced level.

To better grasp the differentiation because it is key, one of the Chinese words for danger, for example, contains within it three individual pictographs. One for "the individual," one for "a cliff," and one for "a measured response." The "measured response" then further carries the connotation to be characterized by slow and cautious movement which enables one to preserve one's dignity. Ultimately, combining all three of these pictographs together, this word for danger implies that this type of danger is actually a potential cliff for the individual in its ability to cause the person to lose their dignity. The second level of implied meaning is so they must have slow and cautious movement in order to maintain their dignity. This word for danger is different than other words for danger in the Chinese language, due to its inclusion of the element of potential loss of dignity.

There is connotation achieved by the choice of adding in the particular radical that signifies this element of dignity. Radicals are these more subtle aspects to the Chinese language that are usually simple lines independent from the main characters, added in to complete the overall meaning. We are dealing here still with word choice, or diction, to encapsulate the most precise meaning possible. We do this when communicating in any language, yet most languages are alphabets. In Chinese, the interpretation is dependent upon the combination of characters, that began as pictures where each essentially contain their own meaning. These get memorized, which is the left brain.

But then the combination of these memorized characters based on pictures require some sense of interpretation that typically is more idiomatic than understood literally, or directly, or logically, or with the left brain. The Chinese language is known for, and frustratingly so, for its idiomatic base. We do perceive literal meanings of words formed by meaningless letters in English; a word has a literal, direct meaning. We'll play with which words to use to capture more precise shades of meaning, and that leave the desired connotation. Yet in Chinese, there is an inherent act of interpretation and then metaphor to the Chinese language. Both of these acts use the right brain. And again, the right brain is where we go to see things holistically.

So you've just walked through a very typical Chinese experience of how to express subtle meanings through these abstract combinations. Yet it is, obviously, a word that for the Chinese carries a common meaning for all collectively so that the culture can communicate. The central point here though is, yes, the Chinese words have to get more interpreted with subjectivity in their indirect communication system, and result in more differing personal meanings. Because of this level of subtlety and interpretation, it allows for a lot more personal interpretation dependent upon the listener's perceptions of the interaction with the speaker. This is where the Chinese rely on the subtle cues of body language, rank in hierarchy among those in the interaction and all the other accompanying info available to the perceiver/listener to create the connotation's most accurate meaning possible. You can see all the room for misinterpretation.

English words contain this too, yes, but not in any way to the degree that the *subtlety* of the *listeners' interpretation gets involved, and is expected to occur.* It's somewhat similar to speakers dropping hints. Their system is known as an indirect communication system, whereas English is considered a direct one, with America being considered the most direct English speaking culture. Yet each culture has within their language an inherent communication *system,* an inseparable intertwinement between these two: language and cultural values. So that Americans are seen in contrast by the Chinese as direct, due to both English and the cultural communication values combined. Americans may view the Chinese as pensive, quiet, subtle (all descriptions for non–extroverts, right?), indirect, or even passive.

Quite genuinely, this indirectness coupled with the abstractions behind their words creates their unique system of communication. So much is left up to the interpreter of my word choice, or my facial expression, or my body language. All are of near equal importance. Within this indirect communication system to a Westerner, particularly a directly spoken, "let's get down to business" perspective, there can be a frustratingly, seemingly dysfunctional lack of clarity. And what seems like over-analysis, and over-thinking of what was said. In English, particularly American English, we're used to saying something, it being understood for what was said, and moving on, message communicated and thus, moving forward.

Whereas culturally, it is part of the art of being a Chinese person, *using the subtlety* from the potential abstraction–due to the pictograph and the act of interpreting it–and the value of not communicating directly. It's considered crude to do so. To a Westerner it seems like a lot of song and dance, a lot of secrecy, deception and unreliability on their words, or on what is said. This is true; they *don't* value clear, direct honest communication in the general sense comparatively as the Western culture does. So much is left unspoken. And it's expected to be inferred, whether it is accurate or not is more a question of the listener's responsibility.

This focus on the subtle that we've just discussed is actually an excellent example of the Chinese culture's typical type of circularity and irony, that makes Chinese thinking and communication sometimes nearly impossible to understand to the non–Chinese. It is ironic, that due to the system being indirect, we should not be focusing on the subtle–for that is too direct or obvious. As in, if we can speak of it, it's not the Tao.

This is a central tenet to the Tao. To Taoism, we should just naturally get it, like being in a flow with the implied connotation. Furthermore, the connotation is rather obvious if we are indeed in this flow, along with the situational context, our relationship and relative positions within whatever hierarchy may exist amongst us, and the used body language. *All of these parts should add up to a whole*, which results in my making an accurate inference in what the Chinese communicator indirectly implied, to appreciate the real meaning. Even if what the words you've said as a Chinese person are the opposite of your meaning. This also can result in what Westerners typically construe as a lie, however, in order to maintain some level of surface harmony within this *collectivist culture* as it's been classified sociologically, *all units must work together to contribute to the larger whole*. This can mean preserving a feeling of non–emotional, non–reactive harmony or lightness even when one is personally seething inside, as we also do in the West. *Yet this sacrifice of not individually honoring one's feelings in the Chinese culture for the preservation of the whole when in social contexts is expected. This includes knowing one's part within the larger circle, or the hierarchy.* Although the hierarchical concepts come less from Taoism and more from Confucius and the Chinese historical institutions of Emperors and governments. It is both these forces that are interwoven in Chinese culture –Taoism and the societal, historical, political structures that Confucius was such a strong organizer for.

As you can see, the language, the sociological structure and the communication style used are all supportive of everything being part of a whole, that is, *units are seen in relationship to the whole.* They are not reduced, broken down into separate units, as we are focused on as individual, separate units in the West—especially America. *The individualists' rights, and the separation of the whole into understandable, observable parts is very much a result of the Enlightenment ideas that the West went through.* Remember that both the America Revolution and the French Revolution came out of the Enlightenment's ideas. As did the American Constitution, itself. Scientific materialism, along with the sociological philosophers, such as John Locke, spoke of an individual's rights to speak out against their government and to have their own voice heard because each individual matters.

The act of looking into how individual phenomena is related, as opposed to breaking it down and examining it as separate parts as we do in the West, is a central aspect of Taoism. One can see how this importance of seeing phenomena's relationships runs throughout the Chinese culture. You were just led through the most typical traits of communication within the Chinese culture, and saw how the holistic view took precedence. This holistic perception of the world can also be seen behind the Traditional Chinese Medical System (TCM), and in the therapies, preventative, diagnostic, and treatment practices of TCM, such as Chi Gong and acupuncture.

When attempting to wrestle out a clear picture of TCM, or acupuncture, or Chi Gong, the relationship of the practice to its greater whole, or context, is essential. Thus, when transferring to and studying these practices within a Western context with Western methodology, frequently much authenticity and, at times, effectiveness, of the practice gets lost in translation. *We end up reducing it to what we see through our own reductionist analysis of the separate units, with our scientific materialist eyes' focus on the direct tangibility of each phenomena, separately, on its own.*

Some of the Taoist concepts that need to be mentioned to see this thinking in relationship form, or holistic form, Rosen covers in his *Tao of Jung*. Rosen quotes an ancient Chinese text, the I Ching, "All movements are accomplished in six stages, and the seventh brings return...Seven is the number of young light, and it arises when six, the number of the great darkness, is increased by one." Also, Lao Tzu said when speaking of *The Tao* as *The Way*, "The Way is to straighten oneself and await the direction of destiny...Find out destiny, govern mental functions, make preferences orderly, and suit real nature." This contains a sense of the mental discipline needed in order to see clearly that which is real and lasting. In seeing that which is real and lasting then one's destiny will become "found out." So then when engaging in mental discipline once knowing one's destiny and making preferences ordered from the destiny seen, this will suit one's real nature. Or–the individual's life will be aligned with that which is real and genuine.

Furthermore, the "Tao is Great in all things, Complete in all, Universal in all, [Tao] causes being and non–being, but is neither being nor non-being," (Rosen 1996). This last one is quintessential Taoist philosophy in that it reflects an understanding of Chi–following much the same pathways as The Tao–and a higher order to the cosmos at this level. But at the same time it is also at the micro level. *Everything contains the whole, no matter what level, microcosmic or macrocosmic, the phenomena is; a rock, or a cloud or a tree or a cell or a human.*

Another prototypical Taoist practice is then to seemingly churn up what feels like the comfortable understanding one has finally gained from the defining of what the Tao is, and blast this understanding apart, by then saying something that totally confuses this gained understanding. That it is in all things, complete and universal, but at the same time even though it is this fundamental to life in that it can cause both being and non–being, it isn't either of these things. *Instead, it's not the cause, it's not the effect. It's beyond that. The Tao is unknowable, in fact to speak of the Tao, means you don't really know The Tao, for the Tao is really unnamable, or unspeakable, it is that all encompassing, and at the same time that elusive. And yet it runs through everything.* As Lao Tzu also said, "It turns in a circle and does not endanger itself. One may call it 'the Mother of the World.' I do not know its name. I call it Tao," (Rosen 1996).

One of the clearest depictions of the Taoist Chinese concepts contained within the yin–yang's larger conceptual framework is quoted here by Lao Tzu, "Whosoever knows his maleness...guards his femaleness," and "When male and female combine, all things achieve harmony," (Rosen 1996). While this does in fact speak to sexual and romantic coupling, it also refers to the masculine and feminine as archetypal energies, and that each person has both inside them, regardless of their biological gender. So this can then make one see that in the black half of the yin–yang symbol that small white dot is to represent "the other," and the same in its opposite with the black half of the circle. *Each contains a part of its opposite.* This concept of *opposites still being united* is central to Taoism, and to achieving balance and harmony within a human being; meaning mental and physical health, vitality, and well being.

Another quintessential concept of Taoism is to flow with that which is natural, as expressed by Chuang Tzu, who is considered the second primary voice creating Taoism. "Do not force things...Can you afford to be careless? So then, flow with whatever may happen and let your mind be free; stay centered by accepting whatever you are doing. This is the ultimate. How else can you carry out your task? It is best to leave everything to work naturally, though this is not easy," (Rosen 1996). This is expressing a principle that runs throughout Taoism that fighting the flow, or going where there is resistance as in swimming upstream against the current, is a useless expenditure of energy. It won't get you anywhere. In fact, it typically backfires on us, forcing, resisting, and going against the natural flow. It actually then creates more to resist against. I know; I help most of my clients and students understand that this sense of forcing comes from the mind. And when we're more successful at managing our mind's dominance, we have access to our being, or spirit, or Higher Self. This connection, or other part of ourself different than our "ego-mind" or cognitive mind, has a knowing of natural timing, the kind in nature, in the universe and in all life that is being described here with this Taoist concept.

This philosophy can be seen in many Chi Gong movements within a Chi Gong series, as most of Chi Gong's movements mimic either natures' or animals' movements. (This is also the case in yoga, where most of the postures are also based on either nature or animals, such as "the tree" pose, or "the cobra.") One Chi Gong movement that encapsulates this teaching is the "pushing and pulling of the waves," in which the Chi Gong practitioner first steps forward with elbows bent, hands up at the chest with palms facing out, as if to push something away as one steps forward with one foot, followed by the other foot. The second half of the movement is where one then flops ones' hands down at the wrists so that the palms are now facing the body, perpendicular to the wrists, with the arms still out and elbows still bent, while the person steps back one foot at a time, as if to say "OK, I surrender" with the second half–or the pulling–of the waves.

The first half of the movement gives a sense of pushing against and stepping out to meet. The second half then gives the sense of pulling back, receiving, withdrawing. This movement overall yields the intuitive mental realization of giving and receiving or advancing and retreating through the movement's rhythm. This forward and backward movement is repeated nine times before going to the next movement in the series. These mental constructs are then expected to be teachings on how to better manage oneself and approach situations in life.

Carl Jung's own study and professional application of Taoist concepts to his own psychoanalytical work, particularly with archetypes, probably reflects more of the reason for his splitting from Freud's focus on the madness in the subconscious. Jung also is known to have used Taoism in his own personal development. Jung said, "The Tao (like the Self) encompasses all opposites...The Chinese have never failed to recognize the paradoxes and the polarity inherent in what is alive. The opposites always balanced one another–a sign of high culture. One–sidedness, though it lends momentum, is a mark of barbarism." Our reductionism and our focus on the external and the physical within our scientific tradition is an example of this one-sidedness.

Traditional Chinese Medicine

Ted Kaptchuk earned his doctorate in Oriental Medicine (DOM) from the Macau Institute of Chinese Medicine in China in 1975. He is the author of the popular TCM-for-westerners classic *The Web That Has No Weaver: Understanding Chinese Medicine*. He is now associate director of the Center for Alternative Medicine in Research and Education at Boston's Beth Israel Deaconess Medical Center, an associate professor of medicine at Harvard Medical School, and is considered one of the top translators of Chinese Medicine to the West. He also says that TCM is rooted in the philosophy, logic, sensibility, and habits of a civilization that is thousands of years old, and *one that is entirely foreign to an American.* He says that TCM has developed its own perception of health and illness as a "coherent and independent system of thought and practice that has been developed over two millennia. Based on ancient texts, it is the result of a continuous process of critical thinking, as well as extensive clinical observation and testing. It represents a thorough formulation and reformulation of material by respected clinicians and theoreticians," (Kaptchuk 2000).

He goes on to help explain that it is not as effective to uproot TCM from its context, and import it to our own system, studied with our own methodology for our own societal uses. For it divorces TCM from its whole system's strength. Due to our reductionist and scientific materialist approach, we end up stripping it of much of its inherent worth and total functionality that it is *on its own as a complete system, a complete interwoven web of understanding.* This interweaving and web mentioned in his title of his classic is this holism we have been talking about. Kaptchuk describes, "The differences between the two medicines, however, are greater than that between their descriptive language. The actual logical structure underlying the methodology, the habitual mental operations that guide the physician's clinical insight and critical judgment, differs radically in the two traditions... These two different logical structures have pointed the two medicines in different directions," (Kaptchuk 2000).

Lao Tzu said, "To be bent is to become straight. To be empty is to be full. To be worn out is to be renewed. To have little is to possess." Chuang Tzu also said, "When there is life there is death, and when there is death there is life. When there is possibility, there is impossibility, and when there is impossibility, there is possibility. Because of the right, there is wrong, and because of the wrong, there is right...The 'this' is also the 'that.' The 'that' is also the 'this.'...Is there really a distinction between 'that' and 'this'?... When 'this' and 'that' have no opposites, there is the very axis of Tao," (Kaptchuk 2000). *So that change and transformation, or that which is in flux, are the constants in Taoism, and it seems they are also the constants of a larger universal truth, or transcendent truth.* This is reflected throughout the Chinese culture, particularly within their medical practices and theory. If there is a system suffering, it is because some other system within the body is being greedy, or taking more due to a "weakened" state. Thus, this is again, an interactive, how–things–relate–as–a–part–of–the–whole perspective, not a reductionist theory.

This is a cultural paradigm for the East. It helps us to see new light in what we construe as problems and solutions. It is a logic that assumes that a part can be understood only in its relation to the whole. This can also be called synthetic (as in synthesis, as opposed to analytical as in analysis). In Chinese early naturalist Taoist thought, this logic of the Yin–Yang Theory explains relationships, patterns and change. It is based on the philosophical construct of two polar compliments, called Yin and Yang. These complementary opposites are neither forces nor material entities. Nor are they mythical concepts that transcend rationality. Rather they are convenient labels used to describe how things function in relation to each other and to the universe. And they are used to explain the continuous process of natural change. So that these two factors combine to be the Yin–Yang theory: *no entity can ever be isolated from its whole.* This is within the interactions between the entity and its whole that then corresponds to how things behave together. So this means changes in one effect changes in another. For example, if the spleen is cut out it, using our reductionist based medicine, this will affect the whole system in some way, even if the spleen can be viewed as a more "unnecessary" organ by a Western surgeon. Setting the system out of balance and out of harmony, this remedy then will somehow require methods to make up for this imbalance .

On another note "The Chinese never tried to tame the elusive and changeable qualities of the Tao," (Kaptchuk 2000). Compare this to the Western scientific materialism's theory of objectivity that has Western science and biomedicine trying to tame what it is that it is working with. It's as if forcing something to become something other than it is by attempts to have it conform to being studied, dominate it, cut it out, or suppress it. All of this is done by manipulating with surgery or drugs or other chemical treatments, as is done in our medical system. In this action, one can see the act of projecting onto the object the concept of separation and reducibility to just its part. It has been reduced in order to be dealt with. So this is when it's able to be manipulated in one of the ways just described.

There is a sense of force here against the inherent nature of the way one thing functions within its whole system, such as the spleen and then the whole body. Kaptchuk continues, "The word Tao, although sometimes translated as 'The Way,' cannot really be translated into satisfactory English, and even its meaning in Chinese frustrates the attempt to pin it down...And so the Chinese have developed ways of alluding to the Tao-in aphorisms, parables, and tales that are more like poetry than like the systematic presentations of Western thought," (Kaptchuk 2000). So this relates back to what was earlier described as the lack of seeming linearity that the Chinese language has, to the eyes and mind of a native English speaker.

This brings us to understanding that this elusiveness to the Tao is deeply interconnected to understanding the activity of chi. Chi, based on these concepts of the Tao, is then directly and profoundly applied to working with the forces within the human body and nature for harmonious living and health. Through working with chi, the subtle energy that follows the same behavior as The Tao, is directed in health giving ways. Longevity is one of the results. Talk about a slippery abstraction.

The Chinese emphasis on interconnectedness and change takes on a very specific character in the context of medicine, due to this. "When the young Chinese physician examines a patient, he or she plans to look at many, many signs and symptoms and to make of them a 'diagnosis,' *to see in them a pattern. Each sign means nothing by itself and acquires meaning only in its relationship to the patient's other signs.* What it means in one context is not necessarily what it means in another context," (italics mine) (Kaptchuk 2000). So that the universality principle of scientific materialism is absolutely in opposition to the practice of TCM. Additionally, scientific reductionism and objectivism are also in direct opposition here because a doctor of TCM considers a patient's subjective experience as an important aspect of the patient's whole system's symptoms. We're getting to that!

Chinese medicine considers important certain aspects of the human body and personality that are not significant to Western medicine. As Kaptchuk concisely points out the differences between Western and TCM, "Biomedicine, a more accurate name for Western medicine, is primarily concerned with isolable disease categories or agents of disease, which it zeroes in on, isolates, and tries to change, control, or destroy. The Western physician starts with a symptom, then searches for the underlying mechanism–a precise cause for a precise disease. The disease may affect various parts of the body, but it is relatively well–defined, self–contained phenomenon. *Precise diagnosis frames an exact, quantifiable description of a narrow area.* The physician's logic is analytic–cutting through the accumulation of bodily phenomena like a surgeon's scalpel to isolate one single entity or cause," (italics mine) (Kaptchuk 2000). This clearly exemplifies scientific materialism's focus on the tangible, as well as reductionism's focus on the analysis or splitting apart of the whole, by reducing the whole into separate, more understandable parts.

Whereas the Chinese physician, in contrast, "directs his or her attention to the complete physiological and psychological individual. All relevant information, including the symptom as well as the patient's other general characteristics, is gathered and woven together until it forms what Chinese medicine calls a 'pattern of disharmony.' This pattern of disharmony describes a situation of 'imbalance' in a patient's body. Oriental diagnostic technique does not turn up a specific disease entity or a precise cause, but renders an almost poetic, yet workable, description of a whole person. The logic of Chinese medicine is organismic or synthetic, attempting to organize symptoms and signs into understandable configuration. The total configurations, the patterns of disharmony, provide the framework for treatment. The therapy then attempts to bring the configuration into balance, to restore harmony to the individual," (Kaptchuk 2000).

For example, if four patients go to an American biomedical doctor or a Western trained biomedical doctor in Taiwan or China with a complaint of stomach problems, the typical response is for the M.D. to use upper–gastrointestinal x–rays or an endoscopy by means of a fiberscope, in order to diagnose the part causing the problem. Again, this is an example of scientific materialism in dealing only with the physical. It is also an example of reductionism in dealing only with the one area that the patient suffers pain in. From the M.D.'s perspective, based on the non-holistic view there is an analytical practice to narrow, and from the scientific materialism's principle of universality, they thus center diagnosis around one underlying entity. So all these patients would suffer from the same disorder; peptic ulcers, stemming from stomach pain.

In contrast, the Chinese counterpart would question and examine the first patient. The doctor of TCM could find that the patient has, for example, a robust constitution, broad shoulders, a reddish complexion, and a full, deep voice, as well as pain that increases at touch but diminishes with the application of a cold compress. In observing the outward indications of the patient's emotional and mental state, he seems assertive and even aggressive. His diet is full of wheat and unrefined carbohydrates. He seems to be challenging the doctor. He does not exercise, focusing instead, mostly on his work in which he is a manager. He is constipated and has dark yellow urine. His tongue has a greasy yellow coating; his pulse is "full" and "wiry." At this point, the pattern that the Chinese physician characterizes is the pattern of disharmony called, "Damp Heat Affecting the Spleen."

The second patient has a different set of signs, which then indicate another overall pattern. The same with the third, then the fourth. "So a Chinese doctor, searching for and organizing signs and symptoms that a Western doctor might never heed, distinguishing (four) patterns of disharmony where Western medicine perceives only one disease. The patterns of disharmony are similar to what the West calls diseases in that their discovery tells the physician how to prescribe treatment. *But they are different from diseases because they cannot be isolated from the patient in whom they occur. To Western medicine, understanding an illness means uncovering a distinct entity that is separate from the patient's being;* to Chinese medicine, understanding means perceiving the relationships among all the patient's signs and symptoms in the context of his or her life," (italics mine) (Kaptchuk 2000).

This method of the Chinese TCM physician is based on their idea that no single part can be understood except in relation to the whole. So therefore, a symptom is not traced back to a cause. Instead, it is looked at as a part of the total information of a whole person. When a patient has a certain complaint or symptom, the Chinese doctor wants to understand how it fits into the patient's entire being and behavior, life and biography. In context, not separate from its parts, is how the TCM doctor will approach a patient. Whereas a Western biomedical doctor approaches the diagnosis as separate from the person's/patient's entirety–or from a "parts" perspective, not holistic.

Now, in even more direct regards to the mind body connection Kaptchuk illustrates the point brilliantly: "Any discussion of emotions in East Asia must consider the complex cross–cultural questions embedded in the continuum and interaction of the psyche and soma." Psyche means of the mind, or psychology, of the person, and soma means the body. Here Kaptchuk is referring to metaparadigms. He continues, "As we have noted before, *East Asian medicine has always recognized the psychosomatic assumption that psychological and physiological processes are interactive and have a shared clinical significance,*" (italics mine).

This can be viewed, on a very simple level, in how Traditional Chinese Medicine can see anxiety and heart palpitations, fear and sweating, revulsion and nausea, anger and changes in metabolism, despair and sighing as all being emotional and physical concomitants of a single yin–yang manifestation. All of these are pairs of examples of how the emotion has a corresponding physical affect, or change. As Kaptchuk goes on, "Nevertheless, Eastern and Western people may tend to experience different ends of this [emotional with physical concomitant] continuum in their actual lives. What may be a single 'energetic' phenomenon in Oriental medical theory may appear to be a different experience for people in different cultures. Any discussion of emotions must ultimately take this (difference) question into account," (Kaptchuk 2000).

What Kaptchuk seems to be speaking to is that in addition to how the metaparadigms within cultures influence people of that culture's perception towards the mind body connection and health, these same beliefs then show up in the experience of emotions in their lives. They then gets reflected in the daily behaviors. This contains a very important difference between Chinese and American culture. Meaning, because the Chinese give the subtle primary positioning, they will think and act differently with their emotional expression from their American counterparts, who give the physical primary importance through a direct communication style.

The Chinese for centuries have lived in a system that is built on acknowledging the role of emotions as part of the subtle energy system. Due to the emotions being part of the subtle energy system inherently tied into the mind body system, emotions are not typically brought up and out to the mental, or intellectual level, to be separated out from the subtle energy. And if they are, they're only reserved for the most intimate relationships. So it would seem there is less, as an American knows it, "emotional intelligence" within the culture. This can be observed in the lack of social support systems for doing so; guidance counselors in the school system, for example, are non–existent.

Within the Chinese cultural practice, children are not to express their feelings about anything to their parents within the hierarchical system. "Seen but not heard" is a saying that they're brought up with. Additionally, typically, employees do not consult with their bosses offering their creative ideas; it's a top–down system. To "grin and bear it" no matter the feeling is the mainstream, traditional Chinese behavior. In fact, there is a cultural value placed on those who can bear the heaviest of burdens, silently, gracefully, and still endure–no matter the level of internal suffering. The more healthy members of society will then find an outlet such as sports or music to release the emotional pressure. Yet the dialoguing, the acknowledging of an emotional response to a situation is not typical to their culture, as it is ours.

But the diagnostician, the Chinese physician, acknowledges the role of emotions in illness, and will have developed an eye for a different flavor of emotions and conditions in their Chinese patients than, say, the typical American who does not suppress his or her emotions in this Chinese way. Some of these conditions, the doctor's culturally trained as well as medically trained eye will know. Certain disorders come from bottling up certain emotions as reactions to certain cultural practices. They will be familiar with it from the population they've worked with, who hold certain cultural pathos in their bodies' manifestations of symptoms. This is what Kaptchuk meant when he said that "Eastern and Western people may tend to experience different ends of this [emotional with physical concomitant] continuum in their actual lives. What may be a single 'energetic' phenomenon in oriental medical theory may appear to be a different experience for people in different cultures."

A easier example, possibly, is American acupuncturists having to create new places for the placement of needles for stress. The Chinese had not developed this specific to the type of stress an average American experiences. This condition has not been seen within the Chinese cultural milieu with as much regularity as within the States. ADHD, OCD are more examples. Although, as the World Health Organization amongst other international organizations acknowledge now "affluent" or "developed" countries' afflictions - meaning diseases change with the level of development and financial security - this stark contrast is beginning to fade a bit. Nonetheless, this changing scenario is still in addition to cultural values and practices that trickle down to typical daily lifestyle choices and behaviors.

Emotional Expression, Buddhism, Self-Management and the Chinese

Another key example to understand how valuing the subtle is reflected in Chinese cultural practices is what is reflected in what is said and not said, facial expressions, and body language. Keeping one's emotional self–and therefore one's energy–in check when within a social setting in order to preserve harmony for the collective is one of the most highly valued traits within the Chinese culture. This cultural, societal practice of the Chinese we've already discussed. Yet in another domain in life, this practice results in a socially valued skill that could be considered an "energetic awareness" of the way people "feel" in their "energy"–which then their "energy" could be defined as how a person's emotions and thoughts are interacting to create a tone or even more strongly, a "mood," with that mood being sensed as "the energy." While in America we do acknowledge moods, and not tones, the importance given to them is dealt with differently–not as sensitively nor subtly, nor as a cultural value *in the same way as the Chinese value it.*

This should yield the conclusion that in America we don't then, therefore give the equivalent importance to what could be deemed a social skill within the Chinese culture as "energetic awareness" or "sensitivity to others' energy." Nor do we give as much weight to emotions as our Chinese counterparts. Yet, again ironically as there are so many ironies in these differences between particularly a Chinese and American, there's a surface level observation of the contrasts, and then when getting to the layer beneath the surface, the ironies become much more complex.

I said before that the Chinese in comparison to the American culture seem to not be as emotionally intelligent because they don't discuss them. Upon more examination though, this is due to their consideration that emotions are so important, and that they contain subtle energy. Then couple this with their indirect communication style, and you can see a more complete picture why it is considered rather crude to outwardly express oneself emotionally, when in public. Home life is an entirely different story, but that's not meant to be explored here. If emotions are a part of a system that is composed overall of subtle energies, then emotions should be indirectly implied, and then inferred by the other. So in this indirect system, to regard emotions in this way seems an inherent appreciation to the power and role of emotions within us and life.

Therefore, they don't get to be discussed at a rational, almost intellectual level, as we are more familiar with in the United States. Even though as was stated before that emotions aren't as valued as reason within the Western metaparadigm, nonetheless comparative to the Chinese, Westerners articulate their emotions. Articulation of one's emotions in America is considered a social skill, and one that is considered a necessity within making relationships work—all relationships, but particularly the male/female romantic one. Yet it seems that somehow in the articulation of the emotions within our culture, some of the power given to emotions–if they are discussed–is then let out. It seems then that the emotions are not perhaps felt as intensely. An image of the value of karaoke singing in the Asian culture overall comes to mind to this author. Seriously! It's a main part of what they do for social entertainment, with entire high-rise buildings that we expect to be business offices instead filled with private rooms, floor after floor, to sing karaoke. Just a thought.

For a foreigner who wants to succeed in interacting with the Chinese in their own environment it is of critical importance to learn to take a "read" of a room as they enter. The same with taking a "read" of a person before they interact with them, so that they can adjust their own behavior accordingly, in response to the person's "energy." In fact, it is a typical bar of measurement for a foreigner working within the Chinese culture to be measured on how sensitively they interact with their Chinese counterparts, reflected in tone of voice, facial expressions and body language–all indirect forms of communication.

This is the ideal, of course, that is meant to communicate that one has to be sensitive in a way within in the Chinese culture to the more subtle energy of those around him or her. Particularly as a foreigner. This, to an average American, can seem like almost being what's been labeled as "over–sensitive," in our culture. Notice what is considered a value there is considered, however unspoken, to not only be of no value here, but a negative trait. In the West a level of sensitivity to a person's mood is necessary for successful social, personal and professional interpersonal relationships indeed. Yet it's not done at the same level of silence, or indirectness, or presumption that everyone will be operating from this awareness necessarily, as it is presumed at the metaparadigm level there.

Here in the United States, a supportive comment or action would typically be made so that the American can voice what they're "upset" or "in a mood about," or left alone until we know that "they're able to talk about it." Eventual articulation of the mood, or emotion or feeling is the common expectation, though. Not silence and dismissal, as is the norm within the Chinese culture. It is one of the most befuddling aspects to the Chinese culture for an American. For it seems a lack of concern for "the other," when in fact it is intended to be supportive and hence respectful. Somewhat. But that's an entirely different discussion. Another contradiction, when supposedly the indirectness is meant to happen out of respect to the person's face and their feelings. It ends up seeming like lack of concern or disregard to a foreigner within the Chinese culture. The saving of face, or pride, is the central most important value throughout Asian culture. However, interestingly enough, this is not the case with the sub–continent of India.

This description is meant to help elucidate the everyday experiences of how the emotions and mental state are contained within a subtle energy, within a system that acknowledges subtle as valuable and primary. Yet at a whole other level, to an American eye, it can seem a glaring contradiction, in that it is the silence and the avoidance that is the loudest communication of all; that there *is* something there. Therefore, the whole subtlety gets lost on a Westerner because our cultural values do not value the subtle, or the power contained within the subtle "energies" and aspects of life. One's actions, and particularly one's management of emotions and energy, speak even more loudly than they typically do in the West. It's used as a measurement of one's social refinement and elegance. It's almost a game is: if you react, you lose. Perhaps this is because in the East Buddhism is their spiritual philosophy—not religion—as their major backdrop to their society? And the central tenet of Buddhism, as you have seen, is about successful mental management.

In fact, I had many games played with me by local Taiwanese Chinese to get a reaction out of me. This is what they do with foreigners, because their stereotype of us is that we're highly reactive emotionally. This is their eyes, from their system, interpreting us, without knowing all the values of our directly expressing system. Nor are they aware of the valuing we do in the States of self-expression.

A final point to this onion of ironies is that even though it's indirect, and this acknowledgement of emotions doesn't get verbal articulation, it's still examined and "spoken," perhaps to even more of a degree.

Again, the direct system does not acknowledge the subtle in an active obvious way inherent within its communication system, as does the indirect system. Americans are not trained to "tune into" energy, or the subtleties within a situation to the same degree or in the same way as are our Chinese counterparts, or even Asians in general, who all come from varying degrees of indirect systems, when compared to the West. Indeed, this behavioral trait is still relatively disrespected and not, by any means, a cultural value within America, as can be seen by the remaining typical pejorative jokes in pop-culture when speaking of "someone's *energy.*"

Although degrees of this acknowledgement of someone's energy do indeed exist within American culture. Right? But then why are Americans so much more emotionally articulate? Where does this come from? Making emotions, or the subtle, physical enough happens in the West because in our metaparadigm of scientific materialism, it has trained us to approach life as a whole in a more tangible way, or more direct way, which means thus, an open discussion of emotions. *What seems to come even more into play here is the Enlightenment's scientists and philosophers ordering of the era by the use of reason and rational thinking.* Therefore, it seems that these two factors combined–scientific materialism's primary focus on the physical, and the Enlightenment's focus on using reason–are what contribute to the "emotional intelligence" aspect to American society. At least, that is comparatively to a more closed, or indirect system that values the subtle.

However, the key aspect here to this discussion, if you think back to the introduction to this section with that long list describing the chaos in Asia through an American expat's eyes, is that as a hemisphere Asia has not been "cleaned" in the same way the West was of the chaos and disorder. By the ordering of the universe using reason, and then projecting this reason onto the external world, objectively, order was created by the Enlightenment's creation of scientific materialism. Then the Industrial Revolution's production of technologies, and industrial and consumer goods reinforced the focus on an orderly production. This retained and deepened the focus on order and on what is tangible. So this focus on the objective at the expense of the subjective within the West may have also produced order on the surface of life. It also has us in the West living life more on the surface, of the possible choices between the tangible, or surface, and less intangible, or inner, aspects of humans and life.

The Archetypal Feminine Cognitive Style

The archetypal feminine cognitive style is typically more internal, passive, and intuitive while the masculine is more active, linear, and external. Yet each person and culture possesses both masculine and feminine traits. It is not uncommon to see some women focused more on active, linear, external accomplishments of tangible, measurable goals. The stereotype of "American women have balls" even said by our Western counterparts in England reflects the observation of the masculinity of American culture. This previous stereotype I heard over and over again throughout the world, but particularly in Asia. On the other end of the spectrum, some men tend to be more inclined to introversion, less active, and more passive in their typical behaviors, and more intuitive. This actually seemed to be the typical Asian, whether male or female, compared to Americans. It does not matter whether American women or men, just the American more masculine style of "getting it done" and "being all you can be" and the directness. Now think to our very own stereotypes of Asian men, and you see the reverse.

It might be thought that scientists should stick to the facts and avoid judgments of meaning. Right? But most of the questions we ask demand answers that realistically fit facts into larger, meaningful patterns. This is like the web of holism mentioned with TCM. Or the entire Chinese system. We've just basically assessed the Chinese system as an archetypal feminine cognitive style, and the West, particularly the United States, as an archetypal masculine cognitive style.

"'Scientists cannot help but tell stories, which require the selection of narrative frameworks that necessarily go beyond the facts,' (Haraway 1989). This selection may depend both on their fit with the facts and on their fit with the background values of the storyteller," (Stanford 2000). Ultimately, Anderson concisely states at the start of her article, "Studies of how biases toward working with 'masculine' cognitive styles—for example, toward centralized, hierarchical control models of causation–as opposed to 'feminine'–contextual, interactive, diffused models—have impaired scientific understanding, for example, in studies of slime–mold (Keller 1985) and molecular biology (Spanier 1995)," (Stanford 2000).

So that the inclusion of emotions as causal factors, or subtle phenomena worth being recognized at a systemic level has not happened. To begin to study the role of emotions means, by implication, to acknowledge not only the relevant importance of the subtle, but also emotions' inherent value. The reality of their role in life alongside that of the physical as just as important would also be acknowledged, should we choose to start to see emotions as causal factors of something else, say an illness. This has been blatantly disregarded historically within the Western scientific materialist model. Hence, the model, or paradigm, is incomplete.

The archetypal feminine cognitive style and approach has also been missing in other domains of sociopolitical life, such as positions of authority, power and decision making. Since this has occurred under patriarchy, it seems that the women's rights movement has caused this dominance of control to gradually give way. As it does, we have begun to be able to appreciate what this historical lack of the archetypal feminine perspective has caused us to miss, through the contrast. *By finally seeing some of its inclusion,* as some of the new sciences are reflecting, we are able to have other options that expand the available options for ways to do life, understand life and enjoy life. For example, Candace Pert with the opiate receptor ultimately leading to validating how the mind and body communicate. She saw value in studying how a brain causes a human to feel good. And so she discovered the opiate receptors. We may never had gotten that from a more masculine cognitive style, without the balance of some of the feminine also being present.

This factor plays a major role particular to the "new sciences" as can be seen by both what is slowly being studied—or chosen to be focused on—increasingly, as well as the results from these studies that are being done by both female and male scientists, philosophers, natural healers, and doctors. What is being chosen to be written about from within the new sciences also indicates this shift of focus. For it has been shifting the focus away from the physical and into the recognition of the subtle. So studies are being conducted more on stressful emotions, physical effects from mental and emotional stress, the effects of tai chi, chi gong, yoga, and meditation on the human system, and vibrational medicine—i.e., flower essences and essential oils—to name a few. The view of mind body connection given to us by male Enlightenment scientists has placed primary importance on the physical and it has operated under the scientific materialism model, which has then infiltrated our society as a metaparadigm. It is based on a system of patriarchy. This has been changing slowly, but within the same metaparadigm, on its own terms.

Materialism itself reflects a focus on the material, or the physical, and this is typically ascribed to the masculine archetypal energy, as well. Or as a stereotype, guys like the tangible, "to get their hands on stuff" and "their bodies moving." Then, the counterpart to this stereotype is girls like the "touchy–feely" stuff, or the world of emotions. This includes the connections found in relationships, and to generate these connections, and to take care of emotions. Yet the role of emotions has been historically relegated to the domains of mothering, and all things feminine, in the traditional, patriarchal model. However, as the women's rights movement has gone through backlashes, and as the ensuing dust settles, into the next wave of the gender roles' configuration within our society, it seems that a rebalancing and a wholeness can be considered to be in its infantile stages. You can see it more commonly in the men of generation X on down.

This also contains individuals who possess both masculine and feminine traits, who embrace both traits, and who insightfully know when to utilize either in the most appropriate contexts. It is the healthiest, wisest and most advanced members of our society who are in the process of mastering this balance, and accessing this larger framework of wholeness, or balance. And it is ultimately, a model for what we are seeking within our discussion.

In order for our sciences to yield more accurate information, and our health care system to be more focused on models of health and not disease, the role of emotions has been coming out of the domain of "women's stuff" and into valid areas of study. This results in acknowledgement of a mind body connection becoming more of a focus due to it being a "whole systems," or "holistic" model. It embraces acknowledgment of the subtleties of emotions, of mind, and as we shall see as in its infancy stage in the West–in consciousness.

Again, from Elizabeth Anderson, in the section of her article entitled, "Feminist Critiques of Objectivity," she states that "Feminist critiques of objectivity are directed not against all claims to objectivity, but against particular conceptions of objectivity. The conceptions of objectivity considered problematic by feminists include the following: (a) Subject/ object dichotomy: what is really ('objectively') real exists independently of knowers...(b) Detachment: knowers have an 'objective' stance toward what is known when they are emotionally detached from it. (c) Value– neutrality: knowers have an 'objective' stance toward what is known when they adopt a neutral attitude toward it, declining to judge it either good or bad. (d) Control: 'objective' knowledge of an object (the way it 'really' is) is attained by controlling it, especially by experimental manipulation, and observing the regularities it manifests under control. (e) External guidance: 'objective' knowledge consists of representations whose content is dictated by the way things really are, not by the knower. *These ideas are often combined into a package of claims about science: that its aim is to know the way things are, independent of knowers, and that scientists achieve this aim through detachment and control,* which enable them to achieve a perspective and external guidance. This package arose in the 17th–18th centuries, as a philosophical account of why Newtonian science was superior to its Scholastic predecessor," (Stanford 2000).

Furthermore, "The ideal of objectivity as detachment, according to which *good scientists should adopt an emotionally distanced, controlling stance toward their objects of study,* is defended as necessary to avoid projective error. Keller suggests that it is responsible for the symbolically 'masculine' standing of science that marginalizes women in science (because women are stereotyped as emotional). Moreover, it reflects an androcentric perspective, in that *it serves mens' neurotic anxieties about maintaining sharp boundaries between self and other,* and keeping the 'feminine' at arms–length (Keller 1985, Bordo 1987 in Stanford 2000).

Her entire discussion is pointing to the dysfunctions of the "masculinized" scientific materialism model. She shows that it is incomplete and outdated, and in some instances, simply wrong. That it is not possible for a scientist to remain "detached and objective" and "neutral" at any step of the way throughout the scientific process. Anderson's argument echoes those of many contemporary male scientists, frequently quantum physicists. They are not necessarily pointing towards the masculinization of the scientific materialism model, but are acknowledging the inability to reach this ideal of objectivity. This ideal in scientists who have been exposed to Asian thought, or quantum physicists (who are frequently one and the same) are examples of scientists who purport this position of scientific materialism's dysfunction at this point.

In regards to neutrality, "The ideal of objectivity as value–neutrality *is justified as a psychological stance needed to guard against temptations toward wishful thinking* and dogmatic, politically motivated or ideological reasoning. Feminists argue, on the basis of historical and sociological investigations of the history and current practice of science, that this insistence on the value–neutrality of scientists is *self–deceptive and unrealistic* (Potter 1993, 2001; Longino 1990, 2001; Harding 1991, 1998; Wylie 1996). Indeed, it is self–defeating: *when scientists represent themselves as neutral, this blocks their recognition of the ways their values have shaped their inquiry, and thereby prevents the exposure of these values to critical scrutiny,*" (italics mine) (Stanford 2000).

This reflects an awareness of the subjectivity, or the mind with its own biases, beliefs, etc. that is at work within the scientist himself/herself which was previously denounced as non-existent and the ideal that scientists strove for. Meaning, that scientific certainty we have all come to know and rely upon is not realistic. Perpetuated by the Enlightenment scientists of the scientific materialism model and Newtonian Physics, now critiqued by modern scientists favoring a more balanced and more honest, self-effacing, non-idealistic system of inquiry, it seems now that quantum physics itself has actually negated the possibility of objectivity. This is clearly central to the crumbling scientific materialist metaparadigm via the discoveries of the Observer affect. We shall soon discuss this discovery.

Finally, and just as importantly so that this last idea needs to be included here to round out the discussion, Anderson explains scientific materialism's approach towards the belief in controlling their experiments: "Experimental contexts, in which scientists elicit regularities in the behavior of the objects of study by manipulating them under controlled conditions, are often taken to generate *epistemically privileged evidence* about the objects of study. *Such evidence is thought to ground knowledge of how the objects 'really are'*, (sic) *in contrast with evidence about the objects of study generated through 'subjective' modes of interaction with them,* such as participant observation, dialogue, political engagement, and caring for their needs." Anderson seems to be speaking to the effects still felt from the Enlightenment scientist's propaganda targeted at elevating science's role in society. That is this sense of authoritarianism and elitism of the scientist, through distance and detachment. We'll get to that, looking at the first hard scientists of the Enlightenment and their promotion of science in just a bit.

Could it be that scientific materialism is a creation of the male brain, reflecting some masculine archetypal ideas and behaviors? And that some of the principles of scientific materialism are the unbalanced aspects of the masculine, such as the archetypal masculine cognitive style when feeling threatened or afraid to then seek control and order?

It can be said, particularly when contrasted to a more chaotic environment where people, laws, cities, organizations, the marketplace–life in general–are unpredictable, that a more orderly structure is desirable. Indeed, when communicating about emotions, the orderly nature that the rational focus yields through the use of reason is quite effective for communication, resolution of conflicts, and the preservation and cultivation of relationships. However, all things in balance, as the Buddha said. The Chinese acknowledge that contained within chaos is order. While as many think in America–on the other side of order is chaos, so keep it away.

Enlightenment science, and the scientific materialism model along with Newtonian physics emerged very much as the counter–balance to the previous centuries of chaos. It would seem at this point now, that this system reliant on order, control and stability is being shaken at its foundation by the increasing levels of chaos. Worldwide, *the consideration of its effectiveness and continued usage needs to be re–examined, and not only within the field of science.*

More societal support for a scientific method that is more aligned with reality is emerging particularly within the "new sciences" and at the fringes of mainstream science, even against the resistance, at this point. It's also occurring at the grassroots level, as participants in studies are volunteering so that they can help themselves through alternative means of natural healing with a health concern. Other factors influencing this pressure on the existing model will be addressed in the section on globalization and the current demographics of the profession of scientific research within the United States. We will soon see how quantum physics is also exerting pressure, intense pressure, on the scientific materialism model to give way to a new paradigm.

Chapter 3—Becoming Reasonable, Yes? Scientific Materialism's Metaparadigm and the Emerging Industrial Era

The West's Strengths are the East's Weaknesses and Vice Versa

B ACK IN THE WEST BY the end of the nineteenth century, with both the modern era and the industrial age firmly geared up, two centuries after Newton, there was widespread certainty that the overall program of scientific materialism and Newtonian physics had been a general success. In the realm of physics, a tremendous amount had been explained by Newton, and in chemistry the theory of atomic activity as the basis of everything had been considered to have been proven valid. There was strong confidence in the scientific approach because so much of its program had been carried out, at least in the realm of physics and chemistry, in application to objects *believed not to have life.* This completely and perfectly fit the Industrial Age's needs, as well. *Objects were created from scientific discoveries, with practical application to mechanizing* many, eventually most, aspects of life so these processes could be quicker and more uniform. Massive improvements in the time and means for travel were gained, as well as improvements for the lifestyle of Westerners, particularly in America, thereby bringing us into the modern age.

The analogy of a "clockwork god" became prevalent, as many in the time period in the mid to late 1800's–which is deemed the start of the modern age–analogized the increasing sophistication of their ability to craft precise machines, with the universe being so, or nature and the skies, also seeming to run in an orderly fashion, like the smooth functioning of a clock. Therefore our understanding of the universe, as well as our material creations using this same science both created the sense that it all runs like a machine. Science seemed to fit together all the pieces of the universe as if it were a clock whose individual parts all have a function, functioning precisely and orderly, and then creating machinery and technology based on this same idea.

The machines and other inventions helped to create the appearance and unconscious feeling over time of facilitating and keeping order by the consistent rhythm the mechanization created as a background, or undercurrent to life, and by the uniformity contained within mechanization's processes and products, as well. These inventions also expanded potential and opportunities, some of which had never before been thought possible for humans to mimic nature. Once the general public then began to increasingly have access to and use these inventions, they too began to gain this same feel that the scientists had already had; mechanization and smooth running. *This stability that permeates through almost all aspects of society is one of the most distinctive, differentiating characteristics between the Western and Eastern hemispheres–up until the last decade or so..*

In other words, this was a good, comforting feeling from this perspective of everything having its place, neat and tidy. In fact, it was so precise in its tidiness that it did indeed resemble the finest sense of subtle measurement and precise mechanistic functioning of the clock. This was a clean, objective feeling of order. Everything being able to be figured out with reason. This rendered the Church seen not to be needed as much any more as a force of authority *due to the influence of reason.*

Further adding to the changes the use of reason and the Enlightenment brought was that each individual had their own rights, intellect, and will and could compete to use them to his or her highest advantage without limitations set by a theocracy or monarchy. Instead, each individual could have a voice in their own republics/democracies/parliaments. *Both these factors thereby made everything feel cleaned by the end of the Enlightenment. All was then cleaned up, after the near millennia of chaos and irrational, unpredictable, mysterious phenomena from the "Dark Ages," or the Middle Ages.*

The Middle Ages had still allowed for an acknowledgement of the subtle. But that had also been dominated by the Church's hypocrisy and abuse of its proclaimed power, particularly in the realms of what had been considered unexplainable, or "supernatural," as the subtle was categorized in the West.

The scientists and intellectuals of the Enlightenment were able to do this through the belief that there is a mathematical foundation to the universe. This has become a cornerstone of science, within the scientific materialist metaparadigm. This belief is an essential aspect of metaphysical realism, one of the key principles of scientific materialism. Metaphysical realism states that the *universe is ordered* by ideas, such as mathematics, that lies beyond or transcends the senses. According to this view, these ideas are the very ideas that are implicit in the actual nature of reality. Meaning, that it's what the universe really boils down to. Even though it has the word metaphysical in its label, metaphysical realism as it has been applied within the greater scientific materialist paradigm has seen matter as the fundamental building block.

Mainstream science still does operate under the principle that everything in the universe is ordered by ideas such as math, even with quantum physics proving differently. We can now see this order reflected in the resultant mass–cleansing and ordering that the Enlightenment's scientific discoveries and revolution provided, using reason as a basis for society. The previous chaos had taken place without this order successfully projected onto external, physical phenomena and onto and within our societies. Chaos after the Enlightenment had been successfully and strategically ordered right out of the metaparadigm —or so it seemed.

Another main aspect of what the Enlightenment provided for the West was based on the understanding that each person differs and so their views and perceptions are different, to varying degrees. This wasn't necessarily a positive view. Something was needed to help regulate against this rampant, inconsistent and at times irrational subjectivity so the irrationality seen in the previous "Dark Ages" would not continue. Thus, one of the key designs behind the scientific materialism model is the use of reason because it was viewed as a panacea to be able to both guard against, as well as override, this human tendency commonly understood in our culture as the subjective world; presumed to be irrational and operating by wishful thinking.

Meaning, we may each have a different perception, or interpretation of the same things, such as colors and fruit and music–but this is the land of the soft sciences and art, like psychology, sociology, and literature. The hard sciences, however, are where we can go for clear, unambiguous, *certainty* that *this is* the way the universe *is*, because it's been proven with reasoning and mathematical formulas. Opinions by the human with their own subjective perceptions affected by their own personal beliefs, histories, cultures, gender, general mental makeup–i.e., optimist, pessimist–etc was not intended for the sciences.

According to the principles of scientific materialism, science can show us what these external objects are really like in an objective way, separate from and independent of any human's perceptions, feelings or beliefs. They saw this as *a way that we can all accept and agree on and acknowledge as reality*, because these are scientific facts, proven with the scientific method. Because of this and because rigorous, solid methodology was developed to obtain these understandings, it became understood, it became the consent, that this is reliable and consistent information. This is otherwise known today as the facts. Whatever science produces that has used the rigor of the methodology accepted within the field, such as replicable results, then it is another fact for us to believe in, trust and know.

We, the general public, are in agreement with this system. Remembering that initially, this reliability and consistency was deemed needed as well as desired by the male scientists of the Enlightenment, is quite important here. Because, again, after such a long period of instability that included the witch trials, they felt they were doing a service by stabilizing life for society. They did provide quite a service, indeed, *at that time.*

This is what is meant partially by saying that the East differs from the West in both acknowledging the subtle energy(ies) in life, and by actually placing it in primary position over the physical–metaparadigm wide. Comparatively, the West places more of its primary emphasis–metaparadigm wide–on the physical, or that which we can see and thus believe in, because it's tangible, quantifiable, measurable and hence able to be proven to be some *thing*. Because of this form of tangibility that yields measurement, science has been able to verify nature and existence. This has been our measuring bar in the West for anything whose credibility is in question. i.e., "What does science have to say about this phenomena?" We now yearn for solid reliability-the facts, proven.

There is another major factor at play here distinguishing between the way the two hemispheres seem to have divergently split at this point post–Enlightenment. The West, from what was just described, has the societal/

hemispheric sense that life is more ordered and less chaotic, compared to the East's feeling that is chaotic. *However, this chaos, after a bit of time and closer examination, can be understood to be some type of a harmonic relationship. It's just not as obvious, or direct, and it is different from the order within the West.* This second major factor of chaos vs. order is built off of the belief of what has primary positioning of influence in life–the physical or the non–physical. And it is resultant from minds that were desiring order. Order and control are creations from the mind. The spirit, or soul, knows and is comfortable with chaos. This will gradually become more clear.

By acknowledging subtle energy as an integral and primary part of life, in the East this shows up everywhere throughout their culture. It's in their main cultural beliefs, institutions, organizational structure, values, and behaviors—as explored within the Chinese culture. Yet accompanying this structure for their valuing subtle energy, they have "some" work and wisdom produced through millennia of attempts at understanding both subtle energy and chaos.

So this yields different societal priorities, laws, structures and rhythms. And this is perhaps where life in the East to a Westerner's eyes can be seemingly chaotic. Whereas in the West, by placing the physical primary this creates a contrast–society wide–that is polar opposite in its organizational structures and rhythms. In this case, we've built upon order. *An important question here to ask, then, is if this order in the West is natural, or is it being imposed from humans' minds using reason? Is chaos actually what is more natural? Or are both natural, but each is at different levels of the evolution of humans and human consciousness?*

We could ask, is it as simple as just different perspectives? But the differing perspectives are what they are due to what's been previously discussed. By following the scientific materialist paradigm, it has yielded our perspective. So we focus on what we do and leave out what we don't focus on. Both of these factors creates our perspective. *This can be appreciated when only having access and understanding to another perspective that does not operate from this cultural, society wide metaparadigm.* And this is what is being given to you from this book.

So, for example, within the Western metaparadigm of scientific materialism, take gravity, the very phenomena Newton worked with. It is in the transcendent reality–meaning that which exists beyond the five physical senses, and so the phenomena of gravity must be either inferred through a process of reasoning, (the scientific method of scientific materialism) or accepted on authority, (scientists). Science had accomplished this by modern day, the ability to be both–a source of reason *and* authority. Science is able to do this because the general public, including the Church now–*us*–we believe what science does, and what it can do, what it proves, and what technology it creates. On a daily basis, we are in consent with this system being our metaparadigm. We continue to rely on it as our source of validation and proof for what reality is. Our consent is also given by investing in the technological innovations that this system produces.

Because we are so used to operating within our metaparadigm, life just appears to us to be the way it is. Attempting to pull out of our system and analyze and discuss it appears awkward and challenging. In order to better appreciate this key distinction, here is a bit more to help. Let's use gravity because it's such an outrageous example, it'll help make the point. Gravity has been taken to be its own separate entity that can be measured and understood in our metaparadigm. Yet if we lived in Asia, gravity could be viewed as part of a larger system, functioning in some level of coordination within the larger system. By it being unable to be extracted out and reduced to its own entity, we are unable to make it more tangible. Instead, we'd have to examine how the whole system worked together. In our metaparadigm in the West, this reductionism feeds into a greater system, over time, of living a more physically based life.

Put another way, gravity was seen to be its own force, and many other discoveries and inventions were made based on the one understanding about gravity. The holistic approach might instead see it as part of a larger system of forces at work, where there is gravity in some parts, and a lack of gravity in other parts. What might also happen from within this holistic view is observing this whole system from a more passive, detached observant role, where we don't believe that we fully understand it and can therefore not fully work with and manipulate it on its own. We must instead approach the whole system that contains gravity within it.

But the key difference in perspective here is that in some way this force—gravity—was relatively beyond our reach, if we came from the holistic perspective. We were limited in some way of what we were able to do with it. Or we were not of the same level that whatever this force was, so we didn't have the ability, nor right, nor were we meant to, be able to understand it enough to then "own it" enough to then create from it and with it. And thus the technologies produced from this understanding would be working from the whole systems approach, not just with technologies using gravity reduced out from its context. We could work with its natural tendencies as it exists in the larger whole system. This would be another way that we could possibly approach the universe and its phenomena in a non scientific materialist approach. Perhaps it would lead to more sustainable technologies in the long term? Isn't this where we need to get to in today's post–modern world?

So by approaching gravity with the scientific materialist approach and its five principles, it has been reduced to be its own phenomena with *reductionism*. Gravity had sophisticated mathematical calculations applied to it by using both *objectivism* and *metaphysical realism*. These are the combined beliefs that the objective universe can be known by the subjective human mind, but the external universe exists above and beyond the subjective human mind and is "out there,"– objectivism. Because the universe is ordered by ideas (such as mathematics) that lie beyond or transcend the senses, these ideas are implicit in the very nature of reality—metaphysical realism. In this case of gravity, the efforts are the subjective reason of the human mind using mathematical calculations to know the objective world's phenomena, gravity.

This force of gravity, when applying the *closure principle, central to the scientific materialism paradigm,* takes out any and all possible metaphysical or supernatural causes or forces–because the closure principle declares that anything other than material influences can not impact and affect any part of the natural world. Once understood, inventions using the same principles of gravity soon followed based on *universalism*, the last one of the five major tenets of scientific materialism. It contends that these rules are universal and that they are the same in any and all parts of the universe whether it is a physical entity such as a cell, a gun or a planet.

As a result, because gravity is a part of how the unseen, or intangible, dimension of space works, and it is only one part of it, by taking this one part and applying mathematical calculations to it, we have turned it into something tangible, by making it something that can then be discussed, manipulated, understood, worked with, and used for our own purposes. Rather, than say, left alone within its larger system, and then us understanding the larger system of space at work, without dividing out the one phenomena of gravity. We have then further made it tangible by the common pool and cue ball example: that if one takes a cue ball and pushes it towards the pool ball–say the nine ball–it will then, with the force of gravity, impact the nine ball with a predictability expected from applying the universalism concept of the scientific materialist approach. From this, we can then base other understandings, and create physical machines that operate on these same premises.

There is one other key point here, with scientific materialism's metaparadigm. The closure principle denies that anything other than material influences can impact and affect any part of the natural world. If there is a larger system at work here that gravity is just a part of, and then if this larger system is unable to be reduced, or broken down, to be measured and quantified, *then we are negating the possibility of its existence*, particularly by this one principle from scientific materialism of closure. Also, what if there is a larger system, or force, at work behind gravity, that is metaphysical or supernatural, not even necessarily of a divine sort such as a punitive god watching over everything we do, but just a force that is not able to be considered of a physical, or material, essence?

This latter concept seems to be much like the subtle energy of prana (from India) and chi (from China) that permeates through all animate life forms as the Indians and Chinese–not limited to only these cultures who hold this belief, but as the two explored in depth here–believe. It seems important to consider that these two cultures have each developed complete medical systems–including diagnostic tools on through to treatments. Not only their medical systems, but also their sciences of the mind (Buddhism and meditation; yoga and the chakra system), and their using food and nutrition medicinally are all geared not towards hitting a problem once it has become a problem. Their holistic medical models do not view physical symptoms as the only indicator. They are also working within a framework of what health, vitality and well–being is, meaning in Western terms– *preventative medicine*. Do you see the parallel to what scientific materialism has done with gravity?

By acknowledging the subtle, they have been able to acquire this vast bank of knowledge and have a working definition metaparadigm wide of what vitality, stamina, longevity, health and well–being all mean. By operating from within the metaparadigm of scientific materialism, is it possible that we are limiting what we're able to see? Are we possibly therefore, limiting what we're able to believe? Why does the East have this system of preventative medicine–again, a label we've given to practices focused on, in their terms, words that translate to, "vitality," "stamina," and "longevity"–at such a metaparadigm level? Whereas we are only just now even beginning to incorporate this concept of longevity into our American culture. And this is only at the levels of those who are working outside the metaparadigm, in either the new sciences, or as "natural healers" of some type (nutritionists, chi gong practitioners, yoga teachers or practicing students, or energy medicine practitioners). What are we missing?

What is seems like the scientific materialism paradigm has given us is an outstanding ability to produce useful, tangible technology that makes life more convenient, indeed. However, this metaparadigm coming to us from the sciences keeps us locked into a certain way of seeing the world. With globalization and increasing crises over the past ten years, we're only starting to get glimpses of other ways to approach life that are more focused on the subtle in life, such as our emotions and the role they play in health, our general mind set, tone, mood and the role it plays in our lives. Breaking things down, reducing the whole into parts has us focusing more on the parts than the whole. And at this point it seems a detriment.

Our Beliefs Are Our Choice and How Many Are Inherited?

As B. Alan Wallace says in *Embracing Mind: The Common Ground of Science and Spirituality*, "So, just as God transcends the universe, his divine language allows the scientific mind to transcend the senses and *reach true understanding of reality*. Often, *according to this perspective*, reality can be reduced to a mathematical formula," (italics mine)(Wallace 2008). And so, this metaphysical realism aspect of scientific materialism–that there is a mathematical foundation to the universe–seems to us, by now, just as natural as that there is an objective world–some of it animate, and some of it inanimate–that we can know experientially through our five senses. *That is separate from us and our perceptions*, as we have been taught to believe by these very principles of scientific materialism, goes without saying. Right?

This ability to calculate, this belief in the fundamental utility of mathematical calculations in application to universal phenomena that is "out there" has enabled scientists to be able to create materials and machines–technological innovations and products–due to their use of mathematical calculations, like electricity and the tangible light bulb. The average citizen also takes the abstract phenomena and brings it into a more concrete concept.

For instance, calculating our expenses for the month against our income is one way that we don't have to just rely on our senses, instead we can reason, using math; it's the same when we want to estimate how long it will take us to drive a certain distance, based on our expected speed we'll drive and the length of time spent driving. These examples are abstract, right? I have never touched my percentage of my salary that is spent on expenses, it's an abstract idea of thirty–nine percent. This then represents a certain physical phenomena–how much cash I have to spend after expenses. But typically, with these abstractions derived from calculations and mathematics, scientists have then used these formulas towards practical applications of science. Thus, giving us industrialization and technology, rather than stopping at general understandings of the world "out there." And this has been what the West has been appreciated for.

This reflects how the abstractness of scientific calculations has been used for tangible, physical goods and services, like electricity, the internet, and wireless technology. It's historic since its inception. The USA more so than any other country has excelled at applying science to inventing technologies and machines we end up taking for granted and relying on. Steam power, the train, the refrigerator, the oven, the television are all examples. Again, B. Alan Wallace helps to paint the picture, "Of course science in the Renaissance [and more so, the Enlightenment was not propelled merely by the curiosity of talented intellects. Expanding commercial interests demanded improved technology in the field of navigation, and governments needed better military engineering to protect commerce and advance the interests of their domains. *As science provided this technology, it gradually gained enough credibility to prevent the church from censuring it each time a new theory or discovery contradicted religious doctrine. Rather, a delicate balance replaced the previous religious dominance over scientific ideas. Once the prestige of science had grown, theologians themselves began to rely on it.* For example, science could be used to determine what was and was not a miracle: if some phenomena could not be accounted for by a scientific law, it could be declared miraculous. *Over time, as scientific knowledge expanded* and *God's role diminished,* he would be called on merely to fill in the gaps in scientific knowledge–*gaps that grew smaller and smaller as science advanced,*" (italics mine)(Wallace 2008).

As the Industrial Revolution progressed, in order to be able to produce relevant technology and a more perfect understanding of the heavens, laws of motion needed to be more specific. Captains in the military needed to be able to calculate the best angle to point their canons in order to destroy the enemy. According to the principle of universality, the same laws of motion that the planets followed should also be followed by canons, and bullets. This was of major interest for such leading scientists as Descartes, Leibniz, and Newton. So what had to then be worked out was whether any nonphysical factors played any part in the motion of objects. Descartes was the first to theorize that there existed nothing in nature that could not be explained by purely corporeal, or tangible, causes. This is the closure principle of scientific materialism. It successfully closed off nature from all but physical influences. "Frightened soldiers couldn't cause cannonballs to fall elsewhere by wishing or praying. Nor could demons start fires or cause objects to levitate. Only matter could move matter," (Wallace 2008).

Wallace then cautions that Descartes was careful to make two exceptions to this principle: *biblical stories and the human soul, both of which he believed could affect the body–and the physical world of matter.* "But the influence of the church had already weakened considerably. Leibniz, born only four years after the death of Galileo (1642), boldly theorized that mind and spirit had no effect whatsoever on nature," (Wallace 2008). Clearly, this is central to the deepening of the mind and body split in the West. The mind is of the non–physical and matter is, well, physical. This is also where the departure from Descartes' acknowledgement of the soul and mind, the non-physical, get left behind, as scientific materialism gets put more firmly in place, alongside the growing industrial revolution.

Interestingly, though, Isaac Newton was deeply religious, and believed that the physical universe was composed entirely of inert matter created and put into motion by God. And the universe had God's laws imposed upon it. So Newton argued against Leibniz's view of a universe completely self–contained and isolated from spiritual influences. *Newton claimed that this would lead to materialism and atheism.* Yet, in another irony within the field of science, it was Newton himself who laid the groundwork for a totally mechanical model of the universe, one that God may have set in motion, but was no longer required to be kept around for the upkeep and management. It seems that the scientists who succeeded Newton grew further away from Descartes' acknowledgement of the mind and soul and Newton's acknowledgment of God's role. This was replaced by the deepening emphasis on the mechanical model. Focusing on the physical at the exclusion of anything subtle enough to not be classified as "physical" grew alongside the growing metaparadigm of scientific materialism and its marriage to industrialization.

The theories on the laws of motion then led to Newton's theory of gravity, and this then "put science on a roll for over two centuries," (Wallace 2008). In fact, much of the ongoing resistance—as we'll soon see—once quantum physics hit the scene with its theories that again seems to take us back into what seemed like chaos, is because of this very stability and reliability of these tenets of the mechanical, solid world of matter based around these very laws. This resistance is at an almost unconscious level within the masses. This belief, and the conditioning resultant from the mechanical universe as presented by these Enlightenment scientists using Newtonian physics has been what we've built our physical world and our understanding of the way the physical world works around since the start of modernity and industrialization. We are deeply steeped in both, by now.

This conditioning runs so deep that these laws feel almost intuitive. So that to state that the world is not really as it seems, that the physical world breaks down to what some modern day physicists refer to as "energy soup" or quanta, or particles, or waves, or a bunch of energy pulsating beneath the surface of solid, physical matter that is waiting to be collapsed *into matter,* seems to sound more like science fiction. It feels not right according to world given to us by Newtonian physics—another label, realistically, for the metaparadigm of scientific materialism. If it is not science fiction it is, at least, incredibly destabilizing. Then what do we do with the certainty we've gained from "to see it is to believe it?" What about how the physical world seems to be so solid and reliable? What do we do with that? Is this starting to reflect a bit more of what life has been like here in the United States over the past decade? It should be. What we once relied upon as steady and stable is breaking down at this point of massive shifting from one era to the next.

Our Fears Are Our Choice, So if We've Inherited Many of Them...?

There's one more major factor at play here that reinforced this emerging metaparadigm's dominance: the Renaissance and Enlightenment's

Europeans' increasing tendency to mistrust the subjective, imaginary, mental realm. This heightened even more with the Protestant Reformation at the start of the 1500's. This birthed the Puritans. They then in great part birthed our American, Anglo–Saxon nation. Particular to this final point, Wallace states, "The new religious reformers condemned the priestly magic of the Catholic Church–the sacraments and saintly miracles–*and warned of the dangers of diabolical influences of the mind*," (italics mine) (Wallace 2008).

This view is central to how the majority of us today still unconsciously and typically unbeknownst to us, view the mind. It is a dangerous place, the depths of which we should avoid because contained somewhere within it is a sense of darkness, or irrationality, or even madness. *There is still much conditioned, deep–rooted hesitancy and resistance in our culture with examining the mind, so that the mind body connection remains held at an arm's length, pushed away. This is obviously fear–based, as our Western tradition has taught us to be of the mind,* and it is reinforced by the avoidance and absence of any real science of the mind with the subjective world not taken credibly–as credibly as the "hard" sciences, as psychology struggles to be.

Not only that, but what about the West having an understanding of the mind that goes beyond focusing mostly on the madness, or the maladies, or the diagnoses, disorders, and problems with the mind? Rather, one that is informative, instructional and helpful to people who seek guidance about how to better use this primary tool that is central to every aspect of our lives; this seems most functional. How we view, value and perceive anything from behind our eyes influences every aspect of our lives, in every moment. We just don't typically hold this awareness as we are busy having our perceptions concluded for us by the mind; we just think it's us as we go about life. This is a turning point; to recognize this is key.

"The most important choice a human being can make is whether they view the universe (outside world external to one's mind) as a hostile or friendly place," said our much beloved genius and philosopher, Albert Einstein. This speaks to the importance of how our perceptions are formed from our beliefs and how we then see the world the way we do based on our beliefs. This discussion also reflects how we've had our collective perception of the mind created for us in our culture, by our cultural values, practices, and ethos.

As we have seen, other cultures do engage in this type of instruction and focus–the opposite of what our value system is. *So it is not "the way it is," rather it is cultural, and it is value laden, and it is a choice.* This is a choice that human minds make. And it was made for us by our science's founding fathers due to their own beliefs influenced by their own experiences, their grandparents' experiences, and their time.

Also, this cycle is a circle of no escape. Meaning in this choice, avoidance of the mind is inherent to it. But it is the very mind, and fear of the mind, that leads to this avoidance, allows for this avoidance, and reinforces this avoidance, creating all sorts of diversionary tactics to perpetuate this avoidance. As the avoidance gets fueled by fear of the madness in the mind and more fear builds, we move further and further away, fueled by fears from the very thing creating this fear–our minds.

Further, it has become, for many, a chosen tactic to disbelieve that something so potentially diabolical could also have control over our health, or at least effect our physical health. That could then mean a lot of things. *Namely, that we would then have to deal with and face what is inside our minds.* So, interestingly, this is cyclical–or the circle of no escape just mentioned–in that the *fear is mind based. It is this very fear that keeps the status quo of ignoring the impact and effect of the mind locked into place.*

To get beyond this fear, and begin to actively question the content of our minds–our thoughts –means to have to eventually, or even initially understand consciously that we have this fear and admit to it. Think of how painful reading this discussion may have been for you. Which means another list of a lot of things, including again, going into the mind at least enough to observe it rather than let it run our every moment by the thoughts in it *and thus believe the thoughts that it produces.* This means giving it some higher level of prioritization for study. To do this, *we need to deprioritize some other things. Which means possibly, making some changes? And the mind doesn't like that.* Especially when there is a lot of change needed or a fundamental change needed. So, avoidance and the status quo becomes the chosen tactic, achieved through a range of superstitions, fear and distractions.

Ironically though, this metaparadigm is originally built upon and centered around the use of reason. However, what was just examined to see how we got where we are today culturally with our avoidance of genuinely studying the mind and subtle, unseen energy, uncovered fears and laziness. It was not solely reason. This deserves repeating: the choices made were based in large part on emotional reactivity to the chaos of the Dark Ages. They wanted order. Ironically, emotional reactivity is one of the key aspects that lessen once the mind is worked with in a meditative practice. To allow for things within one's life, or one's self, or one's society to become uncomfortable to the point of a nagging feeling that change is needed, or a nagging feeling of running away from something out of avoidance takes a lot of effort. Yet because the effort goes unexamined, it becomes habitual, coped with, and just ends up feeling like "well this is just the way it is."

This is frequently labeled "resistance." This resistance happens within individuals as well as societies. It represents a divided individual, or a divided society, somewhat at battle within itself, however unconsciously. Specifically, this behavioral cycle of fear, leading to the checkout reaction of laziness masking avoidance, in resistance are all actually resulting from mental behaviors. But they became infused–as a reaction occurred to the initial observation and judgment–with an emotion, say of resistance, and then a behavioral choice, say of avoidance or laziness. Again we're talking about behaviors within a system that is modeled around reason, and believing in and relying on the reason contained inherently within each individual. *There is a contradiction here.*

It is culturally accepted, as if this fear and then avoidance is acceptable because others are avoiding themselves and this internal work as well. We see signs of reinforcement within most aspects of our society. The entertainment industry and pop culture, the internet, and computer games are easily accessible examples. Group think is at play here. An example is the cultural acceptance–read the word "approval" here–of participating in following team sports, and attending team sporting events at stadiums, and even giving tax dollars towards new stadiums. This remains acceptable at a mass level. While self–examination of this type, observing our thoughts and questioning where they come from is not. The validity or truth contained within our thoughts, and acknowledging some level or responsibility over our typical state of mind, also is not accepted at a mass level. It is simply not what we in the majority do.

Getting to know ourselves in this way is banned by the group think mentality because of these cultural choices made by our ancestors, who set up this, *our* inherited metaparadigm *for us* a long time ago, based on their needs at the time, and their cultural, historical, current circumstances

Alison J. Kay, PhD

within their lifetimes. Again, they made a choice what to focus on, and by doing so also made a choice what *not* to focus on.

Changing this means a whole lot of rethinking that needs to occur, and some re-working of what we value as individuals and as a group culturally. It very likely could lead to some initial inconvenience and discomfort. *It could also lead to the question as to who or what is responsible for one's health.* Is it each individual's contents of his or her mind, our minds connected to a god in the sky, a divine being only, biological factors only, or a combination of any or all of the above?

Then there's the factor of who is benefiting from the current model? If the individual and his or her mind is not affecting the body, who is benefitting from this view? If the lack of health gets diagnosed and treated as biologically–physically–based, then who benefits from this view? Just as importantly, who does not benefit? Considering what the holistic models discussed in the examples of India and China's medicine use for their diagnoses and prescriptions, and the level of importance they place on the patients' daily lifestyle choices, what happens when we don't have that emphasis in the Western medical model?

This leaves the field of medicine very busy, and in a very integral, heroic role. If there were to be a more substantial focus on health, wellness, well–being and preventative medicine, then this would yield a different configuration to the way disease and health are dealt with. Our scientific materialism metaparadigm of an industrialized, technology driven culture used to a certain level of convenience replaces a certain level of self–discipline. This type of self–discipline is part of the yogic path, and the Buddhist path. In these same cultures' metaparadigms, it is understood that tending to one's own state of mind and well–being leads to one's health and longevity. Yoga, Tai Chi, Chi Gong, acupuncture, and using food as medicine, are just a few examples.

Buddhism's science of the mind terminology shows the less functional parts of the mind as "afflictions" which implies understanding that the mind has states that are less than optimal. Beyond focusing on the afflictive states, Buddhism then provides volumes of concrete remedies for these afflictions, as well, throughout the Buddhist scriptures. While Buddhism does not have the Freudian view of a wild beast of darkness hidden in the subconscious, it does have a model for "the neurotic mind," *which is quite simply, the average human being.*

Everything in the mind needs to have light shed on it in the Buddhist model. Once it does, it can then be worked with. First, there is the stopping and facing of one's self rather than running from one's self and the thoughts driving one's mind. Then the ensuing shining of the light into the darkness to expose these thoughts creates understanding, dispels darkness, and provides clarity, light, and health. Sounds like a simplified model, and it is, but that is the long, arduous process of facing one's self through the Buddhist model, in a nutshell.

Remember the Dalai Lamas' definition of the mind body connection? "The mind body connection is the idea that the mind affects physiological functions in the body," (The Dalai Lama 1991). So if the mind is clear, light and healthy, then in this equation of the mind body connection, the physiological functioning of the body should be clear, light and healthy. Likewise, the inverse: with an unhealthy mind, then the physiological functioning of the body then follows this lack of health. It also works that following the lack of clarity and light, there is less vibrancy and vitality. A simple way to understand this theory is when do you have more energy, when you are happy or when you are a little down? What about when you're exercising verses when you're depressed?

As Wallace continues to discuss the splitting apart of science from anything metaphysical and also, the Church, he helps to conclude this section of the discussion: "Moreover, the Protestant ethic, aimed at humans improving their lot in the world through hard work, mistrusted magic, (they had just witnessed the witch trials, so they're meaning earth based spiritual practices, or paganism) not only because it was an inner phenomenon but also because it was a kind of easy way, a shortcut to achieving one's ends. If a magic spell could bring one wealth, why work? It is not surprising, then, that three centuries would have to pass before an experimental science of the mind, psychology, would emerge in the West." As Wallace continues to describe the times and sentiment when science began to carry equal weight as the church, this sword of mistrust cut both ways. The increasing decline in this belief in magic paralleled a questioning of God's role as this supposed miracle–worker. "It was a painful dilemma: If God could intervene at will by magically producing miracles, a universe of consistent natural laws based on the closure principle, universalism, and physical reductionism *was illogical*. On the other hand, if this mechanical model of the universe didn't need God, it was heresy. Even so, science was soon to squeeze everything

Alison J. Kay, PhD

nonmaterial out of the universe—spirits and demons, the human mind and God himself. Before long, the astronomer Pierre Laplace (1749–1827), when asked about God's role in the world of nature would say, 'I have no need for that hypothesis,'" (italics mine)(Wallace 2008).

Wallace's insightful commentary reflects the mutual exclusivity historically deemed to the two institutions of church and science, since modernity began. It further reflects the focus on the physical, while leaving behind a focus on anything deemed subjective, metaphysical, or whole systems focused. *Caught up within what got left behind in the West since the industrial and modern age began, comparatively, is also the spiritual. For the spiritual is encased within the subtle and is beyond the Church and Synagogue. It is not measurable, perhaps not reducible, is different within different moments so is not predictable, and perhaps a bit too elusive* for science to get its calculations to prove, as we shall see in the quantum physics section. Besides, quite frankly, what does studying the subtle energies, or the metaphysical, or spiritual, help us produce and consume?

Alison in Bali getting a treatment from a traditional, aboriginal
Balinese Healer/Medicine Woman—it seems to be the same one Elizabeth
Gilbert of *Eat, Pray, Love* went to later. Part of what they're
rubbing on my bare skin not covered by the sarong is garlic, with some
other freshly steamed herbs for a general detox. You
can see some on the left side of my left knee.

Alison doing Chi Gong in the Thailand sunrise on an island in the Gulf
of Thailand, Koh Samui. This island is considered an energy vortex on
the planet. There are many detox clinics and healing spas there.
Alison worked out of a few during her month or longer stays
when on her breaks between semesters. It became one of
her favorite places in Asia; she returned there 9 times.

Alison with her some of her favorite students at Five Fingers Mountain
in Taiwan. She had taken them on a field trip to go for a hike on a
mountain during a Transcendentalist unit studying the writings of
Emerson, Thoreau and the rest, helping them tune into the "Transparent
Eyeball" Emerson writes about that dispels "mean ego."

Teaching meditation to sophomores in their
Honors level of American Literature class
during the Transcendentalist unit, helping them get in touch with the
oneness and disappearance of "mean ego" Emerson refers to.
Realistically, they loved the opportunity! You can go to my website
and towards the bottom of the testimonials, read some of these
teens' - and other teens' - genuine gratitude and appreciation for
being shown this tool. Particularly among the juniors and seniors,
as the college application and acceptance stress begins to kick in.
I also taught many year long meditation practices to
her AP Psychology students, and in her first
psychology course she designed as a non-AP elective, "Global Psychology"
a merger of Western Psychology and Buddhist Science of
Mind, at the International Bilingual School of Hsinchu. In
an activity, "Fitness & Nutrition" meditation was also taught
to teens, as well as a "Stress Reduction" club while still in the
States, prior to entering the international school system.

This is me in India next to the type of Buddha image you see in India,
where Buddhism originated. In Southeast Asian countries like
Thailand, it's Theravada Buddhism, and Buddha's head is more pointy.
In Mahayana Buddhism—Chinese—Buddha's
head is usually much rounder
than these two - and frequently chunkier. Fun
little tidbit learned from traveling!

This is a purely Taoist temple—the ancient Chinese that the
yin-yang comes from. Most temples in Taiwan are a mix of Taoist and
Buddhist. This was a rare find. Notice the angry male gods. They
act as guardians and protectors. I never saw a smiling male Chinese
god. They're supposed to be fierce protectors, so... Only once Buddha
entered the scene can smiles be seen at temples—
on the Buddha's face, that is.

This is a blended temple in Taiwan of both Buddhist and Taoist cultures. The ornate design of dragons on the roof—symbolizing mystical power—is the Taoist part. The reverse swastika, ironically, on the other side of the planet is representative of Buddhism, where compassion is a key teaching. The swastika, translated from Sanskrit literally means "to be good." This took a bit of getting used to when I was first there and seeing it everywhere. Then my eyes got reconditioned, as I integrated this new meaning of the symbol into my perceptual set.

Alison J. Kay, PhD

A Chinese tea stand—they were everywhere!—with the herb selection
and their medicinal qualities displayed.

One of my favorite partners in crime during my India yoga teacher training, German Katarina Slavikova, and I doing *urdhva dhanurasana*, or wheel or upward bow pose, during an afternoon Ashtanga yoga primary series two hour session. We did two two-hour sessions a day five days a week, and one two-hour session on Saturdays. That's on top of all the class work! The Wheel Pose, appropriately nick-named Chakrasana, is good to open all the chakras—and test your upper body strength. I love it too because of the opening of the front body; it's great for those who are at a computer all day. Overall -it's one of my favorite yoga poses of all! FREEDOM!

My first trip I took once back living in the States was to the Mayan
ruins in Mexico. This is me doing a version of the
Virabradrasana III, or Warrior III Pose,
at Chichen Itza, a World Heritage Site. This is where they created the
Mayan calendar. Antonio Leon, a Mayan elder, energy healer and who
holds a masters degree in Archaeology lead, me through the site. We
had much time to talk over our shared interests, and the Mayan
predictions for 2012. He asked me to do an energy healing on him.
What an honor!

This is one of the many monasteries I visited in Asia. This is a simple one
in Thailand. I also experienced a natural steam room on the grounds of
this monastery - it was the first one in Asia I ever visited - where a monk
fed the steam room with freshly picked lemongrass. It was heavenly! I
love this particular picture because the monk had just finished sweeping
up his area of the grounds for the morning. Sweeping with natural brooms
on a daily basis became a very symbolic act for me in my own daily life.

Chapter 4-The Modern Industrial Age: How Did We End Up Where We Are?

Survival of the Fittest-How Much Have You Bought Into That One?

S O, BY THE BEGINNING OF the 1800's, it was classical Newtonian physics without any obstructions from either philosophy or religion anymore that provided a string of important discoveries, causing scientists, and therefore society increasingly, to believe in this power of science to account for the entire universe using sophisticated mathematics. First, there's Joule, Mayer and Helmholtz in the physical sciences, who devised the principle of the conservation of energy, which evolved into the first—of what was to be three—laws of thermodynamics. This law revealed the relationship between heat and energy, via mathematical formulations. Next came the wave theory of light from Augustin—Jean Fresnel. After this, Lord Kelvin and James Clerk Maxwell ascribed precise mathematical formulations to magnetism and electricity. Electromagnetic waves, it was theorized, caused magnetism, light and electricity.

Radio waves were then detected. Mendeleev's periodic table came in next with the elements based on the assumption of subatomic structures underlying all chemical qualities. The earth was not left untouched by science in theorizing and formulas, either. Charles Lyell probed the earth's geological past via rock studies in the then embryonic field of geology. Next, the classical principles regarding the physical properties of matter and the mechanisms of their interactions—which were derived from Newton— were then applied to the life sciences. The cell theory was formulated in 1838, which revealed at the microscopic level a basic structure of life. This then opened up into the study of cell structure, where chemical principles were seen to govern the activities of cells and therefore, all living matter. Chemistry, remember, is the interaction between physical matter that can be measured, either in gasses, solids or liquids, and minerals. Jacques Loeb then took this reductionist view a step farther, claiming that the instincts of lower animals are simply physiochemical reactions. Then there's Darwin, who proposed his purely mechanical explanation—natural selection—for the evolution of animals and plants, and us.

Charles Darwin's theory of evolution appeared in 1859. Darwin asserted that over a long period of time the more complicated kinds of living things developed mechanically from some very simple kinds of living things. Darwin's theory suggested an even more mechanical, automatic process to life and nature than what Newton had. According to Darwin's followers, all natural processes are simply mechanical. *Darwin's theory helped along materialism. Not only scientific materialism, but now also the materialism of society, or individuals engaged in competing. It became as if it were survival of the fittest for not only basic survival needs, but beyond, into physical goods at a level above basic needs.* These have become today standard measures of success and gratifications possible within a modernized market economy.

These and many other scientific discoveries of the later nineteenth century led to practical knowledge and inventions that rapidly transformed human life, as well. Understanding the role of bacteria in disease ushered in dramatic advances in medicine, *bringing the biomedical model firmly into place, along with pharmaceutical prescription drugs, and the eventual overriding of its competitor, homeopathic medicine.* Today, our biomedical system is quite a bit different from the earlier biomedical model. This is due to the current emphasis on biotechnological innovation, featuring new technologies for surgical and diagnostic use. The research and development from the pharmaceutical industry for drugs is also a part of this.

The Historical Battle in Medical Care: Did You Know Our Medical System Started with Homeopathy?

Nonetheless, the growing practice of prescribing medications from the pharmacy had begun to push out the practice of the earlier forms of other therapies. These other therapies were natural, such as homeopathics. Healing through the diet and lifestyle, hydrotherapy and even a rudimentary acknowledgement of the mental and emotional state affecting physical health existed. Particularly the emotions of hysteria and other stress—induced emotions—were, in what was even then in the late 1800's, termed the wellness field. In fact, it wasn't until up through the turn of the century, through World War I and then the Great Depression that pharmaceutical drugs really began to be used.

There was awareness and resistance to prescribing pharmaceutical drugs during the introduction of and growing reliance on them. However, not from the general public. At first this reluctance and skepticism was from the then current doctors. They were aware of what the shift towards reliance on pharmaceutical drugs was doing to their profession and their patients. In fact, there has been a long-standing battle over dominance of health care by two sides. One side has been elitist, educated doctors, and the other side has been known as "folk healers." These folk healers could be equated historically to homeopathic doctors; present day to naturopaths, holistic healers or energy healers.

Yet prior to the biotechnology industry of today as we know it, which really kicked in around 1950, even trained medical doctors had a belief in and prescribed varying degrees of folk remedies for keeping healthy (preventative medicine), and for healing illnesses, including homeopathic prescription medications, and prescribing lifestyle adjustments as their prescriptions. In fact, this system existed before the trained medical profession in both the USA and in Europe—homeopathy. It is still presently used today by Western M.D.'s in the European Union.

Dr. Dana Ullman is one of America's leading advocates for homeopathy. He has authored ten books including the best selling *Everybody's Guide to Homeopathic Medicines*, with Stephen Cummings, M.D. He is the founder of Homeopathic Educational Services, America's leading resource center for homeopathic products, and considered the leading authority in the United States on homeopathy (www.homeopathic.com). He says in an interview for the Wellness Revolution Summit web telecast in August of 2010 that, "in the 19th century Americans were using homeopathy; it was wildly popular in both the United States and Europe, but it is not frequently known just how popular homeopathy was in the United States. By the turn of the 20th century, America had 22 homeopathic medical schools, including Boston University and other prestigious medical schools."

Ullman describes just how big homeopathy was until the early 1900's. "And because those using homeopaths were the wealthiest and most educated people of the country, like the Transcendentalists, i.e., Emerson and Dickinson—almost all of them were advocates of homeopathy. This includes our literary greats; eleven American presidents were advocates of homeopathy, as were the monarchs of Europe, (i.e., Queens of England), czars of Russia, Mozart, Beethoven, and the list goes on. If you're interested, consult my most recent book that traces the history of homeopathy in the West," (Ullman, The Wellness Revolution Summit with Adoley Odunton, 2010). His book that he is referring to is *The Homeopathic Revolution: Why Famous People and Cultural Heroes Choose Homeopathy*. Ullman's implication is that this shows how the "educated and sophisticated" people were the ones who knew enough to know good medicine. The other implication he's making is that this very fact antagonized the AMA (American Medical Association).

Ullman then goes on to tell a true story about what happened on the night Abraham Lincoln was assassinated, "Lincoln, on the night that he was shot, his secretary of state, William Seward's, personal doctor was a homeopath. Seward was Lincoln's most trusted advisor. Booth not only shot Lincoln, but also had someone go to Seward's home and stab him (Seward) seven times. To help Seward, once he was discovered, they tried to get in touch with his homeopath, but the closest surgeon was the surgeon general. So the surgeon general treated Seward, and was then reprimanded for that by the AMA. Because he chose to treat the patient of a homeopathic doctor and because the AMA was so antagonistic to homeopaths, that just to talk with, refer, or to take a patient that was a homeopathic patient was considered unethical," (Ullman, The Wellness Revolution Summit with Adoley Odunton, 2010).

Providing further historical description of how we lost out on homeopathy, and inherited the AMA backed, scientific materialist biomedical model as our metaparadigm when the 18th century gave way to the 19th century and industrialization deepened, Ullman explains, "So we also know how powerful and how tremendously antagonistic the AMA was and the medical drug establishment, right? [Well] the AMA had a very clever president; he created an AMA seal of approval on drugs, and a drug company without doing any research about safety or the efficacy of a drug, see, all they had to do was advertise in every national publication that the AMA supported, and they would get the AMA seal of approval. [It was] Basically a type of legalized bribery. [And this] made the AMA rich—they got a lot of advertising money, and they were able to coordinate a very consistent effort to attack homeopathy." Ullman goes on to complete the historical explanation of why we've been without homeopathy for most of the modern age, "And the AMA was so antagonistic to homeopaths—even though the homeopaths were graduates of the greatest medical colleges. It was unethical, according to the AMA, what the surgeon general had done in helping Lincoln's secretary of state. *It shows you the antagonism was irrational; it was economic.* I am now quoting a member of the AMA, as I do in my book: 'We have to admit that we never fought the homeopaths on a matter of principal, we fought them because they came into the community and got the business.'" (Ullman, The Wellness Revolution Summit with Adoley Odunton, 2010).

Ullman explains that homeopaths spend more time with a patient, because in order for them to get beyond the symptoms and not just prescribe pharmaceuticals that treat at only the symptomatic (or surface) level and *get to the root syndrome that is being announced by the arrival of the physical (or mental) symptoms* they need to interview the patients. This also had them in a more nurturing role than the biomedical doctors. And, it made them more successful. The AMA obviously knew this, hence their feeling threatened and the need to expel homeopathy from the metaparadigm. This continues up until today, even with homeopathy's increasing usage—again.

Ullman also explains that European biomedical doctors do embrace today, still, to varying degrees homeopathy. He gives the example of France, saying that in France you can go into any pharmacy and also buy homeopathic medications. The author has observed this to be true, in Western Europe overall. He also states how most European biomedical doctors work with homeopathy by using at least an herb or two in their general practice of prescriptions to patients. This obviously reflects some general knowledge and a basic belief in homeopathy beyond that of the majority of American biomedical doctors.

Alison J. Kay, PhD

The website Natural Health Perspective also helps explain a bit of this history as to how the AMA and pharmaceutical backed biomedical model became our dominant medical paradigm. "Throughout Western European history there were two major trends: the professionalism of physicians who belonged to the upper classes and the folk healers who lived among the peasant population. The professionals developed in order to enhance their status in life, while the folk healers developed out of a necessity to survive," (Natural Health Perspective 2010).

In addition, as Natural Health Perspective's website discusses the history of natural healing and biomedicine (allopathic medicine, as they refer to the biomedical system); they report that this division between the two goes back to the Church in Europe playing a central role. They also say that natural healing perspectives developed differently in the Old World (Europe) than they did in the New World (U.S.A.). Ask any person in the natural healing profession, or simply an informed citizen/consumer who shops at health food stores, and/or uses some of the natural healing therapies for health and well-being as their own self-prescribed preventative health care system and they'll know this. They'll acknowledge that European countries are more accepting and open to natural healing, homeopathy, and some of the folklore healing remedies passed down through the ages than the United States. Germany, England, and Switzerland are all examples. Statistics thoroughly discussing and supporting this are in a forthcoming book of mine specific to the biomedical industry's monopoly-and its corresponding ineffectiveness in delivery of health.

This book's intention is not solely to focus on the biomedical model. The biomedical model is only part of the overall picture—albeit it is a main area that could benefit, should we reconsider our unexamined assumptions about how the world works. This is, in fact, the bottom line issue: we are operating from assumptions handed down to us from our forefathers' choices and are living lives based on some outdated ideas about how the world works. So this discussion is meant to help us all see that one of the main inheritances is the central role our sciences, and thus technology, have played and continue to play in the West, American society in particular. This is not inherently bad. It's the focus of our science and technology, and how it has been directed and used that is in question for its functionality, today.

This inheritance has framed the world as the physical is what are the more important phenomena in our world. This basic premise we're still

150

operating from has created the society we're still living in. Every part of our society is structured based on this, as is being suggested in this book, unexamined belief. The impact of our science and technology centered society of today, is a result of choices made from beliefs of yesterday. This does include our "evidence based medicine." We've been exploring how we got here, and are about to look at the overall picture of its impact on us today—as we struggle to maintain some semblance of the solid footing we once had as global leaders. So after seeing how we became this way, ultimately I am then asking the question what, if anything, is still working for us based on this model of scientific materialism we inherited from the Enlightenment and Industrial eras.

Frequently Unknown Statistics to Wrap Your Mind Around

For now, to limit this discussion, a few of the key statistics—which are eye opening when added together—will be provided to see where we've gotten to today with this marriage of science and technology that brings us our biomedical model. Also, on PubMed's website (U.S. Library of Medicine's listing of published medical studies' abstracts) you can also view some of this discussion's stats and many others. I highly recommend spending some time there; it's worth the visit. The intention here is not to point out the dysfunction of our medical system from the health care reform perspective. Rather, it is to present information that leads to the observation that it is the basic premises within the actual philosophy behind our medical system that is the problem, at this point. Then to understand the vested structures that benefit from the system as it is kept in place. Exploring how our consent as consumers locks that in is also presented with the statistics, so you can observe for yourself. You'll also probably end up seeing how much we're wasting by preserving this status quo. It seems impossible not to gain this awareness from reading these statistics as a whole picture. Yet frequently, they're not brought together; they are usually treated separately. Science is one aspect; medical care another; natural healing another; our thoughts and how they influence our health—yet another. Therefore, the result here—are you ready to see what else is possible?

The mainstream option for health care, or the metaparadigm that is legislated for us by our leaders, endorsed by our governmental institutions, and presented to us through the commercialization of it all, is the biomedical one. It is the only option, so it seems, for our health care. It is the option provided by any employer. Insurance companies' incentives motivate employers to get more employees on the biomedical care they cover. It is not that well known as an option not to actually choose this mainstream health care system at all. The one provided by our biomedical, western-trained AMA doctors is what we know as our health care system. Period; end of discussion, end of questions, end of options. However, for a growing number, the replacement they are using is a team of "preventative" health care practitioners. A typical team could look like an acupuncturist, a naturopath or some holistic health care practitioner, an energy healer and a yoga teacher, while shopping at health food stores as one's main supply of food. People making this choice, for example, would only use this mainstream biomedical model for what it's best at: trauma. Others who are choosing differently are gravitating towards an integrative team of both western trained, biomedical doctors who team with holistic practitioners. We'll discuss this more in a bit.

The scientific materialist metaparadigm was put firmly in place for reasons already explored. However, when discussing the American medical system and its sole use of the biomedical model, it is not usually explored how it is founded on scientific materialism's principles. Nor is this then connected to the increasing level of awareness, usually, that this paradigm of science is increasingly becoming outdated. These two factors typically have been kept separate in public discussions, and certainly public policy.

Another biggie is that our mainstream biomedical system is *the* major sector profiting from the scientific materialism metaparadigm. It has to be understood that this has been kept firmly in place by an organized, financially and hence politically powerful group of lobbyists, who are some of the wealthiest taxpayers and CEO's in the country. Meaning: leaders of the AMA, the pharmaceutical industry, the biotech industry, the insurance industry, and the university research and development industry that is geared towards medical and biotech research. This also includes the politicians who support these industries, either directly or indirectly. All of them combine to be industries and individuals who give the government huge tax revenue, the country much prestige as the global leader in scientific research and development and medical technologies-up until most recently. This will be discussed soon, as well.

This conglomerate of merged industries in our market economy are also the ones who bring citizens its surgeries and rapid solutions. They deliver these services through prescription drugs and surgical devices using the latest and most innovative technology based on research that is a result of applying our scientific materialism's science. Our science's paradigm, as has been shown, is focused on the physical phenomena of life. Our biomedical model, thus, is based on symptomatic diagnoses and treatments at this physical level only, looking to no sources of anything outside of the physical causes as sources for illness, depression or lack of health. Biomedicine is obviously not working within a whole-systems based approach—diagnostically or in an ability to cure. Instead, through the latest technological advancements that aids surgery, diagnostic imaging, the soothing of any and all symptoms that cause discomfort through pharmaceutical drug use, and the biggies—chemotherapy and radiation—they are working at a reductionist level of "spot" fixing, coming from scientific materialism. This system is focused on quick, tangible results that the patient can see. It's very much what our science's reductionism in practice can deliver. And, it's precisely what we're used to, particularly in the United States. We get quick, tangible results from our customer service whether at a restaurant or at Best Buy, and if something doesn't appear the way we expect, we get our service adjusted, usually free of charge. I have frequently said we have the best customer service on the planet. What this also does, however, is produce quite demanding consumers for results—we want it *now*!

When living outside our country, even in Western European nations, there is a bit of a different pace and delivery around customer service. The anticipation that any perceived inadequacy can be and will be rectified as soon as possible does not translate into other country's market economies. When leaving the West entirely, it can be a mild to deep reconditioning of our expectations as to how quickly and efficiently things are done. To people who live in these other countries that we visit or live in as expats, it makes us seem spoiled and demanding. Yet they also appreciate it, it seems, because others aspire to our levels of efficiency in delivering goods and services. And others not. They instead, appreciate their pace to life, including afternoon siestas and things being done when they are done. We have a unique consumer driven culture here in the United States, and this absolutely affects the delivery of our health care services.

In an article published on September 20, 2005 on www.medpagetoday.com, entitled, "Medical Research Spending Doubled Over Past Decade," by the Senior Associate Editor of MedPage Today, Neil Osterweil, says, "... funding in the U.S. for biomedical research doubled—when adjusted for inflation—from $37.1 billion in 1994 to $94.3 billion in 2003. Industry is picking up about 57% of the tab for medical investigation, with the National Institutes of Health kicking in another 28%, reported researchers in a special issue of the *Journal of the American Medical Association*, (JAMA), previewed at press briefing time. Overall industry spending on *drug, biotechnology* and *medical device research increased by 102%*, from $26.8 in 1994 to $54.1 billion in 2003. The decade was a heady one for medical device researchers, who saw research funds from industry in that sector rise an impressive 264%. In contrast, pharmaceutical companies and biotech firms were somewhat less bountiful with their support, at 89% and 98% growth, respectively."

Again, this has something to do with the "American ingenuity." It's embedded within our national character—that practical application of science to technology, the long history *with*, and the expensive investment *in* the scientific materialist paradigm. This is quintessentially American; our reputation for producing "all things science." The cumulative, ensuing American love and pride for technological and industrial innovation and development, and the resulting reliance on our technology for stunning quick fixes. We want it, apparently, and are willing to pay for it, both as consumers and with our tax dollars subsidizing these industries. Moreover, Wall Street knows this, and builds on it. This *is us*, here in America. It's what we're known for around the world and here at home in America. Until recently. Keep reading.

Richard Gerber, M.D., wrote the 1988 classic *Vibrational Medicine: New Choices for Healing Ourselves*, that in 2000 became *Vibrational Medicine for the 21st Century—The Complete Guide to Energy Healing and Spiritual Transformation*, which then became *Vibrational Medicine: The #1 Handbook of Subtle—Energy Therapies* in 2001's edition. Notice the growth in the field as he changed titles. Trained in the biomedical system, a Western educated and trained doctor, he says "Our current worldview of medicine does not consider consciousness to be an important causative factor in illness but, instead, merely a by—product of the neurochemical and electrical reactions in a person's brain. In the old school, consciousness was seen not as a cause but as something that was an affect by a person's state of illness. True the existing medical model recognized that being chronically ill could make someone feel depressed, but depression was never seen as playing a contributing role in bringing about physical illness. Newer insights gleaned from research into the effects of emotional stress on the body and its potential to inhibit the body's immune system are gradually affecting medicine, though. As the reader will see, stress, consciousness, and our attitudes toward life play key roles in the new world theories of who becomes sick and who stays well. Just exactly how consciousness and the human spirit affect our susceptibility to illness by enhancing or inhibiting our natural immune defenses is a complex subject, but it is one we will endeavor to tackle," (Gerber 2000).

There is a growing awareness within the biomedical community now that admits the connection between stress and the body's illness or health. This has been begrudgingly and slowly admitted to within the biomedical field and the orthodox sciences. These two fields—biomedicine and the orthodox sciences—who are slow in admitting to this connection—are the ones who have lead to and continue to perpetuate our AMA backed biomedical model. Obviously, there is a reason for that resistance to what the new sciences are showing, even when it's good science, using sound methods.

To be clear, the admission within these two fields - science and biomedicine - perpetuating the current mainstream metaparadigm is that there are physical effects of stress on the physical body. In the biomedical model, the brain is *not the mind* that contains thoughts that cause stress. Instead, the brain is hardwired to send different neurochemicals to the body when it is under stress. It is purely mechanical, with the mind and thoughts having no relevance in the discussion. The question doesn't get asked what is the cause of the stress. It's not a part of this metaparadigm. The science that this model practices through biomedicine is based on not looking at consciousness, thoughts and emotions, right? Therefore, the only conclusion they could come to while still working within their paradigm, is that only the body has the ensuing disease. They do not admit to the thoughts and emotions and level of consciousness influencing the body via the perception of stress, as of yet. Because that would then be the mind body connection.

This is a key distinction. It needs repeating to make sure you catch it: it is actually our own reactions seen in our thoughts and emotions that are in response to something in the external, physical environment that produce the stress our bodies show the effects of. The conclusions we make from these potential stressors in our environment as stressful or not, is what creates -or not- a biochemical cascade of responses. So if we perceive something that we then label and conclude that this is something stressful, there is a stressed reaction within our bodies' physiology. It is not the actual stressor itself. Because we could perceive one thing, and then label it as non-stressful and we'd have no corresponding biochemical reaction in our bodies. Whereas, we could perceive another thing and then conclude, "Oh this is something that always causes me stress. It's bad, it makes everyone stressful" (i.e., the economy) and then have our bodies' respond with the stressful biochemical cascade of events that follow a conclusion that something is stressful.

Our biological chemistry is created by our thoughts, beliefs, emotions and then reactions—or non-reactions- as to what "should" cause us stress. And it is our beliefs guiding that "should" judgment of whether this event "should," stress me or not. Are you prone to frustration in traffic? So then, your thoughts, beliefs and ensuing emotions and reactions are geared up anytime you're in traffic. But what about people who love their time in their car as their own time to listen to the audio books on topics that enrich their lives, so they relish this time? Do you see? Our perceptions—beliefs, thoughts and emotions—of the outside event are the turning point to whether we react with stress or not at all. So, this becomes the turning point for whether our bodies then produce the physiological response of stress. Do you see how this turns everything inside out to what we had previously thought? We are not at the mercy of our external environment, or the physical. Instead, the power is in our perceptions.

This is huge, because it's pointing to the power in our thoughts. This means that we have the power to change the perception of the stress. Then our bodies won't be in a physiological state of stress. The implications of this are—you guessed it—the beginning of the mind body connection being proven, albeit within the new sciences. Furthermore, our levels of vitality, strength, and resilience in our underlying consciousness are also a factor in how well we are able to withstand higher levels of stress, and not react with a physiological reaction. This of course depends on how much we've worked with our own consciousness. If my consciousness is strong and optimistic because I am aware of the power my perceptions have, and have chosen yoga and meditation, for example as a way to build resiliency in my consciousness over my mind's tendency to think, think, think, then I am most likely going to choose not to allow potential stressful events to be concluded by my mind as stressful. Or, if my mind is producing thoughts and conclusions labeling something as stressful, with these lifestyle choices of having practices in place that help me create a more resilient, aware system then I am going to have developed the habit of not listening to my thoughts, whether through my meditation practice or another practice I use, geared towards not listening to every thought I have.

I am going to instead, work to reframe my perception, typically with getting a sense of perspective within the situation. Or even by talking back to my thoughts, as Access Consciousness teaches, by asking the question of ourselves in response to a conclusion our mind has made—say that this person was insulting me by not saying hi as they walked by—"Huh. Interesting point of view I have that point of view." Or in cognitive behavioral therapy, the practice is to talk back to the self-talk within the mind. Self-talk is another way to say inner dialogue. Or with yoga and meditation, to help me develop the habit of pulling off of my thoughts no matter the content and coming back to my breath. This way, my mind and its thoughts do not have the same level of power they typically do—where we think we are our mind and our thoughts. These practices all breathe some space into our human system between our mind's thoughts, conclusions, judgments and perceptions and our spirit, heart and Higher Self. Meaning, our mind is not allowed anymore to be the dominant aspect of our character. This typically looks like someone with a rather toned down personality.

All of this means I wouldn't be as ready to, or some might even say poised to, conclude and then label something as stressful, because I'll be humming through life with a consciousness that has more capacity to stay balanced, rather than tight and closed, or jumpy and erratic.

On the other side of the spectrum here, pharmaceutical prescription drugs are designed to work neurochemically, to help one's brain chemistry. In this example, the drugs prescribed would be to counteract the stress, typically by addressing what's construed to be a lower level of the "feel good hormones" or chemicals, such as serotonin. All of this is at the physical, measurable level. The pharmaceuticals chosen by the doctor could also be to increase the chemicals that make us calmer. However, these are targeted at the brains' chemical releases. It is not addressing that these chemical releases that occur in our brain that do stress us and thus shift our body and brain's chemistry is a result of our thoughts. If it were acknowledged that it is from the thinking or perception itself, it seems we wouldn't need these prescription drugs if we can achieve this through our thoughts. If we chose to breath through something that usually gets us to react and then be stressed, or we chose to purposely think of the other person's situation and chose to understand that they may have had a challenging day—or life—then we wouldn't choose to defend ourselves with a perception of their blatantly rushing out in front of us in traffic as a personal offense, and then react, then we wouldn't have the body chemistry of stress. And we'd have smoother, more comfortable interactions in society as a whole.

As one example, a friend of mind was taking care of a foster child who happened to be throwing a temper tantrum at a restaurant. She had taken him outside to help him calm down, being aware of his seven year old mind trying to deal with the recent loss of his mother and baby sister, who he would not see again. He had just shared a day or two earlier for the first time, how hard his life was because of this loss. A woman on the phone walked into the restaurant, visibly annoyed because this child was acting out and this adult, who she assumed to be the child's mother, was not controlling the situation better. If she had known the full story, would she have still been annoyed or would she have exhibited more compassion and generosity of spirit?

Perhaps we have the view, in this case, that the universe is unfriendly, and people are in general, out to cause us harm? Or perhaps we've had the lifelong practice of being the strong one, who allows others to get what they need, while we suffer silently although feeling like we are doing our job of being the strong one, and then we let it out in traffic. Again, these are examples of this aspect of working with ourselves for our own freedom, and not spreading our pent up, unmanaged emotions in reactions onto others, causing more stress in both people.

Nor does our current biomedical system admit to the connection between the quality and texture of one's consciousness (our typical emotions and thoughts) to our daily lifestyle habits of proper nutrition and rest. Although there is growing awareness of the role nutrition plays, it is not part of this biomedical model's paradigm. We'll look briefly soon at some of the typical curriculum offered at med schools, and see that nutrition courses are most frequently if offered at all, as electives. For now, another central weakness that results from our biomedical model being based on the science that it is, also leaves out this component of food's effects on our bodies and our mind's texture of thoughts. Such as carbohydrates have a component in them to make us feel better, emotionally.

We're not talking here about the classification of the different food types, carbs, proteins and fats; this our science does just fine. And I am grateful for this information. Again, there is lack in the current science our country is still functioning from, and it serves to weaken us. That is the point of this discussion. Where is our power, and why has it been weakened, and how do we go about infusing our lives with this power so we can all thrive-particularly at levels well beyond what the current, mainstream metaparadigm offers us for models of wellness, health, vibrancy and thriving? Again, that is why we're asking these questions.

The mind body connection paradigm of healers and scientists do acknowledge these very essential factors, as was evidenced in the examples of TCM and Ayurvedic doctors. A key point here is you can see the *lifestyle* and *individual* is either completely disregarded or completely involved, depending on whether it's the biomedical system, or the holistic system. And you can see where the responsibility lies within each system. And the power.

If I am going to my biomedical doctor complaining about a chronic pain and he gives me painkillers and an anti-inflammatory as the only routes towards relief, and then I am told that my chronic pain is due to a "degenerative issue" (in quotes because with my background and training, I don't believe in such a thing) and there is nothing more that he/she can do for me, then I am relying on my doctor and these drugs. While these drugs make the pain go away, what side effects do they leave me with and what other medications may I end up on to deal with these side effects?

Chronic pain, in the holistic model, can be dealt with in a variety of ways. One example is I use energy healing for chronic back pain to alleviate the mind body connection at the appropriate chakra and its unconsciousness within. For example, sacral and sciatica pain both are frequently associated with worries over basic survival, money and not feeling safe or supported. I can also use supplements known to help flush any arthritic pain, which is viewed as calcium deposits in the vertebrae (joints). I will also show the client yoga postures to strengthen that area, progressively challenging their core. Pilates and core strengthening from the personal training and fitness element usually are brought in as well. So this is restoring the power to the client, gradually. Eventually they're free of the pain, off painkillers, and have remedies they can do to relieve the pain if they ever have it triggered again. You can view testimonials saying this has happened with many of my clients on www.healing-balance.com.

The newer insights that Dr. Gerber mentions are from the studies conducted by the cutting edge scientists who are not as steeped in the old metaparadigm's conditioning, such as Candace Pert, from the new field of psychoneuroimmunology. Or they are—more typically—from the new sciences, such as Bruce Lipton. Lipton is another scientist like Tiller, who was once a microbiologist working on stem cell research within orthodox science, but left the field due to the system's limitations and "the way the 'game' has to be played." (Lipton 2010)

This transition of letting go of the scientific materialism model still has not been at all made. They're holding on tightly within the biomedical community as well. As Gerber said, "newer insights are gradually affecting medicine." Translated, this is the denial stage within the three-stage process of scientific revolutions as paradigms shift, as will be shown in the next section. Or this is one side of the conflict: biomedicine, scientists themselves of the scientific materialist paradigm, the research and development industry, the academic research institutions funded mostly by the government, biotechnology including the pharmaceutical industry, and the insurance companies, and more, including the food industry using pesticides, additives and preservatives produced by the biotech companies, or "big agriculture." All with the government's financial and/or direct or indirect political support of this entire system-metaparadigm -and the investments on Wall Street in these massive industries. All are focusing on the physical dimension of life as dominant. And our tax dollars help to keep this metaparadigm in place. Who is benefiting from this as it is?

The "other side" of this conflict is those already working within the newly emerging metaparadigm: the new sciences' scientists, natural healers working with and acknowledging subtle energy, concerned citizens, informed consumers, innovative entrepreneurs coming up with new options, and our federal government's NIH's NCCAM—who also funds "the other side." This *is* the breakdown phase of Laszlo's macroshift theory, as well as the denial stage within Kuhn's scientific revolutions model of paradigm shifts. Both will be discussed soon. We're still exploring what's really going on.

The admission that stress effects health has been made, yes, but there is still the crux of the conflict over the mind body connection existing or not. If the scientific materialist metaparadigm admits to the function of thoughts, emotions, consciousness and subtle energy overall, the system crumbles. The status quo changes. And their profit margin and monopoly lessens.

In our discussion, "natural healers" are the ones working within any of the therapies using subtle energies including meditation and yoga, but also well beyond these two. There are many more methods of natural healing or vibrational medicine—i.e. acupuncture and reiki, to name two better-known methods. Some, typically those within the field, know energy medicine is the vibrational medicine methods Gerber's book goes into. Interestingly, the National Institute of Health's National Center for Complimentary and Alternative Care (NCCAM) stops at only the most well known—because they are the ones the majority of consumers are choosing as "alternatives" or "compliments" to the biomedical model the most. So, this is money being taken out of the biomedical health care system, and it became noticed once it got to above 40%. Again, this is reminiscent of the AMA's behavior when the threat of homeopathy took away their business. This is this conflict building into the breakdown of the old metaparadigm.

The link between the pharmaceutical industry and the medical system is well known by now. In fact, it's so well known that it's part of the conditioning that most patients still do not question, meaning this relationship is "a given." However, the dynamics behind this relationship aren't necessarily what are well known. The exception is within the informed consumers, and/or people who have had experiences that have caused them to question the industry.

Pharmaceutical drugs are one of the physical approaches that the biomedical field uses in approaching disease, yes. Specifically, they look at the symptoms and help those symptoms "go away." The pharmaceutical industry is part of the larger biotech industry. Stay with me, we're just starting to build now. Biotechnology also covers other areas that include the surgical devices used in the other main approach our biomedical system has towards disease, to cut out the problem using more and more sophisticated devices and technology created from the biotech field. The two combined, pharmaceutical drugs and surgery, are the two main ways any and all illness and disease are handled within our current health care system. The biotech field also is responsible for creating the incredible devices that are used for the high quality diagnostic equipment that the biomedical model offers.

B. Alan Wallace states, "Furthermore, traditional approaches [biomedical] do not always work. For example, drug therapy for attention deficit disorder effectively suppresses the symptoms of this problem in only about 50 percent of the cases, and the widespread use of antidepressants among children has been linked to suicide. The discovery of dangerous side effects of pharmaceuticals is a common occurrence." This last idea is well known, the side effects of pharmaceuticals.

However, in treating the physical symptoms only, this does not require knowing about the patients' lifestyle, moods, diet and other influencing factors on the patient's diseased state, or illness. We've explored that; more than that, it *does* rely on tests and diagnostics from hi-tech devices. Furthermore, the scientific materialist metaparadigm is perfectly suited for mass production based on the very principles it founded its methodology on. Antibiotics come from mass production; a generic product used for general infections. Thus, the biomedical model was able to create separate laboratories with separate scientists from the prescribing doctors creating the drugs. Furthermore, this has now become the pharmaceutical representatives then marketing their companies' drugs to doctors, with the perks on the side for the doctors using their prescriptions that begins when the doctors are in medical school as first year students.

As the model of the pharmaceutical industry has become today, this leaves the doctor totally removed from the contents of the prescribed medication for their patient. This is unlike, for example, how homeopathy can individualize its treatment for each person's treatment, as Dana Ullman pointed out in our earlier discussion. A biomedical doctor's choice of which medication to prescribe is based on what knowledge they have of the possible pharmaceutical products available, and on the doctor's possible biases. Their knowledge is not based on an individual patient's particular circumstances. This is exactly how our science has translated into our medicine. It's that mass-production, assembly line approach. It comes from universality and reductionism, two main basic principles of scientific materialism, where all things have the same fundamental properties, and all things can be reduced down to these fundamental properties. There is no room for the individual there. Nor is there room for any exceptions or irregularities. Instead, it requires a uniform approach. And it is an approach that has historically yielded much industriousness. It is of extreme importance to note that prescription drugs are our medical system's number one treatment, as it is with consumers' prescription drug use within our country—apparently, our number one choice. To gain a realistic flavor of what this industriousness and commercialistic approach actually means in our medical system, look up the history of ADD; Ritalin was actually created *before* the diagnosis of *"ADD/ ADHD."* Dr. Peter Breggin, Director of the International Center for the Study of Psychiatry and Psychology (ICSPP) and a practicing psychiatrist-and parent-testified, saying this and much more, in front of the United States Congress in 2000. Dr. Breggin also presents other commonly unknown information in this testimony (Breggin.com 2010).

The *Wall Street Journal*, on January 8, 2009, published an article entitled, "FDA Scientists Ask Obama to Restructure Drug Agency," authored by Alicia Mundy and Jared A. Favole. In this article they say, "A group of scientists at the U.S. Food and Drug Administration on Wednesday sent a letter to President-elect Barack Obama's transition team pleading with him to restructure the agency, saying managers have ordered, intimidated and coerced scientists to manipulate data in violation of the law. The nine scientists, whose names have been provided to the transition team and to some members of Congress, say the FDA is a 'fundamentally broken' agency and describe it as a [sic] place where honest employees committed to integrity can't act without fear of reprisal. 'There is an atmosphere at the FDA in which the honest employee fears the dishonest employee,' according to the letter, addressed to John Podesta, head of Mr. Obama's transition team," (Mundy 2009).

The marriage between governmental institutions of power and policymakers to the biotech industry—particularly the pharmaceutical industry—is a central part of our metaparadigm. This government and industry marriage has a historical tradition in our country due to our metaparadigm. We're so used to it that it just seems the way it is, and therefore the way it should be. Scientific materialism became established alongside industrialization, as has been mentioned. We'll soon trace through the key ways this historically developed. For now, it is important to note that taxpayers fund these governmental institutions.

Richard Gerber, M.D., says, "There is a kind of cultural bias, a scientific ethnocentrism, if you will, tending to follow research only in the mainstream sciences." This is the view that helps science to be married to both our medical care system and supported by our government. Gerber continues to dismantle our ideas, pointing out the humanness of scientists and doctors, "Perhaps this reflects the fact that scientists are still people, with personal biases, egos, political affiliations, economic needs, and personal belief systems. And scientists, just like people everywhere, are slow to accept change."

Gerber then provides another voice pointing out how supportive our culture is for science and technology, "In our culture, one of our biases is that newer information and techniques are always better than older belief systems and technologies. Doctors often dismiss older medical approaches as outdated and useless. For example, many physicians don't fully appreciate that the roots of modern pharmacology lie in the older approaches of herbal medicine and homeopathy. Most doctors would rather prescribe a synthetic derivative of an herb's active ingredient than give the patient an herbal capsule, even if the two possess similar therapeutic actions." As we have discussed, this is different in other parts of the West, for example the European Union.

Gerber shifts gears a bit, here, and introduces the opening into the new metaparadigm. "Modern scientists assume that older approaches are too outdated to be valuable. However, mounting evidence supports a variety of ancient healing systems based upon views of physiology very different from the current mainstream healing paradigm. Perhaps revisiting ancient wisdom may supply important missing information that could result in a revolution in the field of medicine and healing," (Gerber 2000).

On the other side of this issue is the consumers'-*our*-demand for quick fixes. We live in a culture that has been groomed for this demand. We are not victims to it, but are heavily influenced by it, realistically. The advertising is just one leg, as massive as it is, that contributes to our conditioning for this quickness of being able to get the desired results we want. B. Alan Wallace says, "The materialist approach to medicine has led to the desire for a 'quick fix'—just pop a pill and let chemicals take care of it. Drug, tobacco, and alcohol addiction follow the same logic. There may be more to mental and physical illness than just chemicals, *but the physical bias of scientific materialism has largely marginalized alternative therapies that show promise.*" Wallace himself a scientist seems to be a voice worth listening to when understanding how our scientific paradigm has become our society's view of how the world works.

Wallace then goes on to provide another example of the current conflict, "The slow, grudging acceptance of acupuncture is just one example of this. For example, even though the 'channels' used by acupuncturists, shown vividly on their charts, have not been detected by modern anatomy, acupuncture is often effective in cases where physical medicine has failed. There is also a growing public interest in herbal remedies, whose curative influences may take longer than manufactured pharmaceuticals but which also may not have as many troublesome side effects as the latest drugs. Finally, attitudes they (doctors) may express toward their patients (such as genuine warmth, concern, and confidence) affect healing, this has only recently been incorporated as part of the curriculum in medical schools, and still only to a very limited extent," (Wallace 2008). While Wallace goes a bit beyond discussing only the "magic pill" popping, he does point out the reticence within biomedicine to have any alternatives to their system. The biggest reason is money, of course. But another factor is this resistance to embracing an entirely new scientific paradigm, and the two factors combined would lead to an entirely new metaparadigm. We'll get there in just a minute.

The statistics on drug use point to the use of prescription drugs as increasing among adults. The Center for Disease Control and Prevention has for their statistics on therapeutic drug use within the U.S., as, "Percent of persons using at least one prescription drug in the past month: 47% (2003–2006)," although the CDC's citation for this statistic cites a 2009 source.

CDC goes on to specify for physicians' office visits the following statistics: "Number of drugs ordered or provided: 1.9 billion; percent of visits involving drug therapy: 71%; most frequently prescribed therapeutic classes: analgesics, (*used to reduce pain*) antihyperlipidemic agents (used to treat hyperlipidemias, or *high levels of fat* that produce cholesterol problems) and anti*depress*ants," (italics mine), with their source for these stats being The National Ambulatory Medical Care Survey of 2009.

The CDC next breaks down drug use into the category of hospital outpatient department visits, with the stats: "Number of drugs ordered or provided: 247.7 million; percent of visits involving drug therapy: 75%; most frequently prescribed therapeutic classes: analgesics, antidepressants, and antidiabetic agents (used to treat *high blood sugar* condition or diabetes)," with their source being the same as the one above for the physician's office visits and percentage of drugs presented there.

Finally, the CDC presents for, "Hospital emergency department visits that the number of drugs ordered or provided: 212.1 million; the percent of visits involving drug therapy: 77%; and the most frequently prescribed therapeutic classes are analgesics, antiemetic (used to combat nausea or vomiting) or antivertigo agents (used to combat dizziness, often accompanied with nausea and vomiting), and antihistamines (used to treat symptoms from allergies)," (CDC 2010). It has been suggested from many sources in natural healing and holistic health that the increases in allergies are from an increased burden on our immune system. The increase in toxins in our air, food, and water supply are the main culprits. Also, within this list of drugs, one is able to observe that the majority of these health issues, including depression, can be treated by eating certain foods, while staying away from others. In other words, the majority of these health concerns that people are receiving medications for can be treated preventatively, with relatively simple dietary changes. *The bottom line is that the majority of these issues people are getting medication for come from their lifestyle choices.*

In a March 2005 article from the *New York Times Magazine*, author Roger Lowenstein interviews David Cutler, a former junior economics faculty member at Harvard, and now a full faculty member at Harvard, who left Harvard to go to Washington DC as a drafter of the healthcare bill under Hillary Clinton. Cutler left Washington DC—in 1994—with the question nagging at him as to why the health care reform had failed back then. It had seemed to Cutler and the Clinton's team that corporations, consumers, the uninsured, and doctors had all been clamoring for reform. Cutler came up with his answer; curbing the health care growth is the reason *any* health care reform fails. His epiphany: most health-spending is good, and it is rising because it is delivering products of economic value. Cutler says that, "Spending has been rising *because it can do more things that Americans want,*" (italics mine) (Lowenstein 2005).

Yes, the U.S. spends more than any other country, while it only has the eighth-lowest life expectancy in the OECD. Japan, though, spends $2,878 per person - about $5,000 less than the U.S. - and has the highest life expectancy among developed nations, reports the Huffington Post on their business page, in March of 2012. So with the statistics hovering around America spending 15 percent of its gross domestic product on health care, what are we spending this much on? Well, aside from medications, another dynamic with our health care system that describes American behavior under our scientific materialist metaparadigm is the option to have surgery. These surgeries, which again are the other most used treatment method next to prescription drugs in our medical system, utilize devices. These devices come from the biotech industry.

So when Cutler then wondered if Americans might be spending more because they were getting more and better treatment, he joined with Dr. Mark McClellan, another economist, to see if this was the case. They chose to look into heart attacks, and to see if they were occurring less frequently. They were. Still, spending on heart attacks has been rising. The cost of the surgery rates have been relatively stable. What they found is,"*But as the technology improved, the operation was being performed far more often,*" (italics mine) (Lowenstein 2005). It's ultimately the same with medications. For example as there have been improvements made to the side effects of prozac, more people are taking antidepressants.

Richard Gerber, M.D., helps us here, "As science grew more sophisticated, so did the nature of the biomachine we were thought to be. That is, as our technologies became more powerful with the discovery of the optical and electron microscopes, the parts and gears of the human machine were studied at smaller and smaller levels," (Gerber 2000). What Gerber is reflecting is the scientific materialist's premise in reducing; and reducing the physical to as small of a level it can, as applied to biomedicine.

Yet mainstream science is what is giving us our biomedicine and technology. Remaining unapplied from theory are the quantum physics' concept of energy being the fundamental building block to the universe and not the physical. This would mean that they would be working with energy as opposed to the physical within biomedicine. The biomedical techniques, of medications and surgeries, do not focus on any of this. Prescription drugs are still working with the physical; they're going through chemistry, which is still a physically based pathway. So it stays with the physical approach of the older Newtonian based, scientific materialist paradigm. Again, notice the focus on the physical only, while the newer quantum physics' discoveries are left to the wayside. Why is that? Who is benefitting from that? The holistic healing modalities, for example energy healing and acupuncture, both address energy, and not just the physical, although they do impact the physical. The focus is different; eradicate the fundamental problem at the energetic level, and the physical will also adjust back into balance, and health. It just happens slower than surgery or chemicals, typically.

Dr. Gerber continues to reflect this focus within the scientific materialist metaparadigm, "While early European physicians could analyze the human body only in terms of dissection of organs at the time of autopsy, today's medical researchers have the tools to study our physical makeup at the cellular and molecular levels. Modern medicine's current Newtonian biomechanistic viewpoint suggests that if we could only understand how all the different tiny parts fit together in the human body, we could develop better ways of fixing and repairing the body in the event of illness. This mechanical approach to fixing the body is nowhere more evident than in the field of surgery. Surgeons are the ultimate biomechanics. Orthopedic surgeons work with unique surgical 'carpentry tools,' which included drills, saws, screwdrivers, and screws that allow them to replace arthritic joints with better, synthetic joints of metal, Teflon, and plastic. Vascular surgeons work to cut out clogged arteries and replace them with newer synthetic Dacron grafts to restore adequate blood flow to the oxygen-starved limbs of individuals with vascular disease. While these surgical approaches do indeed provide a very sophisticated 'fix,' they do not fully explore the reasons behind 'why' diseases occur in the first place," (Gerber 2000).

This area of study is relegated to medical researchers, scientists within the scientific metaparadigm, known as molecular biologists, who are the ones who study the body's most minute parts—the structural molecules, the enzymes, and even the genetic structures that compose and direct the function of the body at the cellular level. Gerber explains that the thinking behind this is that if they could only know which enzyme was defective or which gene was abnormal, then they could invent a molecular solution that would circumvent the disease process and thus "cure all illness." There have actually been many medical breakthroughs resulting from this line of scientific inquiry, Gerber claims. Greater knowledge of the structure of human insulin, genetics, and the way insulin is manufactured ultimately led to the development of genetically engineered human insulin, thereby helping countless diabetics.

The cost of having a medical system based on these technologies is staggering. Lowenstein continues, citing that six of the seven G-7 countries, have seen spending growth on health care, regardless of how it's financed and organized. The rise in the American health care costs is close to the middle of the pack. Yet when attempting to understand what is the driving force behind this growth in costs, Lowenstein reports that Sherry Glied, of Columbia's School of Public Health, concludes that there is no specific aspect of any of the health-care systems in any of these countries that is "'the main determinant of growth in costs.'" Lowenstein adds to that, "*Technology is,"* and that, *"Better treatments lead to higher use,"* (italics mine) (Lowenstein 2005).

Important to remember is that our medical system works, according to Cutler, *because it produces more of what Americans want.* There is a full equation here; it is not just those in power. It is not just the biotech companies, the pharmaceutical companies, the doctors, the AMA, and the insurance providers who are inducing in us this artificial demand, right, as if they were selling us iPhones? This is different, this is our health, and this involves life and death. We're demanding these technological devices and these pharmaceutical designer drugs from biotech. It's not just for entertainment value; it's for life quality, or life versus death. This is huge. So this is a different story than with technology, and the use for it. It's helping to save lives, right, so how can it be anything other than virtuous?

"Contrary to the fears of many on the left, higher prices are not the chief culprit. Thanks to continued pressure from H.M.O.'s, doctors' rates have been held in check. So have the prices of pharmaceuticals already on the market. But because new drugs are more expensive, and because people take more pills, *total spending on drugs since 1990 has quadrupled.* As Cutler says, *medical spending isn't increasing because of inflation so much as because of people consuming more 'good stuff.'* This view is beginning to course through the health–care world. Scanning the literature, you now happen upon sentences like, 'We believe that some of the concern about the growth in spending may be misplaced' (Health Affairs) and 'On average ... society is better off exchanging more money for better health' (The Journal of Economic Perspectives). No one disputes that spending will continue to increase; limiting the rate of growth is the most we can hope for," (italics mine) (Lowenstein 2005). The key question here, obviously is, are we actually enjoying "better health" as the Journal of Economic Perspectives suggests?

Every year the Organization for Economic Cooperation and Development (OECD) publishes data that allows for comparisons of health systems across thirty industrialized countries. *Health Affairs* has been a publisher of many papers that use this data. The leading journal of health policy thought and research, *Health Affairs,* is a peer–reviewed journal founded in 1981 under the aegis of Project HOPE, a nonprofit international health education organization. In an article entitled, "It's the Prices, Stupid: Why the United States is So Different From Other Countries," by Gerard F.

Anderson et al., they say, "In that first report featuring 1984 data, the United States led the way in per capita health care spending at $1,637, nearly double the OECD mean of $871. In the latest offering, featuring data from 2000, the situation is much the same, although the absolute numbers are much higher. The U.S. per capita spending is $4,631, compared with an OECD median of $1,983. *The U.S. level was 44% higher than Switzerland's, the country with the next-highest expenditure per capita*...Over the entire 1990–2000 period the spending gap between the United States and the OECD median actually widened slightly," (italics mine) (Anderson et al., 2003). *These statistics attest to our role as leading spenders on health care of any industrialized nation,* and that figure has been producing a widening gap, increasingly.

"Measured in terms of share of GDP, the United States spent 13.0 percent on health care in 2000, Switzerland 10.7 percent, and Canada 9.1 percent. *The OECD median was 8.0%. Ability to pay*–measured here by per capita *GDP–has repeatedly been shown to be a powerful predictor of the percentage of GDP allocated to health care*...Private spending in the OECD data falls into the broad categories of (1) out of pocket spending for deductibles, coinsurance, and services not covered by health insurance; and (2) premiums paid by families and individuals for private health insurance...This varies considerably across OECD countries. *The median country finances 26 percent of its health care from private sources. The range is as high as 56 percent in the United States* and Korea to as low as 7 percent in Luxembourg and 9 percent in the Czech Republic. As a percentage of GDP, the OECD countries spent 0.4–7.2 percent of GDP on privately financed health care in 2000, with an OECD median of 2.0 percent. The United States was the highest at 7.2 percent. *U.S. private spending per capita on health care was $2,580, more than five times the OECD median of $451,*" (italics mine)(Anderson et al., 2003). Comparatively, we're spending a lot of money the most per citizen than any other countries. Yet both our health and even our mortality rate have been decreasing.

"Although the percentage of the health care dollars financed from public sources in the United States is low compared with other OECD countries, the absolute amount is relatively similar to other OECD countries." Please reread that. "Public sources in the United States accounted for spending of 5.8 percent of GDP in 2000, very close to the OECD median of 5.9 percent. In fact, on this measure of public spending, the United States is virtually identical to that of the United Kingdom, Italy, and Japan (5.9% each) and not much smaller than neighboring Canada (6.5 percent)," (Anderson et al., 2003). But the key thing here is only the U.S. and Japan are not socialized systems, although Japan's system runs closer to a socialized system than ours. So why are we still spending as much on public health care as these top producing countries who have socialized medical care? We're a 56% privatized system with an insurance industry. Yet why, when we're the highest % of OECD countries with our health care delivery system privatized for profit? Are we paying equal amounts as *smaller* nations whose entire health care system is mostly funded by public funds (government/taxation) as it is in a socialized system?

Continuing with "It's the Prices, Stupid: Why the United States is So Different From Other Countries," the authors mention that the numbers are actually worse, in that OECD's stats don't specify what portion of the public, or where the publicly financed health care is coming from. "These researchers measured the public sector's share of total health not by who ultimately paid the providers of health care, *but by the fraction of health spending that originated in households in the form of taxes.* On that measure, close to *60% of total U.S. health spending in 1999–7.7 percent of GDP–was financed through taxes,"* (italics mine) (Anderson, et al., 2003). I'm sorry, but why is that the case when we have a privatized healthcare program that has insurance providers functioning on a for–profit basis? If we were in a country with socialized medicine, I could understand these tax rates coming out of public money.

Another valuable statistic from this report goes back to the issue of our global competitiveness. The authors say, "In the United States medical school enrollment has been essentially constant since 1980. The observed increase in the number of physicians has mostly come from physicians who immigrated to the United States following medical education in other countries," (Anderson et al., 2003).

Sue Blevins, a writer for the Cato Institute says, "The American Medical Association (AMA) has lobbied the government to highly limit physician education since 1910, currently at 100,000 doctors per year, which has led to a shortage of doctors and physicians. Wages in the U.S. are double those in Europe, which is a major reason for the more expensive health care," (www.cato.org/).

Blevins' article, "The Medical Monopoly: Protecting Consumers or Limiting Competition?" written in 1995 discusses how nonphysician providers of medical care are in high demand in the United States because of licensure laws and federal regulations that limit their scope of practice and restrict access to their services. So, the result has been less choice and higher prices for consumers. While safety and consumer protection issues are often cited as reasons for restricting nonphysician services, Blevins continues, the restrictions appear not to be based on empirical findings. "Studies have repeatedly shown that qualified nonphysician providers–such as midwives, nurses, and chiropractors–can perform many health and medical services traditionally performed by physicians–with comparable health outcomes, lower costs, and high patient satisfaction. *Licensure laws appear to be designed to limit the supply of health care providers and restrict competition to physicians from nonphysician practitioners. The primary result is an increase in physician fees and income that drives up health care costs,*" (Blevins 1995 www.cato. org). This also provides a limit to their competition because of historically labeling natural healers as quacks. Yet those who benefit from the status quo are the very ones who gave the label of quackery. Thus rendering their competition less competitive by this name calling. And mainstream masses buying this labeling, following their lead, all in the idea that these are the "official" statements from those in positions of "authority" and are thus, the ones in the know. Does it really come down to name-calling and bullying from the dominant system so they can stay in power? "But I thought that science is science. And so if something is proven effective by science, and then science backed medicine, then that is what I believe, right? There's no way people in power would do anything that blatantly self-interested, when the welfare of so many citizens are at stake," is frequently the line of thought that comes up in reaction to the beginning stages of becoming aware of this picture as it is getting painted for you. Don't worry, you're not alone. Facts are facts, right?

Aside from doctor's salaries, the cost of prescription drugs, and surgeries, there is the medical device industry as well. According to Anderson, our spending in the U.S. for medical technology is the highest out of any country's spending on medical technology. "Just as constraining, and possibly more so, can be the availability of medical technology. Canada's health system also delivers far fewer highly sophisticated procedures than does the U.S. system. For example, the U.S. system delivers four times as many coronary angioplasties per capita and about twice the number of kidney dialyses. These data, of course, do not provide insight on the medical necessity of these procedures. Quite remarkable, and inviting further research, is the extraordinarily high endowment of Japan's health system with CT and MRI scanners and its relatively high use of dialysis. These numbers are all the more remarkable because Japan's health system is among the least expensive in the OECD," (Anderson et al., 2003).

The authors bottom line commentary is: "These simple comparisons suggest that Americans are receiving fewer real resources than are people in the median OECD country...The researchers [of this other study they're referring to] estimated that Americans paid 40 percent more per capita than Germans did but received 15 percent fewer real health care resources. A similar comparison revealed that the U.S. system used about 30 percent more inputs per capita than was used in the British system and spent about 75 percent more per capita on higher prices...In 2000 the United States spent considerably more on health care than any other country, whether measured per capita or as a percentage of GDP. *At the same time, most measures of aggregate utilization such as physician visits per capita and hospital days per capita were below the OECD median.* Since spending is a product of both the goods and services used and their prices, *this implies much higher prices are paid in the United States than in other countries.* But U.S. policy makers need to reflect on what Americans are getting for their greater health spending. They could conclude: It's the prices, stupid," (italics mine) (Anderson, et al., 2003).

Statistics from the 2007 European Federation of Pharmaceutical Industries and Associations say that according to the data compiled and published by multiple international pharmaceutical trade groups, the U.S. is the world leader in biomedical research and development as well as the introduction of new biomedical products. Providing these statistics: "The research and development of medical devices and pharmaceuticals is supported by both public and private sources of funding. In 2003, research and development expenditures were approximately $95 billion with $40 billion *coming from public sources* and $55 billion coming from private sources." Public sources obviously equates to spending our tax dollars. These investments into medical research have made the United States the leader in medical innovation, measured either in terms of revenue or the number of new drugs and devices introduced. Further describing the presence of the pharmaceutical industry in the United States, EFPIA states that in 2006, the United States accounted for three quarters of the world's biotechnology revenues and 82% of world R&D spending in biotechnology. They also state that *pharmaceutical trade organizations also maintain that the high cost of patented drugs in the U.S. has encouraged substantial reinvestment in such research and development,* (italics mine) (2010 www.efpia.com). Meaning, they see where their profit is at, so they continue to reinvest. It is within the American public.

The Congressional Budget Office in a report in January of 2008, entitled "Technological Change and the Growth of Health Care Spending" has found that "about half of all growth in health care spending in the past several decades was associated with changes in medical care *made possible by advances in technology.*" Other factors included higher income levels, changes in insurance coverage, and rising prices, (2012 U. S. Congressional Budget Office). Also, according to a *TIME* magazine article, "Why We Pay So Much," prescription drug prices in the United States are the highest in the world. "The prices Americans pay for prescription drugs, which are far higher than those paid by citizens of any other developed country, help explain why the *pharmaceutical industry is–and has been for years–the most profitable of all businesses in the U.S.* In the annual Fortune 500 survey, the pharmaceutical industry topped the list of the most profitable industries, with a return of 17% on revenue," (Barlett et al., 2004). And if you re-read the previous three paragraphs, look how much of this revenue is gained based on taxpayers' dollars.

Wendell Potter, in an article entitled, "Special Interests Target the Independent Board that May Be the Last, Best Hope for Medicare Reform", states that "One of the reasons why Congress has been largely unable to make the American health care system more efficient and equitable is because of the stranglehold lobbyists for special interests have on the institution. Whenever lawmakers consider any kind of meaningful reform, the proposed remedies inevitably create winners and losers. Physicians' incomes most likely will be affected in some way, as will the profits of all the other major players: the hospitals, the drug companies, the medical device manufacturers, and the insurers, just to name a few. The list is long, and the platoons of highly paid and well-connected lobbyists who represent their interests comprise a large private army that conquered Capitol Hill years ago (2012 www.publicintegrity.org).

The pharmaceutical industry has thousands of lobbyists in Washington D.C. that lobby Congress and protect their interests. *The pharmaceutical* *industry spent $855 million, more than any other industry on lobbying activities* from 1998 to 2006, according to the non–partisan Center for Public Integrity. "Pharmaceutical companies argue that the prices they set are necessary in order to continue to fund research. Only 11% of drug candidates that enter clinical trials are successful and receive approval for sale. Critics of pharmaceutical companies point out that *only a small portion of the drug companies' expenditures are used for research and development,* with the *majority of their money being spent in the areas of marketing* and administration," (2010 www.publicintegrity.org). Have you noticed in the recent years an increase in television and magazine ads for prescription drugs? This would certainly coincide with the increase in sales and revenue of prescription drugs, and to the fact that the pharmaceutical industry has been for years and still is the most profitable of all businesses in the U.S..

Stephanie Rodriguez wrote, "Prescription Drug Advertising: Some Advocate Return to Ban," in April of 2005. She says, "One of the fastest-growing areas for advertisers is the pharmaceutical industry, which spends billions of dollars each year advertising new drugs to consumers. While these advertisements may help the undiagnosed, it can also create a demand for unneeded treatment. 'People are attracted to these drugs because they see these positive images on television,' said Lynda Kaid, Telecommunications Professor at the University of Florida. 'They see it as a quick fix to all of life's problems.' Direct–to–consumer advertising reaches 14 percent of all prime time shows on television, according to studies conducted by Kaid. Advertising for drugs in the U.S. became legal in the 1980's. The U.S. and New Zealand are the only two countries that legalize advertisements today...Dr. John Colon, physician for the Florida Department of Health, acknowledges that one of the leading prescription drugs in the market is Strattera, an Attention Deficit Disorder medication. 'I get young kids asking me about certain medications all the time, especially about Herpes or ADD drugs,' Colon said. In the past prescription drug advertising in the United States was directed primarily to doctors, who were the sole decision–makers when choosing prescription medication. Today, pharmaceutical companies are reaching consumers through mass marketing in television ads."

Rodriguez goes on to say that the growth of direct–to–consumer advertising throughout the past 11 years has led the Food and Drug Administration to conduct a national telephone survey of adults and their views on drug promotion, in which the results were seventy–two percent of adults surveyed recalled seeing an advertisement for prescription drugs within the past three months. She then says, "Many doctors said that they are increasingly pressured by patients to prescribe drugs seen on advertisements. 'I think it puts the doctor in a bad situation because people tend to see symptoms and think they have them when they don't,' Colon said. 'It creates a confrontation between the doctor and the patient.' Proponents of television ads for prescription drugs say that the commercials serve as a valuable educational function to the public," (Rodriguez 2005). Stephanie Rodriguez wrote this as a sophomore at the University of Florida's College of Journalism and Communications.

From the *Washington Post*, "For decades, the United States has been slipping in international rankings of life expectancy, as other countries improve health care, nutrition and lifestyles," (Ohlemacher 2007). In this biotech era and its high profile within the scientific materialist metaparadigm, specific to the medical industry, this field has become all–encompassing with its influence. This influence includes the cross–over of many, many different industries of all sizes producing various services and products within the entire medical and biotech fields, along with insurance companies, all of whom have a vested interest in keeping the scientific materialist metaparadigm unchallenged in any substantial way. So it does seem that in the modern age the scientific materialist metaparadigm has been able to remain in place due more to the profit margin and less to philosophical beliefs.

But prior to today, in fact at the dawning of the pharmaceutical industry, we go to John Kellogg–father of Kellogg's Corn Flakes®. Kellogg graduated from New York University Medical College at Bellevue Hospital in 1875 with a medical degree; he was known to be a gifted surgeon, although he was generally against unnecessary surgery to treat diseases. Kellogg is one of the early American doctors who recognized that the reliance of the doctor on pharmaceuticals was not in the best interest of neither the patient nor the medical profession. In fact, he found the increasing prescription writing and reliance on pharmaceuticals alarming. He said so, "This *undue credit to the effect of the drugs prescribed,* when it occurs among medical men, probably arises mostly from the habit and routine of always prescribing in certain approved manners in certain kinds of cases, and *when improvement takes place, forgetting to allow sufficiently for the healing power of time and nature herself*...As nothing but hard–earned experience and frequently disappointed hopes in his scientific prescriptions, will ever thoroughly convince the young practitioner of their *frequent inutility,* so nothing but the proper kind of education on these matters *will ever convince the people of their frequent too great confidence in the efficacy of drugs alone,*" (italics mine) (Kellogg 1905). Implied within Kellogg's comments is the placebo effect; the belief the medication will work, so it does. Remember though, he said this just as this system was beginning. So he had a unique vantage point–regardless of how many studies today show yes, there's a placebo effect and no there's no placebo effect, depending upon who is paying for the study or how it's intended to be used. When, in fact, placebo use and studies started within the pharmaceutical industry. Keep reading below.

There is a rich history of the investigation into the power of the placebo effect, stemming from the pharmaceutical industry and not the natural healing, or homeopathic world. Ironically, this is where the research first began on placebos; when pharmaceuticals first *began to be prescribed* on a more regular basis. The American Library of Medicine holds an online historical documentation of this. In this document, one can see early pharmaceutical, biomedical medications that were prescribed to and used by the public, but were actually placebos, and known by the doctors to be so. The antique bottles themselves with the word "placebo" on it can be seen on their website. The caption of these photos reads, "Placebos were produced for clinical use in a range of different shapes and colors, and physicians even discussed which colors and shapes worked best. Bottles were labeled with simple code names (Cebocap, Obecalp) so patients would not catch on to the fact that they were being given a placebo rather than a real drug," (Natural Health Institute http://www.nlm.nih.gov/exhibition/emotions/self.html 2010).

In fact this document contains much information on the historical discussions by leading American doctors, members of the AMA, as they began to more actively use prescription drugs for treatment. Eugene F. Dubois, Professor of Medicine at Cornell University, speaking at the Cornell Conference on Therapy in 1946 from his paper "*The Use of Placebos in Therapy*" said, "You cannot write a prescription without the element of the placebo. A prayer to Jupiter starts the prescription. It comes with weight, the weight of two or three thousand years of medicine." The Library of Medicine then goes on to say, "Thus the groundwork was laid for the serious investigation of the role of hope, imagination, and expectations in the operation of medications and procedures in scientific medicine."

W.R. Houston defined the issue clearly, when he said, "The Great Lesson of medical history is that the placebo has always been the norm of medical practice." The American Library of Medicine's digital publication, *"Emotions and Disease: Self-Healing, Patients, and Placebos"* furthers the discussion by saying, "The issue was quite complicated and compromised for physicians. Many of them were aware that they too prescribed medications whose principle basis of action was the patient's credulous belief...the most experienced and sophisticated physicians knew that many medicines thought to be effective were really not, at least not on the basis of pharmacological principles. The regular profession was itself often guilty of over–drugging. Thus William Osler, the beloved and influential turn–of–the–century Professor of Medicine at Johns Hopkins University could slap down quacks and jab at his colleagues at the same time by saying 'In the fight which we have to wage incessantly against ignorance and quackery...diagnosis, not drugging, is our chief weapon of offence,'" (ibid).

Finally, "Some went even further, Lewellyn F. Barker, Osler's successor as professor of medicine at Hopkins, suggested that whatever success modern physicians had with their prescribed medications depended largely on their ability to awaken confidence and inspire the idea of authority by their scientific training and by their mode of inquiry and of examining the patient. Even more provocatively, Harvard Professor of Psychiatry, C. Macfie Campbell, declared in a much noted 1924 lecture that physicians sometimes brought about the improvement of their patient unwittingly, when the patient is already prepared for the display of power," (Ibid).

Now back to Kellogg, this is the same John Kellogg who is the founder of the Kellogg breakfast cereal; he and his brother Will Kellogg started the Sanitas Food Company at a time when the standard breakfast was meat and eggs for the wealthy, while the poor ate porridge, farina, gruel, and other boiled grains. John and Will argued later over the ingredients for the Kellogg breakfast cereal. Will wanted sugar to be in it, and John was staunchly opposed. So they split ways, with Will starting the Battle Creek Toasted Corn Flake Company, and this eventually became the Kellogg's cereal we know of today. John went and formed the Battle Creek Food Company so he could develop and market soy products. John Kellogg, as a trained medical doctor, held strong beliefs in the benefits of eating healthy to maintain an optimally functioning digestive tract, which he recognized–amongst many others prior to the modern biomedical model, including both the Chinese and the Indian culture's medicinal practices, as well as many "folk healers" and natural healers throughout history–to be central to maintaining health–a healthy gastrointestinal tract.

Kellogg believed that most disease is alleviated by a change in intestinal flora; that bacteria in the intestines can either help or hinder the body. These pathogenic bacteria produce toxins during the digestion of protein that poison the blood. A poor diet favors harmful bacteria that can then infect other tissues in the body. Kellogg also operated on the understanding that the intestinal flora is then changed by diet and is generally changed for the better by a well–balanced vegetarian diet favoring low–protein, laxative and high–fiber foods. This natural change in flora could be sped by enemas seeded with favorable bacteria, or by various regimens of specific foods designed to heal specific ailments.

Kellogg taught these various regimens at the Battle Creek Sanitarium, where he held classes on food preparation for homemakers, and taught classes on breathing exercises and mealtime marches (calisthenics) to sanitarium visitors in order to promote proper digestion of food throughout the day. He also made use of artificial sunbaths and phototherapy (light therapy), while also patenting the process for making peanut butter due, to his belief that nuts were a healthy, strong food choice.

I have been known to often comment in my "Food as Medicine" workshops and food demos at health food stores, in my "Eating for Empowerment" Nutrition classes, on my radio show, and with clients how much I've seen nuts used in other countries. Whereas here in the U.S.A. nuts are frequently just in bulk bins at health food stores, or as salted party snacks in the chips aisle at mainstream grocery stores. An example of this is on the streets of Istanbul, Turkey, particularly in Beyazit Square leading into the Grand Bazaar, where there are individuals with carts that serve roasted chestnuts or walnuts then packed into heated and dried apricots and a host of other nut treats typical of Turkish culture. A warmed walnut inserted into a soft dried fig or apricot is like eating a slice of pie. It's amazing!

Kellogg also invented granola–the American version of the European (German) muesli–and a healthful "granose biscuit." He had many notable patients, such as former president William Howard Taft, aviator Amelia Earhart, Arctic explorers Vilhjalmur Stefansson and Roald Amundsen, economist Irving Fisher, Nobel Prize winning playwright George Bernard Shaw, founder of the Ford Motor Company Henry Ford, inventor Thomas Edison and actor/athlete Johnny Weissmuller.

Kellogg was also a proponent of what he termed "Biologic Living," also known as "The Simple Life in a Nutshell." Biologic Living means health, comfort, efficiency, long life, good digestion, sound sleep, a clear head, a placid mind, and an attitude that is content and happy to be alive (Lifestylelaboratory.com 2010). Interestingly, as a side note, at the top of Kellogg's article, Lifestyle Laboratory wrote as an introduction, "In Dr. Kellogg's time, Biologic Living promoted a vegetarian diet with a limited use of dairy products including eggs. Today, however, animal diseases are increasing rapidly, and chemical usage has multiplied exponentially. Biologic Living has–of necessity–evolved to include a total vegan diet and a lifestyle that deals with the reality of our modern toxic world."

Kellogg, at the time as his fellow doctors were increasing their writing of prescriptions, prescribed what the training and education for medical doctors should be, "To this end the study of anatomy, physiology, hygiene, and particularly the laws of life, *with the influence thereon of habits, conditions, and surroundings, should enter largely into,* and be assiduously carried all the way through, the education of the young, even if this be to the exclusion of almost no matter what other branch besides. And if the use of drugs be referred to at all in their education, it should be with a special care that they be taught the facts as they are,–*that the essential and useful drugs are really few and their administration rarely necessary; that in the aggregate in the world it is probable enough that more harm is being yearly done by their indiscriminate and unskilled use than there is good by their timely and judicious employment,"* (Kellogg 1905). Note the date he said this. One could think upon reading this, "Yes, but we've advanced so much since then." Have we?

Kellogg also went on to say where and how he saw doctors able to be most effective, "Physicians can do much more than is usually done in the direction by their individual influence in practice. Each physician should constantly endeavor to establish in the minds of his patrons the fact that they should seek intelligent opinions and skilled advice *more than prescriptions. And even at an occasional risk of losing patronage, when medicine is not required at all, he should dare to say so, and give the right advice instead. Doctors should be educators more than physic–mongers* [not solely and incessantly focused on the physical only]. Whatever time the occasion demands should be taken *to fully explain the trouble for which persons present themselves, and the best regulation of living to be adopted under the circumstances;* and for this opinion and advice alone, when kindly given, they should, and generally will, expect to pay, [as in even if no action is taken other then advice]," (italics mine) (Kellogg 1905). This sounds quite similar to what an Ayurvedic doctor in India does.

What Makes "Us" Us in the U.S.?

Beyond this growing reliance on pharmaceuticals, at this same point in the modern era–around the turn of the 20th century–pasteurization and the canning of foods soon followed, so that food could be preserved and transported. Chemistry opened the way for the internal combustion engine to power automobiles and then airplanes. Plastics, artificial fibers and chemical fertilizers were developed. The practical application of the discovery of steam's properties lead to steam trains and steam powered, metal–hulled ships, helped along by even more practical applications of extracting ore from iron and other minerals with advances in metallurgy. Military technology expanded as well, with the invention of the bullet cartridge, the revolver, the repeating rifle, the machine gun, and a wide range of new explosives.

Lots of practical inventions that increased the quality of life, were also made available through the practical applications of our science. Modern conveniences entered in at this stage too. The playing around with electricity resulted in the discoveries which lead to artificial lighting, so no more use of whale oil or kerosene nor earth–based rhythmic lifestyle with the sunrise and the sunset. We also got the telegraph, then the telephone, which we've all put to good use. We also got electric generators and transformers which the military put to good use. We also got hydroelectric power, the battery, modern factories and the recording of sound and motion pictures for all of us to now enjoy in our recreational time outside of production time. *The proliferation and success of scientific materialism was married to the industrial revolution. This occurs in the United Sates more than anywhere else in the West; it's what we're known for globally.*

Science and its chosen partner, technology, is our foundation economically. The United States came into being around the Enlightenment, and Enlightenment philosophers envisioned a "republic of science," where ideas would be exchanged freely and useful knowledge would improve the lot of all citizens. From it's emergence as an independent nation, the United States has encouraged science and invention. It has done this by promoting a free flow of ideas, by encouraging the growth of "useful knowledge," and by welcoming creative people from all over the world. Albert Einstein was one of those welcomed; a German Jew during World War II, with huge potential to benefit our society's science.

The United States Constitution itself reflects the desire to encourage scientific creativity because it gives Congress the power to promote the progress of science and useful arts, by securing for limited times to authors and inventors the exclusive right to their respective writings and discoveries. This clause formed the basis for the U.S. patent and copyright system. So creators of original, progressive art and technology would get a government granted monopoly, which after a limited period would become free to all citizens, thereby enriching the public domain, as it was intended. Benjamin Franklin and Thomas Edison could both come to mind here.

The availability of vast tracts of land and labor from a periodic and yet consistent doubling of the population from immigration; the diversity of climates throughout this vast land mass; the ample presence of navigable canals, rivers, and coastal waterways; the abundance of natural resources facilitating the cheap extraction of energy, fast transport; the availability of capital, all can be viewed as contributing to America's rapid industrialization. Most historians and sources seem to agree that the period in which the greatest economic and technological progress occurred was between the end of the 18th century and the beginning of the 20th because it was during this time that the United States was transformed from a primitive agrarian based economy and society, to the foremost industrial power in the world. This is attributed to our science and technology, and the resulting Industrial Age, powered by both of these primary industries of our country. Some sources state that the past twenty years or so are rivaling this period that has been perceived as the most rapid rate of change our country has ever undergone.

Beyond the fever for science and the rational application of reason during the European Enlightenment came a new way of thinking. This was the corresponding focus on the rights of individual's to use their rational reasonable intellects to function in varying degrees of democracies within the West. Their liberty became free of unreasonable, arbitrary monarchies or authorities. The American Revolution is a direct result of this new thinking. Beyond the founding of our country, the constitution has been interpreted to having been written to support the sciences and technological advancements so that any citizen deserves the right to be able to come up with a new invention, or product, and "own" this invention, either through patent or copyrights. This secures a market economy for consumers to have access to these products indirectly, as well. Through the comparatively strict patent and copyright laws that favor creativity and innovation, there are also other factors inherent to America that causes our zeal for technology and science. We are a unique, blessed country that the world is used to looking to for this brilliance–and entertainment and "be all you can be" attitude.

I have first hand experience with this. As an expat living mostly in Asia but traveling throughout the world living in other locations more briefly, this attitude was what locals noticed about me. It wasn't always appreciated, either. In fact, much of the time I had to tone down my "let's do this!" approach. I am remembering one scene in Israel working alongside Europeans, Russians and an Australian and realizing that they were startled by how quickly I was working. I recognized I was making them uncomfortable, so I slowed down. Amongst my fellow American expats in Taiwan, I was considered one of the more easy going Americans, comparatively, by the locals. Yet I still had to learn to tone down my "Yeah! let's do this!" attitude there. It appears this American enthusiasm to be all that we can be just seems too aggressive outside of the American climate. Within America, though, I tend to be perceived by others as laid back and easy going, which is interesting information when contrasted against the international experiences.

It is key to who we are as a nation to remember that the United States grew up as a nation during the Industrial Age. However, backing up to its birth as a nation, this was during the philosophy of the Enlightenment. The Enlightenment's philosophy also birthed the ideas that lead to the French Revolution. This is what our American Revolution was modeled after and what made us separate from England and became our own country. During the Enlightenment the seeds of scientific and intellectual thought, and the activity that went on within both arenas, (science and intellectual arenas) then catalyzed the Industrial Age's activity. The Industrial Age created our modern culture that we are still in today in our post–modern times. In fact we are very much still living a metaparadigm based on these exact ideas. One of the key points to this entire discussion is we are living in a society structured around the ideas that birthed our science and our nation, at the same time. Yet we now have new and different needs in this post-modern time of quantum physics, or consciousness. We are in the process of societal structures crumbling; the ones that are based on the Newtonian physics of scientific materialism and the Industrial Age, as we move into this new age, have become outdated. Thus, they've become dysfunctional. And yet we attempt to band-aid these falling structures with incremental changes, when fundamental changes are what are needed.

The Modern Age *is* the Industrial Age, and this was born from science becoming the scientific materialist paradigm seeded in the Enlightenment. The United States was born and came of age completely as a result of this activity. The U.S. is, therefore, a quintessential prototype for the ideas from the Enlightenment, that drove our democracy's founding principles, and then the Industrial and Modern Ages. Furthermore, as we can see by now, the United States has in its skill set an aptness for practical applications of science to technology. The outcome of that skill can be seen throughout our history of technological innovation. Americans are known for being innovative and creative. We've just briefly looked at the climate our society was founded in. What followed, as our country grew up, and we developed our identity through our national character, is essentially, we became a model prototype for the marriage of innovative technological creations from science to the development of our economy. The essence of our identity got firmly established during the Industrial Age.

Benjamin Franklin, our first millionaire benefited economically from rocking American society with the revolution of "discovering" electricity and creating his bifocals; John Deere and the steel plow; Scottish born American citizen Alexander Graham Bell and the telephone, as well as the research laboratories named after him (AT&T's Bell Laboratories) later coming up with the LED technology, the C programming language, and the UNIX computer operating system; and then Thomas Edison with his light bulb; the Wright brothers with the airplane; Henry Ford with the automobile; William Shockley and his team with the transistor; Robert Goddard with his aiding rocket propulsion systems and hence, space travel; Silicon Valley's SRI International and Xerox PARC both helping to give birth to the computer industry; all the way up to Steve Jobs and Apple® and Bill Gates and Microsoft®. Large money has been made. These innovative pioneers also gave us what has been central to our national identity.

Another reason why Americans have science and technology and the resultant industries driving it to the degree we do can be traced back to America being on its own, so far away from its "motherland." Back in England, or Europe (at first) there already were established societies, with infrastructure, and "modern" developments underway. Yet, America was on its own to come up with her own way of figuring out how to live on the vast wilderness of land that is the United States. Meaning, because manufacturing was already beginning in Europe, and the United States was so far away from the sources of this manufacturing, the colonists, then later the citizenry, has had to come up with its own way.

An example is during the 1800's when Britain, France and Germany were at the forefront of new ideas in science and mathematics (apparently nothing new for Germany), and not the United States. This was when the United States was fresh out of being a colony, and beginning its build itself as its own nation. So while the United States lagged behind in the formulation of theory, it excelled in using theory to solve its problems. This is where the applied science to technology aspect has its roots; the phrase "Yankee ingenuity" has its roots here as well.

In *A Social History of American Technology*, Ruth Schwartz Cowan describes this aspect of America quite aptly. She says, "Science, technology, and industry have not only profoundly shaped America's economic success, but have also contributed to its distinct political institutions, social structure, educational system, and cultural identity. American values of meritocracy, entrepreneurialism, and self–sufficiency are drawn from its legacy of pioneering technical advances," (Cowan 1997). Tracing up through the various stages of America's development, the general predominance of the use of science applied to innovative technological creations is throughout America's history. It first began out of need, and eventually become its own industry in and of itself. Eventually science and innovative technological creations lead America's economy and the technological pace of the world. This has continued throughout American history. American dominance of all things scientific and technological has only come into question recently, during this era of all the dysfunctional structures of our society crumbling.

Where we have arrived at today is the technological innovativeness is being applied frequently to products that are not ones we genuinely need. Rather, the industry now creates the need–or demand–*within* the consumer, mandating that society move into the next level of technological use from the products created. Hence, the perception of need is created, but not an *actual* need. This is the nature of the postmodern era that we're now in. Fun, exciting, increasing convenience, speed and volume of access to more and more is the nature of post-modern technology. Yet many argue, these creations are not necessarily needed for basic needs to be met. Even though who could go without wifi now, their iphone or smart phone, their ipads, kindles or nooks, or the plethora of choice with how to view television and movies, and the high definition huge screens for tv and movie viewing now. Some, in fact, go without basic needs in order to have the latest technological gadget. Who do you know without a cell phone, never mind an iphone or smart phone? Are they homeless too? So it would seem in our post-modern era, cell phones are now considered basic needs.

These technologies are driving the flavor of the post-modern age of convenience, digital living and sophisticated use of consciousness in many different venues and technologies. So again, look, it's technology driving the flavor of our times. It was once the telegraph, the steam engine, the car, the phone, the refrigerator, the television.

Some would say that this lack of necessity could be argued, though, for each of the inventions during the Industrial and then the modern age, such as the light bulb itself. However, in the beginning stages of modernization, these technological inventions created "modernity" itself, moving agrarian based living into urban, and then suburban, based living. Now, in the postmodern age, not only is part of the connotations behind the definition of post modernity the lack of genuine utility that these technological innovations provide, but also, even more so, the cycle of demand we're engaged in as consumers. This includes then the work we engage in so that we can have these–many of them–unnecessary items. Much of the ensuing stress then follows directly on the heels of this process.

There are vast, typically under-examined consequences with the near disease state (stress levels) from both the push on consumers to keep up and buy the latest version, and then the high-tech industry's perpetual momentum to exceed the prior speed or clarity or precision of the last model of the latest technological "breakthrough" that forces us to adapt to new technologies. Both of these come from the drive that the high–tech industry has with their profit driven model, and our American ingenuity and love of technology. There is then an ensuing stress ridden cycle of obtaining these products. Recently it seems this has begun to be discussed within the masses. Stress levels have become so rampant, with such far-reaching effects, that this drive from the high-tech industry with the next cool gadget (at least half of which I have, mind you) has finally begun to be viewed as a catalyst to illness and a result from "the race." So it could be said that there is some good the good to come out of this breakdown of our economic activity within "the race." And that is this incremental progress within the metaparadigm. But this is where we are now, where we've gotten to from the beginning days in our country with our "Yankee ingenuity." It would appear this is the far end of the trajectory.

This trajectory was initiated innocently enough with the loom–from Native Americans as much as from the Anglo Saxon culture–for textiles that could no longer reasonably be imported from England; then the cotton gin and the steel plow for agriculture; next the mechanization from the American mechanical engineer Frederick Taylor, with his scientific management theory that revolutionized industry into mass production; the earlier communication technologies of the telegraph and then later the telephone, or the field of telecommunications, of which "for the past 80 years, the United States has been integral in fundamental advancements in telecommunications and technology," (Cowan 1997); then the automobile; then the airplane; then the World Wars and the military, industrial and technology complex developing their tight union as the primary application of the scientific research and development, on up to the atomic age for World War II and the nuclear energy discovery; the focus of science and technology and the military's applications of both changed and it then became the Space Age, with the rockets and satellites and the race to be the first on the moon; out of this continues to be the military/industrial/technological trinity from the Space Age communications back to the telecommunications' industry of now the internet and cellular technology, although the private sector has been more involved in this than the government; then there's the most well known application currently–as well as the one most relevant to the mind body connection–and that is the application of science and technology to medicine and health care, or the field of biotechnology.

They have the government's support, such as medical research like that with AIDS and its origins, while the pharmaceutical drug companies produce the research on the drug, the drug itself, and gain the profits. *Biotechnology, while still having the government's support through funding for research and development based out of universities, is an industry backed by more power and money in the private sector than any other private industry in the list of our government's active support.* Active support is a.k.a. "funding," or our tax dollars. Remembering thought that approximately 40% of biotech's funding comes from taxpayers' dollars for that practical application of science to technology for what biotech produces. Also remembering that biotech is the highest profiting industry in our post-modern age.

We are now in the biotech era of "Big Science." These developments play a central role in how the mind body connection has been increasingly shuffled off to the side by first our government and leaders and then the masses following, due to this very marriage with the biotech industry. Ensuingly, the mind body connection and its therapies (i.e., natural healing or "alternative" medicine) were antagonistically labeled as "quackery." At the same time the AMA backed biomedical model has been presented as the only metaparadigm available to the general public. The general public, the uneducated and educated masses, has overwhelmingly bought what our government, the AMA and the pharmaceutical industry has sold us! Their metaparadigm is centered around scientific research using and relying on the methods and premises of scientific materialism.

World War II ushered in the era known as "Big Science" with increased government spending and patronage of scientific research. It was during this and then the Cold War that followed when the United States rose to the forefront of the international scientific community. As Cowan explains, "In the post–war era the US was left in a position of unchallenged scientific leadership, being one of the few industrial countries not ravaged by war. Additionally, science and technology were seen to have greatly added to the Allied war victory, and were seen as absolutely crucial in the Cold War era. *As a result, the US government became, for the first time, the largest single supporter of basic and applied scientific research.* By the mid–1950's the research facilities in the US were second to none, and scientists were drawn to the US for this reason alone. The changing pattern can be seen in the winners of the Nobel Prizes in physics and chemistry. During the first half–century of Nobel Prizes–from 1901 to 1950–American winners were in a distinct minority in the science categories. Since 1950, Americans have won approximately half of the Nobel Prizes awarded in the sciences." (italics mine)(Cowan 1997).

Also occurring alongside the development of nuclear energy and as a result of it, the pace of technological developments increasingly became tied into a complex set of interactions between Congress, the industrial manufacturers, university research, and the military establishment; also known as the military industrial complex. Again, as Cowan describes, "because of the military's unique technological demands, concentration of funding, large scale application, and highly centralized control, it played a dominant role in driving technological innovation. Fundamental advances in medicine, physics, chemistry, computing, aviation, material science, naval architecture, and meteorology, among other fields, can be traced back to basic and applied research for military applications."

In today's globalized world our science with its practical applications to technology, along with our pop culture and fast food, are what we've exported, both of which run a distant second and third behind our science and technology. They also both stem from our practical applications of our science to technology, like the television, videos, music CD's, movies, mechanization for fast food production along with the food products themselves, such as the preserved and frozen McDonald's patty and the processed cheese slices. It's what we've been known for, and what is expected from us.

Within the developing global community, these innovative technologies have equated modernization and convenience, and living a life that is seen as a certain successful standard of living. To non-Americans in recently developed nations, these technologies and pop culture iconic products symbolize the luxury enjoying Americans and their infamous luxurious lifestyle. And while Hollywood very much contributes to this image and stereotype, this is not the place to discuss this. Although the technology is behind the big–blockbuster movies that mainly come from America. And once a country has Hollywood films, particularly giant multi–plexes, then it apparently sees itself as having risen to a whole new level of modernity and success.

This has been happening in varying degrees all over the globe, and to the citizens in the nations who have joined in on our form of globalization, i.e. Taiwan, India, Korea, Japan, and all the others, when products such as an iPod, Nike along with its main advertising technique incorporating pop culture–our sports stars–into its technical images used for advertising, the microwave, the air conditioner, the refrigerator, the television, the car, reliable wireless internet particularly with Facebook, McDonalds, Starbucks, and pharmaceutical drugs and vaccinations all mean that they have achieved a level of modernization. So it equates to many in these recently modernized countries that they have made it to a certain level of material affluence. This, as we know from the anti–globalization efforts, has them mirroring in varying degrees, the American lifestyle.

The point for our discussion right now, however, is that American science and technology lead the way globally for citizens in other nations. This is, in particular, when it is considered how to achieve what they equate with living an American luxurious, modern, convenient, and enjoyable lifestyle. The importance to the new generation of citizens in the recently developed countries to feel modern and not like their grandparents is central to how globalization has caught on fire.

Their country's governments, should they have it, choose to invest money–along with the IMF, WTO, and our American international mutual funds–in national infrastructure and businesses that will help their nation compete within the now global marketplace. They then produce products that can contribute to what the United States sets as the global standard for science and technology. As we will discuss soon, some of these nations have now surpassed the United States' technology in both production and quality of various technologies. An even more recent development is that many of their scientists are coming to the United States to train in American labs for their post–doctoral work, and then publish in international peer–review journals. These now surpass the amount of American research scientists publishing in the international peer–review journals. They then typically return to their home country and build a successful professional practice as a Ph.D. in whatever field, including M.D.'s. We'll look at this in a bit more depth in just a moment.

Francisco Varela, a physicist and one of the two founders of the Mind Life Institute's biennial summits with the Dalai Lama speaks to this American dominance in a discussion entitled, "Questions of Method" about the scientific international community. He explains how the United States holds a central role in being the source for all things science, and has an international credibility with its scientific research that most other countries do not. In fact, science, and the ensuing technology–so that the two are not really separated in most consumers' minds within the global community–seems to basically be expected to originate in the United States, and then

Europe. This is the perception that our history and dominance within the fields of science and technology has created.

He tells the following anecdote, "One beautiful example that happened in the United States was the following study: Using scientific articles that had been published in good journals (which therefore contained facts accepted by the scientific community), people changed the names of the authors and the names of the place where the paper was written. Instead of saying the research was done at Stanford or Harvard, or some place like that, they said it was done in Chile, or in Tibet–someplace that people wouldn't trust too much for scientific reliability. They sent these articles back to the same journals (of studies that were originally done in such places as Stanford or Harvard). The result was that out of a hundred papers submitted, 80 percent were rejected with comments saying they were not good science, their method was bad, and the interpretation was bad! Yet these same papers had previously been published by the very same journals! This means that a fact, just because it comes from a place that is not considered reliable, isn't reliable...This phenomenon is a lot more subtle and pervasive than one might think. It is part of this sociological matrix that science sits in the midst of, and is not separable from why a theory is accepted and why one fact is considered good and another fact is not," (Hayward 1992).

In this same vein, Varela provides an example with European–American neurophysiologists. David H. Hubel and Torsten N. Wiesel won the Nobel Prize for the discovery of specific neurons within the retina and the cortex. Later, in the former Soviet Union, the same experiment was done, but taken even further, with the science more dynamic and thorough, but the international community did not receive these Russian scientists' data. Apparently, it has been very difficult to get these findings published in the West (Hayward 1992).

The Dalai Lama then asked Varela if the work of the Russians was helpful in the field of research work, and was told that indeed it was, but that it wasn't listened to. It was a good experiment with good data but it wasn't listened to. Varela explains, "That point is important, because for people like myself, who come from a place that is not a dominant center like the United States or Europe (although I have worked most of my life in the U.S. and Europe), (he is from Chile) it is very clear that what is called international science is a particular style of science. This is not to say that the system prevents different voices from coming in, but today what ordinary citizens all over the place would consider real science is fundamentally European–American science," (Hayward 1992).

How did this race begin? This race for all things technological, all things industrial, all things science; how did *modernity* begin? Physicist Fred Alan Wolf, considered one of the most important pioneers in the field of consciousness, points out in *Mind into Matter: A New Alchemy of Science and Spirit* that even though thirty years ahead of Darwin, in 1830, scientists already knew the ideas contained in Darwin's theory, but *the ideas weren't popular yet because society didn't need them yet. Darwin's theory became useful as the industrial age emerged.* Wolf states, "In other words, Western society was rampantly exploiting the world and had begun what we now call the dog–eat–dog world of commerce. And Darwin's *On the Origin of Species* was just the right bible for this new enterprise. *You see, science and industry go together hand in glove, not only in devising the technical means of production, but also in the employment of the alchemical forces of the imaginal realm that fuel such enterprises (scientific discoveries),*" (italics mine). Wolf then goes on to explain that thus, particular heads of industrial states of a society, upon reading Darwin, create the industrial environment as the "proof" that the theories are correct and these heads *then* adopt Darwinian theories of science, and make them popular with people, readying them to accept the theories, by advocating them, "further fueling these machines of society. This circuit becomes dominant and stable wherein what we think is supported by the environment we live in, which in turn limits and directs our thinking, thus enabling species survival," (Wolf 2001).

Further reinforcing the marriage between scientific materialism and industrialization, and strengthening the separation between the church and science to the level of a divorce was the sales and marketing of this mechanical form of science by a number of scientists. It seems that a good amount of scientists in the mid 1800's emerged from their dark basement laboratories and entered the light of society to crusade for political and religious changes that they felt were now necessary, because this new scientific knowledge was in fact demanding these changes. These scientists became public speakers, writers, popular educators. A general "sales team" for Newtonian physics.

Ludwig Buchner, a German physicist, was one of the most popular spokesmen for scientific materialism. He wrote *Force and Matter* in 1855, "which essentially reduced the mind and consciousness to physical brain states produced by active matter. Buchner rejected religion, God, Creation, and free will, and in a later work denied there was any difference between mind and matter at all," (Wallace 2008).

Even more intense marketing of scientific materialism occurred in the beginning days of our colony becoming a country. In England there was a group called the "X Club." This informal group of nine men included the distinguished biologist Thomas Huxley, the philosopher Herbert Spencer, the physicist John Tyndale, and the botanist Joseph Dalton Hooker, amongst others. All were preeminent in their fields. Huxley in particular was an assertive storm of influence, nicknamed, "Darwin's bulldog." Huxley is also the man responsible for coining the term *agnostic*–the view that the truth value of certain claims especially claims about the existence or non-existence of any deity, but also other religious and metaphysical claims, is unknown or unknowable. So Darwin's theory of a mechanical, survival of the fittest, competitive–origin–of–our–species, dependent–only–on–genes–and–not–any–divine–source–for–creationism–or–continuance, became a tidal wave. Once this tidal wave crashed onto shore, what was left formed a thorough scientific overtaking of the West's metaparadigm–scientific materialism. This bulldog of a man Huxley was not only Darwin's fiercest advocate, but he was also agnostic, and he was committed to having science take over. "Huxley claimed that science could achieve 'domination over the whole realm of the intellect,' and even spoke of the creation of a 'church scientific,'" (Wallace 2008).

In Huxley's scientific research he sought to explain physiochemical laws as the basis of living processes. Nothing mysterious was left. It all became explained between Huxley and Darwin, so Huxley promoted. What was left to still be explained could be, and would be, *by science*. Huxley has been described as a brilliant and pugnacious speaker who promoted science in public education and worked for the creation of a scientific elite–both efforts clearly overwhelming successes. Ironically, Huxley himself had "little formal schooling and taught himself almost everything he knew. Remarkably, he became perhaps the finest comparative anatomist of the latter 19th century... In November 1864 Huxley succeeded in launching a dining club, the X Club, like–minded people working to advance the cause of science," (Barton 1990). All members of the club were Fellows of the Royal Society, England's governmental body for Science, and most were Huxley's closest friends. Huxley himself, and the philosopher Spencer, both went on to become presidents of The Royal Society, with Spencer succeeding Huxley.

In fact, the philosophical basis for the group was provided by Herbert Spencer, who was himself another high profile figure in Victorian England. Spencer's contribution to science was reducing social philosophy to scientific concepts. It was actually Spencer, and not Darwin, who coined the phrase "survival of the fittest" (Wallace 2008). All of these X Club members, scientists turned promoters, believed in a natural order to the universe determined by cause and effect, one that might prove unknowable, but one that was to be investigated by science, not religion. They saw religion as bankrupt as a useful guide to truth and that physical science held the answers to all important questions. "So strong was their enthusiasm for an all–embracing scientific worldview that they often allowed their hopes, dreams, and beliefs to masquerade as facts," (Wallace 2008).

They also believed that to further the interests of science, public education needed to include science, for it was science and not the previous classical training (of classical literature, Latin, Greek, rhetoric, history, and moral philosophy) that was going to properly and effectively develop the intellect. Obviously, this is a key shift in the West, and we can still see the impact of this sales job today in our public education. "Members of the X Club held prominent positions enabling them to lobby successfully for official support of science and the teaching of science in all levels of education. *Most importantly it was they who interpreted science to the public–a public that was becoming increasingly industrialized and secularized*," (italics mine) (Wallace 2008).

So that by the end of the nineteenth century these beliefs had become the scientific "gospel." These six principles of scientific materialism–objectivism, metaphysical realism, the closure principle, universalism, physical reductionism and determinism–became sold and packaged to the public simply as "science." *And they have become our metaparadigm, extending way beyond the laboratories into all aspects of our society, our culture, our very minds. It's how we've defined our reality for 300 years, at the mass, mainstream, metaparadigm level.*

"And although the roots of many of these beliefs could be traced to the Bible, their original cause had been forgotten, replaced, banished. God was now at most a ghost passively observing the machine that he had supposedly engineered with his 'intelligent design.' The object of scientific inquiry, originally the heavens created by God, had been replaced by 'objective reality.' God's sacred language, mathematics, had become a subset of the scientific method. The resulting universe could be likened to an immense clock–work, operating automatically–without morals or miracles–driven solely by the laws of nature. Humans and their thoughts and emotions were ruled by that machine. Scientists now saw themselves and the rest of humanity as organic robots," (Wallace 2008).

For these scientists, the "survival of the fittest" was a biological parallel to the impersonal, clockwork universe of classical physics. For them, the no–nonsense, hard–nosed fact of this struggle for survival was the pattern behind every facet of life. Ring a bell? Social philosophers then took this concept further and created social Darwinism, the view that nations and individuals competed for economic supremacy in an area where only the "favored races" or *toughest individuals would succeed*. Sound familiar? Neither idealism nor softness could be allowed here; this was the big leagues. *So, of course, the usefulness of these theories transferred right over to war, industrialization and commercialization–and on into our modern lifestyle, with all of this tied to science as its justification*. Marx himself called his philosophy "scientific socialism." "*So nineteenth century scientific materialists created a philosophy based on a set of beliefs that was not arrived at scientifically, or to put it differently, was supported by modes of inquiry that focused exclusively on material phenomena*," (italics mine) (Wallace 2008).

This set of beliefs, not facts, was that existence is purely physical–there is no other reality. Furthermore, the sources of this reality, they asserted, are the laws of nature, forces that are entirely impersonal, having no connection whatsoever with the mind of human beings, their beliefs, or values, and that these laws operate in isolation from any supernatural, spiritual influences, all of which are illusory any way. All of these leading scientists and promoters, by the way, were men, having the masculine archetypical cognitive approach behind these beliefs and choices without a feminine archetypical cognitive approach as a counter balance.

Remembering that Jeremy W. Hayward holds a Ph.D. in Physics from Cambridge University and spent several years at MIT as a molecular biologist conducting research, as Hayward continues to explain Western science to the Dalai Lama in the first official summit of The Mind Life Institute, he clarifies the scientific certainty that has been resultant from the scientific materialist model. "*By the beginning of the twentieth century, this sense of certainty about scientific knowledge had made science the dominant belief system in Western countries*. During the two hundred years from Newton's time to the turn of the (20th) century, this belief system was unfolding amid great debate between the Christian viewpoint in which God was creator and the so-called scientific viewpoint, *which was gradually diminishing any role for God,*" (italics mine) (Hayward 1992). Once Newton had shown that the planets move around by themselves, Hayward explains, there was no more need for God. When Darwin suggested that different kinds of organisms just evolved mechanically, Hayward interprets this to have meant that even in the creation of humankind there was no need for God. Hayward sums up by saying, "Thus began a fierce debate between people who hold the Christian viewpoint and those who hold the evolutionary viewpoint; the debate has continued into the present. However, by the end of the nineteenth century, the view that science was the one and only true belief system began to prevail and continued to do so, at least in the popular mind. This rather simplistic belief is also held by most working scientists, who do not reflect much on what they do," (Hayward 1992).

Most people, if asked about the tenets just explored, would state, "Well, yes, this is the way the world works," or, "yes, that's what science tells us about the universe and life. It's how it is, yes." This is due to the extent that these theories, and this line of thinking and inquiry have permeated Western, particularly American, society.

Thus, it has been necessary to review this past so that we understand that this is the reason we see unclearly the world the way we do. It's due to what our perception has been cued to. And our perception has been very much influenced, in fact to an almost unconscious level, by the scientific materialist view of the physical aspect of life being the more valid than the nonphysical. The ensuing metaparadigm was then sold to us over time. Reductionism treating things as separate and then specializing in these separate parts is one example of what we accept and expect—again almost unconsciously. The majority of us are still holding onto this view. Not all cultures see the physical world as we do; as primary, while all that is of the subtle or energetic world is deemed secondary or even irrelevant. To many of us within this materialist's metaparadigm we go even further in that the subtle is unbelievable, or even non-existent. Remember that the subtle includes the invisible, the mysterious, the seemingly "unprovable" aspects of life.

This single point strikes such fierce responses in people. The physical is what is real, it is what is solid and dependable, and look, there's measurable results defining and proving it's something to believe. The non–physical, or the metaphysical is what we cannot sense with our five senses. And within this scientific materialist metaparadigm, because it is intangible and can't be picked up by our physical five senses, nor is it easy to observe and measure, it is labeled anything from not credible to something to be feared due to its unknown power. Right?

This metaparadigm has given us the mind body connection split and anything that diverges from this and contains elements of the "unexplainable" gets mistakenly deemed either as supernatural, or skeptically deemed as theories that are just quackery. This hasn't seemed to change since the division between Church and State started back in the Enlightenment. I am not suggested that Church and State merge, at all, so please don't misconstrue that. I am presenting information and observations about how our society has historically, since the Enlightenment and on up through now, divided along the lines of secular/science/medicine and religious/spiritual/natural healing. I am clearly asking the question of functionality at this point. As well, I am pointing out that perhaps this split was even made in the first place in emotional reactivity, or as we would say in Access Consciousness, "resistance and reaction to" the seeming irrationality and lack of reason and order in the Dark Ages. I am inquiring, and asking of you to consider if we are now missing something by continuing to perpetuate this model.

I am also asking you to genuinely consider with an "unconcluding" mind - a mind open to considering other ideas that it is not used to considering, without judging them out of possibility - that because metaphysics was overtaken by what came to be the hard sciences; and the hard sciences, as we have seen, had no practical use for the subtle energies of the mind, emotions, or consciousness, are we not then missing something? Does it not seem that this metaparadigm is nearing collapse, in great part due to the discoveries of quantum physics starting back in the 1920's, as well as from the "new sciences" of today? And that we are in the midst of a macroshift globally, having the influence of other cultures to compete against or to learn from? This idea of a macroshift will be explored next, from one of the leading voices of this school of thought out of Budapest.

Two examples of the most recent studies that I've seen do a perfect job of enriching our understanding. The first is from *The Journal of Medical Ethics* from a study conducted in 2007, with its article approved for publication in 2009, "The Remote Prayer Delusion: clinical trials that attempt to detect supernatural intervention are as futile as they are unethical." The author of the article, Mr. G. Paul, - the information given doesn't indicate he is an M.D. or, in fact, what his background is for that matter - says in his abstract for the Journal that basically due to the potentially adverse psychological impacts of these studies, it renders them unethical, and that resources should not be "wasted" on medical efforts "to detect the supernatural and paranormal," because this large series of clinical trials he is referring to indicate that remote prayer is not effective. In the very next sentence he then accuses the methodology used in these studies that renders the studies inherently ineffectual, due to "mass contamination of sample cohorts," and that there is less premature death in First World Nations while there are also lower rates of prayer, and that these first world nations are only having lower rates of premature deaths since the advent of modern medicine, " (2012 http://jme.bmj.com). Clearly both the journal that he published his article in, and his favoritism for "modern medicine" make his allegiances clear.

Precisely encapsulating this conflict is another article a year later in the *Journal of Religion*, written by Wendy Cadge of Brandeis. Sociologist Wendy Cadge is considered an expert "on the intersection of religion and medicine in contemporary American society, and set out to research medical studies of intercessory prayer going back to 1965, the first year such studies were published in the English language medical literature. Said about Cadge's work "Her novel social history of intercessory prayer studies reveals growing religious diversity and diminishing belief in science to measure the value of prayer," (2012 www.brandeis.edu). Cadge apparently in 2009 won the Suzanne Young Murray Fellow at the Radcliffe Institute for Advanced Study at Harvard University. Cadge herself states, "This analysis in the Journal of Religion is the first to trace the social history of intercessory prayer studies and to situate them in their medical and religious contexts." Pointing to her findings on the difficulty of measuring this subtle phenomena historically deemed an area of religions, she says, "With double blind clinical trials, scientists tried their best to study something that may be beyond their best tools, and reflects more about them and their assumptions than about whether prayer 'works.'... Reflecting a recent shift toward delegitimizing studies of intercessory prayer, recent commentators in the medical literature concluded: "We do not need science to validate our spiritual beliefs, as we would never use faith to validate our scientific data." (2012 www.brandeis. edu). Hhmm. Such clear lines drawn, right?

While prayer is an example chosen to specifically point to the science vs. religion divide we've done historically in the West since the Enlightenment, other forms of subtle energy as it is applied to health are as diverse as Reiki, yoga therapy, meditation, diet and nutritional programs, panchakarma treatments from Ayurveda, acupuncture and medical chi gong from TCM, working with the consciousness of the body as Access Consciousness does, ThetaHealing, and Pranic Touch. These "natural healing" therapies have had studies applied to their effectiveness as well. Unless these studies have been done by the New Sciences, typically the same conclusions are made as Mr. G. Paul above. Again, this goes back to the question that perhaps using the premises and methods of the scientific materialist paradigm are not subtle enough to pick up subtle energies, in the way that they require. Think back to Tiller's comment that we can access this field through our consciousness, but machines and technology are not able to access it. So looking for proof with something that may not inherently allow for proof is seemingly futile, yes?

Nonetheless, there have still been many efforts to do so. As an example, in 1992, Bruce Taino of Taino Technology, an independent division of Eastern State University in Cheny, Washington, built the first frequency monitor in the world. Why would we want to measure frequencies, if we're not working with radios? According to Dr. Robert O. Becker in his book *The Body Electric*, the human body has an electrical frequency and that much about a person's health can be determined by it. Frequency is the measurable rate of electrical energy flow that is constant between any two points. Everything has frequency. Taino has determined that the average frequency of a healthy human body during the daytime is 62 to 68 Hz. When the frequency drops, the immune system is compromised. If the frequency drops to 58 Hz, cold and flu symptoms appear; at 55 Hz, diseases like Candida take hold; at 52 Hz, Epstein Bar and at 42 Hz, Cancer. Taino's machine was certified as 100 percent accurate and is currently being used in the agricultural field today, (2012 http://www.stopcancer.com/essentialoil1.htm).

As we'll see next, quantum physics and the "new sciences" shine a different light on this historical split we've made in our thinking in the West since the Enlightenment. And that in fact, the merger of science with subtle energies/consciousness/spirituality/mysticism/the supernatural that religion has dealt with - you get the point - is what is actually happening within the new metaparadigm. It just looks different than our eyes are expecting science and "proof" to look. So how does that make you feel? Uncomfortable? Excited? Both? This is all good because those are the feelings that typically accompany the new.

Chapter 5—The Breakdown of Newtonian Physics and Scientific Materialism: Quantum Physics Emerges and Scientific Certainty Begins to Falter: Where Are We Headed?

"I now believe that rather than trying to explain consciousness in terms of the material world, we should be developing a new worldview in which consciousness is a fundamental component of reality," Peter Russell (Russell 2000).

Science and Common Sense

INDIAN BORN AND TRAINED PHYSICIST and University of Oregon Institute for Theoretic Physics retired professor of 32 years, Amit Goswami is perfect to turn to at this point: "To grasp the meaning of someone else's system it is essential to understand the metaphysical basis behind that system. And there is the rub. The metaphysics of science, as developed mainly in the West in the last three hundred years, seems diametrically opposed to the metaphysics behind the dominant religion of the West, Christianity." Goswami continues, by introducing us to this new time and quantum physics' discoveries, explaining that by the twentieth century, science's success had led to a series of metaphysical notions of reality based on science. Each one of these was antithetical to notions of popular Christianity. One of these ideas is strong objectivity, which was already mentioned–reality is independent of us, "so our free will, our decisions to love God or to follow ethics, does not make any difference in the affairs of the world. Other ideas are material monism and its corollary, reductionism–all things are reducible to matter and to its elementary particles and their interactions. The dualism of God and the world was openly questioned: if the God–substance is different from the world–substance, how does God interact with the world? Therefore, it makes sense (to the scientists) to postulate that there is only substance, matter," (Goswami 2000). There is irony intended behind Goswami's words. Since retirement, he's been applying quantum physics' mechanics to the "mind body problem," including serving as a member of the Advisory Board on the Institute of Noetic Sciences, stated by former astronaut Edgar Mitchell, the sixth man to walk on the moon.

Goswami's understanding come by him naturally, as a physicist. What would cause Goswami's perspective that would make him retire from physics, and choose to apply quantum physics to the mind body connection—and to work with the sixth man to walk on the moon? What could these three seemingly divergent fields have in common? Let's check out what went on in physics. By the 1920's, the classical Newtonian outlook began to break down. The relativity theory from Einstein–stating that time and space are no longer absolute, but relative–and the development of quantum mechanics with its new understanding that it is not particles but actually waves at the subatomic level chipped away at the Newtonian outlook. That energy is the basic building block of the universe and not matter, and that these waves of energy are within a bigger sea of energy and are without predictable behavior also hammered away at the solidity of the foundations of Newtonian physics. Combined, all of this unraveled the scientific community. And it hasn't been the same since. Even more baffling, within this unpredictability, these waves of energy are affected by subjective influences from the human mind, and its thoughts and expectations of what it is observing. It is interesting to note that those of us outside of science have no clue of this.

These discoveries undermined Newtonian physics most fundamental principles. As a result of the nature of these discoveries, the question then followed if the possibility of pure objective perception in and of itself is even possible. So then doubt arose that eroded scientific materialism's model of the physical as the basis of our universe. But what also arose as well is doubt about the effectiveness of the methodology science uses–the scientific method itself–which assumes objectivity as its basic functioning premise. *How could the scientific method in fact produce certainty about an objective world, when it seems like we can't even observe the objective without causing it to change, according to the Observer effect as seen in the wave/particle duality of quantum physics?* Which actually brings into question the definition of "the objective world" and doubt of its actual existence. These questions result from a long, complex line of questioning that has resulted from the bewilderment that physicists have faced because of these discoveries. We will explore and clarify the most important ones.

However, as apparently set up by Descartes' successors in the Western tradition of science and ultimately the West's metaparadigm, when you doubt the existence of a real objective world, the only alternative you have is subjectivity. So everything is thrown back on the individual subject and his or her own mind. In our materialist metaparadigm, this subjectivity then automatically leads to the leap all the way to the conclusion that the subjective is messy, unreliable, bad. Objective is rational, reliable, and good. Further implied conclusions about the subjective are that if left to "just the subjective" (as if that were possible) we would simply perceive whatever we invent or wishful thinking, with nothing in–between. Simply, the world becomes whatever we make up in our minds and we can't be trusted with our minds' regions that are "not–objective." Compare this view to the Buddhist and Yogic understanding of the mind and this view itself seems unreasonable. Ironic, isn't it?

Meditation, Mindfulness and Common Sense

Our society hasn't endorsed actively going within and working with our minds, so subjectivity is a dangerous unknown. The power in the mind is its ability to objectively reason. In fact, objectivity and reason go hand in hand is the unconscious assumption in our culture, yes? Why are we stuck with only these two alternative extremes of subjectivity and objectivity? Because deeply rooted in Western thinking is a belief in the duality of mind and matter, subject and object and that it is the objective *only* that is reliable.

Our entire functioning of our metaparadigm, our society has developed around this central tenet.

Robert M. Young, in his chapter "The Mind Body Problem" from his book *Mind, Brain and Adaptation in the Nineteenth Century: Cerebral Localization and its Biological Context from Gall To Ferrier,* provides a quote from E.A. Burtt, author of *The Metaphysical Foundations of Modern Physical Sciences,* that helps to illustrate what has happened, "...it does seem like strange perversity in these Newtonian scientists to further their own conquests of external nature by loading on mind everything refractory to exact mathematical handling and thus rendering the latter still more difficult to study scientifically than it had been before. Did it never cross their minds that sooner or later people would appear who craved verifiable knowledge about the mind in the same way they craved it about physical events and who might reasonably curse their elder scientific brethren for buying easier success in their own enterprise by throwing extra handicaps in the way of their successors in social science? Apparently not; mind was to them a convenient receptacle for the refuse, the chips and whittlings of science, rather than a possible object of scientific knowledge," (Young 2010).

We inherited this split, and from this split have left the mind basically unexamined. Instead, we have ignorantly labeled it as unmanageable; again save for the cognitive functions, such as memory recall, processing sensory information, fact and data retrieval, perceptual processing, and analysis. Which are–these cognitive functions–ensuingly, a rather large percentage of what is studied in psychology. Psychology has chosen to focus mostly on the physical because it struggles to be considered worthy amongst its big brothers of hard science.

It is this very factor that is part of the great resistance to the implications of what the quantum theory unveiled. Namely, the discovery that our world is quite a bit more dependent on the subjective than what Newtonian physics had determined–and wanted. The discovery of the "Observer effect" in quantum physics has left quantum physicists coming up against this long held, strong belief that had so many invested historical reactive emotions contained within it–that the subjective is messy, so go to the objective. *It goes directly back to the creation of science in the beginning of the Enlightenment, emerging from the Middle Ages and the Renaissance, where these beginning scientists were all men making these choices of what to focus on. There is no ground for consideration in this model we've inherited that there could be healthy, successful management of our mental landscapes and emotional worlds; not from what they'd seen.* By the time we'd gotten into modernity, science had proven a perfect partner for industrialization, leaving us where we are today in the post–modern world.

Mindfulness arises from an introspective observation of our mind. Typically this is coupled with guidance from an experienced teacher providing explanations of what we're discovering in this murkiness of the human mind. Or as the Buddhists put it—in the neurotic human mind each human has. So as more aware humans of our minds' nature, we then go out in the world more mindful of our own mind's tricks as we interact with others. Ultimately, we become therefore less reactive and more successful with our social and interpersonal interactions. This simply has not been looked at until only recently by the mainstream masses of our materialist metaparadigm. And as this entire discussion is pointing towards, neither has it been looked at, nor genuinely considered within Western science and biomedicine. This again reflects the strong resistance to giving credence to the studying of the mind, as well as the effects of the mind on the body. And thus we have the resulting strong resistance to acknowledging a connection between the mind and the body. You probably now see the need for the preamble at the start of the book.

Acknowledging the mind body connection is only the first step, really. Because then, the mainstream institutions and the field of biomedicine would then have to shift their focus from the physical, and yield to an emphasis on the non–physical. This is the land of the not–so–easily–measured. And it sounds like a metaparadigm shift. Which, once it fully happens, would then result in it not just being at the grassroots level that there is an appreciation and demand for the healing techniques based on a different paradigm. The holistic paradigm that includes the mind body connection is where we're headed, it seems, yes? Financial support would change, for one, along with many, many other changes throughout most levels of society. So again, we are in the embryonic stage of a metaparadigm shift.

It has been only the last fifteen years that the mind and mindfulness has begun to be seriously explored within the West. This has ultimately lead to using rigorous scientific methods to compete with the dominant metaparadigm, which the Mind Life Institute with the Dalai Lama's efforts has led to. Non–mainstream scientists have tracked the results of the changes in the specific lobes or regions of the brain and the behavioral changes as a result of long term meditation with Buddhist monks. They've used EEG's to do this. The behavioral and brain lobes they targeted for measure were in long-term meditators, to measure the impacts of meditation and mindfulness. The MLI's biennial summits were directly responsible for much of this activity. *This is the crux of an authentic meeting of the East by the West in our now globalized world.*

Additionally, this historical refusal to truly examine the mind has caused us to avoid systematically exploring the use of much of the inherent mental and metaphysical potential of humans, which is available to achieve even greater things than typically previously considered. Yogic science and chi gong both acknowledge this particularly once we learn about our minds and how to manage them. Tapping into this power source is not something that the West has embraced, because it involves subtle energy, consciousness, and the mind.

Science Goes Down the Rabbit Hole

According to Hayward, "Science, according to the classical view of the nineteenth century, was the great method for overcoming wishful thinking and finding out how the world really is. Many could not let go of the classical belief in an objective world." Hayward then goes on to describe the doubt that began to arise in the 1920's due to the quantum mechanics theory and Relativity. When this doubt began to arise, scientists had to find a way to make the foundations of science firm again. Sounds like resistance at the beginning of a paradigm shift, yes? Refusal to accept the new, and stay with and reinforce the familiar, even when it's been found to be dysfunctional or untrue could be a less charitable way to label this. As was the scientific materialist metaparadigm –being found to no longer be relevant, or functional, in the face of this new knowledge of energy being the foundation to physical life. But this was too soon for the scientific community, the quantum theory was too new; acceptance would have to wait. It could not be incorporated into our metaparadigm either. So it had to be refuted. The old position had to be made stronger, apparently. More denial and resistance, which is one of the stages within scientific revolutions, or metaparadigm shifts. We're getting to that soon. Your clarity will become crystal clear.

Thus, in the 1930's a whole new approach was worked out and *has now become the mainstream view of science,* called logical empiricism. It is still built upon the underlying tenets of scientific materialism. In fact, ironically, in some ways it took science deeper into scientific materialism. Within this description, you'll be able to see the scientific method as taught in school science text books. Logical empiricism has two parts: logic and empiricism. The logic of propositions deals with the way in which several true statements can be combined to produce another true statement, and it is a system of axioms and rules. Axioms are statements one knows from somewhere else, outside of the logic, to be valid. Kind of what gets brought in to form a new hypothesis with two new seemingly unrelated things, and tested to see if there is a relationship between them.

In addition, there are mechanical rules, the laws of logical operations, which show how one can produce new statements by combining different axioms. These are the basic elements of the logic of propositions. "This kind of system is very familiar in the Buddhist tradition, which also has a highly developed logic of propositions. Now we can use this system in science. The axioms are drawn from observations, from experiments. So, in our scientific method, the axioms come from the first step: we look, we derive facts, data," (Hayward 1992). This is the empirical aspect of logical empiricism.

Next is having to rewrite the initial observations in a language that the logic machine, mathematics, can work on. Notice here how it gets even more painfully tight and mechanical by going back to the basics and then adding more onto it, which is inherent to something before it changes. There are really two layers of initial statements, or axioms: there are observation–statements speaking directly about the scientists' observations. These are then turned into theory–statements that combine the conceptually formulated observational elements of their theory with the laws of the theory. Can you feel the attempt at control, the tightness to this process yet?

"Next, we have to process those theory–statements according to mechanical rules of logic, in combinations, the equations of theory, suggested by our theory, to produce new theory–statements. This produces the third step of the scientific method: a new theory–statement that can be turned into a prediction about new observations. These predictions can then be tested, and this is step four of the scientific method...This is how, in a simple way, the logic of propositions becomes the core of science, *with the observations being the input.* You put in the observation statement and turn the logic crank *in the direction suggested by your theory.* Out comes a new statement, and you make a new observation to check this new statement. If it checks, then your theory is correct," (Hayward 1992). We can grasp in that last few sentences a sense of elitism in this process; that only certain people at certain levels are capable of this.

This seems fitting in this stage right before breakdown, otherwise known as denial. Tighter, more constricted and increased strictness with rules, that is. Another name for this is fear. One of the things that is said if we get too far ahead of ourselves with how much change we are creating in our lives and we begin to feel ungrounded—or unstable—it is said to go back to the basics, such as, "Chop wood, carry water," or "go into the kitchen and peel some potatoes." This is a bit different than what was done with logical empiricism in that it isn't fear driven. Yet this is still that nature of when in the face of change, or *expansion*, there seems to be a desire to go back to the basics that seems to almost automatically be a reaction.

One of the interesting things about logical empiricism–and to the general layperson this seems to actually be the very nature of what our science is meant to do –*is that it is a way of satisfying a distrust of common sense*. It is ironic to note that many of our mind body connection solutions are encased within common sense. Like if you frequently feel cold, maybe it is because you need to feel warmer on the inside, not only by putting on another layer of clothing, or turning up the thermostat, but by engaging in activities in your life that bring a sense of "the warm fuzzies," rather than engaging in more "cold" mental and emotional stages of fear, depression or mechanical intellectual activities. The suggestion also might be made to eat spicier foods to heat up your metabolism.

Further irony is contained within one of Albert Einstein's more famous quotes, "The whole of science is nothing more than a refinement of everyday thinking." So it seems that this aversion to common sense and "wishful thinking" is not as regularly acknowledged by the majority of working scientists. Einstein is somewhat of an exception. One can observe a shift in Einstein's thinking from his earlier days in science to his later days–post atomic bomb development–as more of a philosopher. Additionally, Einstein–having dropped out of school–was not one of the scientists so concerned with elitism.

In other words, when the Newtonian world began to break down, apparently it was a breakdown of what feels, again, like common sense. It was a discovery that space is not what it seems to be; time is not what it seems to be; physical matter is not what it seems to be. As physicist Francisco J. Varela explains in that talk he gave at the first MLI summit, entitled "Questions of Method," that as part of the disciplinary matrix required of scientists–specifically from the Enlightenment and on, "The idea was that science went beyond common sense. Answers were no longer just simple; they were complex. So began a notion in science that common sense cannot be trusted. What you can trust is the logical apparatus of mathematics and logic, which is very complex. The distrust of common sense brought about the entire reformulation of science so that it would have a very precise machinery that would not depend on common sense. This is why the results of science often times are contrary to common sense. But scientists are very proud of this... The phrase that one reads a lot in logical empiricist texts is, 'cleansing the foundations,' making things work. This *means clearing out what seems to be just the noise of ordinary ideas that don't match the standard of what should be scientific theory,*" (italics mine) (Hayward 1992). Does this remind you of the Enlightenment scientists turned promoters of the X club?

It is important to keep in mind that these observations are initially being chosen to be focused on while choosing to *not* focus on other objects or phenomena. Then these observations are being made, and then these theories are being formulated from these observations by a human mind within a human being who is a scientist. Werner Heisenberg is the German physicist who won the Nobel Prize in Physics in 1932 for the creation of quantum mechanics. He is best known for his foundational contributions to quantum theory. In the beginning stages of quantum physics shaking up the metaparadigm of scientific materialism, Heisenberg stated, "What we observe is not nature itself, but nature exposed to *our method of questioning.*"

So discussing both what quantum physics discovered about matter no longer found to be the basic building block, and the scientific method itself is necessary. Why? Because the nature of what quantum physics discovered basically makes the scientific method null and void. The scientific method goes against the very nature of what is now known to be that the universe breaks down to, *which is a subtle force;* energy and not matter. Furthermore, as it is understood now due to quantum physics, observing anything causes what is being observed to change (because everything is energy, meaning both the Observer and the phenomena being observed), again, known as the observer effect.

Specifically, the wave, full of energy with the potential to be anything, *once observed or thought of as something,* then collapses from its potential state and into a particle of matter, as *some thing*. Typically, it's that very *something it's expected to collapse into by the observer observing it that it becomes*. Now it's a particle–meaning at the level of matter. One more thing is needed for this to make sense. It's an interactive universe at its core, as the Observer effect implies. It's hugely important to note that it is this Observer effect that starts this chain of events.

Yet also what's implied here—and discussed in other parts of this book—is that all this energy is interconnected. So it's an energy soup, of interaction and interconnection. We are not separate from this energy, or consciousness. We inherently are connected to it, and we interact with it— whether we recognize it or not. So obviously, it would behoove us to learn how to intentionally interact with this bigger field of consciousness, rather than interact with it by default. More on that in just a bit. It does sound a bit like that much loved and hated movie, The Secret. The worth of that movie is to introduce the concept of this interaction existing. Yet if you think to images of people doing Tai Chi or Chi Gong —what are they interacting with? This is an alive universe, fundamentally. In the new sciences, William Tiller, Rupert Sheldrake, and Lynne McTaggart all are scientists who have done work and written on the discoveries of this greater field.

The bottom line here is what has come into question as a result from quantum physics is what the universe breaks down to, and the way this "stuff it breaks down to" works. Interesting that the two come crashing down together–the scientific method's methodology ultimately being unreliable to be objective, and it not being physical matter as the base to the universe. It is almost as if this coupling was a reinforced mandate that it was time to give up the metaparadigm. Still, it's almost 100 years later. And it's still the way the masses view science, and what our society still operates under.

Let's back up though. First, with the development of quantum theory, physicists have found that even subatomic particles are far from solid, right? This means, matter is not solid material at the subatomic level, as scientific *materialism*'s basic tenet claims. "In fact, they–these particles–are nothing like matter as we know it. They cannot be pinned down and measured precisely. Much of the time they seem more like waves than particles. They are like fuzzy clouds of potential existence, with no definite location. *Whatever matter is, it has little, if any, substance*" (italics mine) (Russell 2002).

Backing up even a bit more, "The 20th century is a remarkable story of technological achievement. Within a few decades, electricity, radio and TV, not to mention lasers, fiber optics, plastics and computers, have all become an everyday facet of our lives. I take for granted that I can turn on a TV set in Hawaii and receive, almost instantaneously, a program that originated in Atlanta or New York. Only a short time ago exchanging information between New York and Hawaii required the same time it takes to send a spacecraft to Mars today. Except for power failures, few people in the developed world know what it was like for most of the human species every night, throughout 99 percent of our history, to face the blackness of space and its sea of stars alone without the reassuring lights of civilization. We live in a special time. Never before has such intense, radical technological change taken place...We will see that there has been another radical change: Something very strange has happened to reality along the way," (Pine 2010).

By 1908 one of the atom's basic properties, its indestructible unity as the smallest thing in the universe, had been literally blown apart. Prior to this, in 1897, the English physicist J.J. Thomson had discovered a tiny, fast-moving particle with a negative electric charge that he called the "electron"; the electron is smaller than the atom, it is subatomic. Later, Rutherford in 1911 discovered something very hard within the atoms of gold, harder than a swarm of lightweight electrons, and so he concluded these to be the nucleus. Thus, through the observation of regularities and consistencies found in experimental data, Rutherford and the scientists who succeeded him contributed to a new model of the atom as having a hard, compact nucleus surrounded by orbiting electrons–a solar model. All of this had been discovered by reasoning from scientific evidence, based on the underlying principles of Newtonian physics. This is impressive knowledge about an invisible realm.

"At first physicists assumed that the atom was like a miniature solar system. At the center was a nucleus *consisting of particles*, glued together somehow, and circling the nucleus were the swiftly moving electrons, like little particle planets. This model did not last long. Although we still use a version of this model today to have some visual handle on what the atom looks like, scientists discovered fairly quickly that mathematical calculations based on this model predicted that the electron would crash into the nucleus in an instant. Physicists also discovered that electrons could be stripped from the atoms and made into beams of radiation. This was a great breakthrough, because scientists could manipulate these beams and began to deduce from the beam's behavior the nature of the electron itself. A similar channel of investigation was taking place in attempting to understand the nature of light. From this, another remarkable discovery was made: beams of electrons behave very much like beams of light!" (Pine 2010). Note that this initial, apparently wrong, model of atoms described above is what is still taught today, in elementary and middle school science text books.

This problem with the solar model of the atom's electrons and nuclei was that *according to the classical laws of motion* and electromagnetism, specifically, if charged particles such as electrons moved in circular orbits, they had to emit electromagnetic energy; yet by doing so, they would lose energy quickly and spiral downward to crash into the nucleus. So in 1913 Neils Bohr theorized that the atom's electrons orbited in fixed locations. They were locked into invisible shells around the nucleus according to fixed energy levels, with a specific quantity of energy needed to move an electron from one shell to another.

This idea came from quantum physics, which had been introduced to the world almost by accident in 1900 by the German physicist Max Planck. Planck had been trying to find a principle behind the way light radiation was emitted from materials when heated. During his work, he discovered the experiment did not produce the expected results. He then came up with the quanta theory, as a result. The principle behind the quanta theory is that quanta were energy *bursts* of fixed intensity and *specific frequencies, not the expected steadiness of equal amounts of light energy that should have been emitted at all frequencies,* as according to classical Newtonian physics.

Planck's quanta theory made sense of the atom, "*but largely wiped out Newton and company when it came to understanding the atomic and subatomic world.* This was an extremely serious blow for classical physics; its laws, aimed at obtaining a complete understanding of the 'cause of causes' that scientists had been hunting for centuries, had proven inadequate," (italics mine) (Wallace 2008). *It appeared that the world of the tiniest, yet most basic and important constituents of the universe, might be governed by other, quite different laws.*

This science of the subatomic realm is called quantum physics or quantum mechanics. The word "quanta" refers to the energy at the microscopic, or subatomic, realm that comes in packets, or quanta (think waves). Energy is said to be "discrete" rather than continuous (think no more predictability). The famous phrase "quantum jump" comes from science, to refer to the implications of this discrete motion of energy.

Even though at the beginning of this road 100 years ago or so where physicists just wanted to understand the nature of subatomic objects such as the electron and the photon–again, the basic unit of light–it lead to a revolution. These ideas were thought so radical that even Einstein could not accept them. By now, though, these once revolutionary ideas have been around long enough to have been studied and worked with. Their meanings and implications have now begun to be applied to other areas of life by those on the cutting edge, to the chagrin of most laboratory, orthodox scientists.

This includes the idea that we, with our thoughts, can and do affect reality. Moreover, we are more in charge of what happens in using our free will and thoughts than ever considered possible before. This wouldn't even have been conceived of, unless one wanted to be considered "off," when limited within the confines of the focus on only the physical from the scientific materialist metaparadigm. Yet now, it is an exciting revolution with the possible outcomes hugely positive and optimistic for humans and the evolution of humankind and consciousness. Yet it is still, even having begun a hundred years ago, in its infancy stages as far as our mainstream institutions, our medical system, our schools, our church's and synagogues, and even still in most mainstream science labs. This infancy has quickly matured into its teen years over the past twenty years, though. And it's part of the reason why things have begun to feel so unstable, comparatively. And somewhat why change seems to be happening so much quicker.

It's almost as if what has been discovered by science has mirrored the evolution of humans. Perhaps also propelling humans, or maybe the other way around. Or, maybe it's us being propelled into this new awareness of how life works, coming to us through science and other means, too. So overall, it has been in the collective consciousness, as Jung referred to that place we discussed before—i.e., the field—and the idea was ready to be plucked out of it, first by a few, and then later, gradually more and more people. Perhaps some were the quantum physicists, but this has also been propelled by the non-scientists making use of these discoveries, interpreting them and applying them to other aspects of life, outside of the laboratory. This further fueled some of the new sciences' efforts, and at some point the momentum kicked in as more and more pioneering people became aware of how our thoughts interact with the field and our consciousness is connected to this field, and so have been working with their own consciousness.

These scientific discoveries are only part of the picture of the times of change we're in. Because, remember, these discoveries were first made a hundred years ago, and it is only in the past twenty years or so that they've begun to really be more actively accepted and worked with and built upon, reaching beyond just the scientific laboratories. So now over this past twenty years, the momentum has kicked into a higher gear. Now this information is being spread out to an increasingly wider audience, becoming more rapidly accepted now, as opposed to those first twenty years with the start of this momentum, never mind when it was first discovered by quantum physics.

So, the three decades from 1900 to 1930 were among the most intense and productive in the history of physics. "The quest to understand the dizzying implications of quantum physics (and relativity) brought together some of the sharpest scientific minds on the planet. One of the most puzzling features—and one that must always be born in mind—is that quantum physics was strikingly successful in predicting the results of experiments. Furthermore, like the classical physics that preceded it, numerous important, practical inventions emerged from quantum theory, including lasers, transistors, computer chips, and photoelectric cells, not to mention the mixed blessings that came from understanding radioactivity; the atomic clock, atomic generation of electricity, radiation medicine, carbon–14 dating, and nuclear weapons," (Wallace 2008). Yet this success is considered puzzling because *quantum physics does not in any normal sense explain how physical events happen.* "Quantum theory—even though it is dealing with such uncertainty—is itself highly consistent; and at the very minimum, quantum physics *implies that clear knowledge of physical processes cannot be obtained.* This was a severe blow to metaphysical realism: even if there are underlying, transcendental mechanisms governing matter and energy, *according to quantum physics we cannot know them with any precision,"* (italics mine) (Wallace 2008). This is a huge statement and deserves to be re-read. So what did and does this mean for the future of science's purpose?

At the turn of the 20th century, with the theory of relativity which will be briefly explained soon, both the speed of light and the nature of light were highly controversial and somewhat of a paradox. This made Einstein say, "I want to spend the rest of my life studying light." In 1905 Albert Einstein made the key discovery about how light is emitted and absorbed according to quantum principles; called the photoelectric effect. This earned Einstein a Nobel Prize. What Einstein found ran counter to classical physics, *which viewed light as waves with smooth, variations in intensity,* kind of like a dimmer switch for lights. What Einstein discovered was that *a threshold had to be reached, and then the metal emitted an electron instantaneously, as if a switch had been flipped.* This is considered its quantum, or the minimum payment in photons, needed to emit an electron.

This led to quantum physicists challenging the Newtonian belief just mentioned, that light was a wave phenomenon with consistent, smooth, and predictable variations in behavior; as it was understood by Newtonian physics, this ultimately demonstrated the particle–like characteristics of light. Soon after within quantum physics, it was shown that these particles, or photons of light, could themselves act like waves. Yet waves and particles are viewed as opposites in Newtonian physics because particles are matter and waves are energy–and energy is subtle and unseen.

For clarity now, the definition of subtle from dictionary.com is, "thin, tenuous or rarefied as a fluid or odor." Quantum physics further discovered that at the atomic level, particles–photons, electrons, neutrons, protons, and other subatomic entities–could also behave as waves, creating reflection, diffraction (bending around obstacles), and interference patterns. And they could do so not just through interactions with other particles *but by interfering with themselves.* This is part of where it gets kind of like Alice in Wonderlandesque–a single particle could interfere with itself as if it were a wave.

What was found was that under some conditions light seemed to behave as if it consisted of very small particles of matter, which are now called photons. Yet under other conditions, light showed clear signs of being a wave of energy, considered a disturbance of a medium in whatever ways the intensity of this disturbance was able to be measured. So this is a problem, how can one thing–light–be both matter (particles) and energy (waves and light) at the same time? So it's not just matter, anymore, as it seems is being said to scientific materialism at this point. *This paradox is what led to the quantum mechanics shake up of our understanding of what reality is based on, due to the mutual existence of both the particle and the wave–both of which were found to be contained within light–*previously being thought of as very different things within Newtonian physics.

A particle is much more dependable and would have allowed us to remain–somewhat, anyways–in the scientific materialism metaparadigm. So these dual aspects of light came to be known as the "wave/particle duality," *yet these dual aspects actually mysteriously complement each other, rather than fight for dominance. This is key.* Particularly in its metaphor for the macroshift our globalized world is currently undergoing. This principle is called *complementarity,* coined by Niels Bohr, who said that these two complementary aspects were not contradictory but "'only together offer a natural generalization of the classical mode of description.' *In other words, the only way one can make heads or tails of this behavior is to combine the two opposite activities–wave/particle,*" (italics mine) (Wallace 2008). What this means is looking at the two as a complimentary whole. We could then understand them by looking at their relationship, rather than reduce the whole into two separate parts with our reductionism. This might help us in new ways. Because it's also what's being called for in many other areas of life and society. And it's reminiscent of what we explored in the discussion about the East's metaparadigm of holistic thinking. The Chinese yin-yang is an ancient symbol depicting this; and it has gained a recent resurgence of trendiness, yes?

And because we do; we look at one part–particle–or the other–waves (energy), and not necessarily their complimentary functions with each other, and their ensuing inseparability due to their combined function within the whole. This is what we get when we come from the scientific materialist approach So we miss what this relationship and whole picture means, and implies for us and life. Now learning from contrast is a way to learn, for certain. It's one of the main tools I use in the classroom to make distinctions for people when first learning a concept. It is this, but it is not that. Beyond the initial learning stage—think Bloom's taxonomy—there then is a synthesis phase. This is the last phase in the learning process, synthesizing new information into the whole picture of what else we know, to see how this new information fits and what it means to us.

A particle is a piece of matter, like a Frisbee, that at any given time has a definite size, speed and location. Right? This is still reliable. A Frisbee thrown in Florida cannot be in California at the same time, right? According to Newtonian physics, no it cannot. Furthermore, we assume that we may discover in this incredible universe some very strange objects, yet regardless of how strange they are, if they are objects, then they will have a definite location at any given definite time. This is part of the solidity of the Newtonian model, and scientific materialism, and it is solid, grounded, and predictable. Any object, such as a Frisbee, cannot be in two places at the same time. That is the stuff of science fiction movies, and maybe cool mystical feats of bilocation that wise male gurus of the East can obtain, or perhaps something that the CIA or the military–industrial complex is working on producing with expensive computers, software and gadgets. But as we know it, in our reality defined by the solidity of Newtonian physics, an object out there in the external reality cannot be located in two places at the same time. This certainty is part of the certainty that material, or the physical, offers us within scientific materialism, and our solid, physical world. Safe. Predictable. End of discussion.

But a wave, well, it's quite a different type of a thing. Really, it'd be more appropriate to refer to it not as a thing at all because "thing" is reserved for physical phenomena, and a wave does not behave like a particle. Meaning, a wave does not follow the laws of the physical world, or the material plane, or scientific materialism. This, again, is the beginning of the breakdown here of scientific materialism's metaparadigm. *And it's the beginning of a scientific revolution* as scientific revolutions are defined by Thomas Kuhn. Kuhn is considered the specialist in scientific revolutions, or paradigm shifts. This shift of our time we are speaking of is a revolution, eventually impacting all aspects of life, taking over as the next metaparadigm. And it totally shakes us out of our comfort zone of what reality is here in the West, especially in America.

In America not only do we ground in the material, we celebrate it. This isn't meant as a criticism; it's meant as an observation as one of the outcomes of having the scientific metaparadigm we have had since our inception. One only has to look at the size of our houses and cars, and then comparatively, look at the typical house and car sizes in Europe and Asia, and the contrast makes this factor clearly seen. One possible feed of this American deepening of the materialist paradigm could be the vastness of our country's land, and its relative population size, historically, compared to that, historically, of Europe and Asia. Perhaps also the American Constitution, within which everyone has equal rights to life, liberty and the pursuit of happiness–and big toys make many happy. Big homes and big cars yield freedom, as well, to those who translate freedom this way. Historically, this has been quite American, in the bigger, the better. It's been part of the American Dream, to freely pursue one's dreams and make lots of money. And then if desired, to then focus it on the physical purchases of tangible things, including the cool technology that we typically produce and enjoy.

Additionally, the archetypal masculine mind likes predictability, while the archetypal feminine mind seems better at multitasking and adjusting to variability. Due to our sciences having been dominated by males with the archetypal masculine mind, or the masculine cognitive style, with the male mind tending to appreciate the tangible and feel more comfortable there, helps to also explain this focus on the physical. The resistance to both the unpredictability and the lack of solidity as discovered in quantum physics connects to this perspective. Our country has been a patriarchy since its inception. Finally, there is also the view that American men–and now American women–are typically both more masculine when compared to either gender in other countries, particularly when compared to their gender specific counterparts in the East. This last point will be revisited later. It seems that we've had the land, space, and legal right to be free and to expand as big as we've seen fit–including landing on the moon–here in America, *and all of this speaks to the focus on the physical, and not going internal, not focusing on the subtle nor the subjective.*

So we return now, back to quantum physics. Based on a wave, reality is not solid, it is not predictable, it is not physically based, it is not structured so that everything can be broken down into smaller and smaller parts with a linear sense and the biggest has the most power. It is also no longer the physical that is the strongest, or primary, of the two–the physical versus the subtle. "Things" have a definite localized size at a given definite time, by definition. Waves do not. Picture a common analogy used to explain this wave concept, as a part of quantum physics: dropping a pebble into a still pond of water, where there is a splash at first, and then circular waves move away from the spot where we dropped the pebble. The wave spreads out; it does not stay in one place, in fact it can be in many places at the same time. *Also, it is the medium of the water that transmits the energy of the dropped pebble. The wave is simply a disturbance of the medium. It does not have an existence of its own; without the water in the pond, there would be no waves.* This is critical in appreciating the fundamentals of this new metaparadigm. It should feel a bit like Eastern mystical teachings, or like Taoist Chinese thought as explored earlier.

Ok, now take this visualization one step further to understand more of the quantum mechanics discovery in physics. You're at the beach one day, relaxing while watching wave after wave come in towards the shore. The waves break after their peak into the white surf. This is what then reaches the shore prior to going back out to sea. But suddenly, instead, we see one wave flow in its normal peaking-then-breaking way toward the beach. Then, just as the wave was about to touch the first bits of vulnerable sand, the entire half circle of water the wave is collapsed instantly to a single unpredictable point on the beach and exploded! The wave would have turned into a massive particle located at one place, rather than spread out as waves typically are, and do. Imagine that wave after wave did this, with the location of the collapse being unpredictable each time. Completely odd this would be, right? But this is apparently, something like what electrons and photons do. And it is totally different than the Newtonian physics typical analogy of two pool balls on the green felt pool table. We push with our stick the white cue ball that then predictably comes into contact with, say, the yellow striped nine ball, moving the nine ball into the corner pocket. This is what we relied on Newtonian physics' law of motion to tell us. Cause and effect is completely observable and predictable; solid matter hitting it in a predictable way as it works with gravity.

As Murray Gell–Mann said, "All of modern physics is governed by that magnificent and thoroughly confusing discipline called quantum mechanics...It has survived all tests and there is no reason to believe that there is any flaw in it...We all know how to use it and how to apply it to problems: and so we have learned to live with the fact that nobody can understand it." Murray Gell–Mann comes at this statement quite honestly, due to his own personal experience. In 1969 he received the Nobel Prize in Physics for his work on the theory of elementary particles. He is the author of *The Quark and the Jaguar,* published in 1994, in which his ideas on simplicity and complexity are presented to a general readership. Among his contributions to Physics was the "eightfold way" scheme that *"brought order out of the chaos"* created by the discovery of some 100 kinds of particles in collisions involving atomic nuclei. However, and here is how he comes by this quote quite honestly, Gell–Mann subsequently found that all of those particles, including the neutron and proton, are composed of fundamental building blocks that he named 'quarks,' *with very unusual properties.* That idea has since been fully confirmed by experiment. The quarks are permanently confined by forces coming from the exchange of 'gluons.' He and others later constructed the quantum field theory of quarks and gluons, called 'quantum chromodynamics,' *which seems to account for all the nuclear particles and their strong interactions,"* (italics mine) (Nobelprize.org 2010).

Why has it been so hard to accept? This chaos? The idea that the subjective mind of the scientists affects the outcome of the experiment? The idea that this quanta activity remains elusive to pin down to predictability? Because, as German physicist Max Born, who won the 1954 Nobel Peace Prize for Physics, said, "We have sought for firm ground and found none. The deeper we penetrate, the more restless becomes the universe; all is rushing about and vibrating in a wild dance." Born was instrumental in the development of quantum mechanics–he worked with Heisenberg on quanta "jumping" by bringing the algebraic matrix to quantum mechanics, in order to mathematically work out the jumping that quanta so mysteriously does, rather than the more predictable, linear, sequential movements from Newtonian physics. So, Max Born, with his study and therefore familiarity with this quantum jumping also proclaimed, "No language which lends itself to visualizability can describe quantum jumps," (Pine 1999). What Born says here is strongly reminiscent of what the great Taoist masters said about The Tao being unable to be described; and if you can, then that isn't The Tao. It's too elusive for verbal explanation; instead it has to be experienced.

Robert C. Pine himself, Ph.D. in philosophy and professor of Philosophy at the University of Hawaii's Honolulu's Community College then goes on to say within his online chapter "Quantum Physics and Reality" from his book *Science and the Human Prospect* that Eastern mysticism is also consistent with the results of quantum physics. The mystics have always rejected the idea of a hidden clocklike mechanism, Pine explains. The clockwork precision of the universe is that concept Western science fully developed in the Enlightenment era while still being partially based on the ancient Greek philosophers as well. This is the belief that the external universe is knowable through study and deductive reasoning, and it exists independent of human observation in this precise, dependable clocklike way. Right?

Pine says, "*The number one truth is that reality does not consist of separate things, but is an indescribable, interconnected oneness. Each object of our normal experience is seen to be but a brief disturbance of a (sic) universal ocean of existence. Maya is the illusion that the phenomenal world of separate objects and people is the only reality. For the mystics this manifestation is real, but it is a fleeting reality; it is a mistake, although a neutral one, to believe that maya* [this illusion of separateness between people/objects] *represents a fundamental reality,*" (italics mine) (Pine 1999).

Pine, the philosopher that he is, then goes on to say that epistemologically, *our so-called knowledge of the world is actually only a projection or creation of thoughts, and that reality is ambiguous.* "We have seen that in the realm of the quantum, dynamic particle attributes such as 'spin', 'location', and 'velocity' are best thought of as relational or phenomenal realities. It is a mistake to think of these properties out there; rather, *they are the result of experimental arrangements and ultimately the thoughts of the experimenters.* Quantum particles have a partial appearance of individuality, but experiments show that the *true nature of the quantum lies* beyond *description in human terms.* Our filters (our minds' background and experiences) produce the manifestations we see, and the result is just incomplete enough to point to another kind of reality, an ambiguous reality of 'not this, not that.' For the mystic, the paradoxes of quantum physics are just another symptom of humankind's attempt to describe what can only be experienced," (Pine 1999).

Clearly, Pine is interpreting, as has been discussed, the loss of the distinctive lines between the objective and subjective, which has confounded scientists. Furthermore, the lack of solidity and predictability is implied within Pine's quote. There is also the sense of the human need and desire as shown within the tracing of the history of Western science to explain and to understand everything. This is even if that means taking our projections and putting them out onto the universe, erroneously while hopeful, and doing so, to varying degrees, unconsciously.

"The proliferation of philosophical interpretations of quantum physics is a symptom of a *traditional Western way of understanding, of our inability to 'let go' of our Western torch–our traditional logic and epistemology. It is also a symptom of our inability to let of our egocentricity, our persistent attempt to define everything in purely human terms, as if we were somehow special and separate from the rest of the universe.* Like a nervous, self–centered teenager at a party, concerned only with what others think of him or her, our entire field of vision and understanding is narrowly defined in terms of 'me.' *Because of our fear of letting go, we are missing much that is right in front of us,"* (italics mine) (Pine 1999). This connects back to the fear previously discussed that typically comes up in the face of changes or the unknown; resistance is another label for it.

Pine then goes on to offer that there are quite a few interpretations of the implications of these discoveries of the quantum world, and the one explored above is just one. It is a popular one; it is the same one put forth by

Fritjof Capra in *The Tao of Physics*, and by Gary Zukav in *The Dancing Wu Li Masters* and by Amit Goswami, the retired physics professor who was an advisor to the Institute of Noetic Sciences, by Gregg Braden... and by many, many others, too numerous to list, who have this same interpretation. There are critics of this interpretation because of its usage of quantum physics; and ironically, their criticism of this interpretation is the same as what Kuhn says occurs in the face of a paradigm shift in *The Structure of Scientific Revolutions*.

According to Pine, the critics purport that "it is just plain silly to interpret an ancient belief system, founded upon certain psychological needs and within a historical context, in terms of any modern perspective. It is obvious, they argue [these critics] how the Hindu and Buddhist beliefs could soothe people living under extreme conditions. If our day–to–day reality is but a fleeting manifestation, then the vicious misfortune and meaningless suffering of this world are not real. For these critics, the methodology of psychological need as an origin of these ideas implies there is no connection. *By revealing the obvious psychological motivation for a set of beliefs, it is argued, one can question the truth of these beliefs. To further suggest that there is any connection between these beliefs and the results of rigorous experimental science is ludicrous [according to the critics of this interpretation],*" (italics mine) (Pine 1999).

Yet this is what Kuhn says in his *The Structure of Scientific Revolutions* is the common thread behind paradigms shifting in science–an understanding that the experiments were conducted by outdated assumptions lead the hypothesis testing. Again, many echo this statement in modern day, as the resistance within mainstream science to have applications to life–not technology–come out of the laboratory *especially* if the application matches something ancient civilizations already knew without rigorous scientific testing.

Finally, Pine makes a suggestion after offering a book chapter's worth of the descriptions of scientists' struggle to contend with the implications of what quantum physics uncovered. Obviously, the fact that he spends a chapters worth on this struggle in and of itself should yield the observation by now of just how shattering the quantum physics experiments with the subatomic phenomena of quanta and its behavior are. They are that inherently difficult to reconcile with our normal view of an objective world.

Again, this is due, in summary, to what particles of matter were thought to supposed to be, according to Newtonian physics and the world we thought we lived in. Independent objects are located in one place at a time, independent of any subjective influence. But then when the observation was repeatedly made that the waves can spread out and/or split and could *be in many places at the same time, Newtonian physics' conclusions in this regard were found to be erroneous.* Furthermore, all the experiments with subatomic phenomena show wave–particle duality, so nothing at the sub–atomic level is clearly, definitively able to be pinpointed as matter only. Our observing, or our consciousness' presence, causes change in the wave and particle behavior was another blow to the solidity thought to exist. So that, rather than a definitive, objective world, reality seems to be quite frustratingly ambiguous at the quantum level, and effected if not created, by our own thoughts.

Although a very successful mathematics was developed enabling physicists to interact with, explore, and extend applications of subatomic reality, as Pine says, "The interpretation of the mathematics is a philosophical muddle. One of the most influential interpretations of quantum physics was that of Niels Bohr and what has come to be called the Copenhagen interpretation. According to this interpretation, the ambiguity and complementarity of quantum experimentation reveal a startling pragmatic, epistemological discovery: Our macroscopic experiments must be conducted from the point of view of a human conceptual reference frame, *but nature at the quantum level need not, and apparently does not, conform to macroscopic concepts.* Accordingly, what we measure in our quantum experiments are the results of *our* relationship with nature, *not nature itself,*" (italics mine) (Pine 1999).

Between moments of preparation and measurement of quantum events, "there is nothing definitive to know, understand, or measure, because nature has revealed to us that there is nothing there that can be conceptualized in human terms. Subatomic phenomena such as photons and electrons become definitive objects only after measurements are made with macroscopic equipment," (Pine 1999). What? How can that be? This is where the Alice in Wonderlandesque aspect comes in, as if chasing Alice down the rabbit hole, scientists chasing the quanta around with their microscopes in the lab, trying to pin down the activity at the subatomic level with an explanation.

Because Einstein was convinced that the job of science is to reveal the clockwork mechanism of nature itself, not just the probabilistic results

Alison J. Kay, PhD

of our relationship or experimental tinkering with nature, he objected to this interpretation. "Quantum theory could not be a complete theory. *For Einstein there was an underlying reality that we did not understand yet*; for Bohr, the goal of knowing an underlying, definitive reality was an antiquated philosophical relic of classical physics. For Einstein, the Copenhagen interpretation implied defeatism at its best and classical idealism at its worse. For Bohr, many fruitful explorations still exist, relationships yet to be described and mathematical trails yet to be followed, but the search for a 'hidden' reality will not be one of them," (Pine 1999). Here you can see Einstein's resistance to the changes coming that are implied by what was being revealed by quantum theory. Especially when he is contrasted against Bohr's acceptance of the anomalous behavior of quanta, and Bohr's looking forward to what these discoveries had opened up for a new level of truth about the universe.

The work of Bell and Aspect resulted in a strong experimental confirmation that in the quantum realm it is wrong to think of quantum phenomena as independent hidden entities influenced by independent local circumstances. Pine then clarifies, "Like Newton confronting the problem of gravity, most physicists in this century have been trained to adopt a pragmatic or instrumentalist stance to these results – science is suppose to describe the objective properties of experiments, not to speculate on a hidden reality between measurements. But the compelling need for a philosophical understanding produced numerous proposals," (Pine 1999).

Finally, Pine's discussion comes around; as all do eventually that involve quantum physics, to consciousness. "Some physicist–philosophers argued that the success of *quantum theory shows that far from being a secondary quality, consciousness has a major causal role in the universe; it produces a definitive, relationship–reality from an ambiguous, featureless whole.* David Bohm suggested that an interpretation of radical neorealism is still possible, one which describes a *multidimensional hyperspace of implicate wholeness 'behind' the explicate or definitive reality of our common–sense world,*" (italics mine) (Pine 1999).

Offering yet another interpretation by the seemingly scurrying activity of scientists to explain and interpret these results, includes some who claim that we must abandon traditional realism altogether, that the world cannot be pictured as "sitting out there" for us to uncover. Our "participation" with an intermingled dance of possibilities yields a concrete reality. So this ultimately brings Pine to say that "Most physicists, concerned with the daily demands of obtaining research grants and Nobel Prizes, have simply filed such demonstrations away and continued with the Einsteinian quest, searching for more and more exotic particles, new 'things' that will prove the supersymmetry theories, unifying all the known forces of nature and catapulting our understanding to the first microseconds of the universe and perhaps beyond," (Pine 1999). The tone adopted by Pine here is reflective of many, *many* authors' tones when dealing with the way the majority of scientists have behaved, including a bounty of scientists themselves, in regards to the elusive mystery that quantum mechanics is.

"Yet in spite of Nobel Prizes for the discovery of these new particles and public pronouncements that the end of the Einsteinian quest is near, one senses that all is not well with this approach. Physicists themselves complain that the proliferation of particles necessary to explain everything is too complex to be consistent with a simple universe. One senses many ad hoc approaches and a situation not unlike followers of Ptolemy adding epicycle to make the data fit," (Pine 1999). This is reflective not only of Ptolemy adding epicycles, but of the scientists trying to explain what Copernicus discovered. Ironic that what Ptolemy began, Copernicus picked up centuries later, and then it took another 150 years and three other scientists to finally get the understanding that the earth revolves around the sun. The shift from our metaparadigm of scientific materialism ignited by the quantum physics discoveries is very similar to the metaparadigm shift Copernicus began that brought us into Newtonian physics, or scientific materialism.

Ultimately, what Pine ends his chapter on "Quantum Physics and Reality" with is nearly synonymous with Kuhn's idea of the structure of scientific revolutions. Pine completes with, "Some experiments reveal serious anomalies. Particles that allegedly consist of a 'bag' of quarks are not supposed to pass through each other, but in some cases, if the spins are just right, they do! *One senses that nature is not yet ready to succumb completely to our latest gestures of understanding. Every past success at understanding has produced new mysteries. Why should it be any different now? Perhaps the results of quantum physics...are revealing to us a great discovery after all. This great partner we call the universe is not a static personality, but grows and is formed by us, as we are by it.* There is every reason to believe that our romance will continue, that there are many mysteries left for a new generation of physicists. Although there will have been many pretenders since the time of Kepler, no one has yet read the mind of God," (italics mine) (Pine 1999). This non–static and instead interactive "personality" of the universe is akin to the Chinese concept of Chi and its interaction with humans and all life forms. This is an interactive relationship that is very much influenced by each of us and our consciousness. This is as if co–partners, or co–creators of what we then see as physical reality.

Our Brain Knows the Known Only, So What Happens When We Want Something New?

Peter Russell in *From Science to God* with his chapter, "The Anomaly of Consciousness echoes Pine by first describing the concept of "the hard problem" of consciousness, naming David Chalmers, Professor of Philosophy at the University of Arizona, as the originator of this term. Russell then differentiates between the "hard problem of consciousness" and the so-called "easy problems." "Easy problems" are what we think of as cognitive functioning, or those concerned with brain function and its correlation with mental phenomena. Says Russell, "how, for example, we discriminate, categorize, and react to stimuli; how incoming sensory data are integrated with past experience; how we focus our attention; and what distinguishes wakefulness from sleep." (Russell 2002). Any Western introductory psychology class provides basic understandings in each of these areas. I taught these whenever teaching a college level introductory psychology class.

All of this is the more mechanical functioning of the brain, and related to physical phenomena. Even the incoming sensory data is taught that it is interpreted by our perception processes, and is mechanical. What is not typically focused on is that our perceptual machinery is programmed from our past experiences. If a professor or instructor of the introductory psychology material is aware of the implications of this, then they'll focus on the implication of the importance that our brain's cognition is only able to function based on what we already know. Further, this means our brain, or cognitive mind, is not geared towards being able to access what is as of yet, unknown or unfamiliar to us. This is a key distinction.

The brain receives the sensory stimuli from the environment and then proceeds to run through its data bank of previously experienced stimuli to be able to label the stimuli and hence, create a labeled and understood perception. Meaning, if I sense with one of my five physical senses–see–something foreign in a foreign country like a fruit, my brain will run through its files of previously seen fruit (I'm at a fruit stand so it automatically refers to the appropriate "data bank") and produces a label that will be connected to what I know–i.e., the Asian pear, which is not really a pear. But what I am looking at looks the closest, in the family of fruit that I've seen before, to a pear. Hence, "Asian Pear." We have to have a reference point, and our brain runs through the process of finding one and providing a label so quickly we are unaware that this is what it's actually doing. And even though this is taught in any introductory psychology course within the material that discusses the mechanistic functions of the brain, this is not just dry, mechanistic cognition of the brain's wheels. Yet because of the nature of the field of psychology working to be considered seriously as a hard science, and all that we've discussed about scientific materialism's focus on the physical, this implication is not touched upon at all in the texts, nor usually the classes—nor the field of psychology itself, who we turn to tell us about the mind.

The supremely important aspect that our cognition, again, draws on the databank only of what we know or have known before in order to label the perceptions we're having implies so much, as you are starting to see by now. I ask you to really consider this. Really; spend some time reviewing and thinking about what is being presented here. *All that we see and end up labeling is labeled what it is from our data bank of previous experiences and encounters of a similar nature.* So we end up not stepping too far outside of the familiar, if we go with this momentum. It also keeps us feeling that when in a new environment or situation this is still familiar to us, based on what our brain is pulling up to help us understand what we're experiencing.

This frequently unacknowledged aspect of how and why we perceive what we think we do is mostly overlooked in the field of psychology. And most certainly by the average person going about their daily business within the material plane of work, commuting to and from work, interacting with others at work, home life and cooking, eating, cleaning, television viewing, internet usage and the general existence on the solid physical plane, one remains unaware of this primary way of why we view the world the way we do. If our brain does not have a previous file that it can access when coming across a new sensory stimuli from our environment then it will choose the closest known previous perception and label. Its function is not really to deal with the unknown. Our brain does not like unknowns.

So then what has also gone overlooked and under-acknowledged is how the cognitive brain, or mind, can not be used to access something new, unknown and unfamiliar to us. This carries huge implications for the process of changing ourselves, and becoming something far different than what we were raised to be. In the coaching industry and personal development field it is known by the better practitioners and coaches that to have success with our clients, we need to guide people *away from their cognitive minds* because that is where the conclusions are people use as the limitations to why they can't change. We then engage a different part of a client's consciousness in order to really help them get the huge changes when going for more in their lives. We're helping our clients go beyond what their family had ever gotten to, or their home community or culture. Another way to say this is how to help someone step out of their comfort zone in order to reach for more; particularly, even more than they could even imagine for themselves as to how life could and can be for them. The weakness in being able to imagine this very different existence a client may desire for themselves is this very mechanism we have been talking about within the cognitive brain. So it's not just that you can't change, or you're lame.

In an oversimplified way, this function of our brain is also why we stereotype, generalize, and dismiss new phenomena in our environment. The inherent function of our perceptual machinery in our brain is to render the unknown a known. *So what influences our perception and its files?* Our background, meaning our culture, our family upbringing, our gender, our education, our exposure or lack thereof to new and different people and ideas. All of this contributes to what is known as our "perceptual sets" that we carry around in our brain as our data files on what is possible in our world, *and its due to our background.*

This is a very simplified presentation of the process—books and much involved, lengthy discussions have been written on this topic, frequently in connection to the issues of: is the brain free of subjective influence, and what is influenced by our personal histories—of what we experience? Another typical topic that covers this discussion is what is really mechanical just the brain but not the mind? But again, this aspect of how our cognitive brains are geared towards the familiar is typically left out of the discussion. That opinions, beliefs, judgments and conclusions about how the world does and should work are found to influence what was previously assumed as mechanical clearly causes much adjustment to what we previously thought.

This is necessary to point out especially when clarifying what we had assumed was purely mechanical and free of human bias and opinions is actually not. This includes the scientists making the choices of what to study, how to study it, and what not to study—all of which tells us how reality works. So, to be clear, our perception is not pure, nor able to be pure; it is influenced by what we have seen before, which is influenced by what we have exposed ourselves to, and the surrounding cultural milieu. The lack of training to perceive what is neither solid nor tangible is a subjective choice. This type of training lacking in our culture is influenced by our cultural milieu. So if we are in a culture that relies heavily on the solidity of matter, then we are not going to really question this, even when we see flashes of white light go across our peripheral vision, for example. We'll dismiss it as something from a physical cause, just one that we may not know–like a headache or being close to an electrical or electromagnetic cell tower, without considering that flashes of light in our peripheral vision are actually an opening to higher states of consciousness. We'll look for physical explanations. Or we'll dismiss it as nonsensical, or think there's a problem and we need to go to a doctor. Go to my Facebook page (http://www.facebook.com/AlisonJKayPhdHolisticLifeCoachEnergyHealer) and look for the video "Signs of a Spiritual Awakening," and just consider what it says. Allow it in as another possibility.

Consciousness is Subtle Energy so It Is Subtle: Isn't This a "No-Brainer"?

Yet the "easy problems" of brain function and its mechanics are much less elusive than consciousness and the subtleness of it. Measuring consciousness is extremely challenging. That's why it's the "hard problem." Yet as we've seen with the "easy problems," they have been successfully measured within the field of neuroscience and continue to be studied. For example, they use EKG machines to trace the electrical activity within the various parts of the brain to study the more mechanical functions. Typically it's been to see what lobes of the brain get lit up when certain functions are performed or certain feelings activated. So Russell, building towards contrasting this level of brain function and the study of it to consciousness and the lack of studying that, then says that "to say these problems are easy is a relative assessment...Nevertheless, given sufficient time and effort, we expect that these 'easy problems' will eventually be solved. The really hard problem is consciousness itself. Why should the complex processing of information in the brain lead to an inner experience? Why doesn't it all go on in the dark, without any subjective aspect? Why do we have any inner life at all?" Russell is questioning–and mocking them as he does so–as if a scientist confounded and frustrated with not being able to stop studying the brain at the point where the more mechanical functions stop.

He is pointing out how there is this other existence beyond these mechanical functions that scientists know of, getting back to the "ghost in the machine" concept, and that this is a frustratingly "hard problem" for scientists. This subjective world of ambiguous beginnings and seemingly unknowable origins, with really slippery behavior makes studying it and pinning it down with measurement, hypotheses, theories and rigorous scientific methods next to impossible. This is the same with what has happened within the discovery of quantum physics; the feeling of constantly chasing something elusive that doesn't necessarily want to be known. Perhaps both are the same phenomena. Another way of putting it is that *consciousness, in its inherent nature, is not able to be studied applying the measurement techniques of western scientific materialist methods. It's not material.*

Russell is contextualizing this within his overall discussion of how we have historically missed out on studying consciousness in our sciences in the West, and that we have come to a breaking point with this avoidance. This is particularly due to the impact of quantum physics within our sciences, and their discoveries. As a physicist himself, Russell goes on to say, "I now believe this is not so much a hard problem as an impossible problem–impossible, that is, within the current scientific worldview. Our inability to account for consciousness is the trigger that will, in time, push Western science into what the American philosopher Thomas Kuhn called a 'paradigm shift.'" (Russell 2002).

Right now, as many have pointed out, due to the anomalies and inconsistencies–and still the unanswered questions–that quantum physics has uncovered, there have been a variety of reactions. At first there was denial within mainstream science; in fact, seemingly an almost obstinate refusal to be open to the new discoveries. *Instead, the reaction was to go deeper into the old* scientific materialist model and methodology of rigorous scientific research, by creating the logical empiricism model. Then, as more and more anomalies popped up as some quantum physicists went further into studying what was being discovered, new theories were created in attempts to incorporate the anomalies within the existing scientific materialist model of our world, based on Newtonian physics. Finally, it seems that a few pioneers have continued to plunge on and discover even more, like the string theory and quarks. Nonetheless, they have recognized–as we have seen–just how elusive the substance is at that subatomic level of quanta. It seems to resist being pinned down and studied; *at least with the old methodology created for measuring physical material.*

"In his seminal book, *The Structure of Scientific Revolutions,* Thomas Kuhn showed that the transition from one paradigm to the next is not smooth. *The pressure for change builds over time,* but the shift itself is abrupt. The process begins when the existing paradigm encounters an anomaly–an observation that cannot be explained by the current worldview. *Because our assumptions as to how the world works are so deeply ingrained,* the anomaly is initially overlooked, or rejected as an error. Or, *if it cannot be so easily discarded,* attempts are made to *incorporate the anomaly within the existing paradigm....* Over time paradigms change. For nearly two thousand years Plato's theories governed the way people thought about the motion of heavenly bodies. In the seventeenth century Newton's laws of motion became the paradigm. Today, Einstein's theories of relativity are regarded as a more accurate description of how matter moves in space and time. Similar changes in worldview can be found in biology, chemistry, geology, psychology–indeed, in all the sciences," (italics mine) (Russell 2002).

However, Russell seems to stop here with Einstein, whereas Pine as reflected in the previous discussion, acknowledged that due to these very anomalies most scientists chose to stick with the easier choice–of going after the Nobel Prizes and the research money, both of which get granted more easily when producing results. The "stuff" of quantum physics, as Pine said–again–*"Yet in spite of Nobel Prizes for the discovery of these new particles and public pronouncements that the end of the Einsteinian quest is near, one senses that all is not well with this approach. Physicists themselves complain that the proliferation of particles necessary to explain everything is too complex* to be consistent with a simple universe. One senses many ad hoc approaches and a situation not unlike followers of Ptolemy adding epicycle to make the data fit," (italics mine) (Pine 1999).

Let's move on to a key factor that makes this such a macroshift of a metaparadigm. Russell goes on to say that the problem is, "in essence, one of *type*. When elementary particles combine to form atoms, and those atoms combine to from molecules, they are forming entities of the same type–they are all physical phenomena. The same is true of a simple cell. DNA, proteins, and amino acids are of the same basic type as atoms. Even the human brain, unfathomably complex as it may be, is still of the same essential type." (Russell 2002). This is all speaking to the scientific materialist paradigm being the underlying system of classification. Meaning, basing all and every understanding on the physical being the primary type of phenomena studied, and upon which everything rests and can be understood.

"Consciousness, however, is of a fundamentally different type. Consciousness is not composed of matter. Matter, we assume, does not possess consciousness. We may not be able to account for consciousness, yet the fact that we are conscious is one thing of which we are absolutely certain. This realization was one of Rene Descartes' great contributions to Western philosophy; some three hundred and fifty years ago... Descartes found that he could doubt any theory or philosophy. He could doubt what anybody said. He could doubt what his eyes showed him of the world. He could doubt his own thoughts and feelings. He could even doubt that he had a body. But the one thing he could not doubt was that he was doubting. This revealed one certainty: he was thinking. If he was thinking, he had to be experiencing being. As he put it in Latin, *Cogito, ergo sum*–'I think, therefore I am.' This is the paradox of consciousness. Its existence is undeniable, yet it remains totally inexplicable. For the materialist metaparadigm, consciousness is one big anomaly." (italics mine)(Russell 2002).

It seems that perhaps we're coming to an end of the functionality of the scientific materialist metaparadigm. As has already been stated, Kuhn showed that the first reaction to an anomaly is to ignore it. This is what most scientists have done with both consciousness and emotions, and for what seemed like understandable, and even good reasons at the time, to them. Yet the difficulty of studying consciousness within the scientific materialist metaparadigm exists for a few reasons. Reviewing these reasons briefly helps clarify this rather complex issue.

First, consciousness cannot be observed in the way that material objects can. It cannot be weighed, measured, or otherwise pinned down, as Russell says. Second, scientists–as Wallace has helped to make clear–took on their job as being one that has to arrive at universal objective truths, independent of any particular observer's viewpoint or state of mind. This is what has given science that certainty we all have come to depend on. In order for this certainty of belief to be sustained, however, they have deliberately avoided subjective considerations, such as with emotions and consciousness, and anything of the soul, or the metaphysical. Third, scientists felt there was no need; the functioning of the universe could be explained without having to explore the rather troublesome subject–"the hard problem" of consciousness.

Yet due to the discovery within quantum physics that at the atomic level the act of observation affects the reality that is observed, it has become impossible to disregard this discovery and remain faithful to the scientific tenet of uncovering the truth, no matter how inconvenient it may be. Additionally, as some of the more cutting edge science, or the "new sciences" as they have been referred to within this discussion have all uncovered and reinforced, in fact a person's state of mind, or consciousness, *can* and most clearly *does* have significant effects on the body's ability to heal itself.

Here is the re–emergence of the mind body connection within science; the new sciences, to be specific. And they have as their in–road to the mind body connection the study of consciousness, and the multitudinous ways it manifests. Some examples are: studies of how stress affects the physiology; or how emotions affect hormonal releases that affect our immune system; or how our thoughts and emotions affect the level of our heart feeling full–emotionally–and good; so our health is good, or how our mind becomes more focused and able to concentrate as a result of meditating, and thereby increase cognitive test scores.

Russell says, "As neurophysiologists deepen their understanding of brain function and its relationship with mental phenomena, the nature of subjective experience again raises its head. As a result of these and other developments, a growing number of scientists and philosophers are now trying to explain how consciousness arises. Some believe that a deeper understanding of brain chemistry will provide the answers; perhaps consciousness resides in the action of neuropeptides. Others look to quantum physics. The minute microtubules found inside nerve cells could create quantum effects that might somehow contribute to consciousness. Some explore computing theory and believe that consciousness emerges from the complexity of the brains processing. Others find sources of hope in chaos theory." (Russell 2002).

Yet what Russell is pointing out is the guesswork that is going on, even amidst the pioneering, strong, valid–and replicable–scientific studies, as to what consciousness is and how does it arise from something as unconscious as matter. *This is the problem.* It is the wrong approach. Consciousness seems to not only be different from, but actually absolutely contrary to the laws of matter, or of the physical world. It is not predictable in the old sense of predictable, not objective nor "out there" separate and distinct from the subjective "in here" world, not linear and not solid, to name a few. All that has been discovered in the quantum world reflects this. All that is subjective suggests that the laws of consciousness run contrary to the laws of matter.

Going beyond emotions and dreaming, consider how consciousness shows up in what has been viewed as "supernatural" or "paranormal psychology" in the West. There are so many rather typical examples of life events that happen that remain unexplained and perhaps are in fact unexplainable. In many of the Native American tribes there is a philosophy of "Respecting the Mystery" in life. In many tribes, "Great Mystery" is synonymous with their name for god, in fact. Mysterious events that we each have in our lives that cannot be logically nor rationally explained, events that seem to coincide with eerily perfect timing (something Carl Jung termed "synchronicity"), the power of prayer to effect faith and then increased positive outcomes, why the phone rings with the same person calling who we were just thinking about, why people have spontaneous healing that doctors can't explain and many, many more. We know these occur. They're just not easily talked about everyday, and certainly not by scientists in their work life.

More examples of a less "supernatural" or mysterious nature are why the hairs on our arms or neck rise when we're uncomfortable, which we can explain biologically sure, but why this very design even being present in our system that goes beyond the need to call attention to a possible threat. How did that get wired into us? Why did it? It's a very subtle physical phenomenon for a response to a threat. Why do we turn when being stared at and find that it's true, we're being stared at? What about that small voice inside us that tells us when someone is lying, or when something is wrong? Intuition–where does it come from? Why were we wired with this?

All of these less physical and more metaphysical questions deal with the part of existence that is less easy to pin down and explain using rigorous scientific methodology that measures, quantifies, calculates and "proves," as is expected. This is particularly even more stringently so within the logical empiricist model that arose in response to quantum physics' first discoveries within the scientific materialist paradigm in the 1930's. And then considering that the ushering in of "Big Science" began in the 1950's, tells us some of why we've been lead to believe only what we see, and only what can be proven. But is this a functional way to live anymore? At this point we seem to be having so many red flags within the old systems, and green flags for new systems, pointing to move beyond where we have been.

This inability for our sciences to explain this side of life–that which is beyond the physical, or the metaphysical –has had an impact on our society at all levels. Yet it is a huge part of our lives, whether we choose to admit it or not, or focus on it or not. Frankly, we avoid the non–physical, as we are lead to do so by our culture's metaparadigm. We run too fast and hard on the physical, or material, plane to take the time to acknowledge it, in order to keep up and survive as the fittest in the material race for employment, subsistence, and material gains. We are not guided to, nor are we living in a metaparadigm that values paying attention to our thoughts, beliefs, reactions and emotions to help us thrive. Not yet, anyways.

Interestingly, and perhaps not coincidental, the increase in attempts to study consciousness from within our culture has arisen at the same time that the simultaneous ongoing financial crisis and issues with unemployment has occurred, causing many to reexamine their values as they find themselves in the life circumstances they do, and with the time during unemployment to do so. This is an important co–arising in timing, yet it is one that is mostly overlooked or reduced down to its own separate phenomena rather than viewed as part of a whole picture.

Another important co–arising with the increasing studies in consciousness is that the computer has grown from the mammoth units housed in federal office buildings to the desktop tower and gargantuan monitor to the laptop, to the notebook, to the pad, to the tablet, to the Smartphone. Smaller and smaller it has become, with digital and nano technology being analogous to consciousness, as each increasingly smaller wireless technology has come onto the scene at a mainstream level. There is more and more data able to accessed and stored as we go smaller and smaller in the tools that house this data. Consciousness is much the same, the smaller and smaller we go into the invisible, the more power there is there. The dense, or the big, houses the least power.

A final simultaneous, perhaps synchronistic event is the crisis in health care within our country. Not only the health care system's near collapse under its own dysfunction, but the levels of obesity, cancer, stress related illnesses and chronic diseases. *All of this fits together as cumulative information that adds up to the pressing awareness that somehow, something very big has gone wrong along the way, while we're discovering that the world is not quite what we thought it was at the most fundamental level.* To ignore these factors, as they combine together to give us indicators as to where we are versus where we should be heading, simply spells disaster for our culture. *Meaning, perhaps the primary importance that we've given the physical has cost us, and it's time we rebalance what has been allowed to get extremely out of balance.*

"Although many scientists abide by high ethical standards, scientific materialism gives them no incentive to do so. A mechanical, impersonal clockwork universe makes no reference to ethics or virtue. Indeed, reducing human subjectivity, the human mind, to neural processes operating according to the impersonal laws of physics (which imply neurobiology, chemistry, and so on) undermines any sense of moral responsibility. Given such an amoral background, it is not surprising that crime, selfish attitudes, and public indifference to the plight of the less fortunate have come to dominate modern life. Even in health care, the purely physical approach has drawbacks, since it often attacks the symptoms of disease but not the cause," (Wallace 2008).

R.R. Reno, a writer for the First Things website succinctly says in his article, "The Gospel of Scientific Materialism," much the same thing, but from a different angle. "Self-examination turns out to be endlessly painful and difficult. Therein lies the appeal of reductive explanations. They release us from the task of self-examination and the need to discipline our errant desires and disobedient wills. What matters is something impersonal, something working at a deeper level than culture and its soul-shaping agenda: the Laws of History or Physics, the Unconscious or Natural Selection. We shouldn't underestimate the appeal of this release-and the pleasing rest it provides." It may sound almost religious because First Things is published by the Institute on Religion and Public Life.

To go to an even more elevated statement–and source–"We must rapidly begin the shift from a thing–oriented society to a person–oriented society. When machines and computers, profit motives and prosperity rights are considered more important than people, *the giant triplets of racism, militarism and economic exploitation are incapable of being conquered.* A nation can flounder as readily in the face of moral and spiritual bankruptcy as it can through financial bankruptcy," Dr. Martin Luther King; 1967. Yet aren't we now facing in varying degrees all three?

Russell goes on to suggest that the continued failure of the aforementioned approaches to make any real, or appreciable, headway into solving the problem of studying consciousness is because they may all very well be on the wrong track. "They are all based on the assumption that consciousness emerges from, or is dependent upon, the physical world of space, time, and matter. In one way or another, they are attempting to accommodate the anomaly of consciousness within a worldview that is intrinsically materialist...I now believe that rather than trying to explain consciousness in terms of the material world, we should be developing a new worldview in which consciousness is a fundamental component of reality." Russell then also suggests that "the key ingredients for this new metaparadigm are already in place. We need not wait for any new discoveries. All we need do is put various pieces of our existing knowledge together and explore the new picture of reality that emerges," (Russell 2002).

Chapter 6—So if Our Basic Beliefs Have Become Outdated, What are Other Options?

"Every truth passes through three stages before it is recognized. In the first, it is ridiculed. In the second, it is opposed. In the third, it is regarded as self–evident," Arthur Schopenhauer

"No man can reveal to you aught but that which already lies half asleep in the dawning of your knowledge," Kahlil Gibran in *The Prophet*

How Do We Stop Giving Our Power Away to Sources Outside of Us?

ALL THAT HAS BEEN DISCUSSED so far implies is that there is a need to bring our culture and its metaparadigm back into balance with a new metaparadigm. It is being demanded of us, and much of our struggle and major issues facing the United States today at the systemic level is because we got out of balance at some point with our over–emphasizing the physical, at the cost of recognizing the power that the subtle has within our lives. Much of this has been in the name of profit as materialism picked up its pace.

We need to bring back in the non–linear and the abstract–typically labeled right brain processes–and integrate it more fully within our paradigm, our values as a society, as well as at the individual level. *This does mean the spiritual, or the metaphysical.* Look at that word again; meta is beyond, so *it is looking beyond the physical.* It does not have to mean anything other than allowing ourselves to logically, with open minds, rationally look at that which is beyond the physical. The subtle is then what we will be looking at. We will then not be ignoring the other half (at the very least!) of the experience of being alive, in this universe, in a human body, on this planet.

This re–examination can and should yield very different results done in today's milieu, if done logically and without preconceived notions, and without emotionally driven resistance that blocks access to rational thought, and particularly without attachment to keeping and having things remain or even look the same. For above all else, change, and quick, rapid, quantum type of change is so obviously the nature of the times that we are now living in. This, in and of itself, is a major contributor to so much of the chaos everyone is witnessing and feeling, and then reeling from not being able to successfully–never mind adequately–cope with it. In today's day and age, with the information we now have as a globalized, postmodern world that has had now almost one hundred years to integrate the breakthroughs of quantum physics into our lives, we should be able to do this. In fact, again, we are being shown in such a host of divergent ways that we have been avoiding this, particularly here in the United States at the mainstream, metaparadigm level, and it has been to our own detriment, individually and collectively.

Yes we have plentiful organized religious institutions–and it's no irony that there has been a huge increase in these numbers over the last decade and a half–however, this is not what is meant here. That is somewhat more of the same metaparadigm. Remember, scientific materialism comes from the Christian–Judeo concept of God and the universe "out there." It also comes from hierarchical power structures with authority figures to whom the average person places his or herself in somewhat of a submissive role to. Both clergy and doctors are examples.

Accordingly, this same metaparadigm has each person not typically making the time or cultivating the skills, training, or power to have that "knowingness" deemed necessary to understand much beyond the tangible, physical world, while we consider doctors and clergy, and even to a much less validated, reputable degree–psychics–to have it. Hence, historically within our metaparadigm, this has left us turning these two most essential aspects of ourselves–our bodies' and our minds' health, and secondly, our soul, or spiritual health–*over to an outside authority figure, someone outside of us, whom we imbue with the ability to know ourselves and our human body–mind–spirit systems, and life, better than we ourselves can.*

Within this old paradigm, while there is some turning within to find a moral compass as guided typically by the outside religious authority figure, or some turning within to connect with this divine source when attending church or synagogue; or some turning inward when praying alone but then ultimately reaching out and connecting to this divine source outside of us, or when in crisis, again *we are reaching outside ourselves for some help* from a power source of a divine nature. The bottom line is that when we as Westerners, or Americans, within our cultural milieu want to interact with the divine, even when we go inside to do so quietly, our attention is still typically directed ultimately outwardly to this divine source. This is because it has been told to us to be, "out there." So this means our construing of divinity is that it is not an active part of us, and that the more active part is outside of us. Because of this, our overall metaparadigm has lead to a focus on the objective world, exploring "out there," or on the physical plane mostly. It's also obviously had some other consequences as well, such as a disconnection from the sacred housed within each of us. Think back to the yogic practices, and the meaning of the word yoga.

Bring in the sciences, then, (as we've seen this is how it has gone in the West) to explain to us what reality is and what it is composed of. This then gets elevated to an authoritative level of knowledge, *based on our invested consent back to the scientists to have this level of authority and elite knowledge over us because we don't question what has been "scientifically proven."* This view of reality we then learn in school, believe in, grow up and design our lives professionally around this version, to contribute within this system's metaparadigm. Even though this system is supposedly reason based, with individuals having the liberty to apply this reason as each sees fit, nonetheless, there is a massive umbrella hanging over each of us that tells us what is socially acceptable to believe in. Furthermore, this view of reality from our science is the underlying backdrop that our societal conditioning tells us what the limits are of what seems reasonable–within this metaparadigm.

An example of the sheer power that our metaparadigm exerts at a typically unexamined level is the following process. After science has interwoven discoveries that explain to us what is reality at the subatomic, microscopic level, so that with the principles of universalism and reductionism this then gets applied to all of life, we then live our lives accordingly. This is because the average citizen doesn't own microscopes, and well, that level of life is the scientists' specialty, not the average citizen's, right? So the scientists make their discoveries, and then the industrial business leaders and innovators utilize this to create new technology. Either next or in conjunction with these previous two steps is our government making budgetary choices on where and how to spend our tax dollars, as well as laws and policies that then further foundationally structure our society. This structure rules our lives, based on what science gives us as the backdrop to what life and reality really is–remember we're still dealing with the industrial, governmental and scientific structures of Newtonian physics. Then finally is the consumer focused arm of the science research industry–government--bio–tech industry, giving us such products as pharmaceutical drugs, surgical devices, pesticides, or food preservatives, and more. Thus, we have the basic tenets of what our society should value. Then there's us, the consumers making the choices.

This shows up in as subtle of arenas as urban planning and what our physical environments nationwide typically look like. We then live in these zoned districts designed in a way particular to our metaparadigm, with structure and order imposed onto the land. Cities and all their urban activity are contained within the urban center, such as business, financial and shopping districts, and then residential areas are separate from these districts. Suburban living is an outgrowth of this and the car. Another way it is done in other metaparadigms is rather than having developed our urban centers as described above, all the activities are blended together throughout the city.

For example, high rise towers like many other cities have across the globe that contain both businesses and living spaces on the same block. Europe even has this, as does Asia. And our older major cities, like New York and Chicago do mix the zoning a bit more than the other, newer cities. So instead of just commercial spaces being the primary focus of urban centers there are living spaces actively sought after and used within the same neighborhood. Yet we have developed in such a way that the zoning laws categorize and section off residential from commercial activity with urban planning that is done in a comparatively linear, direct way typical to American cities.

As a result of our neat, organized, typical habits of zoning laws that carry from state to state as the American flavor of thinking is under our metaparadigm, we have spread outward from the urban centers, to use up the land available, as we have so much of it. This has left a wake of revitalization efforts within the last 20 years or so in urban areas throughout the country. Even though much of the discussions surrounding these issues of "revitalizing the inner city" have been socio–economic, underlying this issue is the thinking with the eyes of a scientific materialist metaparadigm influenced mind.

We are in the midst of a massive shift at a new level within the history of humans on this planet. In this post–modern, globalized, one world, there is a revolution going on that some term a spiritual one, frequently referred to as a time of spiritual awakening. As Westerners who think for themselves and modernized, globalized forward–thinking Easterners and others in the "first world" sense the lack within the scientific materialist metaparadigm there is an encroaching critical mass. Hence there is an ever increasing global society of people who work to fill in this hole at an individual level. There are then pockets of people, communities and businesses collectively spiritualizing. This does not mean starting new Churches or necessarily connected to organized religions at all. Although even within the dominant religions of the West—Christianity, Judaism and Islam—there have been growing efforts to modernize their traditions in order to accommodate the increasing demand for spirituality within their inherited traditions.

This macroshift does mean now acknowledging the sacred more, and how the sacred is contained within life, including subtle energy itself. Slowing down enough to enjoy the outdoors, family, and nurturing one's self all are ways to yes, decompress from stress. At the same time, once decompressed from stress, it is easier for the mind to quiet and then to pick up on the more subtle. A loud mind gravitates towards equal levels of loudness in life. The same goes for a quiet mind—it gravitates towards what is also quieter in life. An example of noticing the sacred more could mean acknowledging the mind body connection simply by seeing how you feel when you eat pizza, chips and/or soda, or a plate full of linguini with cream sauce and red wine. Then observe what you end up doing after eating a meal like this; this is a way to observe subtle energy as it shows up in our feelings while digestion occurs. So for example, after such a meal you could observe that you seem to typically want to then space out in front of the television, listlessly clicking through random shows or surfing the internet. Another example is observing how you feel during and after eating a salad and a piece of lean protein. You could observe that you end up having lots of energy, with this alive feeling that makes you want to go outside, or connect with a friend or family member by doing some activity together, turning off the TV or the computer.

Some of the pioneering pockets of these communities have been helped along in their contagion, blossoming into ever increasing numbers of other, closely related groups of like–minded people and communities due to the explosion of Internet 2.0, with the blogging and the social media. So this new line of thinking is spreading even more rapidly, to have more of a presence overall. In fact, a swelling is happening at a grassroots level, that is proliferating like a forest fire. It is somewhat due to the ease of connecting with like–minded people through the use of social networking, and of getting information about how to make these shifts into new lifestyle choices. This makes making the new choices easier, and finding out how to make and where to get the different products, due to mainstream stores still barely carrying the items. Included in this activity are communities beginning to demand our old policies and structures that are still existing but functioning from the outdated scientific materialism metaparadigm, change. Instead, the changes beginning to be demanded by increasing numbers is the shift to a holistic approach in many seemingly unrelated arenas of production.

What some of these changes are include food production from agribusiness and their use of pesticides, herbicides, and genetically modified food sources turning into more of a green, or organic, consumer/demand driven food production model. Another change is the increased offering of better alternatives from food producers and farmers who have already made the shift from chemical use and genetically modified food to safe food production that is healthy for the consumer. The slow food movement is another example. Yet another change is that all this happens while accomplishing food production that is healthy for *both* the consumer and the earth, instead of the opposite–food production that is unhealthy for both the earth and humans. For example, the less minerals in the soil, the less minerals in our food. The less trees, the less vitamins and minerals that get fixed into the soil by the tree roots stabilizing the soil, while the more trees there are the cleaner our oxygen supply to breath is. But these holistic or ecological views haven't taken off in the scientific materialist model of reductionism—or in this metaparadigm that grew up during industrialization. Industrialization reduces and mechanizes, and this benefits the bottom line of profit, right?

Grass fed beef is another example of these pockets of communities seeing the whole picture, and the option for a new metaparadigm. Whether by demanding or supplying, they are making different choices as consumers. The increasing availability of grass fed beef from both the internet and health food stores, the growth in health food stores in general (one of the few fields to grow in the economy over the past seven years) and this growth in organic produce offered at non–green, mainstream supermarkets are all more examples.

Ben & Jerry's ice cream is a food product that is an example of this clean, whole foods approach as well. Originally, Ben & Jerry's went beyond just the ingredients of their ice creams being whole and pure to their business model being socially aware. Their choices of which producer of cream and milk or which distributor to use, for example, was made based on who was doing something beneficial for the community. Nor did they stop there, and with a percentage of Ben & Jerry's profits being funneled back into the community where there is economic need, they held this new metaparadigm that is still emerging not based on cutthroat competition, but on how much good can be done in all aspects with business, benefitting as many as possible. It's a cooperative, community approach.

Obviously this type of a business model is beyond the physical, it is holistic. It acknowledges the emotions of the people involved in contributing their efforts and beliefs and psychology into their products that Ben & Jerry's then uses. For example, the dairy cow farmers they choose to do business with. It shows they respect their consumers' feelings of wellness both physically and emotionally. By not only having these healthy whole–food based products inside of them, but by also nurturing their sense of responsibility, community and contribution to the larger community of people looking for something more, it creates feelings of well-being. So when a consumer approaches this food they do it with an awareness of taking in something that is based on goodness. Ben & Jerry's popularity continues to strengthen. The increasing awareness of food as our medicine is indicative of the pioneering work Ben & Jerry accomplished, and the awareness that the old metaparadigm had become dysfunctional.

Within these food producers who have made the shift are farmers and companies aware of subtle energies. They allow their chickens who lay eggs to roam cage free, so that the emotional life of the chicken is considered in the end product of the egg that the consumer will then take into his or her body. So these farmers and companies are not only producing non–pesticide, non–genetically modified, non–antibiotic infused, non–hormone pumped chickens and eggs, but are also producing food in which the *subtle energy that transfers from the chicken to the consumer eating either the chicken as their meat or the egg as their dairy is considered in their business as important.*

Another way to relate to this is the discussions around organ donors, and the experiences of those who take on a major organ from another human and end up a little bit different as a person. This is what is known as cellular memory, an example of subtle energy, and the chickens and hens and the way they live and the way they die also carry this. It becomes a part of us, even though smaller than an organ from a donor. Then multiply how many eggs or how much chicken you consume that is produced under the mass–produced agribusiness model, a.k.a. "big ag," linked to bioengineered, mechanically produced, industrialized food, and *you have a certain feeling cumulatively digested, along with the hormones.*

In another arena in our society very relative to subtle energy is Joel Martin and Patricia Romanowski's *Love Beyond Life: The Healing Power of After–Death Communications.* They say that after about the 1920's we stopped dealing with death as frequently in our culture. They offer the example that the living room is called "the *living* room" because funeral or memorial ceremonies used to take place, prior to the formal business of funeral homes, in the family's home in the living room. It was named this to take away the association with this connection to death, due to the mourning and the body being there in the living room.

The authors say that we are not dealing with nor facing death as commonly since around the 1920's because our predecessors were dealing with diseases that our biomedical model has helped to wipe out, such as tuberculosis. Also, one–third of the population of child–bearing women could expect to die in childbirth. The contrast is strong against today's standard of health; you can see that in modern society we are not integrating death as much into our lives compared to the times they're talking about. They suggest that this can even be seen in the fact that a person is lucky to get more than fourteen days off from a good job in order to deal with bereavement, and then told to "stop being morbid" and "get on with one's life." For contrast, in Taiwan when a parent dies, a public employee is given both money and time off, gauged by one's salary bracket. This comes from taxes. Support for bereavement of parents.

The authors say, "We avoid the dying, the dead and the bereaved at every opportunity and then wonder why we feel so alone when death touches our lives...All human societies recognize important personal transitions through public ritual and protocol. In contemporary American society, however, we have witnessed a progressively declining participation and appreciation for funerary and mourning traditions. This has paralleled the declining death rate. For example, if you lived in the mid-1800's, when childhood mortality ran between 30 and 50 percent, you could expect one out of every three of your children to die before reaching adulthood. As a child, you probably have witnessed the death of at least one sibling and perhaps several. During common epidemics of measles, diphtheria, influenza, and chickenpox, families could lose several or all of their children in a matter of days. As a woman, you face a one–in–thirty chance of dying every time you gave birth. Faced with such realities, no one could escape, deny, or choose not to deal with death. Compared with today, death then was not only prevalent, it was pervasive," (Martin et al., 1997).

The authors are discussing a topic that connects to our discussion because as humans in a human body, on this here physical plane during a lifetime, our soul's existence or what happens beyond death might just become more pronounced when we face and deal with our own mortality more frequently in the face of so much death. Specifically, we would remain more connected to the act of questioning what happens when someone we love or ourselves is not in a physical body when dealing with death more regularly. As a result, we'd most likely retain more of a connection with the unseen forces, or subtle energies, or whatever is behind the unseen. It kind of, some would say, puts it all into perspective–death.

The authors go on, "One reason much of what we consider New Age seems so new to us is that in closing our eyes to death, we have also failed to see and/or believe our paranormal experiences related to dying, death, and bereavement. Yet for our predecessors, these experiences brought confirmation of religious faith, emotional comfort, and a means of adjusting psychologically to loss," (Martin et al., 1997). The authors go on to discuss, therefore, contemporary psychology's attitude toward paranormal experience and its resistance towards such experiences, due to the scientific materialist paradigm as already discussed. What they say then is that they have interviewed in recent years mental health and bereavement experts who now support the position that we should accept and use after–death contacts and communications as a means to work through grief.

"In 1994 the third edition of the *American Psychiatric Association's Diagnostic and Statistical Manual of Mental Disorders* finally urged mental health professionals to consider more seriously a patient's religious experience. It was a long overdue recognition of the positive role and importance of spirituality in mental health. Psychiatrists Shaun Josh and Colin Ross, writing in *The Journal of Nervous and Mental Diseases* state, *'Paranormal experiences are so common in the general population that no theory of normal psychology or psychopathology which does not take them into account can be comprehensive.'* This is a welcome change from the not–too–distant past, when anyone admitting to such experiences was declared hysterical, prone to hallucinations, or worse," (Martin et al., 1997). While this may seem a "little bit out there" it is still, nonetheless, an impact of living within the metaparadigm that we do. And it may sound a little "out there" *because* of the metaparadigm we live in and the ensuing judgments and conclusions we've been guided to have. But look again; it is just logical.

Our medical system is another example where the consumer demand is catalyzing change from the grassroots level in the metaparadigm, where the consumers are demanding answers to their diseases and disorders that the current medical system of the United States is unable to answer. The biomedical model is limited today for they are approaching medicine still from the scientific materialist approach of the physical only, and we are dealing with diseases and disorders now that require a different knowledge base, one that includes awareness of the bio–energy field, one that is based on understanding subtle energy and the mind body connection.

Dr. William Tiller, professor emeritus of Materials Science and former department chair at Stanford University from 1964 to 1970, says, "For the last four hundred years, an unstated assumption of science is that human intention cannot significantly affect what we call 'physical reality.' Our experimental research of the past decade shows that, for today's world and under the right conditions, this assumption is no longer correct. We humans are much more than we think we are and Psychoenergetic Science continues to expand the proof of it."

Tiller then concludes, "Future medicine will be based on learning to control the information frequencies of the body." Here, the energy aspect of these frequencies of the body, called "subtle energies," include consciousness. Anger has one frequency, while joy has another; shrill screaming is one frequency, while soothing humming is another. Dr. Tiller then goes on to talk about the science that is done under the scientific materialist mainstream paradigm. An interviewer asks him about his departure from scientific materialism science into his current research with psychoenergetic science, "Have you experienced backlash from orthodox science?"

Tiller responds, "Of course there's always backlash when you're trying to walk a different path, or you're trying to create a different path, or you're trying to talk about something that doesn't fit into their internal self-consistency picture. I would love to have a real discussion. There's never a serious discussion, because their minds cannot accept the information. It boggles their mind. When they look at our experiments their eyes start spinning, and they sort of somewhat lose consciousness. If they really pay attention to the data, they can't handle it because they're in violation of internal self consistency, which they've held true to–it's very difficult for them." Here, Tiller's term "internal self consistency picture" means their understanding and perception of what reality is under the scientific materialist metaparadigm, and what that creates for them to expect to see both outside of and inside themselves. This is reminiscent of the quantum physicists who went on to create logical empiricism in the 1930's as a reaction to what was being uncovered about distance, time, and space and it not necessarily being as linear as the Newtonian physics model had presented. This would be a violation of their "internal self consistency," as Tiller calls it. Or as Kuhn calls it within the scientific revolutions context, "denial."

Tiller goes on to say that there's nothing wrong with what science has done, but that they're limited and "they're now stuck in distance/time. They cannot allow themselves to deal with categories of phenomena that are not distance/time related, and they don't even realize that. Orthodox science doesn't really seek the truth about nature. It seeks internal self consistency with respect to a *reference frame that they hold about nature*. That reference frame has come from their study of space and time and the *unstated assumption* since the days of Descartes by orthodox science that has been no human qualities of consciousness, intention, emotion, mind or spirit can significantly influence a well designed target experiment in physical reality." Obviously, Tiller is parroting Wallace, Russell, Goswami, Hayward and many other scientists here. He speaks as well to this denial these orthodox scientists have, *this disallowance* of a mind body connection within the scientific materialist metaparadigm, because of its core principles. Again, this disallowance comes from a choice, however consciously or unconsciously, of what to focus on and what *not* to.

As Tiller continues in this interview, he begins to shift into contrasting "orthodox science" or scientific materialism, with "new science," discussing what the "new science" is that he has uncovered, termed "Psychoenergetic Science;" meaning psycho–the mind, and meaning energetic–subtle energy. Therefore this science is the science of the influence of the mind on subtle energy. (Within the field of the "new sciences" there are many different names for what is being studied, as it has yet to all gel together the disparate efforts into one main metaparadigm as of now; hence, the umbrella term "new science.")

In fact, it would be helpful to retreat for a moment from Dr. Tiller's interview and go to a basic definition that he provides on his website: "I have written this out very clearly in my book *Psychoenergetic Science: A Second Copernican–Scale Revolution* so here I will be brief. Today's orthodox science has constrained itself to the use of a distance/time–only reference frame for the study of positive mass/positive energy types of interactions occurring in electric charge–based matter via a host of experimental variables that exclude any aspect or manifestation of consciousness. Psychoenergetic science *expands the host of allowed experimental variables for the study of nature's many manifestations to include those associated with consciousness and intention.* As such, this includes all aspects of orthodox science and orthodox medicine in the limit of those natural phenomena that are distance/time–dependent and also includes a host of natural phenomena that are not distance/time–dependent but are consciousness–dependent."

Tiller further confirms where it is that he has seen he and his team have had to come out of the conditioning from scientific materialist science. "To do this, it has been necessary to (1) *expand our reference frame* for the study of natural phenomena, (2) *expand our allowed range of substance velocities...* (3) *expand our allowed range of substance energies* ...(4) *expand our concept of nature and its natural phenomena* to many different classes of substance that express themselves in multiple dimensions *beyond just space–time.* In this way we, at least, have an experiential and *potential experimental field large enough* to allow humankind to quantitatively explore the vast domain of nature *separating coarse physical reality and spirit!*" (italics mine) (www. tiller.org). According to Tiller, it's not only consciousness, but spirit that also needs to be included in order to be true to scientific inquiry about the nature of life in this universe for humankind.

What Tiller then goes on to say will echo Russell. Talking about the difficulty in breaking from the old scientific materialist paradigm, he includes the initial discoveries of quantum physicists, "Now the issue is this other aspect of reality, the higher dimensions ...–phenomena are not distance and time phenomena. *Therefore, the present paradigm cannot deal with them in any way.* Quantum mechanics, relativity theory can't touch anything to do with consciousness because it's (consciousness) not a time/space subject, or phenomena. And once you see that you realize that nature is so much more and *you have to be willing to expand your paradigm, your reference frame for viewing nature.* Mathematical formulas of orthodox science have to be distance/time related, somehow connected with that..."

Now—can I hear a drumroll please?—central to how to get to sense this immeasurable energy, Tiller explains, "We have found over the last decade–maybe a little more–that *there are two general states of physical reality*–there's our normal one–the electric atom molecule one and that's the distance/ time related one. The other one appears to function in the physical vacuum, *and the physical vacuum occupies the space within the fundamental particles that make up the electric atoms and molecules, so it's also in outer space,* but the really key place is that it functions there, and it goes faster than the velocity of light–which you can show mathematically. We can't–*normal equipment in our normal world cannot access that–but with the use of consciousness, which we've shown experimentally, you can begin to access this other level of reality* and you can bring about what we call the coupled state of reality. And it's a higher–it's called the electromagnetic gauge symmetry– state of the very conditions of space, and the state phenomena occur there very differently," (italics mine) (www.tiller.org).

We'll return to the vacuum theory later, but for now, what Tiller offers here is reflective of his experience as a scientific materialist scientist, or a scientist within "orthodox science" as he refers to it, who leaves the field to remain true to his scientific mind in a quest for the truth, and ends up working within one of the "new sciences" that he himself is responsible for much of the discoveries within–Psychoenergetic Science. Of particular importance is what he says about the challenges for an orthodox scientist to let go of the thinking from the old paradigm, in the face of today's new sciences that have stepped away from the scientific materialist metaparadigm. Also worthy of notice is the fact that he was even asked the question, "Have you suffered backlash?" as a result of his departure from mainstream science. The backlash he suffered as a result is a part of the process of our metaparadigm shifting, with pioneers leading the way out of the old, dysfunctional one. And then his description of how to access consciousness, and all the implications of what he and his team have uncovered.

What's Beyond the Personality "Small Me" Perspective?

Those remaining in the old, dysfunctional paradigm are either in: (1) denial; (2) criticism and attack of the validity of the new discoveries; (3) a complete lack of being able to see beyond their own conditioning and thinking under the paradigm being shattered; (4) or tentative support. Kuhn noted this as the typical reactions when paradigms shift with his work on scientific revolutions. We will also see that this is a typical series of somewhat sequential responses as macroshifts are made in societies with Ervin Laszlo's work; conflict and chaos are inherent to an old system breaking down, prior to the breakthrough phase of a new metaparadigm being put in place. Tiller, once a highly respected Professor of Science at Stanford, has taken a lot of risks and suffered somewhat professionally, in order to remain true to his search for the truth as a scientist, no matter the costs. He is hence a pioneer, but also someone somewhat cast out and attacked, due to not going along in acquiescence with the metaparadigm's system(s).

But, as of right now, the overall metaparadigm of scientific materialism is still in place. Hence the increase in chaos. On a more personal level, there is also an increase in the overall "darkness" individually and collectively in reaction to the rising levels towards critical mass of enough people making the shift out of the old metaparadigm and into some new choices that are more conscious, *and "lighter."* The increase in darkness is an almost unconsciously triggered reaction to the increase in light. It's an example of a metaphysical law. Those who are experiencing more darkness are not yet ready to embrace the new metaparadigm with its concurrent new lifestyle choices modeled around more conscious, aware choices. These new choices reflect taking responsibility for one's self, in a whole new way, comparatively. The "lighter" choices are made as they shift away from the "darker" parts of themselves sometimes referred to as the shadow; or, their more unconscious self and its ensuing lifestyle choices. The new choices obviously are not just focused on mindless avoidance, or physical gratification as quickly and conveniently as possible, but are more selective ones that include within it the understanding of the inherent need to have self–awareness and self–knowledge. And then make choices, accordingly.

This means ceasing surrendering one's self over to being told what to do by doctors, clergy, or even scientists. Or, another typical reaction seems to be open resistance or denial or refusal to shift to this awareness and this level of responsible living. This resistance frequently is unconscious. It's a mechanism built within us as our higher self wants something better for ourselves and the smaller personality self, commonly referred to as the "ego–mind," (as Wayne Dyer puts it, "EGO–Edging God Out") feels the threat of change looming. So it holds on tighter.

Think of the homeopathic function of our body generating a fever to burn out an infection; it has to peak before it breaks. This new model, or metaparadigm, is where one cultivates the strength of one's mind and consciousness, and interacts with others and makes consumer choices from this basis. This resistance can be a conscious choice made while others are starting to shift into these more alive behaviors that is not only felt but seen as a shift, while the person or community resisting resist purely because they just don't want to do it. Laziness is a factor here, as is fear; both are ego–mind based reactions towards change and evolution of self.

Living in the old metaparadigm at a quick glance, *is* easier in the short term. Therefore at this point what we're experiencing individually and collectively is a corresponding increase in conflicts. This is in reaction to the increasing light on the planet brought in as more humans open up their consciousness and evolve beyond the mere physical ego–based personality level of living for a material existence. Typically, connecting to something beyond the material has been accomplished by attending religious institutions semi-regularly in order to still feel some connection to something bigger than one's self, as in a divine source. Though this frequently does not necessarily transfer over to living with this connection themselves on a day to day basis. Light has the ability to activate the ego into becoming even more childlike, particularly when it comes to taking responsibility for one's own thoughts and behaviors. The ego throws obvious temper tantrums, or it gets moody, or sticks its heels in the ground and engages in old habits and thinking even more.

But these are the times we're living in. This is the change we are feeling and living through right now. "This light being brought down" simply means people who are working with the denser, or darker, parts of themselves. This could be through yoga, meditation, a new exercise regimen, energy healing, chi gong, tai chi, acupuncture, or a host of other ways that work with increasing the flow of subtle energies throughout one's self. Whether through choice, or forced because of a medical crisis that our medical system can't offer solutions to. So they seek alternative healing, that leads them to open up to the therapies that use subtle energy, causing a new awareness in them. Or perhaps through personal, familial or financial crisis, so they seek help and gain a new level of self-awareness, resulting in an overall increased awareness. People who make these choices are basically cleaning themselves up of some or much of their ego–based personalities, and hence ego–minds, or their "issues" or their "stuff." They are becoming more aware of this part of themselves. Concurrently, They are also making choices that are less focused only on the ego–based desires, but ones from a more disciplined, more responsible, more mature "higher" version of themselves.

My Brahmin teacher of Yogic Philosophy and Patanjali's sutras from my yoga teacher training in India calls this "spiritual maturity." Meaning, when you're about to make a choice, think of how you've felt before when with the result of making this same choice. If it is a bad feeling, we then do not choose the same way again. Instead, we make choices that will lead us to feeling authentically better and lighter, and not just for momentary gratification.

As a result, the level of one's human system has opened up from a more dense physical nature to one of a higher, or more evolved state, so it is "lighter."

It can and does mean more than this, but for now, this is all. We have to start somewhere to understand the dynamic we're all going through in one way or another. After this, there is the next level of working with our consciousness. Albert Einstein said in 1921, "A human being is part of the whole, called by us 'universe,' a part limited in time and space. He experiences himself, his thoughts and feelings, as something separate from the rest – a kind of optical delusion of consciousness. This delusion is a kind of prison for us, restricting us to our personal desires and to affection for a few persons nearest to us. Our task must be to free ourselves from this prison [by widening our circle of compassion to embrace all living creatures and the whole of nature in its beauty]," (Center for Investigating Healthy Minds, 2010).

The term "spiritual" here is not necessarily meaning divinity, but paying attention to the quieter parts of ourselves. It's that soft voice that whispers; our spirit. Further, what is also then meant by the term "spiritual" is that we are working with our consciousness, looking inward rather than mostly outward in an attempt for self-awareness. And when we go inside we observe both our light and dark sides to ourselves. This includes looking inward enough to shine a light on our shadow selves, or the parts of ourselves that are not so nice and thus we haven't wanted to see. Many refer to this as the darkness within us. The more reactive behaviors are a part of this. Frequently, rather than look at our shadows, we will react when our ego-mind, or personality self feels offended. We react from our shadow, and if not worked with, our shadow causing us to react, also causes us to fling what I call "green gook" onto the person we are reacting to. This green gook is like the green slime we used to fling on the walls and it would stay. That's what we're flinging on to each other when we react from our unexamined shadows.

Cleaning our consciousnesses individually in this way is what is meant by "doing our spiritual work." With enough of us doing this collectively then this is what is meant by a "spiritual revolution." Facing ourselves is the start of this process. Nothing more, nothing less. Facing ourselves when alone, *with self-effacing honesty and with detachment,* as if an observer observing a little child, observing and listening to what our mind tells us. Then dealing with the less healthy thoughts that our "smaller self" mind has, from this Higher Self perspective. Meaning a cleaner or less reactive, less controlling, less selfish, less ego-based, less "small minded" self. Again, this does not have to mean divinity. It can simply mean looking at one's self without that sense of taking everything so personally. Rather, having an approach with a sense of humor coupled with a sense of diligence. Some call this self-discipline, grace, or effective self-management. This also means getting help from a coach or a holistic practitioner when we know we're running or hiding from ourselves.

In the act of working with the ego-based personality, and lessening its control in our lives and its desires and demands, a natural opening occurs that makes room for lighter thoughts. These lighter thoughts lead to lighter moments, and *also lead to noticing lighter aspects of existence.* This is another key that I gladly share with you because it's one of the fun ones! This has a momentum to it. So once one lightens up one's darkness the space created allows for less physically dense thoughts, naturally resulting in magnetizing more of the transcendent qualities of life, to one's self a bit more, and increasingly. Our perception, due to its lightening, begins to notice these more transcendent aspects quietly showing up more. We've quieted, so we're more attuned to the quieter aspects of life, or the subtle. Then we'll notice these more subtle and sacred aspects of life more, like a breeze as we walk by some trees or a row of flowering high pink azaleas.

Once a little bit of room is made for something else, we'll notice more a smile, or someone's unexpected kindness, or sun on one's face and the warmth and light gained from it. It is a matter of retraining what our consciousness is used to feeling and then looking for. It's kind of similar to once you decide you want to buy a new red BMW you start to see more of them. Our consciousness has a frame of reference, or a "rut," and it can get stuck. The law of magnetics is involved here somewhat. Our perception gradually get attuned by lightening up our overall consciousness and system to a softer way of being in our minds, bodies, and world. So in order to create a new life and new experiences, we need to plant something new here and build a level of momentum to what we are focusing on. It's a retraining and redirecting of our focus. More conscious discipline and direction is needed at first. But there are a whole host of holistic tools to aid in this; I find energy healing and meditation primary methods.

Ultimately, this does lighten up the density, or the heaviness, of physical existence, comparatively. As the ego–mind's high strung demands and force lessens, a person lightens. This less noisy mind–or as some would now say, our Higher Self–is able to make its presence a bit more known. This is the process. It does not have to include a divine source. However, the lightening of the dense part of our consciousness naturally leads to this lighter existence, which can then lead to connection with what is more light, or more attuned to the divine in life. But this "spiritualizing" does not have to mean a belief in God, or a divine source; at least at the onset.

However, yes, what is being alluded to here is that sensing more of a divine, or sacred source is a natural outcome, experientially and eventually. This is, of course, in varying degrees for each person. Really it is just a restoration of noticing, making room for and having awareness of the sacred in everyday moments. And it can just mean some level of a higher intelligence that pulsates underneath the rhythms of life; like what the Chinese think of as Chi, or like what the quantum physicists seem to be chasing. Think back to the definition of yoga: to "yoke" or to "tie with" or "connect with" the Higher Self, or a higher source to life. But this again, does not have to translate into a belief in an external divine being.

The Dalai Lama said in 2008 at the Synthesis Conference with Western pioneers of this very shift we are discussing from all fields possible–educators, scientists, sociologist, doctors, and many other fields–"I feel there are signs whether in Japan or America or in Europe...in many places now, more and more people begin to feel there is something wrong. We need some sort of new effort or some sort of, I think, way to go."

Going Beyond: What Are the Missing Links?

Gregg Braden, best–selling author of *The Divine Matrix* and *The God Code*, writes in *The Spontaneous Healing of Belief: Shattering the Paradigm of False Limits* that now is the time. He says that even if we don't clearly know all there is to know yet about how the universe works or our role in it, we know enough by now to know that we need to change our current direction. We can do this by taking more personal responsibility for ourselves, so we are much more aligned with living a life of integrity and meaning. Braden cites some emerging studies from "powerful voices in the scientific community, such as Sir Martin Rees, Professor of Astrophysics at the University of Cambridge, who suggest that we have only a '50/50' chance of surviving the 21st century without a major setback. While we've always had natural disasters to contend with, a new class of threats that Rees calls 'human induced' now have to be taken into account as well. Emerging studies, such as those reported in *Scientific American*'s special issue entitled 'Crossroads for Planet Earth' (September 2005), echo Rees's warning, telling us: 'The next 50 years will be decisive in determining whether the human race–*now entering a unique period in its history*–can ensure the best possible future for itself," (Braden 2008). Braden is not intending a message of gloom and doom. Rather, his meaning is that it's a clear time of opportunity. You'll see this soon.

Braden ultimately puts forth a call to action to take advantage of this opportunity inherent to our times we're living in. Prior to this call to action, he explains that there are series of essays written by experts in fields ranging from global health and energy consumption to sustainable lifestyles that all generally agree that we simply cannot continue with the way we use energy, the direction of technology, and an ever–expanding population if we expect to survive another hundred years. Also threatening the United States as well as the global community are other issues beyond those that Braden refers to, such as the health status of the average citizen in a modernized, globalized country; this includes the rates of cancer, obesity, depression, and anxiety as well as other chronic conditions–most of which are referred to as "*affluent illnesses.*" The financial crises that are ongoing are another example of crises that are pointing towards the need for another system, another way of doing things. Braden cites Harvard University biologist E.O. Wilson as saying that we are about to enter what he calls the "bottleneck" in time, when both our resources and our ability to solve the problems of our day will be pushed to their limits.

The various issues just mentioned, and the intensifying threat each of them pose to humanity is again, not meant to be a doomsday picture. Instead it is to act as a very loud arrow pointing out that *we have all of these crises converging at this time to peak the perception of very real threats at crises level separately, that then add up to a collective message that we have to do things differently. Meaning, our metaparadigm has got to change, and not just incrementally.* Within crisis is opportunity, according to many wise philosophers–including the Taoists. This is happening at the same time that there is globalization of information; meaning that each hemisphere has much to offer the other, East and West, in the context of these times.

As the western metaparadigm of scientific materialism has been globalized, materialism has become globalized in any country participating in "modernization" or globalization. There is a lack, or a need fulfilled within each hemisphere by the other. For example, sanitized water and less poverty has been a welcome relief for citizens of any country who have taken on the current metaparadigm of globalization. Also, offering relief has been the results of the Enlightenment science–to a degree–so that superstitions passed down through the ages in their cultures have been able to be countered with reason.

As an example, a Chinese cultural belief and practice includes worshipping deceased ancestors during August, referred to as "ghost month." It is common in Taiwan or China that *waipo*, or grandma, warns not to swim out in the ocean during ghost month (August) because there is a chance of a ghost messing with you, causing you to drown. Ironically, though, in Taiwan during this month there are the most drownings...check the local papers' archives there, such as *The Taipei Times*, or *The China Post*.) This is at an over–generalized level, admittedly, for there has also been reason within the East, long before Westerners entered. But again, nonetheless, however generalized, the import of the Western paradigm with the scientific materialism at its core still has had an affect. Somehow, with the advent of "westernization" the scientific materialist ordering of the universe along with its pharmaceutical drugs and surgeries of the biomedical model has also gotten exported. Anyone with an infection is grateful for antibiotics, indeed. And it seems there is also a gratitude for "stuff," for the outward materializations of inward ideas that are cool, rather than perhaps, a continuing emphasis on what their elders say is important. There is a sense by this author that while the West, and particularly the U.S. are really good at manifesting ideas into physical, tangible goods, that this has been– comparatively–a weakness in the East.

Yet, along with these benefits also has come materialism. This materialism has been out of context for the East, for this "development" or "modernization" has also typically come at a cost to the country in losing much of their inherent organizational structure, and a taking on of the modern race, or consumerism, in order to participate at the global level. However, this has been done at a much more rapid pace for the East than the West did. Another key factor here is the nature of the technology being much different and of a nature that is vastly quicker to change, without the historical, grounded, relatively slower paced, contextualized, gradual lead–up to the present technology and the evolving lifestyle and older infrastructure that accompanies it, as we in the West, particularly in the U.S., have had. This causes a rushed, hectic, and off–balanced general sense to this development.

For the West, the hole missing is this imbalance with the over–emphasis on the physical, on materialism, on technology and lack of valuing the inner landscape. Buddhism with its understanding and science of the mind and how the mind can be worked with for optimum well–being has much to teach us. The medical systems of the traditional Indian and Chinese culture's and how they construe subtle energy to be both within an individual and the universe combined, have much to teach us. Knowing how to successfully cultivate and work with this subtle energy and enhancing our overall sense of well–being, general health and longevity is what we can gain. Much of what they know about subtle energy seems to echo what quantum physicists and the new sciences have gradually been uncovering, as our scientific materialist metaparadigm has been in the midst of this breakdown and shift. The timing of this all coming together demands some consideration.

The world is modernized, and the Indian and Chinese who work with subtle energy are also modernized, so that this subtle energy knowledge is not just for application to the ancient times. However, western culture does not have the cultural metaparadigm as its backdrop or context, as the East doesn't have the cultural metaparadigm or backdrop for scientific materialism. So the languages, idioms, lifestyles able to be seen in grandparents, diets, stores, and restaurants serving food prepared with its medicinal purposes in mind, don't have this cultural backdrop accompanying the practices that the West has imported thus far. Nor do family and societal anecdotes with acknowledgement of the subtle to refer to within its history exist in the West with the practice of acupuncture. So again, the teaching surrounding what subtle energy is, what it does and can do, is a bit out of context here. What is frequently a result is a stripped–down version that a typical Western mind living in the scientific materialist metaparadigm ends up with. An example here is using acupuncture for pain relief as its primary usage, or yoga for athletic fitness and pleasing bodily aesthetics only, such as power yoga. Power yoga actually is closer to plyometrics used in the strength-building fitness world. The richness of what each has to offer the other can get somewhat distorted in the translation.

The Mind and Life Institute's summits between the Dalai Lama with his panel of Tibetan monks and geshes–equivalents of Ph.D.'s–and Western pioneering, visionary scientists are a prime example. MLI provides a model for this mutually beneficial merger of the East and West. Yet, obviously meditation by yogic gurus to lower body temperature in the Himalayas is not applicable to a novice of meditation in any city in the United States. Whereas cultivating attention and focus, or calming the mind and hence the central nervous system from incessant sensory stimuli and stress, is more applicable. Applicability to the local culture still needs to be considered as these mergers continue between the teachings of the East and West.

Braden says, "If we can accept the powerful evidence (from quantum physics and now quantum biology) that consciousness itself and our role in it are the missing links in the theories of how reality works, then everything changes. In that change, we begin anew. *This makes us part of, rather than separate from, all that we see and experience.* And that's why this revolution is so powerful. *It writes us–all of humankind–right back into the equation of the universe.* It also casts us into the role of solving the great crises of our day, rather than leaving them to a future generation or simply to fate. *As we are architects of our reality, with the power to rearrange the atoms of matter itself,* what problem cannot be solved and what solution could possibly be beyond our reach?" (italics mine) (Braden 2008).

Braden really works with our perception of reality in his book *The Spontaneous Healing of Belief: Shattering the Paradigm of False Limits.* He describes our lives from the morning rituals that we go through, the technologies that we do or don't use to make our lives better or worse, our personal routines, to our religious ceremonies and in fact, entire civilizations, saying that all of this is based on our beliefs. With his examples, Braden clarifies how our beliefs provide the structure for the way we choose to live our lives down to the finest details and the smallest choices. Adding in that the new sciences and quantum physics are negating the discounting of our inner experience done by the Enlightenment scientists, Braden continues to reflect ideas parallel to our discussion. He says that the new sciences and quantum physics are instead showing us that the way we feel about the world around us is a force that extends *into* that world. This is an awareness of how subtle energy works.

Thus, in this way, the science from the new sciences is catching up to the spiritual and indigenous traditions–both the Indian and Chinese have been our examples–which have always told us that our world is nothing more than a reflection of what we think and believe. For clarity, remember that this then connects back with the Observer effect "discovered" by quantum physics. Our subjective expectations contribute to what happens on the physical plane; in collapsing a wave into a particle in certain ways that align with our thoughts, feelings, and expectations of what will happen. Then the particles take over, which is when physical matter begins. This is over–simplified, but ultimately it is what was uncovered. So these factors combine to therefore justify Braden saying that we are architects of our reality. Without going any further into the mechanics of how our thoughts create reality–for there are many other resources doing this, and more importantly this is not the point of this discussion–this basic understanding implies enough to see that how we think affects to a degree what happens on the physical plane. We are interacting with and co–creating to a degree what shows up in our physical world. But this is also metaphysical; remember, meta means beyond, bigger than. *And this is key to the motivation to clean up one's thinking.*

Life and managing to live it successfully goes well beyond the physical, right? Then why should we allow this to remain our collective–and individual, for many–dominant focus of our metaparadigm? Furthermore, it seems more than just irony behind the spiraling nexus of crises within our culture that these crises are from the very institutions built on the metaparadigm's belief and focus on the physical. Hence, it's these very systems that are crashing, and also screaming out that they need to change, suffering from their own dysfunction caused by this very imbalance. Quite possibly the banking system and the housing crisis all came about due to greed, focus on the physical, or the material. Do you see?

Pioneer, teacher of intuitive energy medicine and author of *The Anatomy of Spirit,* Carolyn Myss says, "The Divine is coded within paradoxes." She was speaking about being able to read the hidden meanings of the bigger picture, or perspective, within life's events, saying that the divine communicates to humans within paradoxes. This is something I provide for my clients consistently because it's what they require. Most seem to get lost in the small-me personality created me of the cognitive mind and so they lose the perspective that could tell them how to view symbolically what they're going through. What is needed for them to change their situation is what they're looking for from me. I help steer them back to what their own system is saying it needs, by helping them reconnect to this higher perspective. Realistically, it seems like, by using the energy medicine modalities I do, I am helping them reconnect to the their soul, and their ability to sense the soul, or spirit, in life in general. At the same time, I am using energy medicine and other tools to help them move beyond their minds. It seems that this is precisely what many experts, including myself obviously, agree is lacking in our culture. This mystical perspective, or soulfulness, that ancient cultures still have gives a sense of perspective, or a higher backdrop to life, beyond the mind and the small me personality. It is what seems the key to well-being that we're currently lacking in the United States.

So by adding the crises within the major systems in our society built upon the foundation of the materialist scientific metaparadigm, to the growing consensus that we are not just separate from nor uninfluential on the subtle power *behind* what we see as the physical world, this then equals the conclusion that there is a need for a metaparadigm shift. This recognition requires that we see how at the subjective and subtle energy level we are very much influencing, if not creating, what then manifests on the physical plane. And that we are doing this with the power–or lack of, and so creating by default–of our consciousness. This is the shift in thinking needed. *Our thoughts and beliefs*–beliefs are thoughts that have been thought over and over again with an emotional charge–*direct this power. So if we're not managing our thoughts well, or if we're not examining our beliefs, we're still creating from this mayhem of mismanagement, and if we're not aware of the power of our thoughts, we're most likely creating mayhem.* So at the very least, we're not creating what we want in our lives. We're only reacting to what's in our lives if not consciously engaged in some form of "mental management." The shift here, now, is the belief of where the power exists. Is it outside of us, or within us? Or both? And where inside of us?

It is not that the physical plane exists and we are subject to it, as thought within the Enlightenment scientists' ordering of the objective world. Instead, this next stage, or phase, or metaparadigm definitely involves the importance of the mind. For within the mind is our consciousness, or consciousness both underlies and branches up and out of the mind. It does so more fluidly and cleanly when not hindered by a rather unsettled, unstable, discordant mind in struggle or ego based afflictions. Focusing on the physical, or the material to the exclusion–or near exclusion–of the subtle, or consciousness, leads to a more afflicted, clinging, controlling ego based mind. The ego is created for operation and navigation on the physical plane; it's its partner. *So if we are focusing more on the physical, we are coming more from the ego, more than we are coming from the Higher Self, or the sacred self with a sense of a larger perspective than just the human made, physical world in mind.* This is where we are; at this nexus of having to work out of what we've created from the entire scientific materialist metaparadigm that emerged during the 1700's.

As the Buddhist and Hindu scriptures point out, getting beyond this ego based personality part of ourselves allows us to then connect more with a higher state of consciousness. Perhaps even to the point of a higher consciousness of unity with a divine source, with others, and with the universe overall. If one is an atheist or agnostic, substitute "universe" for "divine source" here. Typically, historically, this kind of transcendent focus was left to those who had "dropped out" of the material "race" and pursued a life of solitude. It has been an either–or lifestyle choice traditionally. Henry David Thoreau of the American Transcendentalists is a well known example. So are the baby–boomers who dropped out of their teaching positions at Harvard, or their professions and went instead to India, in search for something more in the 1960's and 1970's.

However, as Carolyn Myss has said, it is the time now to become "urban monks." Meaning, this historical dichotomy of either focusing on the material and physical and being an active member of the scientific materialist metaparadigm, its' institutions, businesses and "game" (as it has deemed it is played,) or withdrawing from it and going off into solitude to focus on the inner life is no longer an option. Instead, we are to do both together, each in a modified, yet genuinely unified, balanced way that keeps the little me, or the ego–mind in check with a cultivated Observer, or a "Higher Self." This can be—and now needs to be—while maneuvering on the physical plane of daily life of family, careers and all its accompanying necessities that we keep ourselves so busy fulfilling.

Complimenting this cultivation of the Observer is the need to also more fully work with the archetypal feminine qualities. These are the more subtle qualities; the non-reactive emotions and what they're telling us about a deeper understanding inside, intuition, and the less tangible, right–brained traits, such as creativity, abstraction, seeing things as a whole or synthesizing, multi–tasking, and compassion. For clarity, this is not the left brain objective labeling, measuring, reducing and analyzing traits. The more archetypal masculine cognitive qualities have led to us focusing on the tangible, objective, hard, raw data to quantify and utilize. The masculine cognitive style, therefore, has a focus on separation-duality–and competition. These traits of the masculine cognitive approach sound like what we typically construe as the cognitive brain's functions.

Duality, or separation, is implied when needing to label, categorize and compare. When comparing, one things comes out as A, and one thing comes out as B; one of which is usually connoted as better. This is inherent to the ego-mind, or the cognitive mind's functions. It separates the whole into this and not this, or that and not this. This is polarity. The counteraction to this is holism and going beyond polarity, to unity. So our framing of this but not that could also include the awareness of how the two have their own contribution to the whole. This is echoing the concept communicated by the yin-yang symbol. In other words, to then not temper this separation-in-order-to-label mechanism within the cognitive mind's functions with a more balanced approach of bringing in more feminine cognitive approaches like holism seems rather foolhardy.

Additionally, there is a an aspect of receptivity in the archetypal feminine approach, and this involves being receptive to what our inner knowing is sensing from the "outside" consciousness of the "outside" world. Yet the connection to this information happens inside us. The connecting point is when our consciousness reaches out beyond our own cognitive mind. So what we are talking about, in fact, is *beyond* the cognitive mind as a whole. We access this through the right brain traits. These right brain traits are the ones historically likened to the more feminine cognitive style, and to the more abstract, spiritual, and intuitive abilities. So we can go beyond, to sensing what else our intuition is receiving, which is back to that connecting to something bigger, beyond the small-mind, little-me, personality based cognitive mind we typically use to go through everyday life.

Relying primarily on the physical and the predictable–*or that which we can control*–so that we can observe, measure and study systematically and then use to compete with has been our metaparadigm's approach since Enlightenment scientists created the scientific materialist approach that we applied to the Industrial Revolution. Again, relying on the physical, when seen from the "hierarchy" of consciousness we just described, causes us also to rely on the "little me" or the ego, in order to navigate the physical plane. While the higher Self, or the "bigger me" is the one who is aware of this quantum field, or the unity of consciousness, or chi, or prana, or life force, and our connection to it and therefore, to each other.

Amit Goswami, the Indian born physicist in *The Visionary Window: A Quantum Physicist's Guide to Enlightenment* provides an example to help understand what happens with interconnectivity. He states that it has been discovered that when many people focus on a single event such as a football game or the O.J. Simpson trial, they may become correlated, or connected, in our terms. He states that this correlation produces a measurable anomalous behavior. Researchers Radin and Rebman in 1996 studied random number generators, and showed this correlation behavior with the numbers generated. "But what is producing the correlation at a distance and maintaining it through the entire duration of the measurement? At present, there is only one agency known to be capable of this: transcendent, nonlocal consciousness...Many holistic thinkers, the physicist Paul Davies for example, recognize that consciousness is the missing causal organizing principle in today's science," (Goswami 2000).

Goswami also provides an insiders secret. "A 1984 issue of *Physics Today* quoted what one physicist told another in the corridors of a physical society meeting: 'Anybody who is not bothered by Bell's theorem has to have rocks in his head.' So scientists are bothered. But as people, we have an infinite capacity to delude ourselves; *scientists are no exception*. The quantum window is a huge invitation to the real freedom that consciousness offers us. It is also very scary. Once you see consciousness as the ground of all being, it is hard to carry on the often meaningless, materialist research programs that form the bulk of the academic, governmental, and industrial research," (Goswami 2000). (Italics mine) Remember that Goswami has retired from a university professor of physics three decades plus career and is now joined up with international organizations focused on applying quantum mechanics to the study of the mind body connection.

Gregg Braden then brings us further into understanding what we are faced with at this unique crossroads in human history, "With access to such a power already within us, to say that our beliefs are important to life is an understatement. Our beliefs are life! They are where it begins and how it sustains itself. From our immune response and the hormones that regulate and balance our bodies...to our ability to heal bones, organs and skin–and even conceive life–the role of human belief is rapidly taking center stage in the new frontiers of quantum biology and physics," (Braden 2008). Braden, thus, brings us full circle in understanding why there is so much resistance to the unseen, intangible realms, with this resistance only recently now being countered with relative force. We have been slowly inching towards critical mass by those at the grassroots, pioneering levels, who are embracing the power of subtle energy. So they're working within the paradigm of there being a genuine mind body connection. They are also, therefore, working with the minds' thoughts.

Meanwhile, the contrary reaction is thus leaving others either still in denial, hesitant consideration, or conflictual resistance–again the stages of Kuhn's paradigm shifts. We're talking about a *meta*paradigm shift here, so there is even more resistance, conflict and upheaval. All of this is clearly reflected in the crises we're witnessing within the health care field in the United States, surrounding how health care should best be delivered. I am not talking about funding. That will answer itself when the metaparadigm shift completes. However, other countries using preventative health care practices with less levels of rampant chronic diseases, spend less. Should it be the biomedical model, natural healing addressing subtle energies, or a combination of the two, as in the integrated model? This will work itself out, without forcing the answer.

Braden says, "If our beliefs hold so much power, and if we live our lives based on what we believe, then the obvious question is: *Where do our beliefs come from?* The answer may surprise you. With few exceptions, they originate with what science, history, religion, culture, and family tell us. In other words, the essence of our capabilities and limits may well be based in what *other people* tell us. That realization leads to the next question that we must ask ourselves: *If our lives are based on what we believe, then what if those beliefs are wrong?*" (Braden 2008).

Furthermore, the clinging attachment to relying on what is predictable and therefore able to be controlled must to be released. The mind's grasping at control in the face of chaos is a very predictable behavior, and it is of the "little me." Kind of like Austin Power's "Mini–Me." It's the ego identity that has feelings of being threatened when faced with the new, change, or the unknown. When it comes to studying the mind and consciousness in mental behaviors and afflictions, as the Buddhists do, *this control mechanism of the ego based personality is a very common understanding, basically a novice one.*

So, part of the ego-mind's design is to help us make sense of what we encounter on the physical place in life everyday. So it prefers the status quo. It seems that its job is easier that way. Another way to look at it is the ego–mind versus the Higher–Self as the human condition. Meaning when in a body we engage in the physical, forgetting about a connection to the Higher versions of ourselves. If and when we do reconnect to the Higher Self, this connection fuels us and nurtures us to engage in what causes us to grow even when it's uncomfortable. It helps us have that mountain top perspective. Many say soul in place of Higher Self. Then there's the idea from Yoga and Buddhism that our Higher Self, or Soul, is connected to eternity because it's the part of us that is eternal. The ego-mind is attached to the ego, or personality part of us, and it is more readily accessible when on the physical plane. Again, it's the Human Condition.

The ego based personality "little me" prefers things stay the same. Change threatens the control the ego has been able to gain, however unreal this temporary control the ego feels like it's been able to garner on the physical plane. So it resists change, seeing it as a threat, and works to keep us locked into status–quo behavior, sabotaging efforts to change much of the time. Again, within cultures who work with consciousness and the mind and know of the ego–mind's games, like most Native American tribes, they have an understanding of this mechanism within the ego part of our mind; or "ego–mind." Some Native Americans traditions call this behavioral trait of the ego–mind that we all have, "the trickster" or "the self–saboteur." They refer to the Wild Coyote as the animal symbolizing "trickster" behavior.

Amit Goswami says, "In one of the Upanishads (The Holy Scriptures for the Hindus), we find an exquisite metaphor for our two–self nature: Two birds, united always and known by the same name, cling closely to the same tree. One of them eats the sweet and bitter fruits; the other looks on without eating (Nikhilananada 1964). The one that eats the sweet and bitter fruits of the world is the personal ego; it experiences itself as separate from the world and is sustained by that separateness. The witness is the universal atman, the unity within us, the quantum self, in our terminology. We identify, first of all, with the quantum self, the subject 'pole' of primary awareness. Then we identify with the ego, the self of limited choice, the self of our personal history. We acquire not only the apparent separateness that enables experience but also the limited identity of an individual personality," (Goswami 2000).

Goswami is paralleling the division discussed in the above paragraphs. Where we've been and what else needs to be incorporated in order for us to evolve, and move beyond this "small me" personality that clings, reacts and limits us, yes? Are you getting a clearer sense now of where we can be? Of what life could look like, and what we could be like if we worked with our cognitive minds and Observed our ego-minds? We've done really well operating on the level of the individual ego–personality to the point of imbalance. Do you see that? And yet we also very much need the "quantum self" as he puts it. Yes? The more unified, less divisive self, the self that sees interconnectivity and wholeness–analogous to the quantum level, or the Higher Self, could you see what it would be like? And how different from what we've been doing? Do you see how it's the missing link, that we've not seen, typically, in our culture? Do you see how many more people have been searching for this over the past five years or so? Do you see yourself in this? Did you happen to exhale, sigh, or lighten up when reading this description above? Did it give you relief? Please pay attention to that. Please. It's subtle, but so meaningful.

We need a more soulful society. We seem to have lost our collective soul, with many individuals doing the same. Still, individually there's many reconnecting, and it's starting to gain momentum. Why do you think yoga is so trendy and international travel and expat life? The shows on the Travel Network, "House Hunter's International" could have been me twelve years ago. People are increasingly looking for alternatives to our metaparadigm. To just come out and say that we need more soul in our society, that we've lost our soulfulness somewhere along the lines, is it possible that this statement would be met with dismissal, or the question, "Where's the proof for that? I think we're doing good, the economy is starting to improve. People are going to church more, there's been a revival with Christianity (or Judaism, or Islam) and people are doing ok,"? Or, "What's the benefit of our society regaining its soulfulness?" And "What is having more soul going to do for me?" Guess who is asking these questions. You got it, the ego-mind. The ego-mind who likes the status quo; our status quo of favoring the cognitive mind and a system very much created from cognitive mind in order to escape the wildness of the soul that was once in our culture, prior to the Age of Reason. The cognitive mind has been our dominant approach, society wide, since then. We need to counteract this with more soul. Do you see it now? Thank you. Exhale on my part, then.

Goswami helps us further grasp this parallel from the quantum world to ourselves: "Our two–self nature is of great consequence for our spirituality–how spirituality manifests in us and how we proceed on our spiritual journey. American psychologist Abraham Maslow and Italian psychologist Roberto Assagioli have rediscovered via clinical studies the concept of a transpersonal self beyond the behavioral ego (Maslow 1968; Assagioli 1976). This recognition of a two–level self–identity has initiated the field of transpersonal psychology." But wait, for Goswami is only building a foundation with the already known Humanistic psychology of Maslow and Assagioli, that he then adds to, "Note that the ego and the quantum self are not a dualistic partnership; rather they are 'united always.' Both are apparent identifications that consciousness takes on in the process of manifestation in a physical body and in a self–referential quantum brain. In identification with the quantum self there is unity and joy, there is freedom of choice and creativity, there is tangled hierarchy in the relationship between subject and object(s), and there is two–way relationship and love. *In identification with the ego there is separateness and anxiety, there is conditioning and dogmatism, there is simple hierarchy and solipsistic tyranny,*" (italics mine) (Goswami 2000).

Goswami then goes on to describe the ego as having qualities such as reasoning, continuous, determined, linear, local, personal, and classical logic; whereas the quantum self possesses such traits as creativity, discontinuous, synchronistic, holistic, nonlocal, transpersonal and quantum logic. Furthering his description by saying that the spontaneity of the quantum self is without fixity, he asserts also that while without the fixity offered by the ego, civilization is impossible. Hence, Goswami is showing a sense of hierarchy, *usefulness at each level,* and implied evolution; evolution in the human, and human consciousness–both individually and collectively.

In Goswami's application of quantum physics to humans, it is apparent through his discussion that he has a well developed almost intuitive feel and understanding as a quantum physicist himself, of the nature of the quantum level. Further, it is also apparent why we, as humans across the globalized and "modernized" world, are feeling as if we are in crisis at this point, for we are being asked to evolve along with our increased understanding of the nature of reality. This means to not only operate from the ego level, but get to know our Higher Self associated with the quantum level, or the quantum self as Goswami puts it, and incorporate the quantum level traits more fully.

Ultimately, the ideal is to be able to be in ego when those traits are needed, and to come from the Higher Self with the quantum level type of traits when these are most beneficial and appropriate. This is a skillful dance, and self awareness and self discipline are key in making this happen. Making the ego-mind serviceable is central to this process. And it clearly is possible, I can attest to this first hand as a meditator, meditation and yoga teacher, energy healer, holistic life coach, Ph.D., and a personal trainer. Many are switching between ego level traits and Higher Self/quantum level traits quite gracefully, moment to moment, even. So gracefully, in fact, that their dance between the rock solid, three dimensional physical world and expansiveness of the potential energies at the quantum level's airiness, multidimensional world is not necessarily noticed by an outsider. But we're getting ahead of ourselves here. Suffice it to say there is so much potential able to be worked with. That's what the quantum field is.

The world simply does not function in the solid, physical way only, as presented to us and perpetuated by the scientific materialism metaparadigm. And this rocks Westerner's foundation to the core; particularly Americans. So it seems that we are being pushed, commanded, cajoled by the major events coalescing together now to see the actual nature of reality stemming from the unseen. Ironically, much of the voices pointing the way out are still coming from the sciences, albeit the new sciences. In the West, again particularly in the United States, one of the most respected sources from whom we get our view of reality is science...yet?...Right.

Goswami offers also, "The quantum self gives us creativity, but the ego is essential to bring the creative insight to manifestation and to augment it with reasoning. This creative process ending in manifestation provides the scaffolding for the next insight, and thus civilization can grow," (Goswami 2000). Yet, in order to be able to dance with the two successfully, the little self's areas of resistance and afflictions need be cleared out to a degree that the quantum self can be better accessed. Then with this increased self–mastery, the power available on the quantum level is able to be shaped more readily. It's also why the affirmations and quick miracle work promised within the movie *The Secret* seem oversimplified and why people who claimed it didn't work for them may not have yet had the mastery needed to engage the power at the quantum level. This leads to taking potential out of a vacuum space and creating what we want in our lives using the subjective powers Tiller talks about, such as intention, emotion, thoughts, and consciousness. This possibly sounds like something from Star Trek or science fiction, and that's ok. It is where we are.

I just had an experience of this power that I am talking about. As I lug this manuscript around with me on the weekends, working to put the final tweaks on it, I sit here on one of the last weekends doing so, at a Chinese restaurant. For my fortune from my cookie (that, by the way, contains FD&C, yellow #5 and yellow #7 as its ingredients...) the side that doesn't contain the fortune but does contain the "Learn Chinese" information has the word *mian*, which means "inside." Think of my main message here: we need to pay more attention to our insides, not the external, physical plane quite as much. Right? This was the vocab word given to me in my apparently still ongoing quest to learn Chinese! Then, turning it over, the fortune says, "The Future: Human Evolution: wider freeways, but narrower viewpoints." No kidding! Synchronistic events like this are normal in my day to day life existence. This is a side-effect of successfully engaging with the quantum level.

Going back now to the main discussion, put another way, by David Hawkins, M.D. and Ph.D. and co–author of *Orthomolecular Psychiatry* with Nobel Prize winner Linus Paulding, in *Power Vs. Force: The Hidden Determinants of Human Behavior,* "An important element of chaos theory, which is helpful in understanding this evolution of consciousness, is the law of *sensitive dependence on initial conditions.* This refers to the fact that an extremely minute variation over a course of time can have the effect of producing a profound change, much as a ship whose bearing is one degree off compass will eventually find itself hundreds of miles off course. This phenomenon...is an essential mechanism of all evolution and also underlies the potential of the creative process," (Hawkins 2002). Meaning, that within chaos, there is much potential inherent to the chaos of swirling energies. Emotions, thoughts, events, people's reactions jumbled together in a confused, almost overwhelming presentation occurring simultaneous to each other is an example of chaos. And this is hugely challenging to navigate.

The skill of self-mastery that comes from learning to Observe our little self's behaviors more (think both individually and collectively now) helps us handle what chaos presents to us, and then to create opportunity out of it. We can stay present and non-reactive, or even ride it out while waiting for reactions to subside, for the moment when we then gain that mountain top perspective. Then asking questions about what this chaos is giving to us, and what is the symbolic meaning to it? What can we gain from it? What possibilities are there in it? What inherent creativity is there, that this chaos is expressing? As in the chaos is present to break something down and have newness created. So asking what is there to breakdown and then create that this chaos is pointing out to my consciousness, or Higher Self, can generate an entirely different way to live. This book, my radio show, all my workshops, one on one work with my clients, and products are meant to give voice to gaining perspective. Reading symbolically the small chaotic breakdown of the old as an entire picture of where we each are and where we are as a whole, then emerges. As does a sense of what is next, emerging out of the chaos, *giving reason to the chaos.*

This is the creative process, with chaos an inherent part of it. Pulling out what is intended, needed, and desired from the chaos is what the creative process is–from a position of awareness and mastery. Also, echoed in Hawkin's quote is what has happened due to choices made by the Enlightenment scientists, and then their industrial age counterparts. It also echoes Kuhn's theory on scientific revolutions and paradigm shifts that can start one hundred years before the actual shift in the paradigm happens at a collective level.

The actual challenges that we are really facing are not going to be effectively addressed by slight adjustments to the system at a status–quo level. Or as minor individual changes that are of the same nature–meaning, small adjustments at more of the physical level, say a change of job, switch of health insurance coverage, or moving homes. These changes may well be a part of the type of systemic changes we're talking about, yes, but it's much bigger than one change here, then another small tweaking there. Ervin Laszlo helps us clearly grasp this important distinction. Laszlo, living in Italy, has been nominated twice for the Nobel Peace Prize, and is the editor of the international periodical *World Futures: The Journal of General Evolution*, as well as Chancellor–Designate of the newly formed Globalshift University and founder and president of the international think tanks, The Club of Budapest, and the General Evolution Research Group. He wrote *Quantum Shift in the Global Brain: How the New Scientific Reality Can Change us and Our World.*

In the chapter "A New Vision" Laszlo quotes J. Krishnamurti, considered one of the greatest thinkers of all times, and who was not associated with any religious institution or organization up through his death in 1986, "It seems to me that a totally different kind of morality and conduct, and an action that springs from the understanding of the whole process of living, have become an urgent necessity in our world of mounting crises and problems. We try to deal with these issues through political and organizational methods, through economic readjustment and various reforms; but none of these things will ever resolve the complex difficulties of human existence, though they may offer temporary relief...But there is a revolution which is entirely different and which must take place if we are to emerge from the endless series of anxieties, conflicts, and frustrations in which we are caught. This revolution has to begin, not with theory and ideation, which eventually prove worthless, *but with a radical transformation in the mind itself,*" (Laszlo 2008).

B. Alan Wallace also asserts the importance of working with the mind, that the time is ripe for this in *Embracing Mind* by saying, "'Know thyself,' the ancient call to self-observation, holds the promise of genuine happiness for us as individuals. Indeed, it may also lead to knowledge and wisdom embracing life itself. Without intimate knowledge of our subjective nature, how can we truly follow the dictum 'to thine own self be true'? Self-knowledge clarifies experience, leading to maturity. In addition...the most subtle practices of introspection may reveal a surprising complementarity between the mind and the universe," (Wallace 2008). Meaning, once we make the seemingly wild monkey or roaring lion of the ego mind our ally, we will find that our consciousness works really well with the natural state of life in the universe. So we stop blocking ourselves from so much more, from all the potential and from it *being actually easy*. It's quite a paradox—and again the divine speaks in paradoxes—the ego mind likes control. It has a lot of fear, especially when we are reaching for more for ourselves, into some new area we've not yet gone. Perhaps because it senses just how small it is compared to the vast power that holds unlimited potential and possibilities? But if we just get around, beyond and through this fear of change, the power, the freedom is immense!

What Wallace says comes as a reassuring jolt of the possible gains from introspection. Remembering that Wallace has training as a physicist and as a Tibetan monk, and was one of the Dalai Lama's main translators, participants and scientists at the Mind and Life Conferences makes him someone worthy of listening to about the importance of self-observation. The power of introspection to help us let go of our mental afflictions that may pose limitations on our ability to know ourselves, be ourselves, be happy and grow, and find meaning in our lives and our universe, without sickness, without conflicts, without struggle, with genuine, clean freedom—this is part of what Wallace is speaking to here. Again, we're talking about accessing the clear potential that can be used to assist us in actualizing our lives as we desire, lives retaining meaning and a connection with the sacred—instead of being so tripped up by the little me's habitual thinking habits and patterns.

In fact, the entire Mind Life Institute's establishment was created in acknowledgement of this lack of knowing the mind from introspection in the West–again, particularly the United States. Seeing the compliment that the Eastern contemplative practices, or specifically Buddhism's science of the mind, could do for Westerners *to fill this gap of understanding about our own minds, and how to successfully know them and work with them for overall well being* seems to be one of the main intentions. As Daniel Goleman, author of the New York Times bestseller *Emotional Intelligence,* says in the introduction to *Healing Emotions: Conversations with the Dalai Lama on Mindfulness, Emotions and Health,* (the transcribed recording of the discussions at the third Mind and Life conference), "On the other hand, the dialogues have also shown that Western science has much to gain from these insights from the East. Tibetan explorations into the psyche have yielded a sophisticated phenomenology of mind that could guide modern scientists, if scientists would listen. One fruit of these dialogues is an ongoing research project that stems directly from this third round of the Mind and Life meetings: *a neurophysiological study of brain states in adept Tibetan yogis* to better understand the potentials of attentional training," (italics mine) (Goleman 1997).

Remember, this was only the third Mind and Life Conference that took place in 1990; much has advanced in, and has actually become the new sciences over these past twenty years. This study Goleman is referring to is one of the first of its kind to measure with scientific rigor and methodology skilled practitioners of meditation for claims that Buddhism makes of the benefits of meditation. In this regard it is the gained skill of attentional training, meaning to be able to concentrate better. This is also the Mind and Life Conference that lead to the founding of the Mind and Life Institute, with its seed money from the Hershey Family Foundation.

Beginning in 2000, and as an extension of the research begun in 1990, members of the Mind and Life Institute again began to research meditation in Western brain science laboratories with the full collaboration of meditation adepts. Using fMRI, EEG, and MEG imaging technology, this research has been carried out at the Centre de Recherche en Epistemologie Appliquee de l'Ecole Polytechnique (CREA) in Paris, the University of Wisconsin in Madison, and Harvard University. Additionally, measures of emotional expression and autonomic psychophysiology have been gathered at the University of California at San Francisco and at Berkeley. *These were the pioneers;* many others have joined in on this research, including, for example, UCLA's Semel Institute of Mindfulness Awareness Research Center (MARC) and others.

And from the Dalai Lama himself in his opening remarks of the first Mind and Life Conference as recorded in the book *Gentle Bridges:*

Conversations with the Dalai Lama on the Sciences of Mind, "Western civilization's science and technology bring society tremendous benefit. *Yet, due to highly developed technology, we also have more anxiety and more fear.* I always feel that mental development and material development must be well–balanced, so that together they make a more human world. If we lose human values and human beings become part of a machine, there is no freedom from pain and pleasure. Without freedom from pain and pleasure, it is very difficult to demarcate between right and wrong. The subjects of pain and pleasure naturally involve feeling, mind, and consciousness. So it is most important for Western science and material development and Eastern mental development to work together," (italics mine) (Hayward 1992).

Evidence Based Medicine & Conflict: The Breakdown Phase

Laszlo also does an extremely good job at summing up the current state we find ourselves in, in his chapter entitled, "Macroshift: The Dynamics." Laszlo states, "In its present form, industrial civilization is not sustainable. In the opening years of the twenty–first century the industrial age is shifting into a post–industrial age, impelled by the 'second industrial revolution'–a revolution hallmarked by the advent of the technologies of information and communication. These technologies are more powerful than the steam and fossil fuel–based technologies of the first industrial revolution, and the 'revolutions' they catalyze are unfolding much faster than the first industrial revolution: in a matter of years instead of decades or centuries. In the past Macroshifts were local, national, or regional. Today's Macroshift is global. Humanity's second evolution has reached the dimensions of the planet," (Laszlo 2008).

Laszlo then goes on to outline the four phases of macroshifts; the trigger phase, the transformation phase, the critical (or chaos) phase, and the final phase broken into two with the first being the breakdown phase and the second being the breakthrough phase. He describes the trigger phase as having innovations in hard technologies that bring about greater efficiency in the manipulation of nature for human ends, like during the Industrial Revolution. The transformation phase is when hard technologies, according to Laszlo, create innovations that irreversibly change social and environmental relations and bring about, successively, "a higher level of resource production;

a faster growth of population; a greater social complexity; and a growing impact on the social and the natural environment," (Laszlo 2008). This can be seen in both the 19th and 20th centuries in the U.S., during which there were two separate periods where the country's population quadrupled, co-occurring with leaps in industrialization's productivity.

The critical, or chaos phase, is described by Laszlo as when changed social and environmental relations put pressure on the established culture, *thereby placing into question time-honored values and worldviews, along with the ethics and ambitions that are associated with them.* It's not that society becomes chaotic in this phase; it's that the order is subtle and one who is extremely sensitive to fluctuations can sense the pending changes. Just as importantly and key to our discussion is what Laszlo points out about this critical, or chaos phase. "What determines the way the society's developmental trajectory forks off, *is the evolution of the dominant culture; meaning the way people's values, views, and ethics respond to change,*" (Laszlo 2008).

Yet finally, in the first of the two stages of the last phase in Laszlo's macroshift discussion that he says we are currently undergoing globally, is the breakthrough phase. He describes this as, "the *values, worldviews, and ethics of a critical mass of people in society are resistant to change, or they change too slowly, and this is accompanied by the established institutions being too rigid to allow for timely transformation.* The social complexity, coupled with a degenerating environment, creates unmanageable stress. *"The social order is exposed to a series of crises that soon degenerate into conflict and violence,"* (italics mine) (Laszlo 2008).

We are in this breakdown phase globally and currently, and more so specifically in the United States. While your cognitive mind may have judged Laszlo's referenced levels of violence, which we'll touch upon in just a bit, nonetheless the conflict is clearly there. We need to reconnect to the central issue here–the mind body connection –in order to better understand both the breakdown phase and where we're at with the mind body connection now. This breakdown phase can be seen in the battle grounds that are centered around the mind body connection's two sides, as they show up in the health care arena. The side that acknowledges the mind body connection and fully works from it–natural healing, while the other side that is still resistant to it, either in theory or application, or both–biomedicine.

Alison J. Kay, PhD

We can see Laszlo's "rigidity of the institutions" by the lack of the mind body sciences taught at the medical schools for the biomedical model *even as half of the public now uses healing methods based on the mind body connection model* (The National Institute of Health's Center for Complimentary and Alternative Medicine (NCCAM 2010)). We can also see this "rigidity of the institutions," as well, when looking to the AMA's and the pharmaceutical industry's control, as they control thru holding the dominant position within our health care industry as the only governmental supported deliver of healthcare. Whereas acupuncture and even more so any form of energy healing are usually out of pocket expenses. The mandate that businesses make of their employees that they use their AMA backed health care benefits is another example of this rigidity—as are the financial perks the businesses get to enroll more of their employees in their health care. There isn't much, if any, real choice when it comes to health care in our system. They're holding on, and this rigidity isn't only signs of their monopoly, but it's also an entire structure that is held together with rigidity at this point. This is the physicians, the pharmaceutical companies, the insurance companies, the AMA, medicare, medicaid and any other part of the entire health care industry—it's all rigidly controlled at this point, the structure allows for very little freedom or choice. And our science's paradigm is at the root of it.

We can also see this resistance and rigidity on our federal government center's website for their version of the mind body connection. This rigidity is there in the repetition of their use of the phrase "evidence based science" to a near mantra level. They make a demand, The National Institutes of Health's National Center for Complimentary and Alternative Medicine, of the citizen to validate the use of these very healing methods before they engage in using them. In order to seriously consider these "new" modalities of healing, NCCAM strongly advises over and over again that it be evidence based, (NCCAM 2010). This is a clear example of government bias and support for the scientific materialist science that the AMA backed biomedical model is based on. It's the official governmental–read metaparadigm here–stance. And it's on lock down, system wide throughout our society, rigidly. Any other choices outside the biomedical model, from our sources of authority, seems to be strongly frowned upon. Quite paternalistic, yes? No. Quite authoritarian, yes.

Upon use of their website, the taxpayer can see this demand repeated to the point of redundancy that clearly implies resistance to natural healing, Ironically that is what they claim to be for—a national center for complimentary and alternative medicine. Yet when reading their website it comes across more as a national center to "make sure that the science is evidence based." Their resistance is predictable within Kuhn's model of scientific revolutions; it's one of the stages as metaparadigm's shift. And the scientific materialist paradigm has become our country's metaparadigm, so the government is a main part of upholding it, along with the fields of mainstream science, the insurance industry, the pharmaceutical industry, the research industry and the AMA. Even though they are a national center for the mind body connection's healing methods, as they call natural healing, "complimentary and alternative medicine," it is nonetheless glaringly obvious when exploring their information on their website that they are more supportive of the scientific materialism metaparadigm's approach to health care.

Of course they are, because as seen, we're discussing a metaparadigm, which means the government is also a central player in perpetuating the sciences' paradigm. The name they use for natural healing methods in and of itself reflects that there is resistance: "complimentary" to what, and "alternative" to what? Complimentary and alternative to the dominant system of biomedicine that the AMA, the pharmaceutical lobby, the insurance industry's lobby, and the other power players along with the federal government keep in place. This is accomplished through its funding and support via policies and laws and then our inherited monopoly of a health care system.

Another example on their home page under the title, "NCCAM's 10th Anniversary Research Symposium: Exploring the Science of CAM," they say, "Ten years of rigorous research and advances in the science of complementary and alternative medicine (CAM) were celebrated at NCCAM's 10th Anniversary Research Symposium on December 8, 2009... Prominent researchers shared exciting findings on a wide range of topics– the body's microbial communities and their role in health and disease, the neuroscience of acupuncture and meditation, and the behavioral science of stress and coping–with an in–person and online audience of approximately 400 health care practitioners, researchers, and members of the public." This is fantastic, admittedly; especially since more funding has just recently been granted to NCCAM at the time of this writing (2010). They've done some really good funding of research, certainly. In fact, interestingly, there is acknowledgement of this in England, about the amount of funding the American NCCAM has for research that the English hadn't allocated by that point.

But it is nearly impossible to get to real information that is helpful to the average citizen, as their website invests so much of its space repeating the need for these "complimentary and alternative methods" of healing to have the back up of rigorous scientific evidence, to the point of it now being called "evidence based medicine" that it drowns out what there is of any real information. *Meaning, the resistance is so blatant that it manifests a fear in the uninformed citizen trying to make heads or tails of if they should actually try something different than what their doctor may have failed to help them with. We're talking about someone just trying to get informed of their alternatives.* That seems to be the actual experience of the average person with our government's website for natural, or "alternative" healing information. That is they end up being led to be skeptical and fearful, while at the same time, marginally hopeful for there being alternatives to the mainstream biomedical model and most likely their own personal diagnosis, only because of the increase in scientific evidence.

Additionally, this redundancy of what they've funded being "evidence based medicine" screams of self-defense within its redundancy. Why the defensiveness? Because there is an attack from those within the old metaparadigm as it is breaking down, the one of biomedicine, and the institutions and structures that include massive amounts of power and money within our country surrounding the biomedical model with the government being both a part of it and stuck in the middle of it. This attack from those trying to uphold the status quo is against the mind body healing modalities, or holistic approaches to health. This "battle" has been getting intensified by the increasing number of breakthroughs in the new sciences about the benefits of holistic health practices, and the importance of consciousness. This reinforces the need for holistic health practices that address a human system of the level of consciousness. These breakthroughs have been helping to reach near critical mass for a different metaparadigm, one centered around a different set of beliefs that acknowledges more than just the physical. It is the same battle as what eventually kicked homeopathic medicine out as the dominant medical model in the 1800's.

Yet it seems that the NCCAM may be so emphatic about its "rigorous scientific methods" used because it is in defense of itself as a governmental institution that both supports the AMA and the biomedical model, but one that is also trying to support the rising voice of the people. This leaves NCCAM in the middle between the power structures set in place that are still dominant under the scientific materialism metaparadigm and the citizens who see change is needed and are demanding something different. Ultimately, this has the NCCAM in a paralyzed, ineffective position. The fact that they've been able to fund the amount of studies that they've been able to fund is impressive, given this dynamic. Since this battle between the two paradigms has been going on for a while now, with growing intensity, there was some awareness of this at the governmental level by the time the NIH created the NCCAM. However, the initial phase was one where there was no support from the government, and those practicing any of the mind body connection based therapies or treatments were labeled as quacks, or pushed outside the realms of what was considered credible. That was the denial stage phase, according to Kuhn's model of scientific revolutions.

So these natural healing methods began to be in increasing demand by the citizenry. Therefore, the leaders of the biomedical community and their other supporters increasingly noticed the field. And once the 50% marker was hit, that means 50% of the citizenry was directing its money towards natural healing at various levels, the government had to respond with some support, right? Typical to the way natural healing benefits get known, in fact it was a single senator who had a family member or friend helped by one of these mind body methods, who initiated the NCCAM. This person who Senator Harkin knew had sought out the natural healing method *not based on rigorous scientific evidence supporting the usefulness of the treatment, but instead based on family and friends' recommendations of the method.* As we will see later, this is most frequently the case with the average citizen who is new to mind body healing methods.

This defensiveness of the NCCAM is also caused by the other half of a public deeply steeped in its own values, worldviews and ethics directly impacted from living within a system that relies on the physical as primary. This is the result—one more time—from a basically unquestioned adoption of the scientific materialism metaparadigm that was handed to us from scientists living in a different time, under a different set of circumstances and within a different cultural, and societal milieu than the current post–modern one. Meaning, scientific materialism's ultimate marriage to industry and technology and biomedicine. Again, this includes the biotech industry, which includes the pharmaceutical industry; biotech corporations conducting research and development on biomedical devices; the university research and development industry involved with biotech research; and the military's own application of these technologies. This has all been so deeply ingrained within our culture's foundation and backdrop, that we have not questioned it–until recently. It's just been the way things are, the way things are done here. It's our metaparadigm.

This is the breakdown phase. It's only begun to be questioned at a more critical mass level, rather than at the level of pioneers only–or visionaries–because more and more people are suffering under this metaparadigm, and have had to go for help outside of this metaparadigm to the healing methods using the subtle energies that are acknowledged within natural healing treatments that operate within the paradigm of the mind body connection, due to this metaparadigm's over–reliance on the physical. This over–reliance led to the imbalance where the biomedical community has focused only on that which is physical. Therefore they've - we've - been missing out on a rather substantial portion of the human experience, as well as missing out on the genuine causes of the diseases, as opposed to the surface level physical symptoms. And then medicating them. Yes, we do have fantastic medicine in trauma cases, for sure. It's what we're considered the best at, remember?

However, in researching the founding of the NCCAM, it was amidst this exact resistance of the breakdown phase that Laszlo is speaking about that the NCCAM was not only founded, but strove to be taken seriously in its beginning years. Much of the reason for the establishment of the NCCAM came from Senator Tom Harkin. It was primarily through Harkin's efforts that the National Institutes of Health had the NCCAM created in 1992, first as the Office of Alternative Medicine (OAM), then in 1998, when NIH Director Harold Varmus tried to place OAM under more scientific NIH control, by elevating OAM to a full and independent Center within the NIH. Thus was NCCAM born. The stormy history of this federal institution attempting to support the visionary work Senator Harkin deemed as important attests to Laszlo's description of part of the breakdown phase, the first of the last two phases of a macroshifts in society, again: "values, worldviews, and ethics of a critical mass of people in society are resistant to change, or they change too slowly."

This conflict is between the supporters of the NCCAM and the critics; more specifically, the stormy history of the NCCAM and "alternative healing," as well as the supplements and vitamin industry, and any preventative medicine practices that can be considered natural healing—even meditation and yoga —within our country, verses those who in this application of Laszlo's model "are resistant to change," who are aligned with the scientific materialist metaparadigm . They also happen to be who are most benefitting from it, such as the AMA and the pharmaceutical industry. This is the "social complexity, coupled with a degenerating environment, creates unmanageable stresses," and "the social order is exposed to a series of crisis that soon degenerate into conflict and violence" part of the breakdown phase, according to Laszlo's "Macroshift in Society" section of his *Quantum Shift in the Global Brain*. We'll get to his use of the word "violent."

An example of the resistance to change in this conflict that Laszlo describes happening as a part of our breakdown phase, comes from the aptly named website and blog "Science–Based Medicine Exploring issues and controversies in the relationship between science and medicine" published by David Gorski. The topic "Politics and Regulation" comes before the "Public Health" and "Science and Medicine" topics as the highest volume of topics on this website, http://www.sciencebasedmedicine.org/." Gorski blasts the NCCAM and Harkin, "I've complained many times about how NCCAM funds studies that, let's face it, are of pseudoscience and quackery (homeopathy, anyone?) and even more about how it promotes unscientific medical practices. I've argued time and time again that there is no research that is funded by NCCAM that couldn't be dealt with as well or better by other Centers or Institutes within the NIH (www.sciencebasedmedicine.com) (Gorski 2009). One can hear the taunting, antagonist tone of the conflict used by Gorski.

Following this Gorski quotes Harkin's address in March of 2009 to Congress that week, "says Senator Harkin, 'I am pleased to co–chair this morning's hearing with Senator Mikulski. And I am eager to hear our distinguished witnesses' ideas on using integrative care to keep people healthy, improve healthcare outcomes, and reduce healthcare costs. It is fashionable, these days, to quote Abraham Lincoln. So I would like to quote from his 1862 address to Congress—words that should inspire us as we craft health care reform legislation. Lincoln said, 'The dogmas of the quiet past are inadequate to the stormy present. The occasion is piled high with difficulty . . . . As our case is new, so we must think anew, and act anew. We must disenthrall ourselves, and then we shall save our country.' Clearly, the time has come to 'think anew' and to 'disenthrall ourselves' from the dogmas and biases that have made our current health care system–based overwhelmingly on conventional medicine–in so many ways wasteful and dysfunctional."

Gorski then goes on to say, "I note that on the video, Harkin does not say 'conventional medicine.' In fact, he says 'conventional allopathic medicine.' And, as any regular reader of this blog knows, anyone who uses the term "allopathic" in such a contemptuous manner to describe conventional scientific medicine has clearly drunk the Kool Aid," (Gorski 2010). Clearly, this is part of the central fire to the current conflict in the United States within this breakdown phase. The insults thrown back and forth at the expense of having a truly functional health care system, one that has side-stepped ego–centric arguments where individuals cling to their values, worldviews, and "ethics" *not for the sake of health*, is not only conflict, it *is* a form of violence.

Because in the midst of this battle are really ridiculous numbers of desperately ill people, or citizens living with levels of pain from chronic conditions for which the biomedical model has no cure, but offers medications that are supposed to help the pain, that then renders more to deal with in the way of side effects. We are one of the most affluent countries on the planet, with a level of lifestyle that others want to emulate.

Yet here, while others are getting rich off of the suffering of increasing sick, diseased, and those "living" with chronic pain, there are prolific testimonies from people who are living in either desperate or numbed out acceptance of there being no real help for them beyond the state that their medications leave them in. Due to following only the advice of their biomedical doctor, who has offered either surgery or medication, neither of which have helped alleviate the fundamental problem, they either turn to "alternative healing" methods for hope, or they give up hope, and just try to deal with their condition on their own, with their loved ones' support. This is violence, even with the comparative lesser number of people who have been helped by the amazing surgical procedures that use these incredible technological innovations of the biotech field, or had their primary symptoms lessened by effective medications with minimal side effects.

The battle in the United States that has been going on for years now between natural healing and biomedical medicine has been intensifying over recent years, culminating somewhat within the health care system reform debates, albeit indirectly. This entire breakdown phase is synonymous with the changing metaparadigm. The mind body connection acknowledges subtle energy and its impact on a human beings' health. The biomedical model does not. So that within the American health care industry this very battle over how to care for and fund the health of people comes from the biomedical model's foundation in scientific materialism and its ensuing focus on the physical, and breaking the physical down into separate parts, and its resistance to change.

Why discuss this? Isn't this focusing "on the negative"? While it may seem to be, that's a quick dismissal of the issue with an easy label. We need to be rationally informed and aware of the fact that this approach is only effective in certain conditions. We also need to be aware of the impact of the metaparadigm's focus on the material, physical side of life, and how that leaves out acknowledging the mind body connection and its ensuing therapies that have been shown to not only provide relief, but also to frequently alleviate illness from its roots. Is it not violence in some form to not support people in having access to this? Never mind steering them away from these options?

One of the key strategies used is anyone *outside* of the biomedical model is not allowed to use the word "heal"–even when they have rigorous scientific studies pointing to this being the case. Translated: How is it that our biomedical model is able to maintain dominance over all other forms of medicine or health care options in our country? When were monopolies written back into law? Wasn't it slid in as a rider on a bigger bill in the early days leading up to the bail out of the financial industry? Yet antitrust laws were in existence longer than not in our country. It was only during part of the chaos of this overall macroshift that they were written out of law. This is not a coincidence. Again, take that holistic perspective. See how the parts fit together as a whole.

The point here is to understand why we have the system that we do and how our thoughts and beliefs and lifestyle choices have been conditioned and effected by it. Equally important to ask at this point is *who is benefitting from the status quo, and who is not.* This control from the dominant paradigm, with the current power structure in their "corner," and the rigidity and resistance locking it further into place—with the creation of "evidence based medicine" much akin to the logical empiricism of quantum physics started in the 1930's—are symptoms of the breakdown phase. Yet in order to break it down, it is necessary to ask such questions. Such as, what are the results this dominant metaparadigm of the marriage between the AMA backed biomedicine, orthodox science, the pharmaceutical, biotech, research and insurance industries are able to have from the status quo that maintains their control? They're able to have our society's laws, regulations and behavior controlled in such a way that *they maintain* this central dominance. Not being able to use the word "heal" calls for very clever wording in a natural healer's marketing. Yet those disclaimers any and all natural healers are coerced into making by the looming threat of attack and the ones on vitamin supplements are to cater to this dominance of the biomedical model.

No natural healer nor supplement nor herb, with or without "evidence based science" is able to put forth its ability to help people's illnesses, mental discomfort, or pain in any clear way to the same clearly marketed degree we see in the advertisements for medications. Nor, for that matter, when surgeries are presented to us by our doctors. Or when insurance companies choose to dictate what is and is not covered by our doctors, directly impacting the flow of economic activity. But then comes consumers' choices. Is there any connection to the increase in health care spending simultaneous to a recession? If we are facing an out of pocket expense for a natural healing method and we're strapped for money, isn't it likely we'll take the less expensive route? Does this connect in any way to the glaringly obvious fact that healthy food produced without chemicals from the biotech industry is more expensive than food made from big agriculture that uses the products of the biotech industry? Going even further into this questioning of who is benefiting from the status quo, is there any connection between the fact that the biotech industry creates the chemicals that are our food additives and preservatives, the pesticides and herbicides that are sprayed on our non-organic food, and the pharmaceutical drugs prescribed by our doctor once someone gets sick? Is it any coincidence, too, what is increasingly being made glaringly obvious within the natural healing field of nutrition and holistic health, that the toxic load tips into disease once our tolerance for the toxins from our food, air, water and emotions reaches a threshold that overrides our natural immune response, and that this toxic load is effected by, and then given treatments from the same industry - namely, cancer?

It is control of the marketplace, essentially a monopoly. Laws exist intentionally to make it tricky; the threat of being shut down makes many natural healers–with relevant credentials–have to be somewhat underground with stating what they do and what their patients/clients have been able to gain from their work, or what has been cured. There is a looming cloud of dominance that acts as an omnipresent threat to those working in this new paradigm. It is more difficult for those engaged in the new paradigm to "get the word out there" in plain English what it is they do and what they can help people with. There are many examples of people having been "cured" from cancer using a few different holistic therapies, all of which have gotten shut down by the powers of the current metaparadigm. Whether it was a technology, or a homeopathic or naturopathic doctor, or healer, or nutrition or a combination of any and all of these, it has been shut down as a cure for cancer by the main powers that be. How can that be, asks an uninformed consumer, my government and the health care system are there to protect and help me. The number of sick people, and the rates of cancer in our country is an indirect answer.

The second stage of the last phase of Laszlo's model of a macroshift is the breakthrough phase. It is described as the mind–sets of a critical mass of people evolve in time, shifting the culture of society toward a better adapted mode. These changes then take hold, and as they do there is improved social order that is governed by the now more adapted values, world views and ethics of the society and institutions that govern it. This social order establishes itself as society stabilizes itself into its changed condition.

It seems that we are nearing this critical mass, now; this can be observed with the activity of the "new sciences" and the natural healers alongside these new sciences putting forth both the theory and the practice applying the subtle energy healing techniques within a paradigm that acknowledges the mind body connection in a system wide, continuous way. Included in this critical mass are the people receiving healing from these "complimentary and alternative" methods, and changing their values, world views and ethics as a result. As the people who seek out healing from the biomedical model and do not receive it either die or get sicker, the outcome of their experience with biomedicine causes them to then have an ensuing change in values, world views and ethics. Along with them, their family and loved ones also change their views.

Furthermore, in regards to Laszlo's "critical mass of people in society resistant to change," due to the vast increases in depression, anxiety, cancer, chronic diseases, autoimmune diseases and neurological diseases, and due to the fact that biomedicine does not heal these, this chunk of "resistance" has been wiped out more quickly than if the biomedical model actually healed. And remember, many of these if not all, as viewed in the holistic health model are seen as more "lifestyle" related illnesses; i.e. toxicity in food and water, malnourishment even when obese, and/or stress leading to illness. All of these are considered "lifestyle" issues because they result from our lifestyle choices.

So many of the ill or unhappy seek out alternative sources for help. They see that the natural healing works, as do their friends and family. Much of the time the person is able to come off of any and all medications, at the appropriate rate, as they heal from the alternative means and implement new lifestyle choices that maintain their restored balance and health. The fundamental dysfunction in the healthcare system as it now is in and of itself what has lead to the (current) debates and attempts at reform. Although as it has attended to the financial aspects, all of the reform efforts have been smelling a problem but haven't gone in the right direction. It is the entire thinking, the foundation to the system and to our metaparadigm that needs readdressing. The country's financial crisis is very much entangled within our health care system. This will briefly also be addressed soon. All of the activity in the health care arena and the health care policy reform efforts are an example of Laszlo's "social order is exposed to a series of crises that soon degenerate into conflict (and violence)."

What are the Options Beyond Stress?

Still another aspect within the health care arena signaling this breakdown phase is the vast increase in levels of stress for the average American citizen. The levels of chronic illnesses amongst the developed countries' populations is secondary to this, and deeply intertwined with stress, as well. Stress is increasingly being seen as the core cause to much of the chronic pain, as well as many of the chronic illnesses. Both appear to have no cure within the biomedical model. This is an all–encompassing issue, needing to change or shift, because it is the nature of our very metaparadigm that is the cause. Meaning, the chasing after and competing for material gains and "financial security," we do, comparatively to how it's done in other countries, causes us to end up with the majority of our lives focused on busyness and activity on the physical plane, including raising children who can compete in this metaparadigm. This devaluing and ignoring of the subtle has caused us to build up to this current point of breakdown. We don't typically catch the more subtle cues and symptoms from our physical, mental, emotional and spiritual selves *as the stress builds*–both individually and collectively as a society. So chronic illnesses results.

Put another way, the levels of stress and chronic diseases resultant *from this stress* are prevalent throughout our citizenry. The rapidly rising levels of depression and anxiety are also resultant from our metaparadigm's focus. This level of impact stress has within our society is flagging us to take a step back and re-examine the cause; our metaparadigm. Suicide rates have been on an increase, as well. Recently, I was listening to my niece and her bff— best friend forever—both of whom come from affluent families, a suburban high school, and are now in their sophomore year in college. My niece's bff said, "Yeah it's a trend with teens. Everyone I know has had some sort of not necessarily full on attempt, but something with it." Over the past two weeks, I have heard of five suicides through my clients' stories about people they know who knew a person who attempted or did commit suicide. And zooming out to an even bigger perspective, we are being told that our entire metaparadigm is not working and is in the midst of breaking down because, for the vast majority of people living within this metaparadigm, their health is breaking down in one way or another, and/or they're asking their doctors for meds. They've been impacted by the emotional, mental and spiritual stress to the point of physical disease. Or it may still be on the level of emotional and metal stress, as in depression.

Those who have sought to get themselves informed earlier on are already engaged in a different lifestyle and are making more conscious choices of how they spend their time, money, and efforts. This includes what they eat coupled with their levels of exercise; how they take care of their mental, emotional and spiritual selves;. what practice of self-care they have; how much they monitor their toxic load by limiting their exposure to and pro-actively garnering against the chemical presence in our food and water supply and environment. This is all compared to that of the masses still fully engaged within the current metaparadigm's structures. The contrast of the two styles of living is stark, including the degrees of health and wellness amongst each population. Yet, again, if one is living within this country, one has to engage within its dominant metaparadigm to a degree. It's just that the former group is doing so with awareness of this, and thus, living (preventatively and) proactively, with an awareness of how to maintain health within this milieu. Historically, there has been effort exerted by these people to find other sources of information, outside of the mainstream paradigm, rather than to unquestioningly go about life.

This group has become aware that by now this metaparadigm's cycle of pushing ourselves to work and produce and raise families and compete within our metaparadigm's structure, rules, laws and lifestyle requires questioning. This is due to the levels of stress the average American is living with. And it is one of the more significant red flags for our metaparadigm. For this dynamic is creating the sense of urgency that clearly, something has gotten out of balance at some point.

The majority still, however, have no sense of contrast that there is a different way, so it's almost a group consensus to remain at this level of stress from the required output to play the game. Then ultimately, we see this impact on the health care system and providers, as well as taxpayers and voters, as we will see next. However, because our system's foundation and medicine focus on the physical, the average citizen still does not have the information that helps them live in a way that teaches them the connection between emotional and mental stress and then a physical diagnosis of a disease. Those who are still actively engaged in the metaparadigm are doing so without question or making changes because "that's how we do it here." Its go, go, go and get things done. It's only if and when there's a physical illness or personal crisis as a result of living this way does one without this information get informed that there are other ways to "do life."

Increasingly, new studies continue to reveal the growing number of reports of stress to patients' primary care physicians so that it has become one of the leading causes to visits to physicians. Also, there have been enough studies by now with findings that show just how stress–based the majority of chronic illnesses are that it is generally acknowledged within the health care industry–on both sides of the metaparadigm now. On Dr. Mercola's website–rated the number one natural health website–there is an article entitled, "Positive Outlook Buffers Damaging Effects of Stress," in which he states, "It looks as though stress is taking over America's health, as up to 90 percent of the doctor visits in the United States may be caused by a stress–related illness." This was posted by Dr. Mercola in 2005. Dr. Mercola is described as: "Dr. Mercola has made significant milestones in his mission to bring people practical solutions to their health problems. A *New York Times* Best Selling Author, Dr. Mercola was also voted the 2009 Ultimate

Wellness Game Changer by the *Huffington Post*, and has been featured in *TIME* magazine, *LA Times*, CNN, Fox News, ABC News, Today Show, CBS's *Washington Unplugged* with Sharyl Attkisson, and other major media resources," (Mercola 2010).

In this posting, Dr. Mercola summarizes an article from *USA Today* from March 2005 that, as Dr. Mercola says, "What impressed me most about this article was it is the highest government estimate of the impact of stress on disease. Here is a direct quote from the story: 'Up to 90 percent of the doctor visits in the USA may be triggered by a stress–related illness, says the Centers for Disease Control and Prevention.' This is quite consistent with my experience and that I find nearly all of the patients I see have stress as a serious factor in the cause of their illness. *I'm glad to see official government confirmation of this observation.* Stress can also play a major role in the immune system, and it can have negative impacts on: blood pressure, cholesterol, brain chemistry, blood sugar levels and hormonal balance," (Mercola 2005).

Dr. Mercola then goes on to explain conceptually how stress creates disease with his post headed by, "Severe stress attacks on a cellular level." Mercola then explains that, "When stress strikes, your body's adrenal glands produce hormones, such as adrenaline, which increase blood pressure; chronic stress keeps these hormones at dangerously high levels. However, studies suggest that severe cases of stress extend beyond the temporary increase in blood pressure and begin to injure cells of the body–which may accelerate the aging process, leaving people susceptible to various diseases." (Mercola 2010).

He then further describes the process of cellular breakdown that makes one more susceptible to disease and accelerated aging, "To determine exactly how stress affects people on a cellular level, researchers analyzed the cells of mothers caring for critically sick children. The goal was to discover if stress affected a key part of the chromosome known as a telomere, thought to be markers of aging. Telomere's cap the ends of chromosomes, which contain the body's DNA. As people begin to age, this cap begins to dwindle down. Disease steps in when the telomere gets too short to work effectively and cells all over the body begin to die." Dr. Mercola cites another study that consisted of caregivers of Alzheimer's patients, who dedicated at least one hundred hours a week to caring for a loved one with this degenerative disease. Mercola cites the results, "Researchers found that a damaging substance in the blood called interleukin 6 increased dramatically among caregivers. Based on the findings the following startling analogy was made: The average caregiver was about 70 but had IL–6 levels that looked like those of a 90–year–old, (Mercola 2005). Clearly, stress causes our cells to age and break down.

Dr. Mercola has another helpful article to further illustrate the process of how stress leads to degenerative, or chronic, illnesses in an article entitled, "Stress Affects Your Immune System: Clearly Defined Patterns Revealed," posted by Dr. Mercola in July of 2004. In this article, he cites what were then recent discoveries. Dr. Mercola says, "For a long time psychologists were aware of the impact stress had on the body's ability to fight infections, but now a study has shown how stress also plays a major influence in altering the functions of the immune system."

In the next section of this article, he then cites the studies, "Studies on Stress and the Immune System," in which he reports that 293 stress–related studies were performed between the years of 1960 and 2001, with 18,941 subjects evaluated in the studies. The findings from the studies were, "Periods of short–term stress triggered the immune system to prepare for injury or infection, similar to a 'fight or flight' response. Long–term stress caused excessive wear on the body and activated a deterioration of the immune system. The immune systems of the elderly and those already suffering with some kind of illness were less capable of coping with stressful situations." Dr. Mercola follows this with, "Researchers concluded that the stressors that most negatively compromised the immune system were the chronic stressors. Researchers also discovered the longer the duration of stress or perceived length of the stress, the less the body's ability to adapt to the stressful situation. It was determined this kind of stress could lead to serious negative health repercussions beginning with attacking the immune system at the cellular level then going after the overall broader functions of the immune system." He then also states that researchers plan to conduct future studies so they can evaluate the degree that stress–related changes alter the immune system, and how this could result in leaving what are called "otherwise healthy" individuals vulnerable to diseases. Note that the source Dr. Mercola is quoting from is the *Psychological Bulletin* of July 4, 2004, so that these follow up studies have been performed since then, as our information about the effects of stress has proliferated in the last six years, which we'll see soon.

Staying with this link between stress and chronic illness, Dr. Mercola himself then comments on the article by saying, *"Stress is a large part of the reason why most chronic illness develops* and this in–depth study reinforces this theory particularly when it comes to individuals facing long–term stress. Stress can seriously impact your health *and when you find ways to control stress in your life you could significantly reduce your risk of developing stress–induced diseases such as heart disease and type 2 diabetes,"* (italics mine) (Mercola 2010).

In another posting by Dr. Mercola, "More Evidence That Stress is Major Factor for Infections," posted By Dr. Mercola in July of 2003, he says, *"Chronic stress, which has been called America's number one health problem,* is not something to take lightly–it can have profound effects on your immune system and your overall health. *Estimates have placed stress–related problems as the cause of 75 percent to 90 percent of all primary care physician visits,"* (italics mine) (Mercola 2003). While this is a different statistic from his first article that was published two years *later* showing the growth in the problem from 75% to 90%, he is already in 2003 reflecting that stress is America's number one health problem. That's a strong statement.

Mercola says, "If you have recently experienced a change in your sleep patterns, feel fatigued, anxious or a lack of enjoyment for life, or have multiple aches and pains, you're likely overstressed." Vast numbers of people report these issues to the point that it seems commonplace with our lifestyles today, and just part of the way it is, right? We're so used to it we chalk it up to just the way it is, or to aging, right? But it's not. I say this repeatedly on my radio show, in my workshops, to my students and my clients, "In other countries, people don't age expecting arthritis, alzheimers, high cholesterol, or high blood pressure." Again, who benefits in our metaparadigm if this is our perception, or belief, created for us about health and aging?

Furthering our understanding of the damage stress does to our system, Dr. Mercola informs us that–again, in 2003, "It was recently discovered that people under chronic stress had above–normal levels of interleukin–6 (IL–6), an immune–system protein that promotes inflammation and has been linked with heart disease, diabetes, osteoporosis, rheumatoid arthritis, severe infections and certain cancers. It appears that stress increases levels of IL–6, which in turn accelerates a variety of age–related diseases. Further, stress can weaken a person's immune response, leaving them more susceptible to infection, and can lead to unhealthy lifestyle habits. For instance, stress often leads people to overeat, lose sleep, and neglect exercise, all of which can create health problems on their own."

Dr. Mercola then cites Dr. David Holland, the medical communications director at MediaTrition, "There is a whole new field called "psychoneuroimmunology" that studies the effects of psychological stress on the immune system. Scientists in this area have demonstrated alterations in the normal function of immune cells in animals during times of stress. Excessive physical stress also changes our immune cell profile. Increased upper respiratory tract infections occur in athletes who overtrain, and a decreased cell–mediated immunity has been demonstrated in such athletes. Without a properly functioning immune system, our bodies are vulnerable to invasion by opportunistic germs such as fungi, viruses and bacteria. By taking an antimicrobial like garlic, some scientists have been able to prevent immune suppression in psychologically stressed mice."

Finally, Dr. Mercola adds, "There is ever increasing evidence that most diseases have an infectious component. Such is the case with most *autoimmune diseases like rheumatoid arthritis* (RA), which–like most all other diseases–*is a result of things that happen, or more frequently, things we allow to let happen to us, such as stress overload,*" (italics mine) (Mercola 2003). It is important to note here that what Dr. Mercola–and many others with evidence from studies–is saying is that *arthritis is not a natural aspect to aging; instead it is ongoing, cumulative stress that eventually erodes our immune system's ability to fight off infections that lead to chronic inflammation.* More sources other than Dr. Mercola could be cited to reflect the varying numbers that various studies attribute to the percentage of all visits to primary care physicians that are stress related. However, it'd be redundant. These numbers are easily obtained from a Google search, from both sides of the conflict–or both paradigms. Yet the range is what you've already seen–most studies state 80–90% of all visits to doctors in the U.S. are stress related.

These findings can then be paired with the increasing numbers of Americans–and any citizen living in a "westernized/globalized" country–suffering from these chronic diseases. *So could all this cumulatively be the red flag for our society that change is needed?* Sure, efforts have been made to now introduce at a more mainstream level the stress–reducing benefits of yoga and meditation, for example. That has been the most recent hotbed of activity with studies. But what if, rather than those of us who are proactive and have learned and incorporated stress reduction tools and techniques into our lives, and thereby live preventatively focused on health and wellness, we instead recognized the issue for what it is? That is, an indication that it is in fact our societal values and our metaparadigm itself, rather than our "inability" or our "need to learn" how to manage the stress? It could make one scratch one's head at the sheer lack of logic. It's like a hamster on a wheel. This is no longer reasonable. It is activity in a flurried state, going in circles.

One positive within the climate of increased studies that have found out the damaging effects of stress is this factor has become increasingly acknowledged within biomedicine. So, realistically, this is their implied initial "admission" towards the mind body connection. In fact, the relationship between stress and physical illness is quintessentially the mind body connection. Some biomedical doctors–not many, as of yet–even go so far as to see and admit to the ensuing primed diseased state that this then pushes the body into, by not ignoring the studies linking chronic diseases to stress, such as rheumatoid arthritis. Typically, it's anti-inflammatory prescriptions as the answer.

However, again, even when discussing the impact of stress on the body, it's done from a physical approach, meaning stress causes wear and tear on the physical system, so it is the physical system that suffers. So that it's not yet realistically being framed as "the mind body connection " so directly within the biomedical model. Meaning, they're not coming out and identifying how it's the mind's perception of stress that creates a body that is under the same conditions. They are just beginning to admit that there is a connection between a stressed out, anxious, worried mental and emotional sate and how that leads to a body that is under the same conditions. The yielding from within the biomedical paradigm is much, much more incremental, and when there has been yielding, it has typically been in response to the increasing demand for what they view as their antagonist, any and all forms of natural healing used for antidotes to this stress. So, it's become that they (biomedicine) have to compete.

This is another key factor that is helping to create this critical mass within the general population of "patients," though. There has been increased use of natural healing methods as treatments for this increased stress. Prevention against this stress prior to physical disease forming has also become more appreciated and consumed. Yoga is an example, as well as massage, energy healing like Reiki, Access Consciousness' bars treatment, and relaxation and stress–reduction geared meditation techniques.

The Completion of Extensive Growth: Are You Up For It?

Finally, one last issue that is another loud red flag for those with seeing eyes can be observed in the very fact that our metaparadigm relies on production of cutting edge technology, right? Yet many of the modern and postmodern high–tech products themselves have been eventually understood to actually detract from our health, as opposed to solely making life easier. Examples are the biotech's pharmaceutical drug industry and all their side effects–particularly the cancer industry with radiation and chemotherapy; the petrochemical industry married to the agribusiness industry that has given us food products with chemicals as additives and pesticides on the food itself; the cell phone, wifi, the microwave and the other electro–magnetic frequencies disturbers that the majority of the newer communications technologies create in our world today of a man made impact that interferes with the natural electromagnetics of the earth and our bodies. This EMF disturbance then disrupts our own natural life based *biorhythms,* also causing a weakening of our immune system and virility. So that somewhere along the way, *somewhere there was a peak reached of positive benefits in the productivity technologically. Then a downward slope has been the central aspect of what we're left with.* Laszlo helps us better understand this factor–and others–of our current state of breakdown at the metaparadigm level, as we are in the throes of, as Laszlo terms it, a macroshift.

Laszlo describes our times by saying, "For states the goal of extensive growth is territorial sovereignty, including sovereignty over the human and natural resources of the territories. The corresponding goal for global companies is to generate demand for consumption, often without regard for the environmental consequences. The ends of extensive growth can be encapsulated in three 'Cs': conquest, colonialization, and consumption. These ends are served by corresponding varieties of means: First, the technologies that use and transform matter, the technologies of production; second, the technologies that generate the power to operate matter–transforming technologies, energy–generating technologies; and third, the technologies that whet people's appetites, create artificial demand, and shift patterns of consumption, the technologies of propaganda, PR, and advertising. The first of these kinds of technologies built habitations with networks of transportation and communication and increasingly powerful production structures for a growing variety of products. The second harnessed the forces of nature to drive these technologies. The third produced the demand–provoking images and the subtle or not–so–subtle means by which the manufacturers of products and the suppliers of services *impose their will* on their clients and customers," (italics mine) (Laszlo 2008).

All of this adds up to meaning that we need to give up a level of perceived control over external events, and instead work more towards where there is control; our individual, internal environments, as the metaparadigm continues to breakdown prior to shifting into something new. Stress and more conflict are the result should we not do so. Being able to relax into that which is easier to see, that which is tangible and therefore yields certainty is not where our evolution is headed–nor where it has been recently. Again–the increasing crises and the seeming overall upheaval of the times that we're living in, as all systems including individuals are thrown into a time of increasing chaos are so that the new can be created. This is indicated by all factors able to be observed should one look at the big picture and add up all the clues. Many of these "clues" have been discussed, with a few more still to come. All of which, when cumulatively added together form a summative statement as to where we are as a human race, and where we're headed, depending on the choices made.

Consciousness and the human mind is popping up in too many places asking to be acknowledged as a reality. And if we were really wise, we'd see that consciousness is pointing itself out throughout various segments of society as a source of power and to recognize this. To learn how to work with it as a primary source of power seems to be the actual intent. The earth with its increasingly erratic weather patterns is not only indicative of global warming, but it is also indicative of alive consciousness. This reflects us and our state of consciousness, collectively. This is not a new theory; ancient and indigenous people all over the globe acknowledge our consciousness' interaction with the earth's. Both contain all life, or chi, prana or life force and are interconnected. It's like when your child or spouse feels moody it's somewhat contagious. The environmental erraticism and threats are too many to be discussed here, and there are enough other sources that cover this.

Alison J. Kay, PhD

The point here from the pressure we're facing with needing to pay attention to our natural environment is that it is another "clue" pointing out that what we've done under our metaparadigm is not working anymore and it needs to change. This change includes acknowledging that the earth and universe contains consciousness, and we are a part of this consciousness, and the environmental issues are somewhat a result of our lack of working with our own consciousnesses–hence the chaotic weather patterns, the increase in natural disasters, and the looming threat of global warming which some consider irreparable damage. We and it both need cleaning and purifying.

Laszlo, in his chapter, "The Cosmic Plenum: The New Fundamental Concept of Reality," *from Quantum Shift in the Global Brain* says, "The quantum shift in the global brain embraces both our *experiences* and our *understanding* of the world. Not only is the world around us in radical transformation, but also our understanding of the fundamental nature of that world–and of the universe itself–is shifting. This is important, for our world is an integral part of the universe; its laws and processes apply on Earth the same as everywhere else. A sound orientation in our world calls for a sound understanding of the universe. Science's understanding of the fundamental nature of the universe is different from what most people believe it is," (Laszlo 2008). Laszlo is about to debunk the common understanding of how our world works, as presented to us by our old scientific materialist paradigm. He also goes beyond that, and tells us the importance for us on the planet, in our country, today. You'll, by now, recognize the information from the previous discussions throughout this book, backed by the voices of new science. So maybe this time, it'll make sense to you in a way that is meaningful for you in your own thoughts. Because now you've heard it enough to go into synthesizing the value of this information into your current understandings, and your life.

He says, "The universe does not consist of bits of matter moving about in space and time. *Matter, in the last analysis, is a bound form of energy,* and space and time are an integral dynamic element, interacting with matter and energy in all its forms. Moreover, *the various forms of energy emerge from and are embedded in a fundamental field or medium* that was not a part of the conventional world picture. This "deep basement" of the universe is variously called quantum vacuum, unified vacuum, physical spacetime, hyperspace, or neuther. Despite these abstruse names, existence is not merely theoretical and–notwithstanding the implication of its names–it is not a vacuum and not just space. *It is an energy–and information–filled 'cosmic plenum,' the womb of all that exists, and the background of all that happens,* in space and time," (italics mine) (Laszlo 2008). Here, Laszlo is informing us of what the vacuum consists of that Tiller introduced us to earlier. The vacuum that Tiller told us was able to be sensed not with technological equipment, but with consciousness, yes?

This "medium" that Laszlo is talking about as the fundamental field is considered to be alive and organic, hence this is why Tiller says that it can be reached through consciousness. As an example of applying this "discovery" within quantum physics and the new sciences, the Chinese have their tradition of chi gong. There is the chi gong warm up exercise of gathering the chi. I do this within the warm up for my chi gong practice of the *shi bao shan* series of 18 movements. One palm is face down over my second chakra area, or the *dan tien*, while the other arm scoops out from over my head as I follow my hand across the opposite side of my body, then across the front, then by the same side the arm comes out of my torso. The whole time I am doing this motion, I am intending—and even sometimes saying out loud—to gather the chi from the heavens, the cosmos, the trees, the mountains, the water (ideally chi gong should be done by a body of water), the earth, the winged ones, the rocks and any other form of life that I choose as my vision follows my hand across the sky. Finally, after my arm has returned by the proper side, that arm's hand replaces the other arm's hand over my lower abdomen area of the *dan tien*, palm in towards this power center that sucks in this intended chi, and I continue the process with my other arm. I do this nine times for each arm. And I immediately feel the results, as do my students and clients. I speak about Shibaoshan style of Chi Gong on my website, www.alisonjkay. com as another method for working with consciousness for our own well-being, improved health and vitality, and longevity.

Laszlo describes further that the latest advances in the natural sciences give us a new picture of reality. He too is yet another voice saying that these discoveries are coming more from the new sciences than classical physics, or "orthodox science." Why do I need to provide so many? Isn't this one of the key points here? Foundations take sledgehammers pounded into them over and over again to be destroyed.

The universe does not consist of matter in three–dimensional space and time, Laszlo states, as we have already discussed. Right. He goes on, "The classical concept of 'mass–points' ... so we can get to the point ... is superseded. *In the new concept the universe is an organically interconnected evolving system. Its origins, as well as its fields and forces of interaction,* are traced to a cosmically extended fundamental medium...The new physics can affirm with a high degree of confidence that ours is not a universe where matter moves about in neutral space, governed by simple rules of cause and effect. Instead, our best insight is that ours is an evolving, instantly and enduringly interconnected fundamentally integral reality, a universe embedded in a dynamic and physically real medium that subtends the familiar world of three–dimensional space and correlated time. What we call "matter" is a wave–form energy pattern in this medium," (Laszlo 2008).

Laszlo also goes on, as yet another voice, to say that quanta, the building blocks that we used to consider the building blocks of the physical plane, turned out to be more like waves, with the wave nature of quanta shown recently by Iranian–American physicist Shahriar Afshar. Afshar's experiment showed that the wave aspect is fundamental, not the particle. The wave's aspects are present even as particles are observed, but particles are not present when only the wave aspect is examined.

What the implications of this are is revolutionary which is why you've needed it in doses in a slow building progression, a little softer than the sledgehammer visual. Perhaps like a hawk flying overhead everyday when you drive in that certain place, until you begin to pay attention more to the sacredness of that place, or you, or both? Genuinely, this information transposes our world view, as we've discussed. The implications of this information are what is stickier for us. Taking this information and translating it into seeing symbolically then what's going on in your life and all around you in all our lives at a societal level is the trick. And that's where I am working to gradually bring you. To help you not only understand first these groundbreaking discoveries that are not frequently discussed out there in our general media or over dinner tables. Then it is to point out what the significance of these discoveries are. Finally, it is to appreciate and apply the significance, to make your life and our lives better, knowing that these changes are under way. So you don't spin out, interpreting certain events as doom and gloom, but instead are able to place it in this proper positioning, *with perspective.* Ultimately, this sets you, and us all, up for benefitting from being informed, and proactively applying these discoveries to our lives so we are no longer at the affect of the results of what these changes are doing to our lives and society. Instead, you're informed, grounded with a clear understanding, and then able to create the effects out into the world that you so choose.

So, repetition is essential with such complex and shattering ideas. Think of the mainstream physicists' reactions. They created a whole other system more entrenched in the old thinking as a reaction to the destabilizing these discoveries caused. Never mind being able to then take it out of the laboratory and apply it to life. Yet that is what I am striving to get you towards. This is big stuff here. Huge, obviously. So, one more time, and this time it is going to hit home in a way that it is now able to: even though what we perceive with our senses seems solid, like that table or desk, this physical material solidity—that table or desk—is actually moving about in empty space. This empty space is the vacuum, or medium we've been discussing. The reality is that the material universe is not material. Matter, like things such as tables and desks, are standing, propagating, and interacting waves in a subtending medium, or a medium that is stretched out and exists *under* the material plane, *or under physical matter.* The medium that Tiller spoke of, or chi, or prana. And then finally, the real important one to us: it is our consciousness' thoughts, expectations and projections and perceptual machinery that then puts out there onto the empty space, focusing on the solidity rather than the floating empty space - a label. These labels get taught to us as vocabulary words as little kids for the solid material, such as a table or a desk, using our cognitive mind's labeling mechanism. Our cognitive mind, or ego-mind, or little personality me mind, is structured to help us do so in order to navigate the physical plane.

Lazlo states, "The concept of a physical field that subtends the three-dimensional world of space and time surfaced in the course of the twentieth century. Until the beginning of that century space was believed to be filled with luminiferous ether that produces friction when bodies move through it. When in the Mechelson–Morley experiments such friction failed to materialize, the ether was removed from the physicists' world picture. The absolute vacuum took its place. However, the vacuum turned out to be far from empty space. In the 'grand unified theories' (GUTs) developed in the second half of the twentieth century (under Einstein's efforts) the concept of the vacuum transformed from empty space into the medium that carries the zero–point field, or ZPF (so called because in this field energies prove to be present even when all classical forms of energy vanish: at the absolute zero of temperature). Ever more interactions have come to light between this fundamental field and observed things and processes," (Laszlo 2008). Laszlo then goes on to trace some of the later refinements to the ZPF and GUTs, ultimately arriving at the statement that all the forces and fields of the universe are traced to origins in the "unified vacuum." You may have heard of the Zero Point Field referred to in energy medicine or energy healing. If it hasn't already, this should by now be making more clear sense to you. Stuff is coming together better for you now, yes? Connections are forming to other aspects of life, yes?

What Laszlo says next is the key for our discussion. "However, in the technical framework of quantum field theory the vacuum is not a part of physical reality. It is a theoretical artifact, a requirement of the mathematics of the field theory. The insight that the vacuum is a real, and indeed fundamental, medium does not derive from the mathematics of quantum field theory *but from significant, if necessarily indirect, evidence accumulated independently in a vast variety of observations*," (Laszlo 2008). This is the same thing that Tiller described, when he said no equipment could be designed to reach this level, but consciousness can.

"The evidence for the realistic concept is of two kinds. One comes from the new physics and cosmology: more and more scientists are coming to the conclusion that the level of quanta, and of space-time itself, is not the ultimate level in the universe. There is also a level below quanta and space-time, a level from which space-time and the quanta that populate it have emerged. The other kind of evidence concerns observations that quanta and the things composed of quanta (organisms and minds included) are *intrinsically* and, as it appears, *'nonlocally' connected*. This raises the possibility that the fundamental level of the universe is not merely at the origin of the things that populate space and time *but is also the medium that interconnects them*," (italics mine) (Laszlo 2008).

The "hugeness" of what Laszlo has said is reminiscent of Goswami earlier talking about the proof for non–locality, and the interconnection studies done. His example for this was anyone watching the O.J. Simpson trial was interconnected as an example of non–local interconnectivity, and another example was the group who is viewing sports together, they are all also non–locally connected. Remember? Meaning, it doesn't matter who is watching from where, just the act of these consciousnesses present and focusing on the same thing allows for a "non–local"–everyone doesn't have to be in the same place, hence "localized"–"interconnectivity," due to the qualities of this medium at the fundamental level within the vacuum that fills up the space between atoms and molecules. *Thus it allows the consciousnesses focused on the same thing to be linked, or connected.*

The idea was presented earlier of how our human consciousnesses have been affecting our planet's living environment, so that the weather patterns are more erratic and stormy and less stable and more chaotic. This is the link. Another way to construe this medium is through the metaphor of the internet, just with everyone on the planet having access to the internet and everyone always online. The medium is an alive, organic energy in and of itself that like the internet, also "carries" or has everyone connected in to it at the sub-quanta level. Most just are not aware of the universe's version of the internet, which is more like Internet 2.0 where we can leave posts and comments compared to the once "authorities only-read only" Internet 1.0 version. Aha! See—it's coming together now! I told you so! I really do not normally have those four words as part of my vocabulary, because my work with clients and as a teacher is shaped for them always as a self-discovery process—as it is for each of us, right? That's the only way, yes? But here, well you've seen a bit of the amount of work put in to how to shape this hugeness together in as small of bite sized nuggets I can. In order to then build it all back up into an overall view. We're doing it now! YES!

Quintessential to our discussion to notice is that the technology of the internet, particularly Internet 2.0 which allows anyone to be able to post on and effect the environment of the internet, has been parallel to the scientific discovery of this medium at the sub-quanta level. It is not necessarily because of business innovation only, as we have already discussed, but perhaps it is from a higher perspective, *we have this technology as a metaphor signaling us to make use of the scientific discovery beyond just the technological innovation and convenience it provides.* Applying what we just learned to life, at the vacuum level or the medium, or the collective unconsciousness as Jung called it, these ideas were ready to be birthed by humans, so different humans brought it forward in different ways, each with their own piece. •

There is a message here. Live life off of the internet as if we are all still connected, which the science now shows that we are. However, the key point here is that we wouldn't be able to appreciate the meaning of this sub-quanta field connecting us all to all animate life as much without the life experience of the Internet 1.0 and 2.0 as a reference. The metaphor had to be made tangible through life experience. Which came first, the technology or the scientific discovery? Who is leading whom? Or what is leading who? And why is all of this happening simultaneously?

It is beyond just that the scientific discovery has been made–it already had been, but was relatively resisted and still somewhat is. Yet we have Internet 2.0 that acts as a metaphor for this interconnecting web that is fundamental to our existence. Are we closer to being ready now to accept this interconnectivity now that we've experienced Internet 2.0? As Braden says, our consciousnesses extend into this medium, into the universe as we are a part of it as co–creators. Did this reality of the Internet come up because there were at the time enough of us–a smaller critical mass–aware of the sub–quanta medium that connects us all at the most fundamental level? So the idea was raised enough out of potential and into more active use of enough of our consciousnesses that enough were ready to then go further with this understanding–meaning getting the idea for the internet from this scientific breakthrough.

Further, did technology get created for the Internet from the same part of this vacuum or field that also yielded increasing numbers of pioneers in the West entering into yoga, chi gong, meditation and experiential practices that lead to experiencing this interconnectivity? Why did these two and the discoveries of this vacuumed interconnectivity all happen relatively concurrently? Or did the Internet come available for us so that the masses could better understand this interconnectivity once the life experience allowed for this relationship to be able to be appreciated? Huh.

Intensive Growth: Are You Happy?

Another red flag is also waving now for change. Your mind and its most typical thoughts -what are they? In general, do your thoughts tend to overall be comforting, attacking, friendly, or authoritarian? Most likely, it's a combination. This additional red flag commanding change is saying that we need to work with our consciousness in its "darker" opposite. Opposite here is meant to mean opposite to the light in consciousness, described in the example of the Gathering of the Chi Gong exercise above. Another way to say this is these darker parts of our consciousness are the ego-mind's afflictions, as Buddhism construes it. I know we've discussed this just a bit, but hold on. This is going in an entirely different direction than your mind may be anticipating, if in fact it is anticipating. This red flag is symbolically seen through the rates of depression, stress and general anxiety, already discussed yes, that pulses through individuals and communities throughout our country and developed, or modernized nations. Yet another shadow form the ego-mind twists into, instead of depression, is over indulgence. The increasing level of greed—seen in obesity, fear, sexual perversions, eating disorders, and focus on one's physical appearance–plastic surgeries, thirst for information about what the rich and famous are doing- in its various forms are all what the Buddhists would label as mental afflictions of greed. There's a few others afflictions in there, but their general flavor is greed. Remember, they're afflictions because it's where our ego-mind has an attachment to something and doesn't let it go, easily. It views the gains from the affliction as necessary and of value in some way. Advertising helps to cultivate this. We'll talk more about this in a few moments.

Here, we're going to be looking at our happiness and this "shadow" form consciousness takes with depression. Yet there it is–consciousness. The power of consciousness–and the human mind–distorted into its shadow form, is very much part of what we're seeing in those increased rates of depression, anxiety and suicide discussed earlier. This is due to the avoidance and negation of ourselves, and our ego-minds. So it's a negation following along the lines of our metaparadigm as to consciousness' importance.

If we valued consciousness and understood it for the power source it is, then we'd view working with our consciousness as important. Instead, taking a pill for antidepressants is what is commonly presented as the antidote. Yet, through observing our thoughts and working with redirecting our thoughts to continually open to the pulsing life force—consciousness—that is omnipresent in all animate life, we'd then flush our life with goodness. We can come to feel, sense, and know that there is a supportive backdrop to all of life.

The rates of depression also come from not listening to our quieter selves, or the voice of our soul as some say. Not working with the mind in order to be more comfortable with it, leaves us then uncomfortable with it, from various trains of thought an unmanaged mind typically goes on. The mind is referred to as a wild, drunken monkey in Buddhism. So we run from what our mind is saying. And we develop coping behaviors. Depression is one. Frequently too with depression we're suppressing ourselves from our next step forward in our own evolution. So we're suppressing ourselves, and the end result is depression.

Here's another bit of bait for you. If we each work with our own consciousness individually, we will then have an affect collectively. We would be indirectly providing the support that maybe a family member or loved one doesn't allow us to do directly. What we're talking about is cleaning up our ego-mind of its distortions and afflictions. We do this by getting to know our mind and its typical thoughts. This *happens by slowing down enough from the race on the physical plane.* First by letting go of the excess that functions as distractions to keep us "busy" and thus somewhat "checked out" from ourselves to face it. So we are in fact, not then using the underlying function of being so busy in place as a value for the ego-mind not to be dealt with. For many this seems to be the inherent value, or pay off, the ego-mind gets by having a mind full of driving thoughts about what to take care of next.

The running and racing away from ourselves is part of the entrainment from our metaparadigm. Who is benefitting from this? We are perhaps doing all of this activity with all these obligations, when there is another voice inside us saying to stay and go within and pay attention to what's being said in that softer voice. This resistance to listening to one's deeper needs, communicated through the softer voice, creates this tension—and depression. Because there is a higher level to life that we could also be in touch with, The subtler aspects of life that connect to the more sacred parts of the life experience come to us through that quiet, softer inner voice. But we don't typically hear it with an ego-mind in full gear, with its demands, judgments, fears and drive to continue to live life from the mind, to "figure stuff out."

This higher level of life gets communicated in those quieter moments. So do the "answers" that the small, personality me ego-mind seeks to figure out. If we don't have the quieter moments to go inside and listen within, then we don't have this sense of the sacred, the "answers" your mind makes you feel like you just can't figure out, nor as much perspective on life's events, either.

Again, this higher level to life does not necessarily need to be about divinity if your ego-mind blocks your ability to hear this, or your desire to work with observing your thoughts a bit of time each day, or even when you're driving in traffic each day. Or even if it blocks overall acceptance towards bringing the sacred more into your life. This "blocking" would come in a variety of forms; such as procrastination, or saying you're too busy, or saying you need to spend your money differently than on that program that would help you learn how to reconnect with this quieter part of yourself. Yet it is being in touch with a Higher, less slovenly, spoiled, demanding, controlling, little child part of ourselves that is always directing the show the way it wants the show to be. This control freak full of fear is otherwise known as the ego–mind. And it has been hugely supported by the structures of our metaparadigm, as we shall see next.

The ego-mind is the part that leads us to getting attached to things and people and situations being the way we want them to be, instead of more patient and accepting and compassionate, for example. If we are sticking it out in a relationship just for the familiarity of it, then this is an example. And depression would frequently ensue from that self-suppression we do of our Higher Self's true desires to move on by listening to our cognitive mind's valuing the comfort in the familiarity.

Our lifestyle today seems to enhance the ego–mind's dominant traits, such as buy this, do more, go further—away from the mind. Again, the inherent design of our metaparadigm turning outward to the external, objective, is very much responsible. That's next. Hold on. So if we silence, avoid, or deny the quieter part of ourselves that is connected to a more sacred part of both ourselves and existence, and we just continue to go along on the material plane without evolving ourselves, or paying attention to our Higher Selves, then tension is created within. So the ego–mind reacts with even more distraction to keep running from being still, and to perpetuate its dominance over our lives, and *our lives not changing*, really. Ironically, the ego breeds more ego. As if blocking out any alternatives to its dominance. So it's able to build a certain momentum to our typical choices, and lifestyle. Sound familiar? It's observed in people going on what they term "health kicks," instead of actually living a healthy life, overall.

Even slowing down enough to hear beyond the childlike demands of what one's ego-mind wants, what the quieter part of ourselves is seeing, feeling, and needing seems a distant reality when the ego is in dominance. This is why a crisis of some sort seems to be needed to shake up the ego's perceived dominance. *You know that strong part of people that comes out in crisis? Yes, that.*

And so living from the ego is compounded and reinforced, and avoidance is perpetuated. It is cyclic. The ego mind may have just been denying that it is any of the things just mentioned; it got defensive, defending its dominance. That's its game–don't let anything of the "other" side of life in, or if you do, keep it contained and controlled. And if you got this far then congratulations on your successful self-management! Because someone in the throes of being controlled by their ego-mind would've tossed this book aside by now, if they had even picked it up, by the ego-mind judging away the newness that could be brought forward from reading this. This is where we are at, collectively, too. Some have stepped outside of their demanding ego-mind's dominance, and have sought help with starting to connect with another part of themselves. Many haven't yet. This is the times we are living in. And it's why there has been so much crisis over the past five years. You see it now! Yay!

Wallace very clearly says the same, "We've seen that in the modern Western world, with its Christian heritage and its science, *the mind has been pointed outward to such an extent that it has virtually forgotten itself.* Whether it sought the laws of the heavens reflecting the mind of God or simply the physical universe, the *Western mind has wanted most to know what lies beyond.* We have been so intrigued by physical objects that the mind itself, the seeker, became unfamiliar–a hidden phenomenon, a black box. *When the mind did come into the picture, it was often viewed as a dangerous place harboring either sinful, demonic entities, or a murky pool of neurotic, subconscious impulses.* Later, when science finally brought itself to study the mind, it was either equated with the familiar physical stuff science was accustomed to–the gray matter of the brain–or deemed non–existent. So it is not surprising that the mind is still a mystery to us. Yet if the mind in the West tended to stare right past itself in its outer quest, in the East the general direction has been inward," (Wallace 2008).

In the first United States' *Surgeon General's Report on Mental Health,* issued in 2000, in the preface to the report, the then Surgeon General David Satcher, M.D, Ph.D., says, "Mental health is fundamental to health and human functioning. *Yet much more is known about mental illness than about mental health.* Mental illnesses are real health conditions that are characterized by alterations in thinking, mood, or behavior—all mental, behavioral, and psychological symptoms mediated by the brain. Mental illnesses exact a staggering toll on millions of individuals, as well as on their families and communities and our Nation as a whole," (italics mine).

Furthermore, in the "Introduction and Major Themes" section, the report states, "This first Surgeon General's Report on Mental Health is issued at the culmination of a half–century that has witnessed remarkable advances in the understanding of mental disorders and the brain and in our appreciation of the centrality of mental health to overall health and well-being. The report was prepared against a backdrop of *growing awareness in the United States and throughout the world of the immense burden of disability associated with mental illnesses. In the United States, mental disorders collectively account for more than 15 percent of the overall burden of disease from all causes and slightly more than the burden associated with all forms of cancer* (Murray & Lopez, 1996). These data underscore the importance and urgency of treating and preventing mental disorders and of promoting mental health in our society." (italics mine). Additionally, in data developed by the World Health Organization, the World Bank, and Harvard University, the *Mental Health: A Report of the Surgeon General* cites that this huge, collaborative effort revealed that *mental illness, including suicide, ranks second in the burden of disease in established market economies, such as the United States.* Finally, the report comments that mental illness emerged from the Global Burden of Disease study as a surprisingly significant contributor to the burden of disease. (Library of Mental Health, 2000).

Another surprising element to the report by the Surgeon General is the following: "Considering health and illness as points along a continuum helps one appreciate that neither state exists in pure isolation from the other. In another but related context, everyday language tends to encourage a misperception that 'mental health' or 'mental illness' is unrelated to 'physical health' or 'physical illness.' *In fact, the two are inseparable.*" Ah. The mind body connection being formally recognized! The report also goes on to say, "Although 'mind' is a broad term that has had many different meanings over the centuries, today it refers to the totality of mental functions related to thinking, mood, and purposive behavior. The mind is generally seen as deriving from activities within the brain but displaying emergent properties, such as consciousness," (Fischbach, 1992; Gazzaniga et al., 1998). Wow! Look at that! Giving hope that the governmental institution is not slow to change, is the statement, "One reason the public continues to this day to emphasize the difference between mental and physical health is embedded in language. Common parlance continues to use the term 'physical' to distinguish some forms of health and illness from 'mental' health and illness. People continue to see mental and physical as separate functions when, in fact, mental functions (e.g., memory) are physical as well (American Psychiatric Association, 1994)."

However, the report then shows the governmental institution still steeped in the scientific materialism approach of the physical being primary with, "Mental functions are carried out by the brain. Likewise, mental disorders are reflected in physical changes in the brain (Kandel, 1998). Physical changes in the brain often trigger physical changes in other parts of the body too. The racing heart, dry mouth, and sweaty palms that accompany a terrifying nightmare are orchestrated by the brain. A nightmare is a mental state associated with alterations of brain chemistry that, in turn, provoke unmistakable changes elsewhere in the body." So even as this report of the Surgeon General is acknowledging the mind body connection, it is also reflecting its resistance to coming out of the scientific materialism's metaparadigm of placing the physical as primary. Nonetheless, the change in perception is noted, however incremental and slow to change.

From the website, "Depression and Perception; It's not what you think, but how you think that's important," their page, "Self–help Treatment; Clearing up the Depression Myths," the authors of the site say, "There are many myths and misconceptions surrounding stress and depression, so it's important to understand exactly what you are dealing with. Depression is nothing more than a term given to define the symptoms exhibited by the *human body's natural reaction to excessive stress on the mind,*" (italics mine). They then go on to provide statistics: mental disorders are common in the United States and internationally. An estimated 22.1% of Americans ages 18 and older (about 1 in 5 adults) suffer from a diagnosable mental disorder in a given year. In addition, *4 of the 10 leading causes of disability in the U.S. and other developed countries are mental disorders*–major depression, bipolar disorder, schizophrenia, and obsessive–compulsive disorder. Also, mood disorders cost U.S. employers 16 billion dollars in lost work time annually." The site also provides that "nearly twice as many women as men are affected by a depressive disorder each year. (12.0 % to 6.6 %, respectively)." Other sources cite this number as much higher, at 30% of women are depressed, and that men's figures were previously thought to be half that of women, but new estimates are higher.

"Everyone will at some time in their life be affected by depression– their own or someone else's, according to Australian Government statistics; depression statistics in Australia are comparable to those of US and UK," (Murray, et al 2005). Authors and psychologists Bob Murray, Ph.D. and Alicia Fortinberry of this website are the creators of The Uplift Program which "draws upon recent studies in neurobiology, psychiatry, and genetics to reveal how the psychological and physical stresses of modern life overwhelm our natural healing mechanisms and foster depression and anxiety by separating us from what makes us human," (Murray, et al 2005).

They go on to site a recent study at Rutgers University Department of Anthropology, which has linked stress to the "mismatch" between our present society and that of our stone-age ancestors. According to this view, *the further we get from our hunter-gatherer way of doing things the more stressed we become.* Murray and Fortinberry also discuss a concept "the tyranny of ends" that is used to characterize certain aspects of modern existence. *"We tend to increasingly do things that we really don't like doing in order to achieve something else which, in the long term we feel (or our parents felt) is more worthwhile. We become fixated with the 'end result' of what we are doing.* To a hunter-gatherer (such as the ones I have observed in Southern Africa) *life is about process, there are no 'end results.'* We modern humans want to 'achieve' things and judge ourselves based on the basis of what we have 'achieved.' We judge others on the basis of what they have achieved. We cannot live for the day, for the moment. We don't give ourselves the option (typically) of changing what we do when we no longer enjoy the process of doing it," (Murray, et al 2005.) What comes to mind is something lifelong that has had the ability to bother me. How, when people in Western nations first meet each other, one of the first three questions always asked is, "So, what do you do?" Think of that plane ride, this party, or that date. See! It's so prevalent! What is your response when asked?

The authors of the website on "Depression and Perception" then go on to say, "Depressive disorders are appearing earlier in life with the average age of onset 50 years ago being 29, whereas recent statistics indicate it at just 14.5 years old in today's society. Depressive disorders often co-occur with anxiety disorders and substance abuse. A recent study sponsored by the World Health Organization (WHO) and the World Bank (the report referred to in the Surgeon General's report cited above) found *unipolar major depression to be the leading cause of disability in the United States.*" Finally, this site says that "over 90% of suicide victims have a diagnosable mental disorder."

In regards to stress, this same site says, "75% of the general population experiences at least 'some stress' every two weeks," citing the National Health Interview Survey as its source. "Half of those experience moderate or high levels of stress during the same two–week period. Millions of Americans suffer from unhealthy levels of stress at work; a study several years ago estimated the number to be 11 million and given events since that time, this number has certainly more than tripled. Studies in Sweden, Canada and other Westernized countries show similar trends." Also, "Stress contributes to heart disease, high blood pressure, strokes, and other illnesses in many individuals. Stress also affects the immune system, which protects us from many serious diseases."

Finally, that "Stress in society is so prevalent that the U.S. Public Health Service has made reducing stress one of its major health promotion goals." High blood pressure and heart related high cholesterol medications are the two most prescribed medications in the U.S., with anti–depressants the third. Are you starting to put these pieces together of our current paradigm? Again, we need to ask who is benefitting from the status quo? Truly, what else is possible here? That's the nature of this entire discussion, book, and macroshift from the old metaparadigm to the emerging one. What are we doing? Can we slow down enough to genuinely ask and see the answers? Isn't it obvious by now, fitting these various puzzle pieces together, what we need to do? Seriously!

Now check this out. Taking it now to the next level, one of the earliest pioneers of mind body medicine–who particularly applied it to understanding the mind body connection within women's systems– is Christiane Northrup, M.D.. In one of her articles entitled, "Depression and Emotions" in which she says, "Autoimmune diseases (lupus, arthritis, multiple sclerosis, thyroid disorders, AIDS, cancer, allergies) are when the body attacks itself. These are first chakra imbalances (authors note: these are issues of feeling safe overall in one's body, in one's place in life and of having food, shelter, and clothing) that go hand–in–hand with depression and affect the immune system. The body gets a destructive message from deep within itself. Mental depression has been associated not only with self–destructive behaviors but with depression of the immune system functioning. Many people with autoimmune diseases also suffer from depression. *If we don't work through our emotional distress, we set ourselves up for physical distress because of the biochemical effect that suppressed emotions have on our immune and endocrine systems.*" This is one of the top statements I repeat the most to my clients and students and audience, who I help with their suppressed emotions.

This is on both ends, before the disease is diagnosed and after the disease is diagnosed.

Northrup goes on to distinguish, "It is not stress itself that creates immune system problems. It is how your body reacts to the stress. If your nervous system and adrenal glands are taxed or your liver clogged, when stressors occur you react to it adversely. This then sets you up for immune system dysfunction as you begin to feel that the stress is inescapable," (Northrup 2009). That is key, central to our discussion about the mind body paradigm, so please, let's be clear. Northrup, M.D., is saying it is not the stress itself that creates the problems, it's how your body, and thus by now you understand this means mind, reacts to the stress. Which means ever more specifically, it's how we *perceive* the stress, not the stress itself. One person perceives a house full of kids as stress while another perceives this as aliveness and love. The perception creates the reaction–or nonreaction–which then results in biochemical (bodily) responses. This means either stressful hormones getting released or pleasing hormones getting released. See, now you finally have it clear. This holistic model requires a whole lot of retraining of a reductionist mind, based on the scientific materialist view.

Northrup then goes on to bring the discussion to a level of spirit, or the soul, providing a deeper context for what depression really is. Please note, again, this is the key difference between the East and us in the West, particularly us in America. In the East they have a context that tends to frame situations in life in this fuller, richer context of the backdrop of *the* biggest picture–meaning soul, soul's growth, soul's evolution, karma and ultimately their metaparadigm, reincarnation. Northrup says, "The message is: What in my life needs new levels of empowerment?" That's it. The biggest perspective.

Northrup continues, "Depression is caused when vital life force energy reverses its flow of direction. Instead of flowing from within us out into our environment, it flows deep into our interior. *By following this energy deep into the quanta fields of our being, our energy body recovers something lost or accesses new levels of power needed for the next level of our expression.* By not resisting this energy and moving with it, we more quickly move through depression. (She notes: this does not refer to mental body depression that can be caused by brain chemistry imbalances. It is a different system," (italics mine) (Northrup 2009).

313

This is quite a mountain-top perspective for understanding depression, yes? In Dr. Northrup's discussion we can see both levels, her training as a biomedical M.D., as well as her understanding of the subtle energy effect within the mind body connection. In her words we also see that *if we avoid expansion of ourselves, it results in depression*. We've also just discussed the vast increase in numbers of depressed people and that it starts at an earlier age now and it costs more than cancer due to its prevalence when the burdens of disease are calculated. So what is the bottom line then? That the majority of us are facing the need to step up to the plate, to the next level of empowerment for each of us? And then collectively, as a society? Hence this entire book. Do you see now?

The vital life force energy, rather than being directed outward into the environment for new levels of expansion and expression, instead gets stuffed back down inside, and directed to flow internally, when it is meant for outward expansion, ultimately. This self–suppression happens out of fear and resistance and whatever other clinging, afflictive thoughts, beliefs and emotions that our ego–mind creates that cause us to clog ourselves, or stop ourselves up from the necessary growth our Higher Self wants. But our lower self, or ego–mind is typically what runs us. So we don't usually see how to direct ourselves towards growth and expansion in new directions. But these answers are inside of us, if we just retrain ourselves to slow down and listen. And find out what that nagging feeling is in the back of our head, or as the undercurrent to our day to day lives that we've been avoiding or running from. We know what we need ourselves. Not an outside authority. This is like when you have that feeling that something is wrong, and you're not sure what, just something feels off. You get these weird feelings now and then, so you go to your doctor to run a battery of tests to help you find out what is wrong. You don't believe the doctor when he or she comes back and says there is nothing wrong. You're either convinced that there is something physically wrong with you and end up talking your doctor into some sort of medication to cover some psychological purpose. Or the doctor comes back and says nothing is wrong and you say ok, but still feel like something is. Now, of course, I am not talking about genuine medical issues. I am talking about catching something mental, emotional or spiritual, before it becomes something physical. If we would learn to practice going inside ourselves for "answers" or guidance, then we'd end up being our own authority on what our system -mind, body and spirit—needs in our day to day lives, effecting our cumulative outcome of health. This is huge and it is a metaparadigm shift.

I help my clients learn to listen to themselves and to have the courage to take the next step into expansion. In fact one of the most frequent things I coach them with is, "If you're uncomfortable, that's good!" It's good because this means that we're entering new territory when we're afraid, unsure and uncomfortable, in the appropriate context, of course. I don't mean if you're in the thick of a national forest and lost, or on a city street at two in the morning. Nonetheless, I am saying to pay attention to that discomfort, it's a message. And that allowing ourselves to be uncomfortable is key to expanding ourselves to our next level of our own potency, or power. How willing are you to feel uncomfortable?

Understanding human happiness and well–being will help us better understand depression. Then we can listen to our level of happiness, or lack of, and work with our mind, emotions (consciousness) and not have depression be an issue. In an article entitled, "Understanding Human Happiness and Well–Being," the organization *Sustainable Scale*, says, "More recently various social scientists have researched human happiness around the world. Some common findings emerge, despite using different experimental and survey methods and exploring the issue in very different countries. *One of the most common conclusions is that money or financial wealth is not the most important determinant. Beyond an annual per capita* equivalent at $10,000 Purchasing Power Parity (this is an ability to provide for basic and a bit beyond basic necessities term), *happiness is a function of non–material factors. The support of family, friends and community, a meaningful role in life, and basic freedoms are much more important at all levels of wealth beyond this range,*" (italics mine). This income range varies amongst other studies that come to the same conclusions, nonetheless, as this study, with 13,000 US$, in relative terms, as the international mean–not the American mean- that people need to get to in order to have basic necessities met. And once they go much beyond it, happiness factors decrease.

These studies, which are increasing in number, all point to: "Studies of the relationship between economic growth measured by GDP and personal levels of happiness report that happiness increases with GDP while GDP is growing up to a certain level, GDP increases do not lead to more personal happiness. *In every country studied, reports of personal happiness level off after GDP continues to grow.* Even five–fold increases in GDP, as occurred in

Japan over the 20th century, do not lead to increases in personal happiness," (italics mine).

The conclusion is: "*The happiness that can be derived from material goods appears to have psychological limits,* just as there are biophysical limits to the services ecosystems can provide," (italics mine) (Sustainable Scale Organization 2009). Sustainable Scale Org further clarifies that this relationship holds for both men and women, and across age groups and income levels, and that this relationship has endured over the decades that such research has been conducted. Meaning, that this is the observed correlation, replicated and repeated over and over again, throughout the decades and the same conclusions have been found. Once basic necessities and a little beyond are achieved (first chakra is feeling good), additional money does not lead to an increase in happiness. In fact, as we're beginning to see, the happiness factor actually decreases at a certain higher level of income.

This has quite a significant role in our discussion of the mind body connection, the usefulness of natural healing methods for our well-being and "preventative" medicine, our society's overlooking the subtle, and all modernized societies' increases in stress and depression—especially ours. There is also that co–occurring increase in the "affluent" diseases already mentioned. So it seems obvious at this point to simply connect the dots. The more we chase after the material, the more we pay attention to the physical at the expense of the subtle. The very mental, emotional, and then physical conditions we put ourselves into in order to compete weakens our foundational systems such as our immune systems. Typically, we ignore the subtle signs–daily low emotions, aches and pains that persist, tiredness, lack of good quality sleep, lack of time and energy to exercise, a perception of no time to prepare wholesome meals–from our body systems.

We then end up with full blown diseases in our physical bodies that are a result of our lifestyle choice to focus more on the physical at the expense of the subtle. This then gets treated by the same physically focused medicine of our metaparadigm –biomedicine. So the problem does not get cured at the core. You can see that now, yes? All of this is on the material plane, with a focus towards the physical. So that, as has been stated previously, a slowing down and a more introspective lifestyle that involves self–inquiry and self–awareness would help us to focus more on the subtle. We'd then catch our emotions' messages and wisdom, and observe our mental states, leading to better self management. We'd catch the messages, and if need be warnings, to change course. We'd have more self–knowledge, and therefore be more self-empowered. Both of these activities–paying more attention to our emotional and mental needs rather than just our physical–are the type of ignorance of the subtle that our metaparadigm has set up for us and reinforced.

How did this viscous cycle begin? How did we end up here? A description that goes back to life in the 1870's and 1880's says, "The pace of life begins to speed up. People began to notice how the acceleration of the perception of the duration of time and the apparent shortening of physical distances was inducing stress in them (i.e., invention of the railroad). Americans who lived through the second half of the nineteenth century experienced the greatest, most fundamental changes ever experienced by mankind: electricity, telephone, telegraph and the railroad. Western notions of stress were a direct consequence of these technological accelerations that began to really take off during the second half of the 19th century. (Yet,) people in our modern times have to do more things, with less and less time to do them in," (Natural Health Perspective 2010).

In tracing back over the field of natural healing, which is not a new field, but one that was actually begun before the biomedical model with the inception of homeopathy as was discussed earlier, we find an interesting parallel to today's situation. In 1880 George Beard, M.D., a neurologist, wrote *A Practical Treatise on Nervous Exhaustion (Neurasthenia)*, in which he defined it as a condition of general malaise, and was attributed by Beard *to the stresses of modern life*. It was the first book in the U.S. to express the concept that one's mental life can have a profound impact upon one's physical health. Natural Health Perspective's website states; "Beard's nervous exhaustion of neurasthenia would eventually develop into the modern concepts of Chronic–Fatigue–Syndrome, Fibromyalgia and multiple chemical sensitivities." That may require a re–read.

Apparently, Beard, who received his medical degree from Columbia University in 1866, wrote *American Nervousness* in 1881, describing neurasthenia as American nervousness. According to Natural Health Perspective, *Beard saw a significant correlation between American social organization and nervous illness*. Inside *American Nervousness* he says, *"American nervousness is the product of American civilization."* On a side note, in England around this same time there was the acknowledgement of the condition labeled *hysteria*. It was thought to affect mostly housewives, and was a nervous condition, associated with the boredom and anxiety of running a household as Victorian women. So the remedy? It was a special manipulation by certain doctors of a manual type of the women's genitalia. This was when the battery operated vibrator was created. No joke. Look it up. There was also an Indie film released in 2012 on this topic. The release given from orgasm feeds a body with feel-good hormones, and calms the system. So it was seen as an appropriate treatment.

Natural Health Perspectives goes on to comment that unlike other countries, *America offered its inhabitants the possibility of unlimited freedom which resulted in unlimited ambition among the populace.* This is a key idea, when reflecting on America's parallel development of itself as a nation with its own national culture alongside the Industrial Revolution. Beard also writes: "It has long seemed the especial province of Americans to abuse their nerves from the cradle to the grave." This is absolutely not the first time I have seen or heard this said. I heard it from one of my Indian yoga teachers in India when he was preparing us to teach Westerners. I also heard it from both the Chinese and Indian friends and acquaintances I made, as well as many other Asian, Middle Eastern, European, and Russian citizens I met while traveling. They all have expressed this same sentiment in their own words over and over again. One example is "Americans love to burn up their central nervous system" meaning because we are so focused on the physical plane, and go go go, and are externally driven, our physical senses are thus being externally driven that much more to external stimuli, *and as we are without an understanding of the role of subtle energies,* we "burn up" our central nervous systems.

National Health Perspective continues this discussion by saying, "A deficiency in nervous energy was the price exacted by industrialized urban societies, competitive businesses and social environments, and the luxuries, vices, and excesses of modern life. Beard wrote: 'The chief and primary cause of...[the] very rapid increase of nervousness is modern civilization, which is distinguished from the ancient [civilizations] by these five characteristics: steam power, the periodical press, the telegraph, the sciences, and the mental activity of women.' American nervousness was alarmingly frequent 'among the well–to–do and the intellectual, and especially among those in the professions and in the higher walks of business life, who are in deadly earnest in the race for place and power,'" (Natural Health Perspective 2010).

This was at the turn of the 1800's into the 1900's, as America was in the throes of the Industrial Revolution's boom. Coming up now to the particulars of our time, Dr. Gregg D. Jacobs discusses the influence of affluence in his article, "Consumerism, Happiness and Health." In it he discusses the point already made, that affluence does not increase happiness, and that although affluence has climbed steadily over the past four decades–save for this present period–we are not happier. Jacobs quotes the well–known Dr. David Myers, an expert on the topic of subjective well–being and a professor of psychology at Hope College, "We are twice as rich and no happier compared to forty years ago, while the divorce rate has doubled, teen suicide tripled, reported violence almost quadrupled, and depression rates have soared, particularly amongst teens and young adults." Jacobs then goes on to discuss how young adults today grow up with much more affluence compared to their grandparents and slightly less happiness and a much greater risk of depression, so that Myers terms this conjunction, as Jacobs discusses, of material prosperity and social recession the "modern paradox." *"In his mind (Myers'), it is hard to avoid a startling conclusion; our increased affluence over the past forty years has not been accompanied by any increased subjective well–being...In short, modern life is built on materialism, which has not improved well–being and may be detrimental to mental health,"* (italics mine) (Jacobs 2010).

On verdant.net's website, there is an article, "How Consumerism Affects Society, Our Economy, and the Environment," in which the authors say that consumerism *sets each person against them self* in an endless quest for the attainment of material things or the imaginary world conjured up and made possible by things yet to be purchased. "Weight training, diet centers, breast reduction, breast enhancement, cosmetic surgery, permanent eye make–up, liposuction, collagen injections, these are some examples of people turning themselves into human consumer goods more suited for the 'marketplace' than living in a healthy balanced society," (verdant.net 2010).

Additionally, verdant.net authors say that many consumers run out of room in their homes to store the things they buy. Hence, a rapidly growing industry in America is that of self–storage. They also offer the "tidbit" of information that there has been a "55% rise in breast enhancements. First time as the #1 procedure since the 1992 silicone implant restriction." Another tidbit offered from the *Wall Street Journal* on verdant.net is that "'each year an estimated 1.5 million Americans choose to have nose jobs, tummy tucks or breast enlargements. Many of these people would be unable to afford these vital surgical procedures if it were not for the public spirited efforts of loan companies like Jayhawk Acceptance Corporation, a used car lender that has turned to covering the booming demand for elective surgery. Lenders in this field face an unusual challenge,' explains the *Wall Street Journal*: 'A lender can take a used car but can hardly repossess a face lift.' Consequently lenders like Jayhawk have to charge a slightly higher interest rate, up to 22.5% to be exact. Says Michael Smartt, Jayhawk CEO, 'We're capitalizing on America's vanity,'" (Verdant.net 2010). And these procedures contribute to each individual's "toxic load." If you think about it, it is the same concept as the carbon footprint concept, just internal.

They go on to say, on verdant.net, that "it is impossible to win a war against yourself or your uncontrolled desires, and that a good example of this is the simplistic materialist psychosis of the bumper sticker: 'He who dies with the most toys wins.' Another example is 'I can imagine it, therefore I want it. I want it, therefore I should have it. Because I should have it, I need it. Because I need it, I deserve it. Because I deserve it, I will do anything necessary to get it.'"

This is quintessential ego dominant thinking, and hence how the ego–mind has gotten piqued during this time. *Consumerism, with its accompanying omnipresent advertising, and affluence have helped to create a new level of hyper–activity within the mind as a whole.* It is what is causing many of the obsessive–compulsive disorders, or in its counterpart or the other end of the spectrum, depression. *Consumerism breeds heightened ego–based thinking as well as low self–esteem just by the very nature of what it is based on. Advertisers prey on one's ego;* that to have the latest is to be cool, or good looking, or more approved of by others, which creates a perpetual cycle of low–self esteem after each item is bought and the fleeting fulfillment gained wears off until the next purchase. This is the consumerism loop. And it's based on the primal emotional fear and need to belong. Buy this, wear this, use this and you'll then be good enough to fit in, and belong, especially to that level of status you don't really feel like you belong to.

In this ego–mind (the part of the mind that is ego–based, acts and thinks in self interest and self–preservation, i.e. greed and competition, or self–sabotage and low self–esteem) dominated milieu that supports the physical as primary in the race for materialism, it needs to be said that consumerism has obviously spun out of control. *In fact, consumerism is the peak of this imbalance that has been discussed throughout this work–the primary focus on the physical at the expense of the subtle.* This consumerism is the mass mental check out, or avoidance of slowing down and going inside and listening. Or another way to label it is symptomatic that we are in the breakdown phase of this macroshift from one metaparadigm to the next.

Noam Chomsky provides this from his *Manufacturing Consent*, as quoted again, on verdant.net. "Sports is another crucial example of the indoctrination system...It offers people something to pay attention to that is of no importance...It keeps them from worrying about things that matter to their lives that they might have an idea of something about...People have the most exotic information and understanding about all sorts of arcane issues... It's a way of building up irrational attitudes of submission to authority, and group cohesion behind leadership elements, in fact its training in irrational jingoism...That's why energy is devoted to supporting them...and advertisers are willing to pay for them."

Verdant.net then goes on to discuss how time is exchanged for money to buy things that there usually is little time to enjoy. "Whatever time is left after work is often devoured by television, basically a series of ever–more mediocre filler programs inserted between ever–more–spectacular commercials whose purpose is to stoke further desire for more things. When the material desires fail to be satisfied, people grow unhappy with their lives...*People become used to the intrusion of advertising into their consciousness*...and so they fail to protect themselves, or worse, their children from being seduced by it. Convinced that their self worth is based on a ($500) athletic shoe or designer clothing, children are already on the road to spiritual dissatisfaction and resentment as well as a perception of diminished self–worth," (italics mine) (Verdant.net 2010). Perhaps this explains the average age of depression dropping from age 29 50 years ago, to now age 14.5.

Noam Chomsky is also quoted in an article from an Indian website, "Consumerism in the Globalized World." On this site, the authors say that Noam Chomsky, one of the world's most noted intellectuals, describes globalization thus: "Insinuation of extension of transnational corporate tyranny...Their first interest is profit but much broader than that it is *to construct an audience of a particular type...addicted to a certain lifestyle with artificial wants, and audience atomized, separated from one another, fragmented enough so that they don't enter the political arena and disturb the powerful,*" (italics mine) (Sukumari 1996).

In the *International Institute of Management's Executive Journal*, there is an article entitled, "The American Pursuit of Unhappiness: Gross National Happiness (GNH)–A New Economic Metric." The author of this article, Med Jones, says that citizens with better emotional and mental health are easier to relate to and work with, tend to be better decision makers, are more creative, and outperform peers in problem solving, innovation, persistence and productivity. Jones says, "I'm not trying to shock you by saying that the current American socioeconomic system does not help your mental and emotional health. A careful examination will reveal the true picture. According to the following independent research studies: The University of Michigan's World Value Surveys (WVS) of 2004, ranks America at number 15th in population happiness. The New Economics Foundation (NEF) study of 2006, uncovered a different world order where *USA ranks at the 150th place*. Regardless of what you or I think of various studies, and of their ranking criteria, the fact is that when it comes to happiness and mental well-being, *the world's most advanced country does not make it into the top 10 and further studies suggest that it's getting worse*," (Jones 2006).

Jones offers as his root cause analysis that the ideologies and governments of this century that promoted happiness, have left people with more material possessions, but less psychological well-being. Many of these people are emotionally bankrupt and unhappy. "The demands of life in our current socioeconomic system require that we keep running and running with little or no breaks. With increasing life costs, economic demands, and social and work pressures, most people are suffering from chronic stress, pain, anxiety, fear or anger. The term 'rat race' applies more today than ever. Many people eventually experience this as burnout, exhaustion and/or depression. Many Americans are feeling unhappy at home and at work," (Jones 2006). Jones goes on to say that to be fair, it is not the government's sole fault that more has changed in the last decade technologically, culturally, politically and economically than the entire past century.

But there is a trump card here; the power of choice.

Chapter 7—Really, What are We Doing?

Out of Order and Into Connection

LASZLO HAS SOME SUGGESTIONS, IN his chapter "A Better Way to Grow," from *Quantum Shift in the Global Brain*. Laszlo, remember, explains the term "extensive growth" to mean growth that moves along a horizontal plane on the surface of the planet, and that it conquers ever more territories, colonizes ever more people, and imposes the will of the dominant layers on ever more layers of the population. Laszlo is saying that this is the current mode, and this is the first half of the macroshift we are now in and coming out of. He goes on to say that the basic end of extensive growth is the extension of human power over larger and larger areas, right? And this is a result from the focus "out there" rather than an introspective one, focused on "in here," yes?

So when Lazlo says that for the states the goal of extensive growth is territorial sovereignty, including sovereignty over the human and natural resources of the territories; therefore then the corresponding goal for global companies is to generate demand for consumption, "often without regard for the social and environmental consequences." Remember that Laszlo says that the ends of extensive growth can be encapsulated in three 'Cs'" *conquest, colonialization,* and *consumption* and that these ends are served by their corresponding varieties of means, with the technologies that whet people's appetites, create artificial demand, and shift patterns of consumption.

These technologies are for the third "C" of propaganda, PR, and advertising of our modern and post modern age. Laszlo describes this third technology as "having produced both the demand–provoking images and the subtle or not–so–subtle means by which the manufacturers of products and the suppliers of services impose their will on their clients and customers," (Laszlo 2008).

It is an artificial demand created for products that profit the producers of both the demand and the products–this is not done with the end consumers' good in mind. Hence the cycle of artificial demand resulting in artificial feelings consumers now have and chase after, attempting to satisfy them by purchasing these products with their money.

So, within our currently crumbling paradigm are nine outdated beliefs. As you read through them you'll notice that they're effects from the scientific materialist metaparadigm's focus, as a result of the Enlightenment thinking that we reviewed.

The Nine Outdated Beliefs of Our Metaparadigm
Everyone is unique and separate
Everything is reversible
Order calls for hierarchy
Efficiency is key
Technology is the answer
New is always better
My country, right or wrong
The more money I have, the happier I am
The future is none of my business

Laszlo explains this first outdated belief, "We are all unique and separate individuals enclosed by our skin and pursuing our own interests. We have only ourselves to rely on; everyone else is either friend or foe, at best linked to us by temporarily coinciding interests." The second outdated belief is that everything is reversible, Laszlo explains, "The problems we experience are but interludes after which everything goes back to normal. All we need to do is manage the difficulties that crop up using tried and tested methods of problem solving and, if necessary, crisis management. Business as usual has evolved out of business as usual and sooner or later will reverse back into it."

This brings up another pioneer echoing Laszlo, Carolyn Myss, who says, "There are no longer problems and solutions. Instead, today we have predicaments," (Myss 2010). Myss says, further, that predicaments do not have solutions. Instead, we have to learn how to live successfully managing them and ourselves. Commenting on the fourth belief that efficiency is key, says Laszlo, "We must get the maximum out of every person, every machine, and every organization, regardless of what is produced and whether or not it serves a humanly and socially useful purpose."

Following along this same track, Laszlo then goes on to list what he calls "Six Particularly Dangerous Myths" as:

Six Particularly Dangerous Myths
    Nature is inexhaustible
    Nature is like a giant mechanism
    Life is a struggle where only the fittest survive
    Market distributes benefits
    The more you consume the better you are
    Economic ends justify military means (Laszlo 2008)

Laszlo offers "A Better Modality: Intensive Growth" as his suggestion for this second half of the macroshift, to replace the outdated model of Extensive Growth with its inherent dangerous myths and now outdated beliefs. "The ends of intensive growth are very different from those of extensive growth. Intensive growth centers on the development of individuals and communities. Its principal ends can be grasped under three other "C's": *Connection, Communication and Consciousness ...One of the great myths of the industrial age has been the skin–enclosed separation of individuals from each other* and the disjunction of their interests from the interests of others. The former aspect of this myth has been legitimized by the worldview based on classical physics. Like the mass points of Newton, humans appear to be self–contained, mutually independent chunks of organized matter only externally related to each other and to their environment," (Laszlo 2008). Reviewing first the three "C's" of extensive growth:

Three C's of Old Metaparadigm of Extensive Growth
    Conquest
    Colonization
    Consumption

Alison J. Kay, PhD

Three C's of New Metaparadigm on Intensive Growth
Connection
Communication
Consciousness

Laszlo connects this now outdated view of classical Newtonian physics with classical economics as well, saying that it has also become outdated. Specifically, the beliefs of viewing the individual as separate, and as a self–centered economic actor pursuing his or her own interests, and that these are then harmonized at best with the interests of others naturally, and that all of this is an inherent working of the market are all getting replaced during this macroshift with more functional views for today. Once the new sciences are taken into consideration, "every quantum is known to be intrinsically connected with every other quantum, and every organism with other organisms in the biosphere. In turn, economists know that there is a direct connection between the interests of individuals, individual states, and individual enterprises and the workings of the globalized international system. In our world these embracing connections evolve rapidly, and it is one of the ends of intensive growth to order them, creating coherent structure in place of random proliferation," (Laszlo 2008).

Linking the second and third ends of intensive growth, communication and consciousness, with the first, connection, he explains that these ends are to deepen the level of communication and raise the level of consciousness of the communicators. He states that *communication unfolds on multiple levels with some of it subtle,* reinforcing this author's experience of the Chinese style of communication presented earlier. The need to observe one's inner dialogues also comes back up here. Laszlo says, "First of all, *we need to communicate with ourselves, caring for and developing our consciousness and personality.* People who are 'in touch with themselves' are better balanced and more able to communicate with the world around them." This alludes to improved functioning in one person's life; and within society, as an individual is healthy, physically, mentally and spiritually their roles in their communities and workplace are all more supportive and less of a burden.

Laszlo continues to state that, "We also need to be in communication with those who make up the immediate context of our lives—family, community, and work or profession. Still wider levels of communication are equally necessary: communication with other people, whether near or far, in our own community and in other communities, countries and cultures. Communication calls for connection, but on the human plane more enters into play than connection: communication also involves consciousness. The full potentials of human communication unfold when communicators apprehend the strands of connection through which they communicate." Again this refers to the style of communication being more attuned to the subtle cues as this author experiences within the indirect communication system of the Chinese. This is not to portray the Chinese communication style as ideal, just that it employs use of subtleties as described earlier. Elaborating, Laszlo says, *"A high level of communication calls for a high level of consciousness* that enables people to make use of the many, *sometimes extremely subtle,* strands of connection that bind them to each other and to their environment. Consciousness of these connections could enable us to shift from today's power–and–conquest–hungry Logos–civilization to a Holos–civilization centered on the growth of individuals and the sustainability of human communities and the biosphere," (Laszlo 2008).

Another significant aspect to this macroshift that clearly needs to increase is feeling more comfortable in what has previously made our culture feel uncomfortable. This is the recognition of the limits to our being able to prove something exists in order for us to be able to acknowledge its existence. We need to let go of expecting the type of proof within the scientific methodology that has been used since the inception of Enlightenment science with physical matter and the physical universe. Because within this domain of existence that is comprised of subtle energy, or the vacuum, or the medium, or the sub–quanta field, or the space that exists between molecules and atoms, or even as sometimes referred to, the God Particle, it is simply not reasonable, irony of ironies.

Within the realm of science, continuing to attempt to study subtle energy with a method developed for studying and understanding physical phenomena, at this point, seems relatively ludicrous, bordering on ignorant. We know enough by now to see that physical phenomena and metaphysical phenomena are too contrary, or different in their inherent natures, to have the same means applied to studying them. Nonetheless, even with the need to study consciousness with new and different tools–such as consciousness itself–we have, in the majority at the level of the masses within our metaparadigm, and at the levels of those in positions of power within the institutions established within this outdated paradigm, continued to expect this.

Our world has changed and we have evolved beyond being able to just get by with most of our focus only on acknowledging what is in the physical domain. This can now be safely said because as we have seen there have been too many overlapping, repeated examples of discoveries of the power of the subtle along with the real need for it to be actively acknowledged within our societal milieu. These various situations and crises occurring simultaneous to each other have been feeding the need for a new way of conducting life throughout the majority of our systems in our society and ourselves. As the Dalai Lama himself said, it seems like we need a new way to go. Remember?

So that by now it is sheer ignorance to ignore the cumulative evidence pointing out that it is actually energy *before* matter and that this energy is effected by humans' consciousness. Thus we need to work with what comprises our consciousness; thoughts, beliefs, feelings, and our essence, or spirit, or vital life force energy. Then coupling this with one of the main impacts of globalization, having more access to how other cultures work with subtle energy and consciousness for health and longevity and have for centuries, and the new direction we're headed in seems obvious. Yet now add in the fact that there have been enough significant red flags that tell us we're ignoring specifically the power of consciousness and that it is something that we can't really afford to do anymore, nor continue to resist its presence and its effect in out lives, and this all adds up to a new way of looking at life, and organizing our lives.

We cannot afford to continue to blatantly disregard that this field consists of something very different, and continue to use old, gross (in the sense of unwieldy due to its dense physicalness) tools that were not intended to catch something so subtle. Nor can we continue to use outdated models of thinking still geared almost exclusively to the physical, obvious and directly observable parts of life. Both of these were not designed to understand the subtle.

At this juncture in history we have far too much directing our attention towards focusing on consciousness, *and the power contained within it,* to continue to stubbornly cling to the old. Particularly while we have other cultures in countries who have now modernized, particularly in the East, embracing what we have offered them as well as what they have taken that we have not necessarily offered. So they're benefiting from globalization by balancing out what their societies may have been lacking prior to globalization, when they were focusing more on the subtle energies and less on manifesting on the physical plane, physical, tangible, useful tools and products. to the same extent that the industrialized West had been.

These freshly modernized countries have been making really good use of what they've seen and learned from us and are "getting ahead," by modernizing and living their version of the American Dream, while they've tweaked and made adjustments within their own cultures in our post–modern era. That's the era they've modernized in, giving them somewhat of an advantage on this side of the equation. Meaning they don't have attachments to how modernization should look, as we do, because it's just now happening. They don't have the industrial age's infrastructure and thinking, like ours, remaining in their cultural metaparadigm. Instead, they have their own cultures' metaparadigm prior to globalization.

It has also been observed during my decade of living in the East during their modernization that they seem to be more malleable, quicker to change than what I'd experienced growing up and living in the U.S.A. I actively worked on change within the U.S. democratic structure during my career as a political organizer and strategist, so I had a decent grasp of this. Couple the political consulting with my minor in my undergraduate program in "Social Thought and Political Economy" and then bring in my Masters in Public Administration and Public (Environmental) Policy and I do have direct experience of the typical rate of change in our democracy. Our democratic system is strong, but also slow to change.

While in Taiwan in my first few years and still gaining familiarity with their society and system, I remember asking my Taiwanese colleagues and my Taiwanese American high school students why they thought Taiwan would seem to me to change so much more easily and quickly than the states. Keeping in mind that my students were of varying degrees of Westernization, who saw their extended Taiwanese Chinese family on the weekends, many of whom had lived in the U.S. for the majority of their earlier school years and who were international students, their answers were from this perspective. Getting their high school education at an international school that teaches an American curriculum thereby setting them up to return to the states for university, they were exposed to American thought through the curriculum, too, beyond having lived there. Their response? Typically it simply was,

"Taiwan is a smaller country." Yet it seems more complex. The democratic structure we have here in the states, comparatively, and the powers that be don't allow for rapid change, to begin with. This is not to our benefit, especially when considering how rapidly other countries are changing and can change in this globalized arena. I am thinking of East Asian countries, India, a few South American countries, and Eastern Europe.

There are less preconceived notions in the newly modernized countries from old systems about how it should be with industry, technology and science other than what they've seen from America and the West. Thus there's no resistance to break through in this way. They've just simply been able to adopt modernization at this post–modern, digitalized stage without any clinging to the way things used to be in Newtonian physics' days. There's other resistance, obviously, but not in this regard. There has been nothing impeding their taking on science, technology and the ensuing industry and lifestyle that accompanies it because there was nothing there before the television, the air conditioner, the internet or the iPod. Except for old lifestyles not as technologically or industrially based but more agrarian from the way they lived prior to globalization. They were a blank slate in this regard. So they've taken to it like a moth to a flame. This has been their "lack" or their empty space to fill,.

In fact, I found these countries in East Asia and India to be on fire. Even with as ancient as their cultures are, they're running a race at top speed with modernization and the West and all that this offers them within their cultural metaparadigm. And it's causing them to change at a rate Americans wouldn't, and couldn't even consider possible as a rate of change. In the U.S. we seem to refuse to genuinely consider, or incorporate what is fundamental to their cultural metaparadigms into ours, beyond Hollywood making good use of martial arts and the mysterious cool power that this subtle art contains.

If one were to go to the East and witness the rapidness with which they take from the Western Modernization model while retaining what they want of their cultural traditions and metaparadigm, it can spin an American's head. Although their rapid modernization is an extremely multifaceted, complex issue, from this angle, nonetheless, it is simple. They change at rates that we can't even conceive of, particularly when contrasted against how slow our rate of change has been to change in this same era. It feels almost embarrassing to an American expat at how quick their rate of change and gobbling up of American lifestyle can happen. Because they are changing and expanding, while we remain basically closed down to what they have to offer us. They take it and run with it. While exporting this lifestyle and accompanying products to complete the image, we are comparatively so ridiculously close–minded to genuinely gaining or receiving benefits from globalization in a reciprocal manner.

They have McDonalds, Starbucks, MTV, biomedicine, levis, Ph.D.'s from American universities, Hollywood movies, Italian food and pizza, the iPod, the iPad, the iPhone and more, particularly since they've made copy cat versions of our original technology or design or entertainment medium without a cultural value to prohibit this. Nor do they have laws and regulations that are either written or reinforced slowing any of this down. In fact, their cultural metaparadigm supports copy cat versions–it's how they compete. Take someone else's idea and call it your own, with little to no change in it, except maybe one letter in the name of the idea or business.

It is not smart on our part. Why do we export what we know? Why do we allow citizens of the East particularly, to come to the United States and learn what we know, and then return to their home countries with knowledge of both countries' ideas, where they will be listened to with gained prestige due to their training in America? Please don't conclude that this is a "close-the-borders" argument. It's not. I'm not even on that planet with where I am going here. By now, I suspect you've picked up on the rhythm of trusting me to develop a discussion and surprise you with where it ends up.

While what we gain, for example, are foreign research lab assistants for their Ph.D. program and post–doctoral work who replace American lab research assistants for many reasons. One of the main reasons is that the economic incentive for American post–doctorate students is too low of a return on their investment of time and money. It now takes many years building into a full research position with tenure, while it's considered good money and a great opportunity by the East Asians. The studies and stats for this are in the next section. The tenure position barely exists anymore, as the main incentive of money has tilted the entire structure of this profession. Furthermore, South Korea, Taiwan, China, and Singapore's scientific researchers are now publishing more articles in English than American researchers. American scientific literature has flattened out as the source to cite, or quote from, while other international sources have become included into the mix, detracting from our strength. Is the profit, or the savings in capital investment or labor costs, as a short–term goal really that worth it? What have we really saved or gained?

Why is that? Because they're hungry for exposure to what we know? Why aren't we more hungry, or why aren't there more of us hungry for exposure to what they know? Because they want what we have as viewed from the lens of Hollywood and pop culture? Or because we think we're already "there," whereas they're "still trying to get there," so we're not striving to learn from them? Because of the prestige associated with American university training, or even American education at any level? Since when is our education system thought of as so good within our own country? What are we missing that they're seeing? So to ask why this is even the case seems like a good place to start, although not meant for this discussion.

The points made are relevant in that it does appear that we are comparatively close minded, and rather egocentric and ethnocentric, and that it is even rather stupid on our part to remain this *wide open,* yes even with the supposed protection of our copyright and patent laws, for others to learn from our culture and our lifestyle, walk away with this knowledge, having gained something, while we have had something taken but nothing gained in return, except for financial savings? For the institution employing them? Realistically, we're talking about two different systems with two different sets of ideals and beliefs from yes, two different metaparadigms. Copyrighting and patents, this constitutional concept in the U.S. of protection for ingenuity and invention is not at all their metaparadigm, as least amongst the Chinese. I remember learning how parents would keep secret the program they were sending their son or daughter to for the summer so their child would have the presumed edge. Secretive behavior and protection of what one knows is not done legally, rather practiced individually–culture wide. Stealing ideas is *so common.* I also remember various students throughout the years amongst my Westernized Chinese students at an American curriculum based international school, where one wouldn't expect it, complaining about other students copying or taking their idea in a way I'd never heard expressed in the American classrooms I taught in prior to going international. It's omnipresent in their culture, the open stealing of ideas, again in a way that is different to copying. It's based on a sense of creativity, and wanting what the other student created, or had. I could see it more in my students who identified themselves as more Chinese, who had been in Taiwan longer, more normalized to this cultural phenomena. The distinction I am trying to make is a challenge; this is another one that may require direct experience. It is just a different feeling behind the protection and guarding against what one comes up with. It's not approached with the same openness, or sharing of ideas we do here in the U.S..

We have been so slow to embrace what is at the core of their system. This understanding they have of the subtle energies as the structure upon which all life operates and the ways to work with subtle energy for health and longevity. Yet meanwhile, we both export and give away what is at the core of ours. Sure, "we" make a profit, or the CEO's of the multinationals and smaller corporations, stockholders, and business owners do. And yes, we consumers get imported, inexpensive cheaply made products at a fraction of the previous costs so we can live a more disposable, "convenient" lifestyle seeing as we're so busy. I love the technology behind my iPod, it's fantastically convenient and ingenious, thank you Steve Jobs!

Yet meanwhile we have a huge imbalance between us and the Chinese with trade surpluses and deficits, and tariffs charged, as the Chinese gain while the USA does not. But this-while related-is for another discussion. And "we" may gain in the research produced from these assistants in technology for academic research or pharmaceutical drugs research with really cheap labor. Yet, what do we gain as a result of this? Apparently, not cheaper drugs. So who is benefitting from this? One would think that as a result of this research being done cheaper, we'd see an effect. This "savings" is not it; this issue goes well beyond capitalism and economics and globalization. We'll return to this in just a moment.

Look at what we've lost. How complacent, miserable, spoiled, stressed out, sick with chronic diseases and cancer, and obese we have become, in general, especially when looking comparatively within our own society even 50 years ago? Look at our reputation around the world. Live the American lifestyle of luxury, a typical Chinese, for example, thinks-but doesn't dare say in a direct way to an American-but don't be like them. They're fat, loud, opinionated, spoiled, arrogant slobs, or they're materialistic, superficial, lazy brats. This is what they're really also thinking. I've heard it, trust me, from Chinese friends once we got close enough, and acquaintances, once I asked them so I could test the validity of what I was hearing and experiencing. In fact, this was somewhat shoved down my throat in that indirect way the Chinese have, so I was driven to understand from my Chinese friends what this was. It showed up in all sorts of ways the Chinese dealt with me, reacting to me and judged me that were all at first completely unfamiliar to me. So I had to eventually ask. I remember asking on of my colleagues, and asking my students because it became such a huge part of living there as an American expat beyond two or three years.

I eventually learned that the Chinese typically have the attitude, "Just take from them (foreigners) what we can, so we can compete in this global arena, and so we can have these cool technologies which we'll then reproduce faster and cheaper with both cheaper labor and cheaper parts, while we won't be slowed down by all their principles, ethics, laws, protests, democratic voices, and regulations due to their Puritan moralistic foundations and freedom of speech so everyone's voice can be heard, protesting whenever something doesn't seem fair, feeling that sense of American entitlement like a bunch of spoiled kids who don't have a perspective of history and patience as our patient, ancient culture does who has seen 5,000 years of strife and struggle and real suffering, and we'll just zoom ahead in front of them."

I am not joking here! A decade on my part worth of wrestling to understand their principles that took me into an administrative position to act as a bridge between the Chinese and American cultures at my international school, allows me to be able to say this. I struggled through so much in order to understand this; what it seemed like on the surface was not typically what it really was there. No this may not be "politically correct" but an observation is an observation, especially if the same one is repeated by many different eyes. Why do we need such cushioning? I paid for the understanding, and hurt for these understandings, as I alluded to above.

While these statements may seem to not be politically correct, after about year number five the generalizations that I'd formed, through many in depth discussions with both other expats and Chinese, consistently seemed accurate to keep. They were functional within the bi–cultural (Taiwanese Chinese, and American) environment I worked in. My home environment there was different then the majority of my colleagues because I chose to leave the comfortable, enclosed grounds providing the ex–pat, or "foreigner's and Chinese who had lived overseas" housing, and instead lived downtown. I sought a more authentic experience, and I wanted to enculturate as successfully as possible with the local Taiwanese Chinese culture. (This is a whole other book.) Part of my desire to authentically experience and learn more about the Chinese culture somewhat atypical to my colleagues, was met by my being asked to help as a bridge in an administrative role as the foreign liason for the school's accreditation process. I was asked to translate and mediate between the local Chinese teachers and administrators and the Western ideas that accompany the accreditation process by a Western accrediting organization, WASC (Western Association of School Accreditation).

Truly consider this line of thinking rather than being turned off by the ugliness of it. Besides, continues the Chinese mind in our example, we have the advantage, we're new at this and we're like little pubescent teens with raging hormones; they're (the Americans and the West) all kind of tired. They've been modernized for how long, and they're how big of a country who can't agree but who need agreement to do anything that would really move them ahead. So while they're busy crashing down under the weight of what they've created in the name of materialism, we'll also become materialistic but we'll do it better, faster, and cheaper than them, *without even letting them be aware of what we're doing.* They won't see it because they don't get our system, besides they're direct. We're secretive. We don't have to honor a direct communication system, and we don't have to be truthful to their face, that's not our cultural value. That's theirs, and *it weakens them against us.* So we'll just play the game their way in the beginning so they trust us and then we'll take over from there, doing it our way without them even noticing because they trust us to communicate about whatever it is that needs communication to honor our relationship as we're supposed to in this global arena as they do it. But that's their rules, not ours. So we'll agree but continue doing business as usual.

(This may sound outrageously politically incorrect to an American's ears, but that's the point, isn't it? Political correctness is quintessentially American. Remaining politically correct at times when stark, painful honesty is needed, even with ugly reflections?)

Meanwhile, South Korean soap operas and pop culture are now the hit of Asia, not American pop culture as much anymore. We now see "Made in China" products now–no longer "Made in Taiwan" because mainland China has become Taiwan's American Mexico with the export of cheap labor to mainland China as Taiwan has become more modernized and white collar while the mainland continues to open up. Chinese products, while they may break easily, can be bought over and over again considered disposable in the quintessence of the term because of "that cheap labor" and "those cheap materials" and they know it. And they know to keep this niche in the global marketplace cornered and dominated. Japan's fashions and music and sexual fetishes are the trend setter for Asia, while American MTV pop culture has begun to be less admired, not really liked or even tolerated as much because that's the way "those easy Americans do things, but we–we're different over here on this side of the world, and they don't understand our more traditional values over here, even though we are modernized now." They've taken modernization, originally from us, and now, have been modernized long enough that they don't need our ideas quite so much anymore; Asia has created its own sense of a modernized self.

Meaning, they have their own modernized identity now, which is coupled with a sleek repackaging of their ancient culture and sold to the West for its exoticism. Our response, from our romanticizing what they know and what they live like—is to believe, for example, that they know to use chi to send people across the room with their hands flowing out this chi. How many times have you seen this portrayed in the movies? Or how they have identified these hidden secrets of the human system and life in the universe that we haven't, and so therefore they are a lot more mysterious and magical to us. Then increasing the romanticism with fascination with the more gory stuff, we also consider them kind of exotic and weird because they willingly get needles stuck in them. We admire how they obtain inner peace, because we think everyone in the East meditates and has some sense of this serenity. We also ascribe more to the East, to the Chinese specifically, because we assume that through meditation and tai chi they have a gracefulness that supersedes what we could realistically hope to ever have. While we also classify them to have these amazingly thin bodies, with delicate skin and serene smiles, eating a healthier diet than us, of fresh fish right from the boats and freshly cultivated grains of rice, alongside growing bamboo that has that ethereal sound that we hear on the meditation CD's we buy, accompanied by the endless pools of water, with waterfalls and orange carp fish. Or so we think, and so they like us thinking and so they seem to like to think of themselves.

Meanwhile, we sit over here, growing more depressed, more obese, less healthy, less employed, less on fire, more complacent, more stuck in our own ways with the mentality "this is the way we've always done things," *refusing to really change in the fundamental ways that we need to,* miserable, and suffering. This is a generalization, yes; but it is accurate, based on the state of our nation, as supported by the earlier discussions and statistics cited. And it's comparative to the "on fire" feeling in the East, to this ex–pat's eyes, who loves her country and has endeavored in this writing to get this message out to the American audience who hasn't had this opportunity, or contrasting view as they instead, raise families, pay mortgages, and work in their careers.

It's like America and Asia were once in a love affair, and America became the fat, out of shape lover who took the relationship for granted, while the Asian got what they needed, learned, and saw what they needed to, went back home and reported to the home turf team via their business or product and have moved on to about five new lovers down the line. Truly, the Asian countries are shocking in their comparative 100 meter sprint to our 12K marathon with how rapidly they've changed and adjusted to modernization and globalization. We're just taking our water breaks on the side and are barely even running our own race anymore. It's like we have actually abandoned ourselves, and become this lessoned shadow version of what America once was, and can be, both here and globally. *Really, what are we doing?*

In order to equal the playing field, we could be, as a wise move on our part, taking on their ideas from their metaparadigm. If we were to do this more actively and authentically, we would gain access to wisdom and ideas that we don't inherently contain within our culture. This, for example, could be in the areas of health and well–being, and perhaps help to reshape our medical care's foundational concepts. Say if we were to be focused on preventative care, or wellness and health, we could use these tools more fully in our system. Right?

To be clear, I do not mean "allowing" acupuncture to be studied for its use as a pain reliever alongside biomedical medicine as a "complimentary or alternative medicine," either. Nor do I mean looking at yoga only as a tool for relaxation, or a 45 minute visit to feel our mind, body and spirit connected, or core toning. This is only taking the surface of what looks the most exotic and inserting it into our societal metaparadigm. In what is considered the countries to have been developed in the "second wave of development"–such as Taiwan, Singapore, South Korea, with India and China being the last wave–they are the closest to our stage of development. So therefore, if we are in a competition, then, as if in a race, they are our competitors, and they have wisdom we don't. This wisdom does not need to be forgotten as ancient folklore, as we've forgotten our ancient tools. We should not simply dismiss what they have to offer us because, as it's usually framed, they had not "caught up" to us yet, or are not as modern as us yet. Meaning just because we industrialized first doesn't mean what we know is any better than what they were doing from what their cultures know, prior to globalization. And now that they are modernized, they've "made it." What about who they were prior to looking and becoming more like us on the surface?

In fact, is the wisdom and lifestyles of the cultures who were not or who are not within the modern, scientific materialist metaparadigm that has now become globalized, a perspective that could teach us a whole lot of what we're missing? We've lost out on some aspect of life as we've been busy up on the material plane creating physical life and focusing on physically geared accomplishments. (It's a progression, as we discussed, with the physical being the last stage of development, with it starting in energy and potential, and then thoughts with strong feelings of desire and intent that then moves the energy in a direction more towards the physical manifestation.) *So their ancient tools, or some of their cultural practices from their metaparadigm more focused on subtle changes, could actually teach us the counterpoint that we're missing, or our balancing point,* so we can come back into balance, and stop being weakened by our going too far off in one direction, yes?

What we don't know, what has not been accepted into our metaparadigm, and what has gotten out of balance within our culture is the loss of what we let go of in order to do things within this scientific materialist metaparadigm. Whenever you make a choice, you go toward one thing, and let the other go, right? So, for example, if you went to acting school and chose to move to Hollywood to follow your dreams, this also means that you did not choose the other option of staying and marrying the boy back home, building a family and maybe acting on the side in local theatre productions with your work outside of the home having little correlation to your "dream" work. This means that when we as a nation began to make it our identity to produce technology and science, to industrialize and modernize ourselves, and ensuingly, anyone who wants to follow our American multinational corporations' lead from around the globe, we ruled out other lifestyle choices as our overall metaparadigm's options of possible lifestyles, realistically.

Today, any "developed" nation is also suffering from the same stress induced, as we discussed, chronic diseases and health problems, such as obesity, depression and cancer. As a country has modernized, the WHO and WTO have observed there is a dropping off of the "developing nation" illnesses that are typically sanitation related, and a taking on of the "affluent disease" like the ones just mentioned, which are so-named for this very reason. So the question here is, are we in the West that far ahead, or that "developed"? And if so, who set this standard, which created this definition of "development"? Furthermore, was it created with any further thought to include the problems with stress and depression? Or at the very least the observed decrease in overall life satisfaction and happiness, as well as the accompanying diseases that have now become termed "affluent diseases"? Isn't there value and worth in what the cultures know who have not had the historical focus America has. They instead have gained wisdom and created entire systems of medicine around living life in a way that understands the power and use of subtle energy, and the correlated significance of happiness and well-being at a more basic level. Can we then learn from their system as our balancer, or our counter part? They have not been busy the way we have, historically. So they logically, know things we don't, and vice versa, as has been discussed.

As has been shown with only the examples of the Indian and Chinese culture, there is that vast depth of wisdom and knowledge that runs counter to what our tradition here in the West has been. If someone knows, especially if this someone is someone who we're seemingly competing against, about something we don't know, isn't that considered to be a lack on our part, and isn't this when we're then motivated to learn this "something," *especially if our system is suffering, or is not clearly "winning"?* Isn't this part of competing, where only the fittest survive? Don't we need to gain what they know? Particularly now that the Chinese are finally starting to share their ancient secrets? Because you can be assured that this is the way the Chinese are looking at Americans–that we are someone to compete against. It's how their vast population inherently and silently–but very clearly–runs. Or have we come to accept the specialist model to such a degree that we allow each person, or culture to have their specialty, *while ours is materialism*? Yet look at the state of our country and citizens. We have been so much healthier and less poor in many ways beyond just economics, prior to this most recent period of the past seven to ten years or so. So materialism as our specialty would be okay, if the state of health of average citizens wasn't what it is. Clearly there's something not working within our system's focus on the physical.

There is a whole other level to this discussion and that is seeing us as the world leaders that we have been and still very much are, but in recent history appear to be in the back wings, taking a rest. We do set the pace in so many ways, as we have with science and technology during the industrial revolution. What about at this point now in history? Yes, we're still setting the pace with technological devices, *somewhat*. Coming out of what industrialization created in this post–modern era, couldn't we be moving beyond even this global competition, as Laszlo said, learn from our mistakes, integrate these teachings that are new to us and that are external to our metaparadigm, as well as what our own new sciences are discovering, and couldn't we then lead the way out of this mayhem?

Isn't that our current positioning? Isn't that the only choice we, as America, realistically have? Since when do we sit back and suffer, and let others set the pace? Truly, couldn't we be the change that is needed on our planet now, as our way for coming out of this crisis ourselves, that we are very responsible for creating, and simultaneously then be setting an example of where the other modernized nations do not want to go? Because they're already headed there, the stats show this. But we've been here for longer.

We do have the opportunity to come out of this current chaos with a new creative direction of balanced, healthy, sustainable lifestyles coupled with economic, environmental and individual health retained if we embrace a new metaparadigm. Or not. The choice is ours. That is all for this topic; there are enough other sources covering it. Except one more thing: the phrase "Yankee ingenuity" defined by Wikipedia is, "It is inventive improvisation, adaptation and overcoming of dire straits when faced with a dearth [of materials]," which later came to be "American innovation." Wikipedia, as a source to reflect the common, or general understandings, gives this definition for "innovation," "Innovation is a change in the thought process for doing something, or the useful application of new inventions or discoveries. It may refer to incremental, emergent or radical and revolutionary changes in thinking, products, processes, or organizations." This sounds quite similar to Laszlo's macroshift concept. And to what this entire discussion has been implying.

Albert Borgmann, German born and American Professor wrote "Technology as a Cultural Force" that appears in *The Canadian Journal of Sociology* in 2006. Borgmann writes that, "To various degrees, the citizens of the advanced industrial countries are suffering from a crisis that is as profound as it is vague and therefore hard to deal with. The problem is particularly acute in the United States, however, ... *In any case, though vagueness obscures the crisis, there have to be symptoms of some sort; otherwise we would not feel troubled.* What are the signs of trouble in the culture of technology and democracy? First there are economic problems—national budget deficits, problems of international trade, newly emerging and powerful competition, viz., India, and China, and the dwindling supply of oil," (Bergmann 2006). Not only supporting our general discussion, Borgmann also addresses the issue with oil and sustainable resources. But sustainable resources come from a holistic view. A reductionist view supports commodification of finite resources, as does a scientific materialist view.

Writes Beryl Lieff Benderly in the February 2010 issue of *Scientific America* in an article entitled, "Does the U.S. Produce Too Many Scientists?' queries our common assumption with, "American science education lags behind that of many other nations, right? So why does it produce so many talented young researchers who cannot find a job in their chosen field of study?" In this article, Benderly's investigative reporting helps to break this myth. "For scientifically trained young people from abroad, though—especially those from low–wage countries like China and India—the calculus of opportunity is different. For them, postdoc work in the U.S. is an almost unbeatable opportunity. Besides the experience and prestige of working in the world's leading scientific power, a postdoc research position is likely to pay many times more than a job at home would. Beyond that, many foreign postdocs erroneously believe that the temporary H–1B visa that admits them to the U.S. will eventually lead to permanent residency. These drastically different opportunity structures explain why more than half of what the National Science Board has estimated as 93,000 postdocs in the U.S. are now foreigners on short–term visas" (Benderly 2010).

Benderly, recently nominated as a fellow of the American Association for the Advancement of Science, is a Washington–based journalist who writes the monthly "Taken for Granted" column on science policy and careers for the website of *Science* magazine. *Science* magazine is the academic journal of the American Association for the Advancement of Science and is considered one of the world's most prestigious scientific journals.

This aspect of our metaparadigms is in direct relation to the science of our metaparadigm having become business. The impact of the field of science having become a field restricted by getting funds to conduct research from those who fund the research is vast. This is because the money dictates what does and does not get studied, and who is typically deciding what does get studied, and who typically decides *how* it gets studied.

Benderly explores the reality behind why it seems like there's a lack of talented Ph.D. researchers, when in fact there's a glut, and why no one in DC seems to be aware of it. Few young Ph.D.'s in science and engineering can get started on the career for which their graduate education purportedly trained them, namely, as faculty members in academic research institutions. "Instead, scores of thousands of them," Benderly explains, "spend the years after they earn their doctorates toiling in low–paying, dead–end postdoctoral 'training' appointments' (called postdocs) in the laboratories of their professors, where they ostensibly hone skills they would need to start labs of their own when they become professors. In fact, however, only about 25 percent of those earning American science Ph.D.s will ever land a faculty job that enables them to apply for the competitive grants that support academic research. And even fewer–15 percent by some estimates–will get a post at the kind of research university where the nation's significant work takes place," (Benderly 2010).

One of the results is that most Ph.D.s hired into faculty–level jobs get so called "soft–money" posts, dependent on the renewal of year–to–year funding rather than the traditional tenure–track positions that offer the long term security we're so used to hearing that professors enjoy. So this is apparently no longer the nature of academic research.

Benderly goes on to define the root of the problem. She quotes Teitelbaum, a Labor Economist for the Alfred P. Sloan Foundation, from a Congressional testimony in November of 2007, "The perverse funding structure for science graduate education…is a recipe for instability." Apparently, since the 1940s, when the U.S. government began to invest seriously in civilian research, the work has been done largely at the nation's universities and "paid for through competitive, temporary grants awarded to individual professors by federal funding agencies such as the National Institutes of Health and the National Science Foundation. Since then, these agencies have become the major funders of academic research in this country, and, indeed, the world," (Benderly 2010).

The outcome of the funding being structured the way it is, according to Benderly, reflects not only why there seems to be an illusion of a shortage of scientific post-doc researchers for academic research when that's not the real issue. The "perverse funding structure" is also why these jobs are going to foreigners allowed in on the country with special visas that the universities secure in order to bring these cheaper workers into the labs. "Despite a longstanding dismal job market in academic science, however, departments continue to recruit graduate students and postdocs because they need skilled and inexpensive labor to do the work promised in professors' grant proposals. Doctoral–level researchers must receive the 'trainee' wages paid to postdocs—generally about $40,000 a year for 60 to 80 hours a week with no job security or promotion opportunities. But paying postdocs a true professional wage would mean many fewer highly skilled hands, fewer publications and less chance of winning a grant renewal...[thus this dynamic] creates distorted incentives, an artificial sense of shortage and a vicious circle," (Benderly 2010).

It seems that until the late 1960s, the majority of young Ph.D.s actually did get those faculty jobs. "But the Sputnik–inspired increase in research funding and graduate fellowships that continued into the late 1960s and 1970s soon began producing more Ph.D.s each year than the nation's colleges and universities could readily absorb. More and more Ph.D.s, educated in a culture that has long viewed—and, in many places, still views—positions outside the academy not as valid career options for serious scientists but as 'alternative employment' at best and 'going over to the dark side' at worst, began accepting postdoc positions in the belief that additional publications would improve their chance to land that coveted faculty post." So that by the late 1970s, *Personnel Needs for Biomedical and Behavioral Research*, an authoritative report issued every two years by the Institute of Medicine of the National Academies "was expressing alarm at the increase in both the number of postdocs and the length of time they spent as 'trainees.' The buildup, as they feared, has continued for three decades, with the growing postdoc pool—enhanced by increasing numbers of foreign Ph.D.s–serving to disguise unemployment among young aspirants to university careers. In many fields, five or more years of postdoc 'training' has become the norm, while the percentage of Ph.D.s who landed academic positions continues to drop."

Benderly concludes that as a result, the average age at which the minority of young scientists who do actually land faculty jobs, who get to launch independent research careers by winning their first competitive grant, "has risen to 42. At that age, scientists of previous generations, such as Albert

Einstein, Marshall Nirenberg and Thomas Cech, were winning their Nobel Prizes for work done in their twenties," (Benderly 2010). If funding to conduct the research were more open and broad, rather than more limited to one system of thinking, this would open up vast opportunities to both access new avenues for funding, and also possibly produce new solutions for our current issues facing our country and planet. If we opened up to more than just the scientific materialist way of looking at the world, and began to have funds supporting actively researching new ways of producing alternative sources of fuel and new ways to heal and work with health rather than the same old ways that invests loads of money into big, tangible equipment or sleek cool technology, wouldn't that seem to be a possible reasonable way to face the various issues all coming together now, at this point in history? That is what macro-shift is intended to be.

Another aspect of our science and research industry that seems to not be working anymore under the rules set up by scientific materialism of how science gets done, is the scientific methodology used. Specifically it's that the results of research have to be replicable by anyone following the original researchers. Anyone following on the heels of the original experiment has to then independently retest the original researchers' results, after the initial publication of those initial research results. This is mandatory and it is the business of scientific research. Susan Gerbi, Chair of Molecular Biology at Brown University, and a longtime critic of the current method of staffing American labs believes, along with others, "that the U.S. needs to establish 'non–replicating' research organizations with many fewer temporary student and trainee lab workers and many more permanent career staff scientists. Such prominent institutions as the Max Planck Institute in Germany, where Gerbi worked, and the Howard Hughes Medical Institution's new Janelia Farms Research Campus in Ashburn, Virginia, follow versions of this model" (Benderly 2010).

In another article by Susan Gerbi in *Scientific American*, she offers some statistics that help us better appreciate the dysfunction of the old scientific materialist approach in today's industry of research and science: "The worldwide science and engineering publications output captured in *Science Citation Index and Social Sciences Citation Index* grew from approximately 466,000 articles in 1988 to nearly 700,000 in 2003, an increase of 50%. Worldwide growth in article output between 1988 and 2003 was strongest in the European Union (EU)–15, Japan, and the East Asia–4 (China,

Singapore, South Korea, and Taiwan). *The EU–15 share of world output surpassed that of the United States in 1998,* although growth in the EU–15 and also in Japan slowed starting in the mid–1990. *The article output of the East Asia–4 grew more than sevenfold during this period,* resulting in its share of world output rising from less than 2% to 8%. *The number of U.S. scientific publications remained essentially flat* between 1992 and 2003, *causing the U.S. share of world article output to decline from 38% to 30% between 1988 and 2003."* This is in the face of continuing growth of research inputs, which represents a trend change from several decades' growth in the number of U.S. publications.

Now in today's globalized climate there has been another shift in the share of publications with authors from multiple countries, which are an indicator of international collaboration and the globalization of science. These publications, "grew worldwide and for most countries between 1988 and 2003. In 2003, 20% of all articles had at least one foreign author, up from 8% in 1988. The increase in international collaboration reflects intensified collaboration among the United States, EU–15, and Japan. It also reflects greater collaboration between these science and engineering publishing regions and developing countries and an emerging zone of intra-regional collaboration centered in East Asia. The United States has the largest share of all internationally authored papers of any single country, *and its researchers collaborate with counterparts in more countries than do the researchers of any country. The U.S. collaboration with the rest of the world continues to increase, but its relative share of co–authorship on other countries' internationally authored articles has declined as those countries have broadened their international ties.* ...The volume of citations to U.S. literature, however, flattened in the late 1990's.... The number of scientific articles cited by U.S. patents, an indicator of the linkage between science and technology, *rose rapidly until the late 1990's.* These increases were heavily centered in academic–authored articles in the fields of *biomedical research and clinical medicine."*

Medicine is getting the research. The question is, who is funding this research for biomedicine? If biomedicine uses two main tools–pharmaceutical drugs, and surgical devices and both come from the biotech industry, then isn't the source of funding for the majority of research obvious? How much of it comes from taxpayers and how much from the biotech industry, comparatively?

We continue to demand proof for subtle energy that fits within our scientific materialist metaparadigm's and biomedicine's parameters of measurement. Yet these substances do not have the same inherent nature to them as what we've been primarily measuring historically within our scientific materialist metaparadigm based on Newtonian physics. Should we then demand that the phenomena that other cultures seem to have more knowledge and wisdom about (that is not phenomena inherent to our metaparadigm's background), then fit into our methodology and way of measuring before we allow ourselves to acknowledge its existence? Shouldn't we now, considering the new globalized climate, and the nature of all that we've discussed so far, be more open minded to allow for an evolution to our sciences, and to our society? Doesn't it sound like some changes are needed within this global arena in order to remain viable? Isn't this the way we can lead out of the old and into the new?

There's another factor here to consider as well, and that is the amount of money that people are willing to spend on natural healing and preventative health, without it having had "rigorous scientific investigation" or "proof." Rather, word of mouth from positive experiences from friends or family seems to be the leading causes for people to expand beyond the bio–medical to natural healing's methods. It seems that there is approximately 50% of our American population willing to use the methods of natural healing. These methods are typically based on both the wisdom from other cultures' practices with subtle energy, and what our own new sciences have shown– which is still pulling in ties to, or validations, with what the ancient cultures seemed to have understood. *So, really, who are we doing this old metaparadigm of science for or why?* This is a really critical question. Who is benefitting from the results of all the academic research and science that is currently getting done within orthodox science?

Furthermore, when we demand that the science be absolutely replicable, and we are working with a phenomenon that is not predictable based on all that quantum physics has discovered about the nature of quanta that it is inherently unpredictable–as was shown in our prior discussion, then doesn't that rule out replicability? This may seem oversimplified, but it is actually simply not over complicating the matter. We need to see our system as it is today and what we're doing that is *based on old methods that are not applicable any longer,* as well as *the clinging to these old methods* that we are doing emotionally and mentally *out of resistance to change,* and *wanting to maintain the status quo,* because change does involve discomfort, uncertainty and instability.

But is this discomfort in the face of change and "inconvenience" of changing any worse than how all the various structures within our metaparadigm, and all the people within these current structures of our outdated metaparadigm, are already suffering? Crisis, instability and discomfort is the least, while distraught with struggle and hopelessness is the worst–or dead from cancer, depression or a combination of lifestyle choices that lead to a heart condition? Who really is profiting from keeping this status quo?

In addition, with all the gains that foreign scientists have made by getting trained in our system, and then returning home to their home countries to publish and continue academic research at a more prestigious level, we need to re-examine our fundamentals here. The level of our scientific journal output, and citations coming from American scientific literature flattening with the foreign competition, does it make sense to limit ourselves to continuing to restrict what gets studied by where the money has been coming from? Couple that with what we deem as scientifically acceptable, or "evidence based." And then rethink this.

Particularly interesting is when what we're dealing with is phenomena that does not easily yield to measurement, specifically measurement developed for physical phenomena–which is not subtle enough to use to pick up subtle phenomena, why would we perpetuate this system? It is an outdated system that no longer applies and should we give up the machinery, the infrastructure and the thinking that accompanies this old, outdated industrial age model, we'd make room for a clearing. This clearing would then yield the room, the space, the openness to fill with machinery, infrastructure and thinking that is more applicable to where we are now, and what we know now. Too many of our fundamental structures and systems within our metaparadigm are in crisis and/or near collapse.

It just seems like we're ignoring what is being shown to us the longer we resist and hold on to the old. This is a breakdown phase of our old metaparadigm, and the sooner we admit to this, the sooner we can begin the letting go of it at the mass level. We could be brainstorming, at the mass level, instead, what would work in a functional way. Now this most likely will not be incremental change. That is not how change happens at the quantum level; it is called quantum leaps for a reason–this is how the quanta changes.

All signs are pointing to us needing to adopt the thinking and behavior that mirrors what we now know about the space in between atoms and molecules. It would be best if this were done with the support from within mainstream science, along with the technology that's already there,. Again, this is not incremental change. The medical system–minus the health care reform discussion–comes in another of my books, after completing this discussion about where our scientific research industry is. The medical system will include a more specific description of biotech's role in the research industry, and from the private sector more so. Whereas the current discussion involves the academic leg of the scientific research industry. What we see there is ever more revealing to the business behind our scientific research industry and its use within our biomedical system. It gives a pretty clear window into why our biomedical model has remained in place even amidst the obvious dysfunction–but from an atypical angle.

Given the problems within the academic research field and job situation, doesn't it make sense to come out of the necessitated "replicable science" methodology, and open up to a change in not only the way our science is done and the way it is funded, *but also what we study*? Which would also open up science to more than just the dominant industries where there is already funding, such as biotech–specifically pharmaceutical drugs and surgical devices? And more than the military or information technology as the other options? Aren't there new possibilities that only the pioneering scientists have explored, compared to our near redundant exposure to our current dominant metaparadigm's opportunities with industry, military, biotech and biomedicine? Aren't there new areas we can open up to apply our new sciences to, say sustainable energy and natural healing? this is the direction it's already going. And both these contain solutions to two of our main areas of crisis. Aren't we funny! Really, what are we doing with what we continue to choose?

This *is* happening at the grassroots level, this seeking of new alternatives, outside of what our current metaparadigm offers, and its building momentum. The movie *Generation Rx* exposes the pharmaceutical industry and it's far reaching influences, even down to school nurses getting a kick back for prescriptions written for kids to be on Ritalin, with both the school and the school district also receiving money for this, as another child/student gets labeled "special needs," (GenerationRxFilm.com). The movie *Food Matters* exposes the agribusiness business as usual, and what goes into our foods, and how that has created so much of our county's ill health. In this movie it is said, "1/4 of what you eat keeps you alive, and 3/4 of what you eat keeps your doctor alive," (foodmatters.tv).

Suffice it to say it is to our continued detriment if we choose to perpetuate this current system of academic research and science within the U.S. with the current level of resistance to the new sciences by mainstream science. Their basic refusal towards studying science using any other methods, or anything other than what has typically and traditionally been deemed acceptable by mainstream science is no longer in our best interest.

The dominance of our dominant metaparadigm is no longer in our best interest. It seems rather like a blind choice when perpetuating a system that is obviously crumbling and outdated and going after only where the funding is–which at this point is primarily from the biotech industry. Does it seem that way to you? Especially when this system appears designed to keep those in power making the financial gains while the masses are not benefitting in the long term, isn't it time this system be genuinely re–examined? Again, are we really that slow to change? Are we really that numbed down or checked out as citizenry under the dominance of consumerism, the pharmaceutical lobby, and the AMA and agribusiness (and oil)?

Well we cannot afford this any longer. We need new sciences. We need new methods of doing science. We need alternatives. We need the new. We have got to become more open minded, and more mentally flexible and mentally agile, overall as a country. Which again, brings us back to working with the traits of the (ego) mind already discussed. Central here is the resistance to change, or anything new, and clinging to maintaining the illusion of control and the "comfort" that the status quo seems to offer. Another red flag here, and again, it's cyclical–going back to working with our beliefs and thoughts and ability to be open to, and catalyze the new. Because as we've thoroughly explained by now, many of the beliefs that our society is run by are simply not accurate anymore.

Al Gore, along with many, many others has spoken to the opportunities presented to us within this chaos of these converging crises, particularly opportunities for new sciences and technologies. And that these opportunities are going to be bold, new and not look very familiar, but that this time is ripe for breakthroughs with new systems–a new metaparadigm, ultimately. One that is able to, out of necessity and gained forces, "overthrow" or "overturn" the power structures that have come to be from our metaparadigm's historical success with science and industry, and now science and biotech.

This is not just the pharmaceutical companies, although they are a major part of it. It is not just the agribusiness companies with their pesticide and herbicide use and their genetically modified foods and their hormones pumped into their chickens, cows, pigs, and turkeys to make them bigger so the animals would yield more profit from more meat being sold off of them. These hormones and genetically modified food and pesticides and herbicides are all from the biotech industry, either directly or indirectly. While girls get their periods earlier, more males have "male boobs," there's more issues with lack of fertility in either the female or male, and there's more chemical imbalances within the body's bio–chemistry that set off a cascade of health issues and disorders, including the sterility. These chemicals present in our food supply are offsetting our own chemical balance–which is our hormonal balance–within our bodies. Nor is this just about the academic research industry having a flawed system that doesn't provide incentive via success for encouraging new American scientists because of the way the system is funded and by whom.

In his Nobel Peace Prize Acceptance speech, Gore says, "We must ensure that entrepreneurs and inventors everywhere on the globe have the chance to change the world," (Gore 2007). This is not just about a collapsed job market, nor about corporations downsizing, outsourcing or financial institutions going bankrupt and needing the federal government with its own cash flow issues to bail them out using taxpayers' dollars. Nor is this about the brutally strong power controlled by the oil industry and those benefitting from fossil fuel usage, as opposed to shifting to alternative, renewable sources. This is not just about the amount of our population taking anti–depressants in order to "kind of" function.

Make no mistake about this timing–it is about all of this *together*. Al Gore's Nobel Peace Prize Acceptance speech contains the words: "We also find it hard to imagine making the massive changes that are now necessary to solve the crisis. And when large truths are genuinely inconvenient, whole societies can, at least for a time, ignore them. Yet as George Orwell reminds us: 'Sooner or later a false belief bumps up against solid reality, usually on a battlefield,'" (Gore 2007). While actual physical war and battlefields should be more of the old way of solving "problems," they're also part of the very metaparadigm that is breaking down. The metaphor for our post-modern day crisis within our country is appropriate. Why would hard, physical war be of this new age? It's not–it's one with working with our own consciousnesses–our beliefs and thinking that leads to our behaviors. War is too gross, this battle is more subtle.

As has been discussed through using both Kuhn's scientific revolutions theory, and Laszlo's macroshift theory, our current battlefield is not only Iraq and Afghanistan, but in reality it is within America, as our old system that contains prolific abuse of power in the name of profit crumbles, and as we continue on through the conflicts of this breakdown phase, into the creation stage of the breakthrough phase prior to establishing a new metaparadigm. Again–this *is* happening at the grassroots level. Gore says, "We must quickly mobilize our civilization with the urgency and resolve that has previously been seen only when nations mobilized for war. These prior struggles for survival were won when leaders found words at the 11th hour that released a mighty surge of courage, hope and readiness to sacrifice for a protracted and mortal challenge."

He continues not talking political fluff, because he had no agenda here during his Nobel Peace Prize speech, other than furthering *An Inconvenient Truth*'s message. "No, these were calls to come to the defense of the common future. They were calls upon the courage, generosity and strength of entire peoples, citizens of every class and condition who were ready to stand against the threat...Have we the will to act vigorously and in time, or will we remain imprisoned by a dangerous illusion?... Mahatma Gandhi awakened the largest democracy on earth and forged a shared resolve with what he called 'Satyagraha'–or 'truth force.'...When we unite for a moral purpose that is manifestly good and true, the spiritual energy unleashed can transform us...*That means adopting principles, values, laws, and treaties that release creativity and initiative at every level of society in multifold responses originating concurrently and spontaneously...This new consciousness requires expanding the possibilities inherent in all humanity,*" (italics mine) (Gore 2007). Remember that quanta are pure potential prior to becoming physical matter. Potential, 'release creativity,' 'initiative'–do you see it? This is all happening con–currently with a common theme for a reason. As Carolyn Myss is known for saying/demanding, "Let's get some perspective, people!" God bless her.

Alison J. Kay, PhD

Qualitative State of Being: Beyond Everyday Mind

There are other ways to do this and these ways require a fundamental shift in approach, or a macroshift, or a scientific revolution. Or a change in metaparadigm of all of the above. Richard Jelusich, an American Ph.D. and core faculty member and former dean of administration for the California Institute of Human Sciences, writes in *Psychology of the Chakra:*–again, India's psychology and healthcare system of subtle energies that acknowledges the role of the soul in an individual–*Eye of the Lotus*, "Why is it so difficult to understand the field of metaphysics, its tenets, and functioning? For the Western world, it is because we are steeped in duality, the separation of one thing from another.

In Western society we are taught to believe we are separate from that which we seek. 'I am here, God is there'–two separate and distinct phenomena, when in reality there is no separation between them. *The separation causes the inception of a belief system that becomes very linear and quantitative.* We see this so often in science, where the observer counts, divides, summarizes the subject of study," (italics mine) (Jelusich 2004). This is the apples–oranges phenomenon, in that we're comparing two inherently different phenomena which share a much more general category of fruit. Or in the case of the physical and the metaphysical they share the same general category. Jelusich describes phenomena of a metaphysical nature to have a physical, linear counterpart, *but it cannot be thought of in the same way.*

Jelusich goes on to clarify this quintessential point to our discussion, "*The nature of metaphysics is rooted in a qualitative state of being, rather than what can be quantified or counted.* We often think of intuitives in terms of 'Where did they get their information from?' or 'How do they know that?' In essence they are tapping into a sea of consciousness that is not separate from them or their existence in any way. This is the manner in which all psychics work. They are merely accessing something that already exists, but that which most people feel is quite separate from their daily lives and activities," (Jelusich 2004). As we have industrialized and modernized alongside the scientific materialist paradigm, following along the Enlightenment's scientists' choice of what to study for their own period's reasons, we have gotten further and further steeped in the physical, as we were initially directed away from the subtle, for the reasons already discussed.

Yet it does not mean that what is subtle does not exist. So why do we continue to resist the incorporation of this awareness of subtle energies, subtle phenomena, emotions, consciousness into our culture's metaparadigm in a meaningful way that can help us? Does this question now resonate more, or make more sense? We could have said the same thing about electricity three hundred years ago. Meaning if within a conversation one person spoke about a wondrous energy that when run along two pieces of metal to a filament, the filament would glow like the sun, this person would be talking about electricity. However, they may very well have sounded like "a quack." By now, it is logical to appreciate that electricity has always existed, *but it's our awareness of it that had to awaken.* Furthermore, it seemed like enough other environmental–societal–factors had to have happened, enough other awareness closely enough aligned or leading up to electricity had to be there already, for the acknowledgment of electricity to happen. No wait, electricity ultimately is tangible, in what it produces—light, televisions on, etc—so this wasn't an abstract principle or theory discussed. It was able to be seen, as well as used as a convenient new technology.

Instead, with the subtle–emotions, consciousness, the soul–we don't have this tangible item to hold in our hands, or see with our eyes, that we can point to and say, "Look, this is the soul!" or "Look, see that's MacDuffy's consciousness!" or "Ha! There's Jason's anger!" Well, we may be able to see Jason's expression of anger as Jason is seen stomping around and slamming items on to the counter with a snarl of unhappiness on his face, but these are all considered, collectively, as *indicators* of anger, not the anger itself. The anger, or the emotion itself, cannot be seen or touched, literally. It is a subtle phenomena, or subtle energy, albeit with tangible indicators of it.

It can be metaphorically referred to. This is the primary way that we have to commonly refer to the subtle in our lives–through metaphor. Poets, musicians and artists render the subtle into a *more* tangible form for us. But this is one of the sticking points for us. We need to genuinely consider consciousness, rather than leave it to the artists, poets and musicians, at the level that it needs to be regarded, for its role in our lives, and our health and well being. We'd have much more power here available to us if we would. So instead, as has been discussed, due to this challenge, it has typically just been negated and ignored at best, and devalued at worst. Yet *this is due to our sciences' method of measuring* and what they measure, leading our cultural ethos, economy, health care and all systems–our metaparadigm our entire society is structured around our science's presentation of what reality is and is not.

So, electricity exists now at the societal and individual's level of waking consciousness. Perhaps most people living in the world today know of it but think nothing of it when entering a room and flipping on a switch as to where this electricity originates from and how it came to be in one's home. However, if one were to ask this question, the answers are traceable back to the coal supply in the earth, and then the conversion facility, then the electrical towers and then the lines strung from those wooden poles up alongside roads that run to one's home. Yet, no one has seen electricity in and of itself. Streams of electrons as lightning bolts and sparks, flashlights and street lamps, chandeliers and televisions all contain electricity as its power source, but no one has actually seen the energy itself. The effects of it and what it does we do see, and yet we don't question it. We live with its convenience, enjoying it and paying for having it.

Jelusich helps to further the understanding about subtle energy and our reaction to it, "Energy from higher dimensions permeates every space, every aspect of our lives, but we are mostly unaware of its existence because of our linear, dualistic approach to life. We see and hear, two of the most vital of our five senses that tell us what in the world is real. Our five senses are the way in which we reach out to our third dimensional physical existence–they inform us of our experiences here. We perceive and interpret differently, according to levels of ignorance and understanding, awareness, karma, mission statement, and freewill," (Jelusich 2004). Jelusich clearly shows how a Western mind is geared towards measuring, and indeed even acknowledging, reality.

Due to this factor, and then coupling it with the current scientific materialism methodology, it has been said that the "best way to teach the Western mind that metaphysics is real, in lieu of an epiphany, is to use the very same model of separation or reductionism. In other words, to use science and technology to explain a qualitative phenomenon that externalizes into a physical realm," (Jelusich 2004). This has been what the new sciences have been attempting thus far, in order to "prove" to a western mind, in western methodology geared towards western perceptions that these subtle energies exist and are a form of power.

Examples abound by now. One is the invention of the AMI, which was created by Dr. Hiroshi Motoyama, Ph.D., (notice he's Japanese) that measures the functioning of the meridians with small enough direct–current pulses to be able to pick up on the subtleness of the energy emitted through the meridians (acupuncture points run along the meridians) at the fingers and toes, which is where the major meridians that run throughout the body end. So the energy emissions are strong enough *to be measured with subtle and precise enough technology.* "The amount of time it takes for the signal to decay is converted into an analysis of the functioning of the meridian system through a series of computerized algorithms and displayed as a map, or radar chart, of the individual's health. The AMI has been in use in Japan for over thirty years, *and has been going through the FDA in the United States for licensure since 1992*," (Jelusich 2004). Why is it's entry into the system here so slow? What's stopping the FDA from licensing it? What is the FDA's genuine M.O.? And from whom does the FDA get its M.O.?

Scientists determined to help "prove" to our society not only that these subtle energies exist, but the function and power of subtle energy in and of itself, as well as its uses for health and well-being, have been working at this increasingly over the past twenty or so years. This is one of the major components to many of the new sciences. However, there is limitation to this, for it is still demanding that something as elusive as consciousness and energy conform enough to the current scientific and cultural metaparadigm based on the physical. What this means is that we are missing much that is inherent to the phenomena itself by demanding it conform to what we deem as measurement, so we can understand it in our usual way of thinking. The confounded quantum physicists described earlier are an example within the field of quantum physics of this sense of chasing after consciousness in order to capture it to measure and study it. It seems wise to take note that the phenomenon has not been allowing itself to be measured by technological machines for whatever reasons. Who know whether this is due to its inherent nature or some other reasons. Perhaps it is meant to be a level of existence all together that we cannot capture with measurement, technology and proof.

Again, there have been compelling techniques created to capture some element of measuring subtle energy, yet typically it is still done with a machine meant to produce a physically tangible result that "proves" its existence so that our cognitive, linear minds have something to wrap around. These initial studies have been revolutionary in that they've been taking a phenomenon that truly belongs in another paradigm, and bringing it down and into our metaparadigm in order for us to understand it. This is not at all easy, particularly considering what the nature of the phenomena is that we're talking about; it's subtle!

Jelusich helps here, "However, no matter how much research and analysis is done in this manner, *it is not enough to bridge the gap in consciousness between the quantitative state and the transcendent qualitative state.* It is, however, enough to pique the interest of those Western minds that would never accept a qualitative state of being that could not be empirically established. There has to be the initial leaping–off point, where technology shows that there is *something there.* Another way to say it is that the best way to change a paradigm is from within itself. The best way to get the Western mind to understand that there really are qualitative states of consciousness that transcend our everyday lives is to use the very same duality that gives us the illusion of separation. In that way a chink in the armor of incredulity is achieved, where we first entertain the *mysterious* in order to get to the *real.*"

He goes on to flatly state, "The metaphysics of our lives cannot be measured directly through our five senses. We must use a part of our nature that is based in an inner knowing, a *trust.* This is where we have the greatest opportunity and the greatest problem of all," (italics mine) (Jelusich 2004). Yet people believe in a higher power, or God, many do, in fact, within our metaparadigm, and this can't be measured or proven. Actually "a subtle energy" if you will, is comparable to this divine source, so why doesn't this belief crossover from a belief in an invisible God to a belief in an invisible source of energy underlying all existence in between all atoms? Because our metaparadigm is steeped in a Judeo Christian foundation and that concept of God instead of say, chi? Or in an either–or framing, either it is all physical and dry of a divine or mysterious force, or there is a divine, mysterious force without any science in between?

Jelusich is speaking to that same behavior that Tiller spoke about; that there really is no equipment that can get to and measure this level of existence, but that it can be touched and interacted with through consciousness–our consciousness. But there is a *whole lot of* intellectual activity and *movement*– including a clearing out of cultural conditioning, a level of questioning and examining, and an opening up of what one's mind will consider, as well as a synthesized "AHA" moment that is needed in order to integrate at a deeper level prior to a Western mind being able to get to the point of understanding what Jelusich just communicated. So to say yes I get it, and then yes, I agree, and finally yes, I already know that and am aware of and do choose to connect with this transcendent reality with varying degrees of regularity is an organic progression.

What is also required is to have observed the nature of the mind and its basically nonstop thinking, particularly the games that the ego–mind engages in. Someone who is far along enough with their own work on themselves that they have wrestled the ego–mind down to a manageable level in order to hear the wisdom coming from their Higher Self will have an easier time with this integration since they have had life experiences that have opened them up to this more qualitative, transcendent state. This really is experientially based, and that's the greatest problem of all, as Jelusich is describing. Because in order to have this trust in this invisible energy there typically needs to be a reason to cause this trust, and usually that reason comes from some experience in life. This feeling of trust is not typically intellectually learned from a book or authority figure saying you should have it. It has to be something alive inside of you, which comes from either naturally being this way and not having one's environment and life experiences cause one to lose it or close it down, or having experiences in life that cause you to reopen it, whether through a health issue, the death of a loved one or a personal crisis, or yoga, meditation, chi gong, reiki, or other subtle energy healing modalities, including prayer.

What Jelusich means by us having to use a part of our nature that is based on an inner knowing, or a trust, is that we cannot have this tangible, sensory driven proof that makes us feel so certain and comfortable with this trust. This inner knowing goes into the territory that has been basically dismissed as unreliable in our culture, historically. This involves the intuition, and we do not have a tradition in our culture of knowing how to respect, cultivate and listen to our intuition. It has not been valued, so this skill has not been typically taught or reinforced culturally.

Within the new sciences, and more specifically, within the natural healing fields overall, intuition is one of the central aspects of one's training as a practitioner. However, even without this training or focus, as one becomes increasingly exposed to how we take consciousness, emotions, the subtle, and the intangible for granted within our cultural milieu, examples abound to describe this level of trust in these subtle energies that we *do* operate with on a daily basis. And because these are all so fundamental to our existence, we typically overlook them due to their simplicity–or lack of complexity. This is the way the cognitive, linear, ego-mind works. It wants complexity to chew on, to use its machinery of cognition on.

They seem too obvious, too close to common sense, so we disregard them as seemingly too base, or too mundane to be worthy of recognition. Yet these are the fundamentals to life. In other words, *we're too busy looking outside of ourselves for more complex things to figure out.* "If you were asked, 'Do you love your mother?' you would most likely respond 'yes.' And if asked, 'How do you *know* that?' you may respond that you 'just know.' Well, *how* do you know? *And if you were asked to produce this love, to set it on the table for all to see, you could not do it because that love is a qualitative state and cannot be quantified.* Yet, the access to true consciousness is not in how many books you've read or workshops you've attended, nor is it in your intellectual capacity, but rather in your vulnerability to trust that not only do you live in Oneness, not only is it accessible in any instant, but the way to achieve (this) awareness is through your feelings," (italics mine) (Jelusich 2004).

Even with the discussions of the medium that interconnects everything at the most fundamental level as Laszlo says, or the vacuum that exists between electrons and molecules as Tiller says, or the interconnectivity of us all through the "non–local interconnectivity" that Goswami says, or the concept of prana for the Indians, or the concept of chi for the Chinese, if the word "Oneness" as used above causes you to squirm or even turn off, pause for a moment: why does this concept have the capacity to do this? It is this exact skepticism that is being pointed to as central to the resistance within the larger context of what needs to be re–examined within our society, and shifted, in order for us to regain our global positioning competitively, and to regain our health and vitality individually and collectively.

It is also this "oneness" that quantum physics has uncovered and the new sciences has built on, as well as what yogis, meditators, and Taoists practicing chi gong work with; a subtle energy that permeates all living things, or that runs through all phenomena that is alive. It is also what the new sciences have discovered that contribute to vital health and are applying to new areas of healing. Or is it because the concept of us all being connected, and each of our thoughts affecting the whole to varying degree, requires a whole new level of taking responsibility? Which makes your (ego) mind fight back with the desire to just relax and go after gains for self? Or is it just too much responsibility overall and we want to just shrink back and simply be told what to do?

This entire discussion has been leading to this precise point; *why do we resist the subtle?* Particularly when we have the validity of it being shown to us, popping up over and over again from a wide range of divergent sources, and yet we remain still, heavily resistant to *believing* in it. What are we doing? Just because it "can't be seen"? Yet "having to see it to believe it" is just not a good enough excuse anymore to sweepingly dismiss this whole other, hugely relevant and quietly powerful aspect to our lives.

Jelusich helps again, "We are taught that our feelings are fleeting and our emotions are based on transitory thoughts, but the reality is that our feelings are the keyhole through which we see and aspire. I've said before that 'The smallest feeling is greater than the greatest thought' because feelings transcend the linear and temporal, quantitative state of being." Here he is referring to how feelings transcend the physical dimension, and the laws of the physical universe, *as do quanta.* Consciousness has also, within the new sciences, as well as within other cultures' studies of consciousness, been shown to exist beyond the physical dimension, and *behave peculiarly similar to quanta.*

"It is the feelings that transcend the *waking state* of consciousness, not the thoughts, for the thoughts are born of the experiential mind and linear existence, based in a third dimension of quantified existence. Here again, you must yield with your heart to what your mind cannot yet know. That is the inception and path of our true greatness and genius. It is the part of our minds that we are not using, the hidden part of the universe that cannot be seen but definitely can be felt. We often have difficulty with this because we are not educated to trust our feelings, to have a high regard for our emotions, or to nurture and take care of our emotional well-being. It is through this avenue, though, that the greatest shifts in awareness can be achieved because it represents direct access to that sea of consciousness, a Oneness in which you already exist, where technology cannot embrace and thoughts cannot count it," (italics mine) (Jelusich 2004). Clearly, what Jelusich has said helps to connect various strands of our discussion together, making the point quite clearly that the subtle exists. We know it because we can feel it, like the subtle energy or the subtle consciousness behind love.

Yet expecting this universal phenomenon to conform to our expectations, the needs from our mind for certainty and proof, and our demands, therefore, that it be measurable and satisfy our lack of trust is responsible for our culture not advancing as quickly as it could have. Yet we obviously still can correct this. But we need to allow ourselves to take a quantum leap, rather than a slow, incremental change at the pace of small proofs from another study using the old Newtonian scientific materialist methodology for measurement of this subtle energy. And rather than small adjustments in public policy, and rather than small changes in the openness of our minds, collectively as a society, rather than just the pioneers and trailblazers continuing to be doubted, or labeled as quacks. In fact, it looks like avoiding the integration of the more subtle into our metaparadigm at a more genuine level appears to be its own version of quackery, or actually ignorance–*at this point*. So we also need to take this quantum leap individually, leaping over our mental doubts, skepticism and demands, and challenge ourselves to evolve, by engaging a deeper knowing from within ourselves, by trusting ourselves. And training ourselves to go in and listen.

Otherwise, at this point to continue to live within the old metaparadigm only remains just sheer resistance. This resistance has to be addressed and then released; replaced by something more functional and healthy.

It is in the face of this skepticism, that reflects more of the same paradigm–people just are not used to things actually being able to be easy or simple; we are used to making "stuff" complicated, we are used to having problems and crises to attend to. *Yet this is only the nature of the mind.* Should we go beyond the everyday mind, or the ego–mind used to navigate the more mundane aspects of our physical/material plane, there is that underlying presence behind life. *It is an irony, more so for the Western mind, that we need to actually NOT use our minds to "know" this. There is nothing to figure out here!*

How can we "know" something without using what we've invested all this time and money developing–our intellect? Another more painful irony–or paradox–is that we are taught to cultivate our mental capacity, and that is what is valued and reinforced at the expense of the heart, emotions and spirit. Again we're looking at imbalance. Yet the twisted part is that we do not use our minds for engaging with the subtle energy of consciousness. *In fact we need to get our minds out of our way in order to evolve.*

We need to get around our minds, and all of its skepticism, doubt and resistance to change, to *be able to ground in the trust of our inner knowing.* This knowing is the feeling you're having now of knowing "in a body way." This type of knowing is not just in your head, it's down deeper than that and feels like a "whole body knowing" that what was just said is truth. Something at a deeper level in you—not heavier—went zing! Yes! It's there, but it takes practice to attune your everyday linear, cognitive mind to identifying it while also yielding to it. It's kind of like the thoughts and feelings that we experience in those moments of stillness. Like on that fishing trip, or that previous Sunday morning before everyone else in the house was awake and we sat outside drinking our morning beverage, or that time when someone we love dies, or that moment when we sat silently with the person we love not needing to talk yet still full of "stuff" to say knowing how right this felt, or that moment when we witnessed a child being born, or that dream we had that had parts of it that came true, or that moment of that déjà vu, or that feeling when we met that person for the first time when we experienced that uncanny feeling that we've met them before when in fact we know we hadn't, or the multitude of experiences that are exactly that–*experiences-of the unseeable.*

Yet notice how these experiences shut up the everyday mind full of its doubts and needs for reassurances *because it transcends the everyday, it is bigger than the everyday mind and goes beyond it.* Now, do you feel the function crisis has? What do you feel like in moments of crisis? Do you panic? No. Only afterwards, once the mind gets re-engaged. Before that, you were caught up in an adrenaline rush, during which the mind is drawn into a very present moment focus, with some of it due to the effect of the hormonal releases to either fight or fly.

Understand that this is not necessarily about faith, as in the faith involved with religions and a belief in God. For this is another typical error, or fallacy. In our metaparadigm we equate almost anything that is from the unseen realm with some kind of mysterious "unexplainable" thing to it, automatically with having some relationship to us having to then have to believe in God. So what happens when someone is uncomfortable with this belief in the one great, higher being, who is typically an all knowing, some might say punitive, God? This is where it gets a whole lot bigger than believing in the worth of valuing what happens in our lives that is of the non–physical. And the framing of the intangible that is in this dualistic, external–to–us way that comes from the main religious paradigms of the West. We have already discussed this. So because the version of God in western religions is external to each of us, this world of the unseen then typically becomes the Church or the Synagogue's domain–or the psychic's, and so then we doubt it and ourselves because we're not the authority in this domain, we thus think we don't have the power to really know of "this transcendent stuff."

So we typically don't trust it, our own knowing, and so we disregard it. Meaning, anything that is not tangible of the material or secular world that we physically exist in, we have given up to an external source, usually for some other authority figure, or specialist, to know. Apparently, it is not for us to know. Either it is deemed to be of the nature that it is something no one could know, or it is for us to place our trust in this "other" authority on these matters who is "more skilled" in "this kind of knowing." This duality is not world wide. Yoga is in fact the direct opposite of this.

Furthermore, nor is the connection between this consciousness–or this subtle energy–about God, as much as it is logical. It is logical to acknowledge that as there is the physical dimension that shows up for our five physical senses to pick up, there is an unseen dimension that the less physically dense parts of us tunes into, such as through our feelings, and our Higher Self, and our intuition, the "sense" that works for the unseen realm, and a way to connect and hear our Higher Self. Watch a dog wait for its owner to come home with their tail wagging, nose pressed against the window. *This is a balance that the universe has; the invisible has to be behind the visible.* A mother's womb hides an embryo in the dark womb of her belly, while the embryo is fed and nurtured in order to properly and fully form, prior to being released fully onto the physical plane, into the material world. This is a rather all encompassing analogy. Another, smaller scale example is how we first feel the feeling of love towards a potential partner before we then go up and approach them on the surface, possibly manifesting a relationship, during which we will hold hands, go out to dinner, have conversations, etc. The feeling happens first, the physical action follows.

Jelusich offers a good closing statement, "You must have the courage to trust with your heart through an abiding faith that what you cannot see exists nonetheless, regardless of religious tenet (or lack thereof). *We must have a balance of mind and heart, of thoughts and feelings.* The technologies we use can help us to achieve some success, but they are not the answer; no more than restructuring a gene sequence will automatically make us more enlightened, no more than doubling our brain capacity makes us smarter. The technologies can only help to point to the answer, for the answer is within us," (italics mine) (Jelusich 2004). This returns the power–and the responsibility–back to each individual, particularly where health and wellness are involved, taking the power out of looking towards external authority figures, or external sources such as technology, and instead becoming informed ourselves and trusting ourselves, our own knowing, and our own individual access to this sea of consciousness to be worked with for guidance and our own answers for health, well–being, happiness, and a sense of nurturing sustenance. Listening to our bodies' responses to what we eat is an example. This is radical in some ways to those used to giving this power over to "the trained specialists with all that education in their field," I know. Or to the food companies to responsibly produce our food.

Not only for these outcomes, of course, but where the mind body connection is concerned, we are so clearly not just the body. The consciousness being spoken of here contains the other three areas of the human experience–our emotions, our mind beyond the physical brain, and our soul, or spirit, or whatever term that symbolizes the eternal part of the human being. Or, if you've ever had a dream during sleep that you then experience on the physical plane while awake. Simply put, that part of you that is connected to, or contains the mysterious aspects of life that seem unexplainable. Now that we've discussed the science behind it, that part of you that is more expansive–perhaps that part of you that you felt when visiting the Grand Canyon or another National Park or Forest or another one of the Seven Great Wonders of the World, or a UNESCO World Heritage Site–that connects to the underlying field, or medium that exists at the sub–quanta level, in between atoms and molecules. If you've never had any of these experiences, then think of that friend or family member who has, and know that you also have that same ability. Newborns are a good source to look at to get this understanding more concrete, as well. So are older people who are close to death. It does not have to be anything bigger than this, to start with.

The emerging models of health care on the cutting edge in our society take these other aspects of the human being into account for healing and curing, rather than treating only at the level of the physical body. As should be happening, a connection to the Indian and Chinese medical sciences of holistic approaches that consider a human's entire system and lifestyle is also clearly linked here. This brings us to a more prevention based model, rather than a treatment of physical symptoms only when the body has manifested these physical symptoms. This, in turn, brings us back to individuals being responsible for successfully knowing themselves, and thus, successful and healthy management of their own mind, body and spiritual elements within their own individual human system composed of the mind, the body, and the spirit.

Your mind influences your body. So then your body to a degree is a reflection of your mind and its most frequent thoughts. This is huge. You may want to re-read that.

Time now to consider working with this thing that seems like it thinks us, yes? Making the mind serviceable helps us get beyond attachment to our thoughts and all the addictive, fear based conditioning from our environment that lead to the thoughts that make us uncomfortable. Move beyond the everyday thinking.

Now we're just beyond the everyday thoughts/thinking mind. This is now an unlimited, magical existence with this field we've just entered. And then begin to sense. That whole body sensing, as if you're a channel able to be tuned in to different fm or am shows, or frequencies. And you'll start to interact more with nature and then the nature of life in this field. Feel its aliveness, the presence of something else, beyond and bigger than the mind. See the slight wave of the trees' branch right by your head. Uh uh uh - no, come off of the thought and back to the sensing, the breath, the now. Tune into hope or excitement, or the passion or enthusiasm for life that once still, and then opening up to this sensing, you'll be able to gradually feel. Reach for it through your wonder, your awe, and in a sense, that wondrous imagination we've been given. Yet it's not that you're imagining this presence. It's just a different sense we're using here, a different entry portal, the likes of which we can barely imagine...Or can we? Einstein also said, "Imagination is more important than knowledge." I wonder what he knew...

Discussion

"The spinning whirling energy in the universe, harnessable by mankind. Now. We are whirling through endless space, with an inconceivable speed, all around us everything is spinning, everything is moving, everywhere there is energy... There must be some way of availing ourselves of this energy more directly. Then, with the light obtained from the medium, with the power derived from it, with every form of energy obtained without effort, from the store forever inexhaustible, humanity will advance with giant strides. The mere contemplation of these magnificent possibilities expands our minds, strengthens our hopes and fills our hearts with supreme delight."—Nikola Tesla, referring to Zero Point Energy in 1891

THE CREATION OF THE SCIENTIFIC materialist paradigm was from a desire to bring balance back to what seemed like a system out of balance. We have been following along the trajectory of that creation, with the industrial revolution alongside it all the way through, leading us up and out of the modern era with the technological products for improving the ease and convenience of life, to the present day post–modern era. As we have discussed, the issues that are at crisis level now are occurring because a new model is needed; we have gotten way out of balance in the name of what claims to be reason based science. Realistically, somewhere in the modern era, it became a metaparadigm based on profit that we have all been swept along into, eventually becoming a metaparadigm out of control based on credit and debt–and not just financial credit and debt, but environmental, human health, and happiness; credit then, debt now.

We can see these choices culminating in the financial crisis that is flagging us with the news we don't really want to face–that we will never return to the expansion levels that were of the industrial era. It is time to both go inside and rather than expansively grow, intensively grow.

Some, increasingly so it's now many, have seen this, understood that living underneath this metaparadigm's systems has felt progressively off, and have made the choice to investigate why and then made further choices for ourselves from right where the spin–out began from. Meaning, they've–we've–returned to the basics, but in an informed way that incorporates what the new sciences continue to unravel and prove. Part of the new sciences also have focused on the field that is at the inter–molecular level, as has been explored; or what is understood as this field of consciousness at the quanta level that runs throughout all, which is basically the same concept as chi in the Chinese culture or prana in the Indian. Within this field, which is also known as a vacuum or a medium as Tiller pointed out, and as zero–point energy as Tesla's quote describes, there is infinite energy, so there is infinite power.

This power can be, and indeed is shaped by consciousness. So, this now brings in the power behind intention and choice.

Wayne Dyer, considered by many to be the father of our current self-help boom, wrote a book called *The Power of Intention*. Intention has a definitive direction behind a choice we make, so that it directs the zero–point energy in a certain direction. We are creating at all times of our lives with the power of our thoughts, choices, intentions–consciousness–and our actions. We can either continue to remain outside of this power source and continue to create by default and struggle and suffer, and then complain and look to power sources outside of ourselves to blame for our misery. Or we can stand up and take responsibility and stop caving in to the cowardly, slovenly, lazy ego-mind that abandons this part of us that contains our own power to shape and mold what we see in our lives.

This means to acknowledge the power of our thoughts, and the act of abandonment we engage in when we don't work with our thoughts, but instead allow the mind to continue to rant and rave as it does, as it will. But it gets a bit different once we are alerted to this information about not believing our thoughts and that there is an option even present to whether to believe our thoughts or not. It's like once we are made aware of this being how it is, we know this is truth and there is no avoiding working with ourselves and our minds without creating even worse struggle afterwards, if one continues to engage in resistance. It's a nasty little trick this process has built into it. But it is there for a reason. That is, we are basically driven to the point of such collapse in our lives, such magnified intensifying of "our issues" hitting us in the face by continuing repeated circumstances of strife and struggle with this one particular—or two—areas of our life, that we have to find a different way, or we perish. The human ego—mind likes problems and struggle; it keeps it in charge. Yet there is a part of us that knows this and that we are avoiding something.

We all know this inside, when we are avoiding something, where that deep sense of knowing resides that is connected to the Higher Self, aligned with the power at the source that is acknowledged as divine in its nature. This source can be experienced as containing the sacred, the power of the light and the power of creation. It is refreshing. Change is a big fear inducing monster for the little mind who likes to stay the same, even if its worn out. And our last ten years or so has been what was just described; an exaggeration of crises. So we are thus left with the choice to change or perish. It has been and continues to be a climb towards the climax of this resistance on one side towards this awareness, and then the other side where there is this taking of responsibility for ourselves and of the power inherent within our consciousness—our thoughts, our beliefs, our habits, our choices, our minds and our ensuing actions. And once the self-management has been successfully worked with enough there then is the actual stepping into and using this vast storehouse of power and unlimited potential. Or not. It is our choice.

As a Reiki Master and an intuitive medic myself, I have seen what fear of claiming one's own power causes humans to do; we tend to be afraid of our own power, because of all that we imagine this connotes, including having to give up anything sensual or fun. We sabotage ourselves to cause ourselves to fall backwards or to not gain in ways that we genuinely desire and are authentically in our Highest Good—like earning money from a means that uses one's passions and strengths, or being in that "dream" relationship —in ways that only concentrated mindful awareness of this behavior can unravel. Wayne Dyer's most recent book *Excuses Be Gone* contains a list of 18 of the most common excuses people responding to a poll he had on his website came up with when asked the question of, "What is the most common excuse you tell yourself from living your life based on your dreams for yourself?" Some of these are, "It will be difficult. I can't afford it. I don't deserve it. It's not in my nature. I'm too old/not young enough. It will take a long time. I'm not strong enough. There will be family drama." In response to this, Dr. Dyer says, "All excuses are misalignment [with source energy]."

Staying in excuses means staying in resistance to alignment with this power source, that helps each and every individual with our own power as a unique human being who is here with a mission—we all have one no matter how mundane or glamorous. Meaning, when we have worked with our mental chatter enough to then side step it enough to then empower our Higher Self enough, we have access to this source of infinite power and energy. It is that simple. And it is what I have found to be the most forceful divinely encoded paradox within the human experience.

We have to get out of our own way means we have to let go of that personality level of ourselves that everyone labels us with, knows us by and that we've most likely used to gain either success - or attention - for our misery as a helpless victim to outer circumstances, otherwise known as "our storylines." Yet when we identify and increasingly align with our higher selves it is good, because we can stop being blocked or limited to only living at the lesser level of the every day mind and thus have more open access to the source of power permeating all life at the subatomic inter–molecular level. And until we do, we will continue to perpetuate habitual patterns in our lives that get us every time no matter how new our environment or clothes or car are, or that make us in those quieter moments—and those raging ones—know that this is a core pattern of ours and that we are sick of doing this to ourselves, or feeling this same way again, or just plain sick of ourselves. Notice that wording, "Sick of myself." Now connect it to the levels of dis–ease and depression. And environmental damage.

And consumption. And political check out. And pop culture check in.

We apparently have to get sick of ourselves enough to want to change. And this has now become collective. Hence our peaking levels of crisis. Grand scale resistance. Eckhart Tolle, author of *The Power of Now*, says, "For the masses, crisis is their greatest spiritual teacher." How much more crisis is required?

Conclusion

T HE BUDDHISTS WRITE OF THE neurotic mind being the human mind, *every human mind*. Advanced meditators do not stop their thoughts from coming in. Distorted perception comes–or perceiving people and events in our environment inaccurately because we are interpreting them negatively by taking them personally or by judging them–from a mind allowed to do whatever it wants; an obese mind, if you will. Distorted perception causes conflict and misery. Conflict and misery get dealt with either by turning it onto someone else and directing it at them, or by turning it inward. Emotional eating is one way to deal with internal misery. So is shopping and unchecked consumerism. Cancer is cells that have gone awry, and have begun to sabotage their own host.

Our cells get communicated with, get imprints from our environment on how to organize. If our perception is that the universe is basically hostile and an unfriendly place, then our cells will organize around the perceptions that interpret our environment's input–our home, our family life, our love relationship, our job, our authority figure boss, our friends–as unfriendly and hostile. It is the thoughts that we think on an everyday basis, it is the way that we hold ourselves as we go through our days as a result of this mental dialogue that creates our biochemistry, which becomes our biology.

If we are too busy, or too focused up on the physical plane of life, or if we have not been taught to manage our internal environment, or not sought out the tools with which to do so, then we will create our biology by default. We won't pay attention to it until a physical symptom has to show up and announce that, yes, indeed, this system is out of alignment. This comes from not paying attention to the subtle in our lives, as has been explored.

The impact of not paying attention to the subtle we can observe in our cultural climate, today. The paying attention to the physical plane of existence we can observe in our cultural climate, today. We have inherited a system that worked for a time when we were in a certain place in our own human evolution as a species—meaning the history of humans on planet earth including moving away from agrarian based lives where the home and community centered around farming, to urban based lives, where the home and community centered around industry—but this system has peaked and run its course. I would say in around the 1980's is when we first really started to go into excess without being able to return back to what we once had.

A base line we could return to without global warming being a crisis, without American debt being financed through credit, without those in the financial and banking industry taking the meaning out of paper money and the dollar by gaining so much that the value of money became permanently distorted, without CEO's of multinationals able to engage in whatever unethical business practices and throw these onto the unsuspecting public while they make an entire country's GDP's from a year of their annual salary, without our values then shifting over to allow sports players and pop stars to make such insane amounts of money that the average person would not accumulate in their lives over a lifetime of annual salaries and savings and investments, without leaving us all focused on consumption and money and materialism, without basically only taking time out for family gatherings on birthdays and holidays, and attending our organized religions' services on the most important religious days of the year, without only attending once a week to be fed a connection—hopefully—to a less materialistic, more eternal, and sacred form of power, without us not having a connection to ourselves.

We have gone into excess, and our health is showing it individually and collectively, as a society. Before I became a natural healer and classroom teacher, yoga and meditation teacher, personal trainer and health and wellness coach, I worked in politics. I have a Masters Degree from a secular university that set me up to work within either a non—profit or a governmental agency focused on environmental protection policy, based on the political organizing work I had done in 1991–1993. I left politics because the machine was too big. I went into classroom teaching because change happens at the individual level, in order for it to happen at the collective. Margaret Meade once said, "Never doubt that a small group of thoughtful, committed citizens can change the world; indeed, it's the only thing that ever has." And this is where we are today, with both the battle and the battle field in our country, in our metaparadigm, over two very divergent systems, one that glorifies and honors materialism and in the process disregards most if not all aspects of the sacred, and the other works to keep life more in balance by honoring the subtle and the sacred. When honoring the subtle and the sacred, the slovenly excessive little child screaming inside of us who wants what it wants, when it wants it, no matter what is kept in check. It has to be. There's something more powerful than it and it knows it, which is why the little mind engage in such resistance when we seek to change into a better, empowered version of ourselves. It knows it can't really even compete in this powerful of a playing field.

I worked as an organizer in politics because I believe in the power of democracy, because I believe in this country's founding principles, I believe in what our country once was and the absolute purity of much of our citizens' intentions, and that we deserve to be living in a system that is healthy and that supports our own health at the individual, family, and community levels. While living as an ex–patriot outside of this country for a decade, while teaching American Literature to high school sophomores who were expats in their own right, I was more of a teacher about what our country is about and not about. This became further clarified by experiencing a contrasting system, the Chinese, to such depth.

Both inside and outside of the classroom, having the stereotypes of Americans projected on to me to such degrees that it caused paralysis for genuine relating and integrating within the local culture, has made me even more aware of what it means, and does not mean, to be an American. The second time I lived overseas, it was in Asia. Living in Asia as an American all happened in the years during Iraq, the war on terrorism, Bush's administrations, and Obama's first two years in office. I was sometimes afraid to admit I was an American in certain settings. I had received enough hostility in the early years, most of all when traveling during my breaks, that I just choose to save myself the trouble. Additionally, listening to the stereotypes of Americans from my American born Taiwanese–Chinese students that I elicited from them in order to set them up to then think for themselves instead of through their more Taiwanese–Chinese conditioning as we then explored the literature of America was eye–opening. I found that I had to engage in this exercise of raising their (and my) awareness of their conditioning prior to even cracking a book written by an American because I had come to see the stereotyping towards Americans can run extremely deep and sometimes, for me, painfully accurate.

This was done so that they could then accurately interpret and actually hear what the American author was saying. Otherwise, the stereotypes took over and they skimmed the literature not able to grasp neither the themes nor the more subtle messages. It also gave me a glimpse, from contrast, about what our country stands for, and the national character that we as Americans typically have, through the eyes of my students who still lived amongst their Taiwanese–Chinese extended families, many of whom were traditional Chinese.

It is something to live outside of this country, literally, as well as figuratively, out of dissent to the destruction one sees the dominant metaparadigm has gone into due to being out of balance. My first year living in Asia, my first month in fact, was when 9/11 happened. I had returned to the U.S. each summer for two months, as well as for 2/3 of a year, four years into my living in Asia due to my mother's diagnosis with a brain tumor, in order to help support her efforts to live, using natural healing methods. This entire discussion has been written as a culmination of the efforts to try and understand why is it that we have been taught to stick our heads in the sand when it comes to acknowledging the power of intuition, the power of the subtle, and the power of *energy* in our lives, as Americans. This awareness is what caused me to move and live amongst the Chinese and travel throughout Asia for a decade, to see how cultures who do hold this awareness manifest a system based on this understanding.

In doing research for this book, I came across some information that could provide another answer that builds on what I've discussed here; what has been done in the name of keeping those in power, in power. This is connected to what Tesla himself went through when working with zero-point energy, as well as many other inventors of technology using zero-point energy, because zero-point energy is a renewable source of energy that is fundamental to this universe.

Wait, then there are also the inventors of alternative fuel sources who have been producing technologies throughout the history of our country, but particularly since the 1970's, and they have "mysteriously been silenced." I heard firsthand accounts of this from other American expats living in Asia.

Others, who have created technology for curing cancer have also been silenced. There is the history of the Rife machine that was invented by Rife and used to cure cancer; he got shut-down by the AMA. The congressional hearings on pure, strong versions of vitamin C being used to cure cancer in the earlier decades of the 1900's that also got shut down for use in curing cancer, so that the AMA and its cohorts have remained in charge of their multi-billion dollar industry, their "war on cancer."

However, none of these cases were mentioned in the body of this discussion, to the fact that all are cases that represent the conflict between the power structures who retain power and profit and those who want a different paradigm and who are working towards a different paradigm. So this discussion is not intended to focus on these conflicts, for it creates more of the same; accusations that go back and forth, confusing some, while building more conflict based on conditioning without true facts. Rather, it was to step outside of the conflict and to explore why we're where we are, how we got conditioned to believe what we do, at a mass level. It was once to have reason at the core of our society, in response to irrational hysteria seen in society during the Dark Ages, while it has now become profit motivated, so that it is materialism at the core of our society—and a different type of hysteria.

But we all know this now. Should you now want to do further research on your own, those are some places to start; the voices who have gotten shut down as we have modernized into this country with a materialistically focused metaparadigm, given to us from the scientific materialist principles that fit perfectly with industrial development.

So now that we are no longer in the Industrial Age, it seems appropriate that we no longer live within and under a metaparadigm created for and during the Industrial Age's purposes. And that we take back our power, each and every one of us, individually and collectively. Over the past few years it seems like one "awake" person counteracts more not-awake people than what this number was even five years ago. As more and more of us choose to become awakened to our own subtle energy circulating throughout our systems and we lighten, this is a use of our power; a choice for what is lighter, or the light.

About the Author

Alison J. Kay, PhD is a Holistic Life Coach, an India trained YA Yoga & Meditation teacher, an ACE Certified Personal Trainer, and an energy healer/shifter of 16 years. The unique blend of credentials, use of multiple modalities, and the wealth of experience she acquired during the 10 years she spent living in Asia studying subtle energy practices, make her perspective and manner of working with people around the world incredibly powerful. She hosts her ever insightful radio show "Create Your Best Life Ever" on World Talk Radio, the biggest online media company, on the 7th Wave Channel of voiceamerica.com. She resides in Florida. Visit www.AlisonJKay.com and www.healing-balance.com to learn more.

2 Free MP3 Recordings

~~~~~~~~~~~~~~~~~~~~~~

Join me, John Robbins and the Food Revolution to be as healthy & happy as you - and we all - can be!

Dare to discover the most cutting-edge information, startling facts & inspirational wisdom that will heal you & have you CELEBRATING LIFE! Our vitality, health, well-being & joy are directly connected to the foods we take into our bodies & that then effect our minds. John Robbins, the "father" of exposing the food industry & to all of the recent movies (i.e. Food Matters, Food Inc) joins me. Poised to inherit the Baskin & Robbins ice cream empire, John went on a tour of dairy farms to see how cream was made. Horrified by what he saw, he then proceeded to poultry, pig & beef farms. Writing the book *Diet For a New America* as a result, John is responsible for thousands becoming vegetarians & many more modifying their Standard American Diet. He'll expose some of the less well-known effects of what is in our food supply that lead to the most common illnesses in our country. We'll learn how to put the POWER IN OUR HANDS to eat for our health, using food for medicine so we can thrive! **To download, go**: http://chirb.it/0GsnxH

Alison J. Kay, PhD

The Science Behind Consciousness & Energy with Dr. William Tiller: We Humans are Much More Than We Think We Are

Another scientist sourced in my book's late December release What if There is Nothing Wrong?, Dr. William Tiller, former professor of Materials Science & department chair at Stanford University from 1964 to 1998, says that for the last 400 years an unstated assumption of "old" science is that human intention can't affect what we call physical reality. This is no longer accurate, as his pioneering work within Psychoenergetic Science shows. One of the leading scientists of the New Sciences, leaving Orthodox science behind to have more freedom to explore consciousness w/science, he says that future medicine will be based on learning to control the energy frequencies of the body. His cutting edge work builds a reliable bridge of understanding thru the various domains of how nature manifests, both in the external physical as our sciences have already studied & the more subtle domains of inner reality typically studied in the East & then how they strongly join w/the domain of spirit.

To download, go: http://chirb.it/52OI0N

Alison's Radio Show

Create Your Best Life Ever! What Else is Possible?

Friday at 1 PM Pacific Time on VoiceAmerica 7th Wave Channel

We are in the midst of a HUGE macroshift on our planet right now. It is not a time of gloom and doom, but a time of rebirth for you to make the exact changes that your life needs in order to restore basic sanity, health, calm, positivity, hope, abundance and joy. FREE ENERGY CLEARINGS ARE A PART OF EVERY SHOW TO HELP YOU, using ThetaHealing,™Access Consciousness™and Alison's own vibratory transmission. A focus on the meaning behind the global macroshift we're undergoing in 2012 and beyond, and how it affects our thoughts, feelings, bodies and lives is central to the show.

Through my guests, and your call-ins, I will address your concerns, as I do with my clients, helping you to understand that within the mind, body and spirit model is the key—holistic living. Holistic living means creating a lifestyle that is comprised of daily behaviors and choices from an overall mental and feeling tone that supports our well-being, health, joy and abundance from our connection with our higher selves and the unlimited potential in the higher realms supporting us now in this transformative year of 2012 and beyond.

Forthcoming Books

~~~~~~~~~~~~~~~~~~~~~

Keep an eye out for forthcoming books by Alison J. Kay, Ph.D.. The next one is tentatively titled, *Gentling Down©*.

Bibliography

~~~~~~~~~~~

Abelson, Reed, 2009. "Following the Money in the Health Care Debate" The New York Times online: Week in Review. Accessed August 2010. http://www.nytimes.com/2009/06/14/weekinreview/14abelson.html?pagewanted=1&fta=y.

"Adrenal Fatigue–Symptoms & Treatment" on Holistic Back Relief Acupuncture & Wellness Center's website, www.holistic–back–relief.com/adrenal–fatigue.html.

"AltMed: Regulatory Challenge" Accessed April 2010. www.naturalhealthvillage.com/reports/coulter.htm.

American Association of Medical Colleges, 1998. "Report 1: Learning Objectives for Medical Student Education: Guidelines for Medical Schools; Medical School Objective Project" Accessed April 2010. www.aamc.org.

American Dream Abroad, (www.americandreamabroad.com).

Anderson, Elizabeth. 2000. "Feminist Epistemology and Philosophy of Science" Stanford Encyclopedia of Philosophy. Accessed May 2010. http://plato.stanford.edu/entries/feminism–epistemology/.

Anderson, Gerard F., Uwe E. Reinhardt, Peter S. Hussey, and Varudi Petrosyan. 2003. *"It's the Prices, Stupid: Why the United States is So Different From Other Countries"* Health Affairs 22:89-105. Accessed April 2010. doi:10.1377/hlthaff.22.3.89.

Health Affairs. Accessed April 2010. http://content.healthaffairs.org/cgi/content/full/22/3/89?maxtoshow=&hits=10&RESULTFORMAT=&fulltext=It%27s+The+Prices+Stupid&searchid=1&FIRSTINDEX=0&resourcetype=HWCIT

Astin, John A., Shapiro, Shauna L., Eisenberg, David M., and Forys, Kelly L., "Clinical Review: Mind body Medicine: State of the Science, Implications for Practice" *JAM Board Fam Pract*, Mar 2003; 16: 131–147. Accessed March 2010. http://www.jabfm.org/cgi/reprint/16/2/131.

Barlett, Donald L. and Steele, James B.; Karmatz, Laura and Kiviat, Barbara, 2004. "Why Drugs Cost So Much / The Issues '04: Why We Pay So Much for Drugs" Accessed August 2010. http://www.time.com/time/magazine/article/0,9171,993223,00.html#ixzz0wQvltxaX

Barnes, Patricia, et al., 2008. "Complimentary and Alternative Medicine Use Among Adults and Children: United States, 2007" *National Health Statistics Reports: U.S. Department of Health and Human Services, CDC's National Center for Health Statistics.*

Barton, Ruth. March 1990. "'The Influential Set of Chaps': The X-Club and Royal Society Politics 1864-85." *The British Journal for the History of Science.* Vol. 23, No. 1, p. 53-81. Accessed 2010. Cambridge: Cambridge University Press.

Bell, et al., 2006. "CAM use among older adults age 65 or older with hypertension in the United States: general use and disease treatment" *PubMed–U.S. National Library of Medicine, National Institute of Health.* Accessed April 2010. http://www.ncbi.nlm.nih.gov/pubmed/.

Benderly, Beryl Lieff, 2010. "Does the U.S. Produce Too Many Scientists?" *Scientific American.* Accessed April 2010. http://www. scientificamerican.com/article.cfm?id=does-the-us-produce-too-many-scientists.html.

Benson, Herbert, M.D., "Mind Body Basics" *BHI Institute-Massachusetts General Hospital.* Accessed March 2010. http://www.mgh.harvard. edu/bhi/basics.

Billert, Bob, "Aristotle" Accessed March 2010. http://www.associatedcontent. com.

The Biopsychosoical Model. Accessed May 2010. http://www.answers.com/ topic/biopsychosocial-model.

Blevins, Sue, 1995. "The Medical Monopoly: Protecting Consumers or Limiting Competition?" *The CATO Institute.* Accessed April 2010. http://www.cato.org/pubs/pas/pa-246.html.

Bohr, Niels, 1935. "Quantum Mechanics and Physical Reality," *Nature* 136 (1935): 65.

Borgmann, Albert, 2006. Muse Project "Today's Research, Tomorrow's Inspiration" Online Journal Collections. "Technology as a Cultural Force: For Alena and Griffin"-*The Canadian Journal of Sociology* 31:3 (2006) 351-360 Muse Search Journals. Accessed August 2010. http://muse.jhu.edu/login?uri=/journals/canadian_journal_of_ sociology/v031/31.3borgmann.html.

Braden "Braden, Gregg", Gregg, 2008. *The Spontaneous Healing of Belief: Shattering the Paradigm of False Limits.* Carlsbad, California: Hay House, Inc.

Brown, Edward, "*New choices for healing ourselves: An Interview with Richard Gerber.*" Share International. http://www.share-international.org/ archives/health-healing/hh_ebnewch.html.

Cadge, Wendy. 2005. *Heartwood: The First Generation of Theravada Buddhism in America*. Chicago: University of Chicago Press.

Capra, Fritof, 1975. *The Tao of Physics*. Boston: Shambhala Publications. Shambhala, 2nd edition 1983

The Center For Investigating Healthy Minds. Accessed July 2010. http://www.investigatinghealthyminds.org.

Chakraburtty, Sneh, 2009. *The Science of Meditation*. New Delhi: New Age Books.

Cheung, et al., 2007. "Use of Complementary and Alternative therapies in community–dwelling older adults" *PubMed–U.S. National Library of Medicine, National Institute of Health*. Accessed April 2010. http://www.ncbi.nlm.nih.gov/pubmed/.

Chopra, Deepak, 1989. *Quantum Healing*. New York: Bantam Books.

Cohen, Kenneth S., 1997. *The Way of QiGong: The Art and Science of Chinese Energy Healing*. New York: Ballantine Books.

Cohen, S. Marc, "Aristotle's Metaphysics" Stanford Encyclopedia of Philosophy. Accessed April 2010. http://plato.stanford.edu/entries/aristotle–metaphysics/.

"Complementary and Alternative Medicine Use Among Adults and Children: United States, 2007" *National Health Statistics Reports; U.S. Department of Health and Human Services, CDC's National Center for Health Statistics*. Accessed April 2010. http://www.cdc.gov/nchs/.

Cowan, Ruth Schwartz. 1996. *A Social History of American Technology*. London: Oxford University Press.

Coveleskie, Kristen. "Chocolate on the Brain" Accessed May 2010. http://serendip.brynmawr.edu/bb/neuro/neuro04/web1/kcoveleskie.html.

Dalai Lama, Mind and Life Institute, Accessed May 2007. http://www.mindandlife.org/mission.org_section.html.

The Dalai Lama, 1991. *Mind Science: An East-West Dialogue: The Harvard Mind Science Symposium.* Boston, Massachusetts: Wisdom Publications.

Dyer, Wayne. 2005. *The Power of Intention.* Carlsbad, California: Hay House.

Eisenberg, David M., et al., 1998. "Trends in Alternative Medicine Use in the United States, 1990–1997" *Journal of the American Medical Association,* Volume 280, No. 18. Accessed April 2010. http://jama.ama-assn.org/.

Engel, George 1977. *Academic Journal of the American Association for the Advancement of Science.*

Evans, M., 2007. "Decisions to use complementary and alternative medicine (CAM) by male cancer patients: information–seeking roles and types of evidence used" *PubMed–U.S. National Library of Medicine, National Institute of Health.* Accessed April 2010. http://www.ncbi.nlm.nih.gov/pubmed/.

Frawley, David, 2008. *Ayurvedic Healing: A Comprehensive Guide.* New Delhi, India: Shri Jainenedra Press.

Fox, Robin Lane, 2005. *The Classical World; An Epic History of Greece and Rome.* Penguin Publishing Group; London, England.

Galileo, 1623. *Il saggiatore (The Assayer),* 1623, quoted in *Discoveries and Opinions of Galileo,* trans. Stillman Drake (New York: Knopf, 1957);

then quoted in B. Alan Wallace, *Embracing Mind: The Common Ground of Science and Spirituality*

Gerber, Richard, M.D., 2000. *A Practical Guide to Vibrational Medicine: Energy Healing and Spiritual Transformation*. New York: Harper Collins.

Goleman, 1997. *Emotional Intelligence*. New York: Random House.

Gore, Al, 2007. "Al Gore–Nobel Lecture" *Nobel Prize Organization*. Accessed August 2010. http://nobelprize.org/nobel_prizes/peace/laureates/2007/gore–lecture.html.

Gorski, David, March 2009. "Senator Tom Harkin: 'Disappointed' that NCCAM hasn't 'validated' more CAM" Science-Based Medicine: Exploring issues and controversies in the relationship between science and medicine. Accessed June 2010. http://www.sciencebasedmedicine.org/?p=394.

Goswami, Amit, 2000. *The Visionary Window: A Quantum Physicist's Guide To Enlightenment*. Chennai, {Madras} India: Quest Books.

Gray, et al., 2002. "Complementary and alternative medicine use among health plan members. A cross–sectional survey" *PubMed–U.S. National Library of Medicine, National Institute of Health*. Accessed April 2010. http://www.ncbi.nlm.nih.gov/pubmed/.

Gross, Rita M., 1993. *Buddhism After Patriarchy: A Feminist History, Analysis, and Reconstruction of Buddhism*. New York: State University of New York Press.

Gummow, Andrew and Janit, Adrian. *Who's Minding the Store;* A web page dedicated to the body–mind relationship. Accessed October 2007. http://www3.niu.edu/acad/psych/Millis/History/2002/mindbody.htm.

Hare, R.M. and Barnes, Jonathan, 1999. *Greek Philosophers, Socrates, Plato, and Aristotle.* Oxford, England: Oxford University Press.

Hawkins, David M.D. 2002. *Power vs. Force: The Hidden Determinants of Human Behavior.* Carlsbad, California: Hay House.

Hayward, Jeremy W., and Varela, Francisco J., 1992. *Gentle Bridges: Conversations with the Dalai Lama on the Sciences of Mind.* Boston: Shambhala.

Heisenberg, Werner, 1962. *Physics and Philosophy: The Revolution of Modern Science.* New York: Harper and Row.

Helfer, Adam, February 2010. "'Chakra Talk' With Dr. Candace Pert." Accessed April 2010. http://communities.washingtontimes.com/ neighborhood/omkara/2010/feb/26/chakra–talk–dr–candace– pert/.

"How Consumerism Affects Society, Our Economy, and the Environment" Accessed March 2010. http:www.verdant.net/society.htm.

International Society for Complexity, Information and Design (ISCID). Accessed 2010.

Institute of Heart Math. Accessed April 2010. http://www.heartmath.org/ research/overview.html.

Iyengar, B.K.S., 1966. *Light on Yoga.* New York: Shocken Books.

Iyengar, B.K.S., 2001. *Yoga: The Path To Holistic Health.* London: DK Books.

Jacobs, Dr. Gregg D. "Consumerism, Happiness and Health" Accessed March 2010. http://www.truestarhealth.com/members/com_ archives10ML3PIA54.html

Jelusich, Richard A. 2004. *Psychology of the Chakras: Eye of the Lotus.* New Delhi: India: Motilal Banarsidass.

Johari, Harish, 2009. *Dhanwantari: How India's Ancient Art of Living and Healing Can Give You a Healthier, Happier, More Joyous Life.* New Delhi, India: Rupa Co.

Jones, Med, 2006. "The American Pursuit of Unhappiness–Gross National Happiness (GNH)–A New Socioeconomic Policy" *International Institute of Management Executive Journal.* Accessed March 2010. http://www.iim–edu.org.

Junod, Suzanne White, Ph.D, 2003. "An Alternative Perspective: Homeopathic Drugs, Royal Copeland, and Federal Drug Regulation" *Homeowatch Organization.* Accessed August 2010. http://www.homeowatch.org/history/reghx.html.

Kahlil, Gibran. 1923. *The Prophet.* New York: Alfred A. Knopf.

Kaptchuk, Ted J. 2000. *The Web That Has No Weaver: Understanding Chinese Medicine.* McGraw-Hill: New York.

Kellogg, Dr. John H., "The Simple Life in a Nutshell." Biological Living. Accessed May 2010. Lifestyle Laboratory. http://www.lifestylelaboratory.com/articles/simple–life–nutshell.html.

Kraut, Richard, "Plato" *Stanford Encyclopedia of Philosophy.* Accessed May 2010. http://plato.stanford.edu/entries/plato/#PlaCenDoc.

Larsen, Hans R., "Alternative Medicine: Why so popular?" Accessed April 2010. http://chinese–school.netfirms.com/alternative–medicine–why–so–popular.html.

Laszlo, Ervin, 2008. *Quantum Shift in the Global Brain: How the New Scientific Reality Can Change Us and Our World.* Rochester, Vermont: Inner Traditions of Bear & Company.

Lipton, Bruce, 2005. *The Biology of Belief: Unleashing the Power of Consciousness, Matter and Miracles*. Carlsbad, California: Hay House.

Lipton, Bruce H., Ph.D., Goi Peace Award 2009: Accessed April 2010. http://www.goipeace.or.jp/english/activities/award/award2009.html.

Lipton, Bruce H., Ph.D. Uncovering the Biology of Belief website. Accessed April 2010. http://www.brucelipton.com/about-bruce.

Lowenstein, Roger. 2005. "The Quality Cure?" *The New York Times Magazine*. Accessed April 2010. http://www.nytimes.com/2005/03/13/magazine/13HEALTH.html

MacIntosh, Anna, Ph.D., ND, 1999. "Understanding the Differences Between Conventional, Alternative, Complementary, Integrative and Natural Medicine" Accessed August 2010. http://www.tldp.com/medicine.htm.

Maha, N., 2007. "Academic doctors' views of complementary and alternative medicine (CAM) and its role within the NHS: an exploratory qualitative study" *PubMed–U.S. National Library of Medicine, National Institute of Health*. Accessed April 2010. http://www.ncbi.nlm.nih.gov/pubmed/.

Martin, Joel, and Patricia Romanowski, 1997. *Love Beyond Life: The Healing Power of After-Death Communications*. New York: Harper.

Mercola, Joseph. M.D. Posted July 2003. "More Evidence That Stress Is Major Factor for Infections." Accessed 2010. www.mercola.com.

Mercola, Joseph. M.D. Posted July 2004. "Stress Affects Your Immune System: Clearly Defined Patterns Revealed." Accessed 2010. "http://www.mercola.com" www.mercola.com.

Mercola, Joseph. M.D. Posted 2005. "Positive Outlook Buffers Damaging Effects of Stress." Accessed 2010. www.mercola.com.

"Monsanto's Roundup Triggers over 40 Plant Diseases and Endangers Human and Animal Health" http://bit.ly/tR2pC1.

Morin, E. L., "Greek Philosophy: Epistemology and Metaphysics," Accessed May 2010. http://www.associatedcontent.com/.

Mundy, Alice, et al, 2009. "FDA Scientists Ask Obama to Restructure Drug Agency" Accessed August 2010. http://online.wsj.com/article/SB123142562104564381.html.

Murray, Bob, Ph.D., and Fortinberry, Alicia, Ph.D. "Depression Facts and Statistics" Accessed May 2010. www.upliftprogram.com.

Myss, Carolyn lecture, "I Can Do It Convention," Tampa, 2010.

National Center for Complimentary and Alternative Medicine NCCAM 2010.

"National Center for Health Statistics. Health Data Interactive" *Centers for Disease Control and Prevention*. Accessed August 2010. www.cdc.gov/nchs/hdi.htm

The Natural Health Perspective. 2010. Accessed April 2010. http://naturalhealthperspective.com

Nilsson, Martin P., 1947. *Greek Popular Religion*; "The Religion of Eleusis" New York: Columbia University Press

"The Nobel Prize in Physics 1969: Murray Gell–Mann" *The Official Website of the Nobel Prize*. Accessed June 2010. http://nobelprize.org/nobel_prizes/physics/laureates/1969/gell–mann–bio.html.

Northrup, Christiane, PhD, 2009. "Depression and Emotions" sent in an attachment to an email to me from another Reiki Master; beyond this, the specific source–which book or seminar–from where "Depression and Emotions" is cited is not known by this author.

O'Grady, Jane. "Emotions–Definitions, How Rational Are Emotions?" Accessed April 2010. http://science.jrank.org/pages/7650/Emotions.html.

Osterweil, Neil, 2005. "Medical Research Spending Doubled Over Past Decade" *MedPage Today*. Accessed April 2010. http://www.medpagetoday.com.

Pert, Candace, 1997. *Molecules of Emotion: The Science Behind Mind body Medicine*. New York: Scribner.

Pine, Ronald C. 1999. *Science and the Human Prospect*. Accessed March 2010. http://personal.tcu.edu/~dingram/edu/pine3.html.

Rodriguez, Stephanie, 2005. "Prescription drug advertising: Some advocate return to ban" Accessed August 2010. http://www.afn.org/~iguana/archives/2005_04/20050407.html.

Rosen, David, M.D., 1996. *The Tao of Jung*. New York: Penguin Books.

Ross, W.D., 1941. translating Aristotle's "Metaphysics" in *The Basic Works of Aristotle*. Edited by Richard McKeon, (New York: Random House, 1941. Accessed April 2010. http://www.angelfire.com/M.D.2/timewarp/firstphilosophy.html.

Russell, Peter, 2002. *From Science to God: A Physicist's Journey Into the Mystery of Consciousness*. Novato, California: New World Library.

Saraswati, Swami Satyananda, 1976/2008. *Four Chapters on Freedom: Commentary on the Yoga Sutras of Patanjali*. Bihar, India: Bihar School of Yoga.

Satcher, David. 2000. "The Surgeon Generals Report on Mental Health." *National Institute of Mental Health*. Accessed 2010. www.surgeongeneral.gov/library/mentalhealth/home.

"Self Help Depression Treatment > Clearing Up the Depression Myths" Depression, Perception: It's not what you think but how you think that's important. Accessed March 2010. http://www.depressionperception.com/depression–self–help–step1.asp.

Sheldrake, Rupert, Accessed May 2010. http://www.sheldrake.org/.

Sheldrake, Rupert, 2005. "Entelechy: Mind & Culture" http://www.entelechyjournal.com/rupertsheldrake.html

Sukamari, Devi, 1996. "Bhotikvadi Upbhokta" Accessed March 2010. www.legalservicesindia.com/article/175–Consumerism–in–the–Globalized–world.html.

Tasaki, K., 2002. "Communication between physicians and cancer patients about complementary and alternative medicine: exploring patients' perspectives" *PubMed–U.S. National Library of Medicine, National Institute of Health.* Accessed April 2010. http://www.ncbi.nlm.nih.gov/pubmed/.

Tiller, Dr. William. "The William A. Tiller Foundation" Accessed July 2010. http://www.tillerfoundation.com

Ullman, Dana 2010. Wellness Revolution Summit. http://wellnessrevolutionsummit.com/

"Understanding Human Happiness and Well–Being" Sustainable Scale Organization. Accessed February 2009. http:www.sustainablescale.org/AttractiveSolutions/UnderstandingHumanHappinessandWellBeing.aspx.

U.S. Department of Health and Human Services, 1999. *Mental Health: A Report of the Surgeon General—Executive Summary.* Rockville, M.D.: U.S. Department of Health and Human Services, Substance Abuse and Mental Health Services Administration, Center for Mental Health Services, National Institutes of Health, National Institute of Mental Health. Accessed March 2010. http://www.surgeongeneral.gov/library/mentalhealth/summary.html.

University of Creighton Homeopathic School of Medicine. "Like Cures Like" Homeopathy Tutorial Pages. Accessed August 2010. http:// altmed.creighton.edu/Homeopathy/philosophy/similia.htm.

Verhoef, MJ, 2007. "Assessing the role of evidence in patients' evaluation of complementary therapies: a quality study" *PubMed–U.S. National Library of Medicine, National Institute of Health.* Accessed April 2010. http://www.ncbi.nlm.nih.gov/pubmed/.

Wallace, B. Alan, 2008. *Embracing Mind: The Common Ground of Science & Spirituality.* Boston: Shambhala.

Whitehead, Alfred, 1926. *Science and the Modern World.* Cambridge: Cambridge University Press. As quoted in Robert M. Young's online excerpts from his book: *Mind, Brain and Adaptation in the Nineteenth Century.* Accessed April 2010. http://www.human-nature.com/rmyoung/.

Winston, Julian, April 16, 2010. "Outline of the Organon of Samuel Hahnemann" *Homeopathy Ezine.* Accessed August 2010. http:// hpathy.com/homeopathy–philosophy/outline–of–the–organon–of–samuel–hahnemann/.

Wolf, Fred Alan, Ph.D., 2001. *Mind into Matter: A New Alchemy of Science and Spirit.* Needham, Massachusetts: Moment Point Press.

Yasha. The Mind Body Connection. Accessed April 2010. http://www. personal–development.com/yasha/mind body–connection.htm.

Young's, Robert M. online excerpts from his book: *Mind, Brain and Adaptation in the Nineteenth Century: Cerebral Localization and its Biological Context from Gall to Ferrier.* Accessed April 2010. http:// www.human–nature.com/rmyoung/.

Zukav, Gary, 1979. *The Dancing Wu Li Masters: An Overview of the New Physics.* New York: Bantam Books.

Index

Chi Gong 1, 8, 69, 83, 86–88, 93, 96, 109, 123, 130, 134, 199, 206, 210, 254, 299, 304, 357, 358
definition of 14, 33, 72, 131, 151, 186, 202, 203, 215, 257, 339
Chinese culture xii, 78, 86, 88, 93, 97, 104–106, 119, 259, 334, 339, 366
Confucius 88, 93
Lao Tzu 88, 94, 95, 97
yin-yang 138, 216, 264
Chocolate 24, 25, 36, 387
mind body connection 13, 14, 15, 16, 17, 18, 20, 21, 22, 23, 24, 25, 26, 27, 28, 29, 32, 33, 40, 46, 71, 101, 102, 109, 110, 127, 131, 155, 156, 159, 160, 187, 188, 197, 202, 205, 208, 233, 243, 248, 250, 266, 277, 278, 279, 281, 282, 285, 287, 295, 309, 310, 312, 314, 316, 363
Consciousness 3, 4, 8–10, 15, 16, 18–20, 22, 29, 31, 33, 34, 48, 49, 52, 62, 66, 72–75, 77, 79, 83, 86, 88, 89, 110, 119, 151, 154–158, 161, 184, 186, 192, 197, 199– 202, 206, 210, 213, 223, 224, 226, 228–230, 232–235, 236, 237, 249–256, 255, 260, 263, 265–272, 274, 276, 280, 296–299, 301–306, 309, 315, 321, 325–328, 351–360, 362, 363, 366, 367, 378
as a source of power 297
definition of 14, 33, 72, 131, 151, 186, 202, 203, 215, 257, 339
Conversations with the Dalai Lama on Mindfulness 275

D

Dalai Lama xi, 23, 32, 48, 60, 65, 71, 79, 80, 131, 190, 191, 195, 205, 257, 260, 274–276, 328, 387, 389
on materialism 33, 259, 319
Descartes, Rene 16, 232
Dyer, Wayne 253, 366, 367, 368, 387

E

Ego-mind 1, 3, 95, 255, 264, 267, 268, 269, 270, 301, 304–308, 357, 366
definition of 14, 33, 72, 131, 151, 186, 202, 203, 215, 257, 339
Emotions and Health 275

G

Goleman, Daniel 275, 388
Healing Emotions 275
Conversations with the Dalai Lama on Mindfulness, Emotions and Health 275
Mind Life Institute summits xi

H

Hayward, Jeremy 65, 66, 80, 191, 192, 195, 196, 206, 207, 208, 209, 250, 276, 389
Mind Life Institute xi, 60, 190, 195, 205, 274
Naropa 65

Mind body connection 13, 14, 15, 16, 17, 18, 20, 21, 22, 23, 24, 25, 26, 27, 28, 29, 32,
    33, 40, 46, 71, 101, 102, 109, 110, 127, 131, 155, 156, 159, 160, 187, 188, 197,
    202, 205, 208, 233, 243, 248, 250, 266, 277, 278, 279, 281, 282, 285, 287, 295,
    309, 310, 312, 314, 316, 363
    examples of 23
Mind Body Medicine 25, 26, 312, 384, 393
    Herbert Benson 25, 26, 385

P

Paradigm shifts 160, 217, 266, 273
    scientific revolutions 160, 206, 217, 225, 249, 252, 273, 279, 281, 351
Pert, Candace 24, 109, 160, 389, 393
    mind body connection 13, 14, 15, 16, 17, 18, 20, 21, 22, 23, 24, 25, 26, 27, 28, 29, 32,
        33, 40, 46, 71, 101, 102, 109, 110, 127, 131, 155, 156, 159, 160, 187, 188, 197,
        202, 205, 208, 233, 243, 248, 250, 266, 277, 278, 279, 281, 282, 285, 287, 295,
        309, 310, 312, 314, 316, 363
    neuroimmunology 24
    neurotransmitters 24
Primary Mind-Body Theories in the West 27, 28, 29, 30, 61, 62, 79, 89, 126, 155, 192,
        195, 196, 197, 209, 225, 230, 231, 261, 301
    dualism 16, 28, 29, 30, 32, 33, 86, 202
    idealism 16, 28, 29, 30, 32, 33, 86, 202

R

Russell, Peter 393
    The Global Brain 33

S

Scientific Materialism 18, 20–22, 27–29, 60–62, 66, 71, 78, 93, 98–100, 107, 109,
        111–113, 115, 117–123, 125, 126, 130, 146, 151, 152, 153, 160, 162–164, 181,
        184, 188, 192–194, 201, 203, 207, 209, 210, 215–217, 225, 227, 236, 240, 244,
        249, 250, 252, 258–260, 271, 279, 281, 285, 310, 344, 354
    roots in philosophy 59
Subtle energy 8, 22, 83, 87, 99, 102, 104–106, 118, 119, 122, 160, 161, 199, 206, 229,
        243, 246, 248, 250, 254, 259, 260, 261, 263, 266, 285, 287, 314, 327, 328, 333,
        339, 346, 353–360, 362, 373, 375
    and chakras 47
    definition of 14, 33, 72, 131, 151, 186, 202, 203, 215, 257, 339
    for power 14, 33, 72, 131, 151, 186, 202, 203, 215, 257, 339

T

Tiller 160, 199, 210, 248–251, 252, 271, 299, 301, 302, 356, 358, 366, 378, 394
Traditional Chinese Medicine 27, 84, 96, 102
   and acupuncture 93, 167

W

Western Psychology 31, 136
   limitations of 16
Whitehead, Alfred North 23, 29, 59, 395
   Science and the Modern World 59, 395

Y

Yoga 2, 4, 8, 25, 57, 69, 72–78, 81–83, 84, 85, 87, 95, 109, 122, 123, 130, 141, 152, 156, 157, 159, 161, 199, 241, 254, 257, 260, 267, 269, 270, 283, 294, 295, 304, 318, 337, 357, 362, 370, 375, 389, 394